Shakespeare in Bloomsbury

Shakespeare in Bloomsbury

Marjorie Garber

Yale UNIVERSITY PRESS

New Haven & London

Published with assistance from the Louis Stern Memorial Fund.

Yale University Press books may be purchased in quantity for educational, business, or promotional use. For information, please e-mail sales.press@yale.edu (U.S. office) or sales@yaleup.co.uk (U.K. office).

Set in Adobe Garamond type by Integrated Publishing Solutions.
Printed in the United States of America.

Library of Congress Control Number: 2023931868
ISBN 978-0-300-26756-3 (hardcover : alk. paper)

A catalogue record for this book is available from the British Library.

This paper meets the requirements of ANSI/NISO Z39.48-1992 (Permanence of Paper).

10 9 8 7 6 5 4 3 2 1

For Augusta and Rhoda

For it seems sometimes as if we were about to say, or had in some previous existence already said, what Shakespeare is actually now saying.

—VIRGINIA WOOLF, "How Should One Read a Book?"

Contents

Introduction

"HOW SHAKESPEARE WOULD HAVE LOVED US!"

The day after a fancy-dress party at her sister Vanessa Bell's London house, Virginia Woolf wrote an appreciative account in her diary. "Let the scene open on the doorstep of number 50 Gordon Square," she begins theatrically, before plunging into a description of the festivities next door. Her husband Leonard carried a Ceylonese sword; she wore her mother's laces. There were charades, they celebrated "old plays," and the painter Walter Sickert, who had once appeared in Henry Irving's company, acted Hamlet. The guests included many of the writers, artists, and critics who would come to be known as the Bloomsbury Group. As Woolf describes the exuberant spirit of the evening, she also evokes an additional, spectral guest: "We collided, when we met; went pop, used Christian names, flattered, praised, & thought (or I did) of Shakespeare. At any rate I thought of him when the singing was doing—Sh[akespea]re I thought, would have liked us all tonight."[1] For Woolf, Shakespeare was a congenial and kindred spirit whose imagined presence on this occasion confirmed the special fellowship of Bloomsbury.

A few years later, looking forward to a summer evening with friends and family at the Sussex home of Maynard and Lydia Keynes, she would call Shakespeare to mind in very similar terms. "Lydia will sing," she writes to her friend, the novelist Vita Sackville-West, and "we will sit out under the downs." Some guests will come dressed in costume, but her sister is more likely to turn up with holes in her stockings, and her nephew with a hole in his trousers. Imagining the scene—"the gramophone playing Mozart, the stars, the heat, the combination of shabbiness and splendour"—she adds, "I shall think, 'How Shakespeare would have loved us!'"[2] Just as she did in London, Woolf here takes special pleasure in the idea of a gathering that, by mingling culture, comedy, performance, and friendship, includes both "us" and Shakespeare.

This is a book about Shakespeare in Bloomsbury—about the role Shakespeare played in the lives of a remarkable set of writers, artists, and thinkers whose influence is still strongly felt today. As poet, as dramatist, as model and icon, as elusive "life," Shakespeare—or, as Virginia Woolf comes to abbreviate him in her diaries, "Shre"—haunts their imaginations and makes his way, through phrase, allusion, and oblique reference, into their own writing. Not only the works they intended for publication—the novels, biographies, economic and political writings, and reviews—but also their diaries and correspondence, their gossip and small talk turned regularly on Shakespeare. They went to the theatre and saw some of the great Shakespearean actors of the day. They discussed performances and speculated about Shakespeare's mind. They read his plays for pleasure, as recreation, relief, and a source of inspiration in the evenings and on sunny summer afternoons in the country. They commented on each other's libraries, and on whether the copies of Shakespeare plays seemed sufficiently worn by constant use. They alluded to phrases, speeches, and characters as familiarly as they discussed the words and actions of their contemporaries. They lived in and through Shakespeare in their everyday lives. They had known his works since childhood, and they called upon and renewed that knowledge as they matured and became famous.

The "Shakespeare" of such vital importance to the members of the Bloomsbury Group was certainly not an edition, a text, or even a set of favorite passages. Nor was it a mode of exegesis or a school of interpretation—ways of thinking about literature that were far from their own experience and inimical to their instincts. Bloomsbury's Shakespeare might rather be described, in terms more amenable to the people most closely involved, as an *attitude,* a *reading practice,* and a *style* both of writing and of thought.

"It seems to me indisputable," Virginia Woolf once observed, "that the conditions which make it possible for a Shakespeare to exist are that he shall have had predecessors in his art, shall make one of a group in which art is freely discussed and practised, and shall himself have the utmost of freedom of action and experience."[3] Her topic on that occasion was "the intellectual status of women," and her mention of Shakespeare was designed to contrast his situation with that of the modern woman writer. But the "group in which art is freely discussed and practised" was also the world of Bloomsbury, where "the utmost of freedom of action and experience" was a strongly held belief, foundational to the writers' creative and personal lives.

For these brilliant friends—who both individually and collectively had such a formative effect upon literature, the arts, and culture—Shakespeare was in effect another, if less fully acknowledged, member of the Bloomsbury Group.

Virginia Woolf's lifelong engagement with Shakespeare—his plays, his language, his characters, his persona—has been frequently noted.[4] From the early reading notebooks and her conversations with her father, Leslie Stephen, and her adored brother Thoby to the very end of her life, she thought—and wrote—through and with him, sometimes taking comfort in a phrase or a word, sometimes galvanized by his brilliance or his example, sometimes comically despairing that she would never catch up to him no matter how hard she tried. He was also for her a confidant and a consoler. Above all for her he was a *writer:* at once a mentor, a rival (never to be outdone), and somehow also a peer.

Thoby, two years her senior, was her first real Shakespeare interlocutor. After his tragic early death from typhoid at the age of twenty-six, he would always be associated in her mind with the playwright and the plays. In a paper she read to the Memoir Club in 1928, she recalled that when Thoby told her stories of his Cambridge friends she imagined them "as if they were characters in Shakespeare."[5] (Several of these "characters" were, of course, present in the room to hear Woolf's droll and affectionate portraits of themselves.) The three key elements—Thoby, his friends, and Shakespeare—were, and continued to be, indissolubly bound in her thought. Throughout her life Thoby's friends remained her friends, the foundation of the group that would become known as Bloomsbury.

From Asheham in Sussex Woolf wrote to Saxon Sydney-Turner: "I'm thinking of reading Measure for Measure this afternoon, and I wish you could be here, and then we'd ramble on about all sorts of things. I daresay you share my feeling that Asheham is the best place in the world for reading Shakespeare."[6] Much later, after a long period during which she and Saxon had fallen out of touch, they resumed their relationship, effortlessly, through Shakespeare: "We take up a conversation broken these 10 years in our natural voices: What about Pericles? & so on."[7] For Virginia Woolf, talking about Shakespeare with friends and relatives was both a pleasure and a sign of intimacy. Such interchanges were an essential part of her Bloomsbury existence.

One evening the theatre critic Desmond MacCarthy, whom Leonard had known since Cambridge, stopped by the Woolfs' house in London for an hour to offer some thoughts about Shakespeare's appearance and personality.[8] On another occasion a visit from the psychiatrist Alix Strachey and Helen Anrep, Roger Fry's longtime partner, led to "talk of Lear; of Huxleys; of this, that & the other."[9] The mixture says it all; to talk about *King Lear* in the midst of a gossipy social conversation was for them the most natural thing in the world. "Virginia was a natural raconteur," recalled the writer David Garnett. "She saw everyone, herself included, with detachment, and life itself as a vast Shakespearean Comedy."[10]

Sometimes Virginia preferred Shakespeare's company to that of her guests. When Leonard's brother Philip, a lawyer, was visiting them, she lamented in her diary that social obligations precluded solitary reading. "One couldn't sink back before the log fire & read Shakespeare. That form of exalted egotism was checked."[11] Reading Shakespeare was its own exultant pleasure. Once she could hardly wait to get back to *King John* and after that *Richard II:* "It is poetry that I want now, long poems."[12] Ten years later she was still as engaged as ever: "I am reading Shre plays the fag end of the morning. Have read, Pericles, Titus Andronicus & Coriolanus."[13] This is recreational reading, not "research"—for Woolf, Shakespeare offered relief from the pressures of the day and of writing.

Turning to Shakespeare could occasionally lead her to make negative self-comparisons, even after her own writing had brought her fame and success. Here is an example, among dozens of similar observations in Woolf's private diaries: "I read Shakespeare directly I have finished writing, when my mind is agape & red & hot. Then it is astonishing. I never knew how amazing his stretch & speed & word coining power is, until I felt it utterly outpace & outrace my own, seeming to start equal & then I see him draw ahead & do things I could not in my wildest tumult & utmost press of mind imagine. . . . Indeed, I could say that Shre surpasses literature altogether, if I knew what I meant."[14] The passage is itself thrilling to read, and offers some insight into how Shakespeare served for her as a model as well as a (beloved) rival. And there is also this dramatic vignette, which begins with one of her favorite time markers, "the present moment"—a phrase that will appear in several of her novels. "The present moment. 7 o'clock on June 26th: L. printing; hot; thunderous. I after reading Henry 4 Pt one saying whats the use of writing."[15] But of course she kept writing—as well as reading and rereading. "Shall I read King Lear? Do I want such a strain on the emotions?" she asked herself rhetorically in her diary.[16] The answer, needless to say, was yes. Long after she had become a famous author, when she was wrestling with a manuscript to "get the last pages right, if I can only dream myself back into them," she decided "to read a little Shakespeare. Yes, one of the last plays; I think I will do that, so as to loosen my muscles."[17]

At moments of joy the thought of Shakespeare often came spontaneously to her mind. "It was so lovely in the Waterloo Road," she writes in her diary in 1923, "that it struck me that we were writing Shakespeare; by which I meant that when live people, seeming happy, produce an effect of beauty, & you dont have it offered as a work of art, but it seems a natural gift of theirs, then—what was I meaning?—somehow it affected me as I am affected by reading Shakespeare. No; its life; going on in these very beautiful surroundings."[18] In this case, and indeed consistently, Woolf equates "writing, "reading," and "living," connecting them all with Shakespeare.

Her life with Leonard was also a life with Shakespeare. Once, on "a pessimistic walk" in the countryside, they took note of their happiness together while Leonard "discoursed on the illusory nature of all pleasures & pains," deciding that "mankind is a wretched tribe of animals, & even the works of Shakespeare no good save as his skill in doing excites one's pleasure."[19] Their shared pleasure in this discussion of unpleasure is palpable in her account.

A few years later, when they had just returned from abroad, she writes in her diary, "L. & I were too too happy, as they say; if it were now to die, &c. Nobody shall say of me that I have not known perfect happiness."[20] The quotation from *Othello* is also one that she cites in *Mrs. Dalloway*—published in the same year as the diary entry—at the moment when the young Clarissa anticipates her meeting with Sally Seton ("'If it were now to die 'twere now to be most happy.' That was her feeling—Othello's feeling, and she felt it, she was convinced, as strongly as Shakespeare meant Othello to feel it").[21] Neither Virginia nor Clarissa mentions the dramatic irony of these lines in the context of the play, where they mark the apex of Othello's happiness. But perhaps the conjunction of love and death, so powerful throughout Shakespeare, is also something Woolf shared with, or derived from, Shakespearean drama. In 1938, with war looming, Virginia and Leonard went to a performance of *Twelfth Night* ("disappointing") and walked home talking about whether they feared death. They decided that they did not, so long as they could be together. ("So we dont think of death.")[22] Was Feste's haunting song in the play, "Come Away Death," a spur to their conversation, consciously or unconsciously? Certainly Shakespeare was one of their powerful bonds. Once, when Leonard told her that he was the only person who understood her, she replied, "You and Shakespeare."[23]

Like the Stephen family, many of the men and women who would later be known as "Bloomsbury" were reared in households where Shakespeare's plays were read in the evenings for entertainment. Lytton Strachey's mother, Jane Maria Strachey, was a passionate enthusiast of Elizabethan drama and often read aloud to her children. Maynard Keynes's parents were avid playgoers. Clive Bell, as an undergraduate at Cambridge, founded two play-reading groups and began another for Bloomsbury friends after his marriage to Vanessa. One of their first selections was *Troilus and Cressida.*

Lytton Strachey, Leonard Woolf, and Saxon Sydney-Turner all agreed, from their first years at Cambridge, that Plato and Shakespeare were the two first-class minds in all of literary history.[24] Their list of how writers through the ages would rank in a Cambridge Tripos—giving only those two "firsts" and awarding them fellowships—was not really a joke, and the dyad of "Plato and Shakespeare," strongly endorsed by Maynard Keynes, echoes through Bloomsbury correspondence and makes its way into Virginia Woolf's novel *Jacob's Room.*

The letters of these friends to one another, as well as their published writings, are full of Shakespeare lines and references, sometimes attributed, often not. Shakespeare offered them a shared language in which they could underscore—and validate—their strongest feelings, whether of love, admiration, fear, or loss. He was for them not just a great poet and dramatist but also an intellectual companion. Often they called him to mind in connection with their own professional labors in comments that, characteristically, could be both serious and droll. Leonard Woolf, turning down a poetry submission, wrote to the friend who had recommended it about the difficulty of deciding what to publish. "I feel more and more that if Shakespeare presented himself in the basement of the Hogarth Press, it is even betting that he would be informed that his work 'interested us but that we regret being unable to offer to publish it.'"[25] In a similar spirit Maynard Keynes told Roger Fry that a certain amount of currency inflation was necessary to foster artistic creation: "If Shakespeare had been born fifty years earlier England couldn't have afforded him."[26] Fry, an artist and art historian, compared Rembrandt and Shakespeare, noting that both "have the almost miraculous power of creating and placing before us in all their fulness and solidity, credible living beings" with "an unparalleled economy of words or pen strokes."[27] These are brief and sometimes incidental observations, but they are indicative of a certain consistent habit of thought.

Of the philosopher G. E. Moore, a fellow Cambridge Apostle, the undergraduate Keynes had written to Strachey, "He lives with Socrates, Shakespeare, and Tomlinson—the trinity of our holy faith."[28] Virginia Woolf would later elevate her friend Maynard—at least for a moment—to a similar "Shakespearean" height, remarking in her diary, "As I truly said when he gave me some pages of his new book [on monetary reform] to read, the process of mind there displayed is as far ahead of me as Shakespeare's."[29] In a letter to Lytton Strachey she wrote that in moments of frustration with the busyness of life she sought her "chief consolation in the works of Shakespeare and Lytton Strachey."[30] Such comparisons were often on their minds—and in their writings and conversations. When Keynes cites *Macbeth* in *The Economic Consequences of the Peace* as he surveys the men who made the Treaty of Versailles, his allusions are not ornamental or decorative but intellectual and foundational. In Strachey's three major biographies, as in his essays and theatre reviews, Shakespeare is omnipresent. And when Strachey channels Cleopatra or identifies with the passion of Antony, he dramatizes as he analyzes, finding his voice through theirs.

Bloomsbury's Shakespearean legacy was institutional as well as literary. Reacting against the declamatory acting style and overdone stage effects of the previous generation, they restored attention to Shakespeare's language and the text of his plays. Major theatre companies today in London, Stratford, and Cambridge owe their existence and their innovative brilliance to figures like George ("Dadie") Rylands, who taught Cambridge undergraduates how to speak the verse—and prose—of the plays with clarity and without affectation, and to Keynes, an economist who loved Shakespeare and, as chair of the Committee for the Encouragement of Music and the Arts after World War II, laid the foundations for generous government support of art and culture. These were collective enterprises and collective achievements. Rylands had worked for the Woolfs at the Hogarth Press. Lytton Strachey reviewed Shakespeare at Cambridge and wrote an eloquent introduction to Rylands's Shakespeare book, *Words and Poetry*. Keynes not only managed the funds that founded the Cambridge Arts Theatre and was its first chairman—he also paid for most of the construction himself. Keynes's wife, the former Russian ballet star Lydia Lopokova, was a member of the Arts Theatre's first acting company, and Rylands would succeed Keynes as its chairman. And it was Dadie Rylands who hosted the sumptuous luncheon in his rooms at King's that Virginia Woolf described so unforgettably in *A Room of One's Own*. Pull on any thread and the same kinds of interconnections will become visible. They are part of the warp and woof of Bloomsbury, woven together with the words and works of Shakespeare.

Over time Shakespeare in Bloomsbury would come to play many roles: as a cultural inheritance and a social code; as an inspiration for work in genres as apparently different as fiction and biography, art history and economics; as a vehicle for expressing—and also for masking—personal opinions; as a structure of feeling and a structure of thinking; and as an example of what G. E. Moore called a state of consciousness in a passage in his *Principia Ethica* that was foundational for many of the Cambridge Apostles and their friends: "By far the most valuable things, which we know or can imagine, are certain states of consciousness, which may be roughly described as the pleasures of human intercourse and the enjoyment of beautiful objects."[31] The works of Shakespeare exemplified *both* these states of consciousness: human intercourse and aesthetic enjoyment. His plays, his language, his characters, and his aura brought Moore's two "most valuable things" together as one—in conversation and writing, reading and performance.

When Virginia Woolf visited Stratford and looked out the window from which—her tour guide assured her—Shakespeare himself had gazed as he was writing *The Tempest,* she noted the peacefulness of the place, the view, and also its "sunny impersonality." Shakespeare was, she thought, "serenely absent-present" there.[32] It is startling to come upon this phrase, more recently associated with postmodernism, in a diary entry from 1934. But it is perfectly apt as a description of the uncanny presence of Shakespeare in the lives and minds of Bloomsbury.

"Bloomsbury" has become something of a shifting term. In this book I will use it in the broadest sense, to include not only the members of what Virginia and Leonard Woolf called "Old Bloomsbury" but also their children (whom the chronicler Frances Partridge called "Young Bloomsbury") and their friends. Of the many, sometimes conflicting, descriptions of "Bloomsbury," from Virginia Woolf's Memoir Club paper "Old Bloomsbury" in 1928 to Clive Bell's puckish suggestion in *Old Friends* that perhaps it had never existed, one of the best is the judicious account provided by Leonard Woolf in his autobiography.[33]

> Old Bloomsbury consisted of the following people: The three Stephens: Vanessa, married to Clive Bell, Virginia, who married Leonard Woolf, and Adrian, who married Karin Costello[e]; Lytton Strachey; Clive Bell; Leonard Woolf; Maynard Keynes; Duncan Grant; E. M. Forster . . . ; Saxon Sydney-Turner; Roger Fry. Desmond MacCarthy and his wife Molly, though they actually lived in Chelsea, were always regarded by us as members of Old Bloomsbury. In the 1920's and 1930's, when Old Bloomsbury narrowed and widened into a newer Bloomsbury, it lost through death Lytton and Roger and added to its numbers Julian, Quentin, and Angelica Bell, and David (Bunny) Garnett, who married Angelica.[34]

He goes on to emphasize a few points that seem to him essential: they "were and always remained primarily and fundamentally a group of friends" and their "roots and the roots of their friendship were in the University of Cambridge," especially in the Cambridge Conversazione Society, known as the Apostles, of which six of the men of Old Bloomsbury were members at the same time (MacCarthy, Forster, Strachey, Sydney-Turner, Keynes, and Woolf). Fry, seven years older, was an Apostle of the previous generation. All of them were strongly influenced by the philosopher G. E. Moore and his book *Principia Ethica*—as were, through them, Vanessa, Virginia, Duncan Grant, and Clive Bell.[35] But the basis of the group was "friendship, which in some cases developed into love and marriage."[36]

These individuals were in many ways very different from one another, as their careers and opinions make clear. Friendship held them together; Moore's philosophy intrigued and inspired them. And Shakespeare provided them with a common language, a set of reference points, and a model for what they did not hesitate to call "genius."

In the pages that follow I will suggest that Shakespeare was, in Virginia Woolf's apt phrase, an "absent-present" participant in the Bloomsbury Group by considering both how his works were understood by its members and how he came to influence their thought, their language, and their distinctive culture.

CHAPTER 1

Shakespeare in Victorian Bloomsbury

In the middle years of the nineteenth century, a fashionable salon led by Sara Pattle Prinsep and her husband, Thoby, brought together artists, writers, and politicians in what has been described as a "Victorian predecessor of twentieth-century Bloomsbury."[1] Sara was one of the seven much-admired "Pattle sisters": Adeline, Julia Margaret, Sara, Maria, Louisa, Virginia, and Sophia.[2] Maria was Virginia Stephen Woolf's grandmother, and the other sisters were her great-aunts. Julia Margaret, who married Charles Hay Cameron, became one of the most accomplished photographers of her age and an important visual interpreter of Shakespearean characters. Two frequent guests to the salon would influence the Victorian (and post-Victorian) understanding of Shakespeare: the poet laureate Alfred Tennyson and the future Shakespearean actress Ellen Terry, then a young woman in her teens. Virginia Woolf would, in time, come to write about all of them.

On Sunday afternoons at Little Holland House, the Prinseps' salon in Kensington, the house and garden overflowed with friends and visitors: Edward Burne-Jones, William Holman Hunt, and Frederic Leighton among the painters, Carlyle, Browning, Thackeray, and George Eliot among the writers, together with Disraeli, William Gladstone, Sir John Herschel, and the Czech violinist Joseph Joachim. The eminent painter George Frederic Watts, known as "the Signor," was a central figure; Sara is said to have remarked that "he came to stay three days; he stayed thirty years."[3] "A breezy Bohemianism prevailed," reports one admiring chronicler of the era. "That time of dread, the conventional Sunday of the early Victorian age, was exchanged for the wit of cynics, the dreams of the inspired, the thoughts of the profoundest thinkers of the age."[4]

Recalling those days in her memoirs, Ellen Terry wrote, "Little Holland House, where Mr Watts lived, seemed to me a paradise, where only beautiful things were allowed to come. All the women were graceful, and all the men were gifted. The trio of sisters—Mrs. Prinsep—(mother of the painter [Val Prinsep]), Lady Somers, and Mrs Cameron, who was the pioneer of artistic photography as we know it today—were known as Beauty, Dash, and Talent. There were two more beautiful sisters, Mrs Jackson and Mrs Dalrymple."[5] "Mrs Jackson" was Maria, Virginia Woolf's grandmother, the mother of Julia Jackson Duckworth Stephen. And "Mr Watts," of course, was the celebrated painter to whom Ellen Terry, then not quite seventeen, was married in 1864. Sara Prinsep had strongly encouraged the suit. He was thirty years older than Terry, and the marriage dissolved within a year, though they were not formally divorced until 1877.

Julia Cameron died before Virginia was born, and Sara Prinsep when she was five, but both were significant figures in her life and imagination. In a playful letter to her sister in 1908, fantasizing about a time when she and Virginia would be "two celebrated ladies," Vanessa Bell offered one vision of perfect happiness: I "shall see you every day and gaze at the most beautiful of Aunt Julia's photographs incessantly."[6]

There was, it seems, as much that was "Victorian" in these gatherings as anything that might anticipate the more irreverent spirit of Bloomsbury. "The Prinseps had claims upon the respect of artistic and literary people," Leslie Stephen remembered. "Their house had a character of its own. People used to go there on Sunday afternoons; they had tea and strawberries and cream, and played croquet and strolled about the old-fashioned garden, or were allowed to go to Watts' studio and admire his pictures." After his marriage to Minny Thackeray, Stephen himself went often to Little Holland House, feeling, he said, somewhat intimidated, though his hosts were kindly and welcoming. He found the eminence of Leighton, the smart set around Val Prinsep, and the talk of "music and the drama and other mysteries" by actors and opera singers very different from the language of philosophy and scholarship, confessing that "I have always been shy with artistic people, who inhabit a world very unfamiliar to me."[7] Nonetheless, he came to enjoy it, and it was there that he first saw Julia Jackson, who would, after Minny's death, become his second wife and the mother of Thoby, Vanessa, Virginia, and Adrian.

As a child Virginia Stephen would often be brought there on Sundays with her parents. "I remember," she wrote, "the ceremony of our visits to great men. For father and mother were equally respectful of greatness. And the honour and the privilege of our position impressed themselves on us." Looking back at that lost world she wrote, "Greatness still seems to me a positive possession,—booming; eccentric; set apart; something to which I am led up dutifully by my parents. It is a bodily presence; it has nothing to do with anything said. It exists in certain people. But it never exists now. I cannot remember ever to have felt greatness since I was a child."[8]

For the men and women of Bloomsbury, "greatness" would be a more problematic category, one often viewed with suspicion. While Plato and Shakespeare could be admired as indisputably great, living candidates for this status were likely to disappoint or, even more problematically, to aspire. Leonard Woolf, in his autobiography, identified G. E. Moore as "the only great man whom I have ever met or known in the world of ordinary, real life"—and Moore was famously self-effacing.[9] Lytton Strachey's succinct title, *Eminent Victorians,* embodied the distrust that such veneration could elicit. And yet one can sense—as in Virginia Stephen Woolf's memories of her childhood—a little nostalgia for a less skeptical age.

When the Prinseps' lease on Little Holland House expired in 1871 and the house was demolished, their social and cultural scene shifted to Freshwater, at the western end of the Isle of Wight. There Watts, the Prinseps, and assorted friends and acquaintances moved to the Briary in 1874.[10] It was at Freshwater that the Tennysons purchased their estate at Farringford, and Julia Margaret Cameron and her husband Charles bought two nearby cottages, combined them into one, and named the house Dimbola Lodge after one of their coffee estates in Ceylon.

To Woolf aficionados, *Freshwater* is probably best known as the title of her comic farce depicting a rebellious Ellen Terry, a solemnly stuffy Tennyson, and the superbly indomitable Camerons, Julia Margaret and Charles, packing their coffins to take with them by ship to Ceylon (as Woolf would later wryly explain, "in case coffins should be unprocurable in the East").[11] First written in 1923, *Freshwater* was then revised and performed at Vanessa Bell's Fitzroy Street studio in 1935 for an audience of some eighty highly amused guests. Vanessa took the part of Julia, whose work she admired; Duncan Grant, a distinctly modern artist, gleefully portrayed a doddering Watts; Adrian Stephen, a psychiatrist, was the poet Tennyson; Leonard Woolf, a former colonial administrator, played Charles Hay Cameron, and the role of Ellen Terry was enthusiastically undertaken by Vanessa's (and Duncan's) eighteen-year-old daughter Angelica Bell.

Freshwater was in many ways a characteristic Bloomsbury entertainment, deliberately transparent in its symbolic *à clef* casting, full of in-jokes and opportunities for on-the-spot improvisation. It is very much of its own moment, when "Bloomsbury" had already become a celebrated—and sometimes reviled—label. But these are affectionate, not dismissive, portraits, devised by a writer who sees her characters' virtues as well as their absurdities, their uncanny modernity as well as their signature Victorianism. The Tennyson so admired by Leslie Stephen, the evocative photographs of Julia Margaret Cameron, and the commanding artistry of the actress Ellen Terry were things not only of the past but of the present. Each became, in different ways, inflection points, as the women and men of Bloomsbury found and articulated what might be called a "Shakespeare of their own."

THE LAUREATE: ALFRED TENNYSON

Alfred Tennyson first met Julia Margaret Cameron in 1850, soon after his marriage. It was through her that he had initially become part of the Prinseps' social world. "The arrival of Julia Cameron in Tennyson's life marks a point of intersection between the Victorians and Bloomsbury," says Tennyson biographer John Batchelor.[12] Tennyson's neighbor in Freshwater, she became "almost the only woman outside his relations whom he called by her Christian name, and who called him in turn by his."[13] This fortunate conjunction, not coincidentally, also marks a point of intersection with Shakespeare.

As an undergraduate at Cambridge—where he was elected a member of the Apostles—Tennyson had been drawn to the stage and was, according to his son Hallam, "famous in some parts of Shakespeare, especially in Malvolio."[14] A contemporary described him as "six feet high, broad-chested, strong-limbed, his face Shakespearian, with deep eyelids, his forehead ample, crowned with dark wavy hair"—though it is hard to know whether this perceived resemblance to the earlier poet was immediate or retrospective.[15] In any case, Tennyson's allegiance to Shakespeare was direct and lifelong. Asked "what politics he held," he declared, "I am of the same politics as Shakespeare, Bacon, and every sane man."[16]

In the spring of 1840 Tennyson visited Stratford-upon-Avon to see Shakespeare's monument in the parish church, and then went to the birthplace. He wrote to his fiancée, "We went also into the room where they say he was born. Every part of it is scribbled over with names. I was seized with a sort of enthusiasm and wrote mine, though I was a little ashamed of it afterwards: yet the feeling was genuine at the time, and I did homage with the rest."[17] When he began

Alfred, Lord Tennyson, photograph by Julia Margaret Cameron, ca. 1865

construction on a grand new house at Aldworth in Surrey, the cornerstone was laid on Shakespeare's birthday, April 23, 1868, and the event was celebrated with friends.[18]

Tennyson himself would not infrequently be compared to Shakespeare—or would himself suggest such a comparison. His own monodrama "Maud, or the Madness," he described as "a little *Hamlet.*"[19] The novelist Anny Ritchie, Leslie Stephen's sister-in-law, reported that in 1874, after an evening watching Henry Irving's *Hamlet,* "the play was over, and we ourselves seemed a part of it still; here were the players, and our own prince poet [Tennyson], in that familiar simple voice we all know, explaining the art, going straight to the point in his own downright fashion."[20]

His opinions, too, were downright. *Hamlet,* he said, was "the greatest creation in literature that I know of." The ghost in that play "is the most real ghost that ever was." As for the tragic death of Ophelia, "The Queen did not think that Ophelia committed suicide, neither do I."[21] Among his favorite Shakespearean moments were several that confirmed the importance of romantic love. Romeo's words after leaving Juliet are "one of the most passionate things in Shakespeare."[22] The teasing love talk between Hotspur and Lady Percy in *Henry IV, Part 1* is "deliciously playful."[23] And, citing "the three repartees in Shakespeare which always bring tears to my eyes," he lists among them Posthumus's exhortation to Imogen in *Cymbeline,* "Hang there like fruit, my soul, / Till the tree die."[24] This passage was so greatly admired by Tennyson that he died with his copy of *Cymbeline* open to those lines, as his son Hallam told Queen Victoria:

> I think that your Majesty would care to know that the volume he asked for during the three latest days of his life was Shakespeare's *Cymbeline.* I said to him shortly before his passing away—"You must not try and read it," He answered, "Let me feel it then," and, after a pause, "I *have opened it.*" He kept it open at one of his favourite passages.—
>
> Hang there like fruit, my soul,
> Till the tree die.
>
> . . . On this his hand rested till he died. I could not part from this precious volume—but we had a Shakespeare buried with him—open at this passage which I marked.[25]

This same passage, as we will see, would be excitedly discovered and praised nine years later by a young Virginia Stephen as "the best lines in the play—almost in any play I should think," as she wrote to her brother Thoby.[26] Later she would make two young men's enthusiasm for those lines part of a key scene in *Jacob's Room,* the novel that she thought of dedicating to Thoby's memory.[27]

Like many celebrities in his time, Tennyson enjoyed performing for (usually rapt and adoring) audiences in his home or the homes of friends. Writing to the tutor of Tennyson's sons, Julia Margaret Cameron described a particularly memorable evening: "the whole range of poetry comprised, every immortal poet brought to life, and living again in the glowing and wise breath of Alfred Tennyson, [and] in the quotations from Henry Taylor's rich and faithful memory."[28] Both of these men would figure in Cameron's own photographic homage to the immortal poets—a homage that focused, directly and compellingly, on Shakespeare.

THE PHOTOGRAPHER: JULIA MARGARET CAMERON

Virginia Woolf's essay on Julia Margaret Cameron was originally published in 1926 as the introduction to a book of Cameron's work, tellingly titled *Victorian Photographs of Famous Men and Fair Women.*[29] The famous men are all there—Taylor, Tennyson, Holman Hunt, J. F. W. Herschel, Thomas Carlyle, Charles Darwin. The fair women, many of them very young, include several of

Julia Margaret Cameron, photograph by Robert Faulkner, early 1860s

Cameron's relatives. (One of her favorite female models was Woolf's mother, Julia.)

Cameron's interest in photography coincided with the fashion among her social set for tableaux vivants and amateur theatricals. Her "fancy subjects"—fantasy or allegorical images—drew largely upon the Bible, the poetry of her friends and contemporaries, and Shakespeare. And as with so many interpretations of Shakespeare, both then and now, Cameron's photographs presented ideas that were consistent with her own beliefs and those of her friends, family, and social peers.

"No woman," Cameron once declared, "should ever allow herself to be photographed between the ages of eighteen and eighty."[30] On the other hand, eminent men seemed to grow ever more photogenic with the years. On one occasion she led a visitor up to the bedroom in which her husband, Charles Hay Cameron, was quietly napping, and threw open the door. "Behold!" she said. "Behold the most beautiful old man on earth!"[31] Tennyson seems to have concurred, in a way, with this assessment; he described Charles Cameron as "a philosopher with his beard dipped in moonlight." Charles Cameron appears in some of his wife's photographs, but more frequently for her "fancy subjects" she used Tennyson, "wrapped in rugs," or their friend Sir Henry Taylor, poet, dramatist, and man of letters, about whom the photographer wrote, "Regardless of the possible dread that sitting to my fancy might be making a fool of himself, he, with greatness that belongs to unselfish affection, consented to be in turn Friar Laurence with Juliet, Prospero with Miranda, [and] Ahasuerus with Queen Esther."[32] The lavishly bearded Taylor is also the model for a number of solitary studies inscribed "Prospero."

But many of Julia Cameron's Shakespeare images follow a different pattern, that of the double portrait—bringing together supposedly wise older men (Friar Laurence, Prospero) and lovely young women (Juliet, Miranda). In *Friar Laurence and Juliet* (1865), Juliet looks up trustingly into the eyes of Friar Laurence as he hands her the potion that will simulate death and provoke the final catastrophe. In *Prospero and Miranda* of the same year, an obedient Miranda likewise looks up into the eyes of a kindly Prospero while clasping his hand.

Even when the play text makes it clear from the outset that the older man is not so wise, as in the case of *King Lear* (or indeed the naïvely hopeful Friar Laurence), the emblematic iconography of the singular father-daughter relationship is still center stage.

In *King Lear Allotting His Kingdom to His Three Daughters* (1872), although there are three daughters in the photograph, Lear's back is turned to two of them, and he faces Cordelia. Together the king and his favorite child take up almost all of the picture plane, he majestic with his flowing white beard and hair, she attentive but clearly also concerned, in a white gown. Goneril and Regan are squashed together behind the heedless king. One tries unsuccessfully to get his attention, raising a finger to pluck at his robe; the other gazes off into space. But

Julia Margaret Cameron, *Friar Laurence and Juliet*, 1865
(Henry Taylor and Mary Hillier)

in the next moment, not pictured, the king's love will turn to rage. The model for Lear is Cameron's husband, Charles; the daughters are photographer Charles Dodgson's favorite subjects: the sisters Lorina and Edith and, as Cordelia, Alice Liddell.

In another *Lear* image—this one from the end of the play rather than its beginning—the bearded, crowned king bends over the dead body of Cordelia (*Cordelia and King Lear,* 1865). Cordelia lies supine, her eyes closed, in a posture similar to those of the many floating Pre-Raphaelite Ophelias. A surprisingly robust Lear fills much of the picture plane, his face expressing solicitude as much as grief.[33]

The taste for dressing up as literary or historical figures was one that would have appealed to Bloomsbury, which had its own penchant for fancy-dress parties and private theatricals. Double-reading such images—taking note of the iden-

Julia Margaret Cameron, *Prospero and Miranda,* 1865
(Henry Taylor and Mary Ryan)

tity of the actor as well as the role—would later enliven many Bloomsbury productions and amuse many Bloomsbury audiences (including those who attended the performance of *Freshwater,* Virginia Woolf's affectionate send-up of these Victorian forebears). It's clear from her own account that Julia Margaret Cameron herself enjoyed both the casting and the role-playing. As did her sitters.

Perhaps the most suggestive of Cameron's father-daughter photographs with respect to Bloomsbury is *Prospero and Miranda.* "Shakespeare" in this period has many avatars, but one of them is surely to point a moral. The characters in the plays become emblematic actors exemplifying social roles enshrined in the culture. Thus the image of Prospero and Miranda can mark the affection—and the status difference—between wise father and adoring daughter—or, as Sidney Lee put it, "tender, ingenuous girlhood unsophisticated by social inter-

Julia Margaret Cameron, *King Lear Allotting His Kingdom to His Three Daughters,* 1872 (Lorina Liddell, Edith Liddell, Charles Hay Cameron, and Alice Liddell)

course."[34] But *Prospero and Miranda,* as we will see, could be an image not only of father-daughter affection but also of parental education: the kind of education Virginia Stephen would receive from her father's reading and philosophy and from his library.

The photograph itself was the subject of a romantic story told by both Julia Margaret Cameron—an inveterate matchmaker—and Virginia Woolf. The model for Miranda, Mary Ryan, was the daughter of an Irishwoman whom Cameron found begging on Putney Heath. Cameron "adopted" the mother and sent the daughter to school with her own children; Mary joined Cameron's household and became another of her favorite models. Some years later, when Mary Ryan was in charge of the catalogues at an exhibition of photographs in Bond Street, Henry John Stedman Cotton, a wealthy young bachelor, was smitten with both the photographs and the model. But apparently—so goes the story—it was only when he saw Cameron's photograph *Prospero and Miranda* that Cotton determined that he would marry her, despite the difference in their social positions. Mary, says Woolf, "grew up to be a beautiful woman, became Mrs Cameron's parlour-maid, sat for her portrait, was sought in marriage by a rich man's son, filled the position with dignity and competence, and in 1878 enjoyed an income of two thousand four hundred pounds a year."[35] This is Cameron's Victorian fairy-tale version:

> Entirely out of the Prospero and Miranda picture sprang a marriage which has, I hope, cemented the welfare and well-being of a real King Cophetua who, in the Miranda, saw the prize which has proved a jewel in the monarch's crown. The sight of the picture caused the resolve to be uttered which, after 18 months of constancy, was matured by personal knowledge, then fulfilled, producing one of the prettiest idylls of real life that can be conceived, and, what is of far more importance, a marriage of bliss with children worthy of being photographed, as their mother had been, for their beauty; but it must also be observed that the father was eminently handsome, with a head of the Greek type and fair ruddy Saxon complexion.[36]

Cotton and Ryan posed as *Romeo and Juliet* for yet another Cameron photograph in July 1867, a few days before their marriage. Despite what the Shakespearean reference might have inadvertently implied—Stuart Sillars notes "the rather curious idea of such an enactment as the prelude to a happy married life"—the couple did live "happily ever after," or at least well into the twentieth century.[37] Cameron's Shakespeare citation, in fact, was clearly by this time what another era would call a meme: Romeo-and-Juliet in the Victorian cultural imagination meant "young love," not "fated to die young."

When freed from the constraints of narrative and the appeal of the tableau vivant, however, Cameron's Shakespeare portraits can look strikingly modern, as is the case with her *Iago* and her two *Ophelia*s. Only one print of *Iago, Study from an Italian* (1867) survives, and it has been speculated that it was produced

Julia Margaret Cameron, *Romeo and Juliet,* 1867
(Henry John Stedman Cotton and Mary Ryan)

for Watts as a study for a projected painting. The professional model, Angelo Colarossi—one of very few models Cameron ever employed—had also posed for Leighton, Sargent, and Watts. The half-closed eyes, the chin with its stubble of beard, the roughly parted hair, and the inward reflection of the gaze—taken at a time when sitting motionless was essential for proper photographic exposure—all effectively suggest the intensity of Shakespeare's character.[38]

Cameron's first *Ophelia* (1867), a head shot of a young woman named Mary Pinnock, looks resolute and passionate, alert and aware. As Philip Prodger describes her, she is "transformed from victim to protagonist, level-headed and determined."[39] A later Cameron *Ophelia,* a photograph of Emily Peacock (1874), runs one hand through her hair and looks straight at the camera; her gaze is introspective, her brows furrowed. She looks worried or troubled but not out of control.

Despite the fashion for images of Ophelia in the period and the stage con-

Julia Margaret Cameron, *Ophelia Study No. 2,* 1867
(Mary Pinnock)

vention that unloosed hair was a sign of "madness," each of these Ophelias is in its way contemporary, not solely dependent upon Pre-Raphaelite models for pathos or power.[40] Julia Cameron would have been familiar with all the Ophelia images of the time. John Everett Millais's famous painting of a supine Ophelia floating on a flower-banked river, completed in 1851–52, was widely—though not universally—admired. A classic of Pre-Raphaelite art with its vivid colors, truth to nature, and "language of flowers," it illustrates an event that is described by Gertrude to Laertes (*Hamlet* 4.7) rather than actually shown in the play. Other Ophelias from the same period are similarly decorative: John William Waterhouse and Arthur Hughes both depict a pretty Ophelia sitting on a branch of a willow tree toying with flowers before she enters the water; in a version by the French painter Alexandre Cabanel, Ophelia, blond and graceful, reclines in the brook on a broken limb, apparently unfazed by her situation.

Julia Margaret Cameron, *Ophelia,* 1874 (Emily Peacock)

Sometimes Cameron titled her photographs imaginatively, with phrases chosen from favorite poems (*The Angel in the House*, *The Mountain Nymph Sweet Liberty*), and other times simply by the name of the sitter (*My Niece Julia Jackson Now Mrs Herbert Duckworth*). Whether the "Ophelia" and "Iago" associations came as she was posing her subjects or after the sitting when she looked at her work, it's clear that Shakespeare was often in her mind, and in her mind's eye.

THE ACTRESS: ELLEN TERRY

It is instructive to compare Julia Margaret Cameron's 1867 *Ophelia,* shown in half profile, her lips slightly parted, her hair loose, with George Frederic Watts's *Ophelia* (1864; reworked circa 1877–80), his painting of Ellen Terry done shortly after their marriage.

In Watts's painting Ophelia leans over the water, her head and hands braced on the willow branches that will shortly give way beneath her weight. But the

G. F. Watts, *Ophelia,* 1863–64, ca. 1877–80

long, tousled hair, the profile, the parted lips—all are there. Terry "brought an expressive inevitability to the pose, as Ophelia gazes open-mouthed at the beckoning water, seemingly in a trance."[41] "For Watts," suggest the authors of a catalogue of his work, "the Shakespearean source provided the framework for what became a study of the interior mind of Ophelia in a far more disturbing scene than Millais' decorous drowning." The result was transformative: "In an era of literal Shakespearean productions and paintings, his deeply emotive view of Ophelia provided a counterbalance."[42]

Yet the painting was entirely an imagined scene. Ellen Terry at seventeen had not yet played Ophelia, though her elder sister Kate appeared in the role at the Lyceum in May 1864. It was not until 1878, after her divorce from Watts and her return to acting, that Ellen's Ophelia could be seen onstage, opposite Henry Irving's Hamlet. The same year, the reworked *Ophelia* painting by Watts was exhibited at the Grosvenor Gallery, where the playwright, critic, and *Punch* editor Tom Taylor pronounced it "pathetically beautiful."[43]

Ellen Terry as Ophelia in *Hamlet,*
photograph by Window & Grove, 1878

Ophelia's "madness" in these works is inward- rather than outward-facing. None of the artists show her giving flowers to the men around her or, as the stage direction to her entrance in the First Quarto says, "distracted, playing on a lute, her hair down, singing" (*Hamlet* 4.5 [stage direction]). Where Millais shows her floating peacefully, and relatively passively, toward her death, Watts and Cameron give us vivid pictures of intense personal feeling. What a modern era would call "agency"—the capacity to act—attaches to these young women as they face their anger and despair.

Terry, the high-spirited young girl who married G. F. Watts and posed for Julia Margaret Cameron, would in due course herself grow up to be a major interpreter of Shakespeare's women. In an era when the "pictorialism" of the stage sometimes threatened to overshadow the actors, Terry was one of the few able to adapt it for her own purpose and in her own style. For her the visual model was not the architectural panorama but a form both more familiar and more intimate: the panel painting and the photograph—the visual arts, in other words, of Millais and Watts and Cameron, of Little Holland House and Dimbola Lodge. The theatre critic Clement Scott, reviewing her performance as Portia in *The Merchant of Venice,* said that she "looked as if she had stepped out of a canvas by Leighton," and the painter Graham Robertson wrote that "she was preeminently the Painter's Actress and appealed to the eye before the ear; her gesture and pose were eloquence itself."[44]

Virginia Woolf's late essay on Terry, published in the *New Statesman and Nation* in February 1941, just a month before her death, probably had its origins in her visit to the Ellen Terry Museum founded by Terry's daughter, Edith (Edy) Craig and her partner, Christopher St. John, at Terry's former home in Smallhythe, Kent. Edy would be a model for the character of Miss La Trobe in Woolf's last novel, *Between the Acts.*

Woolf's assessment of the actress, whom her parents had probably encountered at Little Holland House so long ago, is frankly retrospective. The task she sets herself is to reimagine and bring to life Ellen Terry on the stage as a previous generation would have seen her. "When the part was congenial, when she was Shakespeare's Portia, Desdemona, Ophelia, every word, every comma was consumed. Even her eyelashes acted. Her body lost its weight."[45] And where did Terry learn her Shakespeare? "As for education, she never had a day's schooling in her life. As far as she can see, but the problem baffles her, the main spring of her art is imagination. Visit madhouses, if you like; take notes; observe; study endlessly. But first, imagine. And so she takes her part away from the books out into the woods. Rambling down grassy rides, she lives her part until she is in it. If a word jars or grates, she must re-think it, re-write it. Then when every phrase is her own, and every gesture spontaneous, out she comes onto the stage and is Imogen, Ophelia, Desdemona."[46] Woolf also summons up for the reader "the full-length portrait of Ellen Terry as Sargent painted her, robed and crowned as Lady Macbeth." What she does not say is that this is an invented scene, not in the play, showing the lady triumphantly crowning herself—Sargent's tribute to an actress and her greatness.

Then the focus shifts: in Woolf's imagined scenario, "Pen in hand, she is seated at her desk. A volume of Shakespeare lies before her. It is open at *Cymbeline,* and she is making careful notes in the margin. The part of Imogen presents great problems." She enters into correspondence with "the brilliant young critic of the *Saturday Review,* whose long letter lies beside Shakespeare" on her desk. Characteristically, Woolf does not mention the name of the critic; those in the know will recognize him as George Bernard Shaw. "But what suggestions has the brilliant critic to make about Imogen? None apparently that she has not already thought for herself. She is as close and critical a student of Shakespeare as he is. She has studied every line, weighed the meaning of every word, experimented with every gesture."[47]

Terry in her prime both created and embodied Shakespeare's women for late Victorian playgoers. And yet, Woolf suggests, she even transcended those roles. "Something of Ellen Terry it seems overflowed every part and remained unacted. Shakespeare could not fit her; nor Ibsen; nor Shaw. The stage could not hold her."[48] Something extra or something missing—this is the mark of modernity. Ellen Terry's career as charted by Woolf in this late essay is emblematic of the passage from mid-Victorian to modern, from Little Holland House and Freshwater to Bloomsbury and Charleston, from the young Leslie Stephen, "shy with artistic people," to the artistic innovations of Leslie's daughters, Vanessa Bell and Virginia Woolf.

An instinctive student, a thoughtful scholar, a brilliant experimenter with word and gesture. Is this a description of Ellen Terry or of Virginia Stephen Woolf? Perhaps it is both. After Woolf's death, Vita Sackville-West read her essay onstage in 1941 at the Barn Theatre in memory of Terry and of Woolf.[49]

As has often been the case with Shakespeare, his works, characters, and language were appropriated in the Victorian period to support or sometimes challenge ideas about the social world. Tennyson identified with Shakespeare as a poet and shared—or said he shared—the views of Queen Victoria. Julia Margaret Cameron's Shakespeare images both reflect and redirect Victorian concerns about women, love, and filial obedience. Ellen Terry empowered Shakespeare's women on the stage.

But of all those who had frequented the Prinseps' salon at Little Holland House, it was perhaps Leslie Stephen—scholar, biographer, critic, and father of Thoby, Vanessa, Virginia, and Adrian—who most directly identified Shakespeare's views about personal conduct and the family with his own.

CHAPTER 2

Shakespeare as a (Victorian) Man

"My father always loved reading aloud," wrote Virginia Woolf. "His memory for poetry was wonderful; he could absorb a poem that he liked almost unconsciously from a single reading." These recitations, spoken with closed eyes as he lay back in his chair, imparted a kind of double verisimilitude: "Many of the great English poems now seem to me inseparable from my father," she wrote shortly after his death. "I hear in them not only his voice, but in some sort his teaching and belief."[1]

"Poetry in those days was music," notes Leslie Stephen's biographer Noel Annan, writing of the period before the First World War. "It was an incantation to be chanted, as anyone who listens to the earliest gramophone recordings can tell."[2] As a child Leslie had recited the poetry of Walter Scott in Kensington Gardens. When he brought up his own family at Hyde Park Gate in Kensington, Virginia Woolf remembers, "he shouted Newbolt's 'Admirals All' as he went about the house or walked in Kensington Gardens, to the surprise of nursery-maids and park-keepers."[3] Shakespeare, Scott, and Austen were among his favorites, and he read them to his daughters long after his sons had gone away to school.

His family became accustomed to the rhythmic thump of verses. Often, as he mounted the stairs to his study, Woolf recalled, "he would burst, not into song, for he was entirely unmusical, but into a strange rhythmical chant, for verse of all kinds, both 'utter trash' as he called it, and the most sublime words of Milton and Wordsworth, stuck in his memory, and the act of walking or climbing seemed to inspire him to recite whichever it was that came uppermost or suited his mood."[4] Woolf's own response to Shakespeare's verse at times seems to echo this memory of her father's "strange rhythmical chant," the physical energy he derived from poetic language. Even in sedentary reading she is struck by the powerful cadences of the great speeches, the "volley & volume & tumble of words."[5]

Friends who joined Stephen on his "tramps" through the countryside and up and down mountains became accustomed to his full-throated recitations. "Out of doors he strode along, often shaking his head emphatically as he recited poetry, and giving his stick a flourish," as Woolf would describe it. Indeed she thought that in his later years "he must have put his clothes on automatically, to the sound of poetry, I expect; the waistcoat was often unbuttoned; sometimes the fly buttons; and the coat was often grey with tobacco ash."[6] In *To the Lighthouse* Woolf gives this same propensity for quoting poetry to Mr. Ramsay; the words of Tennyson's "Charge of the Light Brigade" ("Someone had blundered") and Cowper's "The Castaway" ("we perished each alone") resound throughout the novel, intersecting with narrative events in ways that are by turns ironic and tragic.

In his role as the editor of *The Dictionary of National Biography* (*DNB*), Leslie Stephen supervised the writing of some 653 contributors and wrote 378 of the biographies himself, including those of many of the poets and writers. But the biography of Shakespeare was entrusted to Sidney Lee, who was Stephen's assistant at the *DNB* and later his successor.[7]

Nonetheless, Stephen wrote several essays that directly convey his thoughts on Shakespeare. In "The Study of English Literature," delivered as a lecture to the Students' Association of St. Andrews in 1887 and then published in the *Cornhill Magazine,* he claims that "the true object of the study of a man's writings" is "to make a personal friend of the author" by becoming familiar with "the very trick of his speech, the turn of his thoughts, the characteristic peculiarity of his sentiments, of his imagery, of his mode of contemplating the world of human life."[8] This aim is—somewhat paradoxically—facilitated in the case of Shakespeare by the fact that he is no longer alive. "If we could consciously meet a Shakespeare we should be struck dumb; but we are quite at ease with that essence of Shakespeare which is compressed into a book. We can put him in our pockets, admit him to an audience when we are in the humour, and treat him as familiarly as a college chum."[9]

In this essay Stephen makes the earliest of what will be many similar pronouncements about youth, maturity, and the plays: "To enjoy *Romeo and Juliet* the best qualification is to be one-and-twenty (which is compatible with being also thirty or forty). To enjoy *Hamlet* it is, perhaps, better to be, let us say, fifty-four."[10] The extension of the youthful romantic age of "one-and-twenty" to "thirty or forty" marks the dates of Stephen's two marriages, to Minny Thackeray in 1867, when he was thirty-five, and to Julia Duckworth in 1878, when he was forty-six, while the genial "let us say, fifty-four" refers to his age when the essay was written. It is here, too, that Leslie Stephen offers one of his best-known pieces of advice to students of literature: "Never persuade yourselves that you like what you don't like; not if it be *Faust* or *Hamlet,* or the *Divina Commedia,* or the *Iliad.* Sham liking is far worse than honest stupidity. But again, do not presume that your dislike to an accepted masterpiece proves it not to be a masterpiece. . . . Try again, and see if Shakespeare will not improve."[11]

In "Did Shakespeare Write Bacon?" his one satirical piece, Stephen sends up the fashionable Bacon-wrote-Shakespeare claims (including those of the American Delia Bacon), maintaining that as lord chancellor, Francis Bacon was too busy with matters of state to work on the philosophical *Novum Organum,* and that he therefore paid Shakespeare to retire from the stage and become his ghost writer.[12] The essay includes a faux cipher allowing the reader to decode the opening words of Bacon's book to identify "Will Shakespere" as the author. More extended discussions of Shakespeare can be found in "Massinger," in which Stephen compares him to the early modern playwright Philip Massinger, and "Shakespeare as a Man," published after the appearance of Lee's *Life of William Shakespeare.* Both essays, though relatively brief, are revealing, as much about Leslie Stephen as about Shakespeare.

"Massinger" offers an assured statement about Shakespeare's politics: "The author of *Coriolanus,* one would be disposed to say, showed himself a thorough-going aristocrat, though in an age when the popular voice had not yet given utterance to the sentiments symptomatic of an approaching revolution."[13] And on Shakespeare's ideas about maturation: "Shakespeare's Henry or Romeo may indulge in wild freaks or abandon themselves to the intense passions of vigorous youth; but they will settle down into good statesmen and warriors as they grow older. Their love-making is a phase in their development, not the business of their lives."[14] The fact that this was unhappily not the case for Romeo seems almost beside the point; Stephen here reads Shakespeare as a social psychologist rather than a playwright with a tragic plot. And very often, as it happens, Shakespeare's opinions about these matters concur with his own.

On the subject of women, too, it turns out that Shakespeare's views accord with Stephen's, and when his women step out of line they either step back in pretty smartly or suffer the consequences.

> Shakespeare's women are undoubtedly most admirable and lovely creatures; but they are content to take a subordinate part, and their highest virtue generally includes entire submission to the will of their lords and masters. Some, indeed, have an abundant share of the masculine temperament, like Cleopatra or Lady Macbeth; but then they are by no means model characters. Iago's description of the model woman is a cynical version of the true Shakespearean theory. Women's true sphere, according to him, or according to the modern slang, is domestic life; and if circumstances force a Cordelia, an Imogen, a Rosalind, or a Viola, to take a more active share in life, they take good care to let us know that they have a woman's heart under their man's doublet.[15]

This may be the only place in all of Shakespeare criticism where Iago's view of women is regarded as more accurate, or more "Shakespearean," than Antony's. On the other hand, Stephen sympathizes with "poor Mariana," whose future life with Angelo, "her hypocritical husband," seems to him at best "a questionable advantage," intimating that Shakespeare may have felt that "marriage with a hypocritical tyrant ought to be regarded as better than no marriage at all."[16] In general, however, Stephen's admiration for Shakespeare in the Massinger essay is so immediate and so instinctive that it reads like both projection and identification. "In literature," he writes, "the foundation of all excellence, artistic or moral, is a vivid perception of realities and a masculine grasp of fact. A man who has that essential quality will not blink the truths which we see every day around us. He will not represent vice as so ugly that it can have no charms. . . . He will describe Iago as impartially as Desdemona, and, having given us the facts, leave us to make what we please of them."[17]

"A vivid perception of realities." Impartiality. Truth-telling at any cost. "A masculine grasp of fact." These are all qualities that Leslie Stephen valued for himself and the ideals to which he held other men. His later essay "Shakespeare as a Man" begins by setting up a contrast between Sidney Lee's approach and that of the Danish scholar Georg Morris Cohen Brandes, whose *William Shakespeare: A Critical Study,* was published in English in 1898, the same year as Lee's *Life of William Shakespeare.*[18] Lee, he says, "like many critics of the highest authority, maintains that we can know nothing of the man." Lee had, indeed, explained in his book's preface that he had "endeavoured loyally to adhere to the principles that are inherent in the scheme of the 'Dictionary of National Biography'" and to "reduce conjecture to the smallest dimensions consistent with coherence," a nod to his *DNB* colleague that he might have supposed would be greeted with favor, especially in view of the rather unexpected—and rhetorically unnecessary—word *loyally.*[19] And Brandes?

> Professor Brandes, on the contrary, tries to show how a certain spiritual history indicated by the works may be more or less distinctly correlated with certain passages in the personal history. The process, of course, involves a good deal of conjecture. It rests upon the assumption that the works, when properly interpreted, reveal character; for the facts taken by themselves are a manifestly insufficient ground for more than a few negative inferences. If, with Mr Lee, we regard the first step as impossible, the whole theory must collapse. Upon his showing we learn little from the works except that Shakespeare, whatever he may have been as a man, had a marvelous power of wearing different masks.[20]

Where does Leslie Stephen place himself in this scholarly debate between conjecture and what he had called in the "Massinger" essay "a masculine grasp of fact"? "I confess," he says, restating an observation he had made in "The Study of English Literature," "that to me one main interest in reading is always the communion with the author."

The tall, "lean," Stephen, who says elsewhere that he "had the misfortune to be hopelessly unmusical,"[21] gestures disarmingly toward his own presumptive failings: "Some of us have personal reasons for hoping that when his characters express a dislike for the lean or for the unmusical, their words do not give his deliberate judgment. If this were a fatal difficulty it would follow that no competent dramatist reveals himself in his works. Yet, as a matter of fact, I suppose that dramatists are generally quite as knowable as other authors. We learn to know Ben Jonson from his plays alone. . . . That surely is the rule." Yet, he concedes, authors differ. "To read Dante is to know whom he hated and why he hated them, and what, in his opinion, would be their proper place hereafter. To Shakespeare good men and bad are alike parts of the order of Nature, to be understood and interpreted with perfect impartiality. . . . His characters prosper or suffer, not in proportion to their merits, but as good and bad fortune decides or as may be most dramatically effective."

Here is that word *impartial* again. In many ways "Shakespeare as a Man" reads like an extension or a rewrite of the ideas first expressed in the essay on Massinger. The belief that Shakespeare "showed himself a thoroughgoing aristocrat" is restated here: "I do not see how any man could have been more clearly what may be called an intellectual aristocrat. His contempt for the mob may be good-humoured enough, but it is surely unequivocal." Stephen's nephew J. K. Stephen is credited with coining the term "intellectual aristocracy," which came to describe those who valued mental and moral achievements rather than wealth or noble birth, and who worked to reform old institutions.[22] This was clearly the class to which Leslie and his friends belonged, and perhaps unsurprisingly he finds in Shakespeare a commonality of spirit.

Likewise with the fate of the youthful Romeo, now explicitly enjoined to live despite the loss of his beloved—as Leslie Stephen had realized he had to do, after the deaths of his first and second wives. Shakespeare, he imagines, must have shared such a view. "Be a Romeo while you can; love is delightful when you are young; only, think twice before you buy your dram of poison. As you grow older be a soldier, a hero, or a statesman, or, if you can be nothing better, be a playwright, so long as the inspiration comes with spontaneous and overpowering force. But always remember to keep your passions in check." In short, Shakespeare, says Stephen, "sees the facts of life too clearly not to be aware of the vanity of human wishes, the disappointments of successful ambition and the emptiness of its supposed rewards. He is profoundly conscious of the pettiness of human life and of the irony of fate—of which, indeed, he had plenty of instances before him. This, I fancy, implies personal characteristics which fall in very well, so far as they can be grasped, with what we know of the life." "The disappointments of successful ambition and the emptiness of its supposed rewards." "The pettiness of human life and of the irony of fate." Personal characteristics which "fall in very well . . . from what we know of the life." "The life" is an elegant way of saying "Shakespeare's life"—or is it? From whose life are these thoughts inferred or derived? The whole essay is, in its way, a textbook example of projection.

At the close, in a moving peroration, the young Romeo has grown older, his "passions" not only kept in check but now in fact palpably diminished, together with his ambition. Bearing in mind Stephen's desire for a "communion with the author," it is of some interest to see how he imagines the retirement years. Especially noteworthy is the acrobatic management of pronouns in this paragraph, which shift from "one" to "we" before returning in the final sentence to an ostensibly neutral editorial "I."

> When youthful passions have grown feeble, and the delight of being applauded by the mob has rather palled upon one, the best thing will be

> to break one's magical wand and sit down with, we will hope, "good Mistress Hall" for a satisfactory Miranda, at Stratford-upon-Avon. Though we can no longer write ballads to our mistress' eyebrow, we can heartily appreciate gentle, pure, and obedient womanhood, and may hope that some specimens may be found, while we still enjoy a chat and a convivial meeting with an old theatrical friend. This view of life suggests, I think, a very real person, and does not go beyond what is substantially admitted by literary critics.[23]

"Good Mistress Hall" is Susanna, Shakespeare's daughter, married to Dr. John Hall—who is, however, absent from this family portrait. The privileged dyad is father and daughter, Prospero and Miranda, an old man and his young daughter—the image so powerfully presented in Julia Margaret Cameron's iconic photograph. And the "very real person," Shakespeare "as a man," has been conflated with the author of the essay.

Like the imaginary twilight Shakespeare of this happy vision, Leslie Stephen believed in the ideal of "gentle, pure, and obedient womanhood." He "did not care for emancipated women," says Noel Annan, and his wife Julia shared his conviction that the role of a woman was to serve.[24] He would attempt to find "a satisfactory Miranda" after Julia's death, first in her daughter Stella Duckworth, and then in his and Julia's elder daughter Vanessa. Each took her turn as Stephen's main support in the household.

When her mother died, Virginia Woolf wrote long afterward, "Stella inherited all the duties that she had discharged."[25] It was a state of affairs that, under the circumstances, suited Leslie's wishes and his needs. When Stella married, he admitted to himself some "selfish pangs: but—well, I should be a brute if I really complained."[26] In fact he did complain; he was jealous as well as inconvenienced. And after Stella's marriage to Jack Hills (all too soon followed by her own death), Vanessa and Virginia were expected to take her place. Julia Stephen's conviction that a young woman should be "beautiful, dutiful, and altruistic," says Noel Annan, was "an ideal Leslie Stephen was all too ready to accept, since it enabled him to assume that after Stella's death Vanessa and Virginia would continue to regard as their first duty to minister to his own needs."[27] In the same memoir Woolf describes her father, devastated after her mother's death, receiving mourners "like the Queen in Shakespeare—'here I and sorrow sit'" (*King John* 3.1.73; the original line reads "sorrows"). The "queen" in this case is in fact not a queen but rather the Lady Constance, the mother of Arthur, a child claimant to the throne. Woolf is here clearly quoting from memory, her affection and sympathy

Virginia Stephen and Sir Leslie Stephen, photograph by George Charles Beresford, 1902

mingling with her ambivalence, since Leslie had put his own loss—rather than that of his children—so powerfully at center stage.

"One realises that Lear has always been stormy. His daughters have suffered for it," she noted when reading *King Lear* a few years after Leslie's death.[28] Here the attentive devotion of a Miranda seems to have merged, at least for a moment, with the resistance of Goneril, Regan, and Cordelia. All three of Lear's daughters seem to be included in this succinct comment; they are not differentiated into "good" and "bad" or "loyal" and "disloyal." Likewise Leslie's three adult daughters—Stella, Vanessa, and Virginia—had often to deal with his "violent temper," a "temper that he could not control," and his "extreme irritability."[29] "Why have my sisters husbands, if they say / They love you all?" Cordelia asked her father (*King Lear* 1.1.88–89).

Many years later, now a celebrated author and long married to Leonard Woolf, Virginia wrote in her diary on the anniversary of her father's birthday, "He would have been 96 today; but mercifully was not. His life would have entirely ended mine. What would have happened? No writing, no books;—inconceivable." But having written *To the Lighthouse* she is now able to think of him differently. Writing of her parents in that book was, she thinks, a "necessary act"; she was no longer "obsessed" and "unhealthily" haunted by memories. As for her father, "he comes back more as a contemporary. I must read him some day. I wonder if I can feel again, I hear his voice, I know this by heart?"[30]

One of Virginia's chief resentments against Leslie was his refusal to send his daughters to school as he had his sons. She longed for the social interaction and the intellectual stimulation—both of which she would later enjoy with her brother's Cambridge friends. Yet "arguably," says Woolf's biographer Hermione Lee, "as she sometimes argued herself," Leslie Stephen "gave her a better education from his study than she would have had at school or college."[31]

Again the relation of learned father and studious daughter may bring to mind that of Prospero and Miranda. Prospero tells his daughter at the beginning of *The Tempest* that as Duke of Milan he had been "reputed / In dignity, and for the liberal arts / Without a parallel" (1.2.72–73).[32] When his brother usurped his place, exiling Prospero and the infant Miranda by ship, the loyal Gonzalo, "knowing I loved my books . . . furnished me / From mine own library with volumes that / I prize above my dukedom" (167–69). It was this library that allowed him to educate his daughter.

> Here in this island we arrived, and here
> Have I thy schoolmaster made thee more profit
> Than other princes can, that have more time
> For vainer hours and tutors not so careful.
> (1.2.172–75)

Like Miranda, Virginia Stephen was educated from her father's library with his careful tutoring. He assigned her reading and quizzed her on it.[33]

He also helped shape her literary taste. "It was the Elizabethan prose writers I loved first & most wildly," Woolf notes in her diary, "stirred by Hakluyt, which father lugged home for me—I think of it with some sentiment—father tramping over the Library with his little girl sitting at HPG [Hyde Park Gate] in mind. He must have been 65, I 15 or 16, then; & why I dont know but I became enraptured, though not exactly interested, but the sight of the large yellow page entranced me. I used to read it & dream of those obscure adventurers, & no doubt practised their style in my copy books."[34] Here is another teasing glimpse of Leslie and Virginia as Prospero and Miranda, since the travel narratives of both Richard Hakluyt and William Strachey—the latter an ancestor of the Bloomsbury Stracheys—were sources for *The Tempest.*

"I am sometimes pleased to think that I read English literature when I was young," Woolf wrote to Vita Sackville-West. "I like to think of myself tapping at my father's study door, saying very loud and clear, 'Can I have another volume, father? I've finished this one.' Then he would be very pleased and say, 'Gracious, child, how you gobble.'" He would "get up and take down, it may have been the 6th or 7th volume of Gibbons complete works, or Speddings Bacon, or Cowper's Letters. 'But my dear, if its worth reading, its worth reading twice,' he would say. I have a great devotion for him—what a disinterested man, how high minded, how tender to me, and fierce and intolerable."[35] In analyzing their "relation as father and daughter"—including the "temper he could not control," his "worship of reason," his "hatred of gush, of exaggeration, of all superlatives"—Woolf would ultimately have recourse to the language of psychoanalysis. "It was only the other day," she writes in "Sketch of the Past," "when I read Freud for the first time, that I discovered that this violently disturbing conflict of love and hate is a common feeling, and is called ambivalence."[36]

And yet—or perhaps one should say "therefore"—his effect upon her was very great. And her affection comes through with particular vividness when she describes him doing something that was, for her father, very unusual: going to see a play. Leslie Stephen grew up in an educated, upper-middle-class household that "went neither to theatres nor to dances."[37] In general "theatre" for their set included home theatricals, tableaux, and charades—the kind of thing that for his children and their friends and families would later translate into masquerades like the "*Dreadnought* hoax," costume parties at Charleston, or Virginia Woolf's *Freshwater*.

By contrast, Stephen's contemporary the clergyman, author, and photographer Charles Dodgson was a passionate playgoer and a special fan of Ellen Terry, whom he saw onstage as Mamillius in 1856, when Terry was eight years old, again as Puck in 1858, and still later as Ophelia, a performance he found "simply perfect," in 1879.[38] In her autobiography Terry wrote that her friend "Mr Charles Dodgson—or Lewis Carroll" was a "splendid theatre-goer" who "took the greatest interest in all the Lyceum productions."[39]

But Virginia Woolf remembered her father going to the theatre only once. "He was so struck, so normally and masculinely affected by Mrs Langtry's beauty, that he actually went to the play to see her. Otherwise he never went to a play." As a singular exception to a life more regularly given over to the pleasures of philosophy, poetry, walking, and reading, this is in its own way worthy of note. And perhaps more importantly for the writer (and the reader), the memory "gives humanity to his austere figure."[40]

Lillie Langtry was a celebrity from Stephen's younger days at Little Holland

Lillie Langtry as Rosalind in *As You Like It,* photograph by Napoleon Sarony, 1882

House. Her portrait had been painted by Millais, Edward Poynter, and Val Prinsep, the artist son of Sarah and Thoby Prinsep. Burne-Jones used her as a model for one of his most remarkable paintings, *The Golden Stairs*. The "Signor" himself, G. F. Watts, asked her to sit for him at new Little Holland House in 1877.[41] She spent many hours in his studio as a social visitor as well as a model. The mistress of the Prince of Wales (later Edward VII), she was then one of the most famous women in England. "Mrs Langtry" first appeared on the London stage in the early 1880s, when she was admired for her looks rather than her acting: "the finely shaped head, the classic profile, the winning smile, the musical laugh, the grace of the figure."[42] She played many roles, classic and modern, but her favorite was Rosalind in *As You Like It*.

Initial reviewers were not impressed by her performance, so Langtry traveled to New York to hone her skills. When she returned to London at the end of the decade, she resumed acting, attracting better notices. "Mrs Langtry is a bewitching Rosalind," said the *Times*. The *Telegraph* reported that "the improvement in her acting is astounding; she is worthy of her stardom now," and the *Post* declared, "Mrs Langtry joins the ranks of the great Rosalinds."[43] In April 1890 when she appeared in *Antony and Cleopatra* opposite Charles Coghlan, she was given fourteen curtain calls. "She is the finest Cleopatra of our time," said the *Telegraph*, and the *Times* review described her performance as "dazzling!" This was Langtry's greatest theatrical triumph. The play ran until just before Christmas, and was often subsequently revived.

Did Leslie Stephen see "Mrs Langtry" as Rosalind? As Cleopatra? As the heroine of a more modern play? As Woolf's affectionate memory suggests, perhaps it did not matter. He went to see the woman, not the play.

Stephen's contributions to the study of literature were honored by the academic world, and here too both Shakespeare and women play small but indicative roles. The vice master of Trinity from 1888 until his death in 1914 was a Shakespearean, William Aldis Wright, described by David Nicol Smith in the *DNB* as "our greatest Shakespeare scholar since Edmund Malone."[44] Wright edited the Clarendon Press edition of Shakespeare's plays, and coedited, with George Clark, both the Cambridge Shakespeare and the Globe Shakespeare. It was Clark, another Trinity man, whose bequest funded the Clark Lectures in English literature.

The first Clark lecturer, in 1884, was Leslie Stephen, himself a graduate not of Trinity but of Trinity Hall. Despite the honor, Stephen felt the lectures to be onerous (necessitating travel to Cambridge three times a week) and pointless. His report, in a letter to Charles Eliot Norton, makes clear his views about "young women from the ladies' colleges," who were the largest part of his audience: "The female student," he wrote to Norton, "is at present an innocent animal, who wants to improve her mind and takes ornamental lectures seriously, not understanding with her brother students that the object of study is to get a good place in an examination, and that lectures are a vanity and a distraction. I confess that I sympathize with the male and grow half-inclined to laugh in the faces of my respectful and intelligent hearers." Although his reception, "both from the young women and from some old friends and stray dons," was warm enough, he felt himself to be a "humbug" and resigned the post after the first year.[45]

Cambridge lecture series in English literature continued to have a Bloomsbury connection, however. Both E. M. Forster and Desmond MacCarthy would later offer Clark Lectures, and when the university named a lectureship after Stephen in 1905, Lytton Strachey gave a Leslie Stephen Lecture on Pope, MacCarthy one on Stephen, and E. M. Forster one on Virginia Woolf (after her death). Woolf herself had been invited in 1932 to give a Clark Lecture, but she declined, although she was tempted; she noted in her diary that it was "the first time a woman had been asked," reflecting that "father would have blushed with pleasure could I have told him 30 years ago, that his daughter—my poor little Ginny—was to be asked to succeed him: the sort of compliment he would have liked."[46]

In his Leslie Stephen Lecture, Forster noted that Woolf "was somewhat astringent over the academic position of women. 'What? I in the Senate House?' she might say; 'are you sure that is quite proper? And why, if you want to discuss my books, need you first disguise yourselves in caps and gowns?'" Yet he thought that on balance she "would be pleased. She loved Cambridge." And here he indulges in a Woolfian fantasy of Virginia, disguised as a boy, taking her degree there.[47] Woolf's love for Cambridge seems, in fact, to have been imbued with that same ambivalence she described when speaking of her father.

CHAPTER 3

The Shakespeares of Virginia Woolf

All her life, Virginia Woolf made entries about Shakespeare in her journals and diaries, and kept up a lively correspondence about the plays with her friends. A few kinds of comments recur with particular regularity over the years: her pleasure in the solitary reading of the plays, often seen as both soothing and ecstatic; her reports of conversations with friends and acquaintances about Shakespeare and his works; her reflections on life—nature and "human nature"—as inspired by Shakespeare; and her exhilaration at reading Shakespeare in conjunction with her own writing, where his work seems to set an impossible standard but also to be a spur to her creative efforts.

The Stephen family often called one another and their friends by affectionate nicknames. Virginia was the Goat (and therefore Billy). Vanessa was Dolphin. Thoby was Tobs or Grim (as Virginia addressed him in a letter about *Cymbeline*). Virginia's childhood friend Emma Vaughan was Toad (and Toadlebinks and Todger), and so on. At Cambridge Thoby was, more grandly, known as the Goth to his friends, while Lytton Strachey was the Strache, and Strachey dubbed E. M. Forster the Taupe.

It should not come as a surprise, then, to find that Shakespeare, too, accrued a range of nicknames as Virginia Woolf began to think and write about him. In an early letter to Thoby he was "the great William," a description intended to mark her own initial skepticism. In her diaries he was "Shre," a shorthand term for a word she would write over and over again. She also uses "&" for "and" and

Virginia Stephen, photograph by George Charles Beresford, 1902

omits apostrophes (dont, cant, wont) and underlinings (Othello, Measure for Measure). Woolf is writing and thinking quickly, for her own interest and pleasure. When these private diaries are published, what was convenience becomes instantiated as style. "Shre" seems to take on a life of its (his?) own as a familiar, admiring, and affectionate sobriquet. This may be—in fact surely is—an artifact of reading, but it is difficult to overcome completely, especially because when she writes about other peoples' responses to the playwright she typically uses his full surname. "Shre" usually appears when Woolf is thinking about her own writing in connection with his. Of course there are exceptions, but the great passages from the diary about the splendors and rigors of writing, even when they start with "Shakespeare," often end with the more contracted—and private—form.

In her essays and reviews written for journals and newspapers he was, unavoidably, "Shakespeare," the public name. But in the novels he develops a variety of names and titles, each with its own nuance. At one end of the scale is

Orlando's reference to "Sh—p—re (for when we speak names we deeply reverence to ourselves we never speak them whole)," modeled, with the deft tonal irony omnipresent in that novel, on the biblical injunction against pronouncing the name of God.[1] It is Orlando's mind, not the narrator's, that employs this pious deflection (comparable to the spelling of "G—d" in some religious tracts). At the other end are those characters who quote or name the playwright as a way of asserting their own status or England's. The classic example is Lady Bruton in *Mrs. Dalloway,* although there are more naïve and likeable name-droppers as early as *Night and Day*. But the most profound references to Shakespeare are often not references at all but glimpses, guesses, analogies, or fantasies—references that summon to mind a poet, an act of writing, or a hidden story.

LETTERS AND DIARIES

"Had He Been Put On"

Her brother Thoby Stephen was Virginia's first Shakespeare tutor, and his influence on her, intellectually and personally, was to last a lifetime. When he went up to Cambridge in November 1901, she wrote him with what she called a "confession" concerning her views on "a certain great English writer": "I read *Cymbeline* just to see if there mightn't be more in the great William than I supposed. And I was quite upset! Really and truly I am now let in to [the] company of worshippers—though I still feel a little oppressed by his—greatness, I suppose."[2] Still, she had questions to ask as well as an important discovery to report.

> I shall want a lecture when I see you; to clear up some points about the Plays. I mean about the characters. Why aren't they more human? Imogen and Posthumous [*sic*] and Cymbeline—I find them beyond me. Is this my feminine weakness in the upper region? But really they might have been cut out with a pair of scissors—as far as mere humanity goes—Of course they talk divinely. I have spotted the best lines in the play—almost in any play I should think—
>
> Imogen says—Think that you are upon a rock, and now throw me again! And Posthumous answers—Hang there like fruit, my Soul, till the tree die. Now if that doesn't send a shiver down your spine . . . you are no true Shakespearian! Oh dear oh dear—just as I feel in the mood to talk about these things, you go and plant yourself in Cambridge.[3]

Thoby Stephen, photograph by George Charles Beresford, 1906

A twenty-first-century reader might wonder why Virginia had turned to *Cymbeline,* of all Shakespeare's plays, as a test case for his "greatness." But due in part to the admiration of poets such as Tennyson and Swinburne, and also to the performances of celebrated Victorian actresses like Helena Faucit, *Cymbeline* had risen high in the estimation of readers and audiences. The story of Tennyson's death—his repeated request for "his Shakespeare," the book opened at Posthumus's lines, his burial with a copy of *Cymbeline*—was described by his son Hallam in the two-volume *Memoir* he published in 1897, a work Leslie Stephen would certainly have known.[4] Whether it was among the books Stephen read to his children or lent them to read is unclear; nothing in Virginia's letter to Thoby suggests anything other than that she discovered the "best lines" while reading *Cymbeline* for the first time.

In any case, the play would remain firmly in her mind, appearing again and again in the pages of her novels. Clarissa Dalloway sees a copy of *Cymbeline* in a shop window and is haunted throughout the day by its dirge, "Fear no more the heat o' the sun." In *Jacob's Room*, a book Woolf wanted to dedicate to Thoby's memory, the painter Cruttendon, announcing that he knows "the three greatest things that were ever written in the whole of literature," begins to recite "Hang there like fruit my soul," and Jacob joins him in chanting the lines.[5] (The nineteen-year-old Virginia's reversal of opinion on Shakespeare does, however, accord with one of her father's precepts: "Try again, and see if Shakespeare will not improve.")[6]

The artificial quality she had noted in *Cymbeline*'s characters—"really they might have been cut out with a pair of scissors"—would, just a few years later, be discussed at length by Lytton Strachey in his iconoclastic essay "Shakespeare's Final Period." But what we should also see in Virginia's letter to Thoby is her desire to *talk* about Shakespeare—with her brother and with friends like his. "I dont get anyone to argue with me now, and feel the want," she wrote to him in May 1903:

> I have to delve from books, painfully and all alone, what you get every evening sitting over your fire and smoking your pipe with Strachey etc. No wonder my knowledge is but scant. Theres nothing like talk as an educator I'm sure. Still I try my best with Shakespeare—I read Sidney Lees Life—What do you think of his sonnet theory? It seems to me a little too like Sidney Lee—all that about Shakespeare's eye to the main chance—his flattery of Southampton etc.—But the Mr W.H. is sensible—I must read the sonnets and find my own opinion. Sidney says that Shakespeare *felt* none of it—I mean that not a word applies to him personally—But it is a satisfactory book—doesn't pretend to make theories—and only gives the most authentic facts.[7]

In these last phrases Virginia echoes Lee's own claims in his preface ("an exhaustive and well-arranged statement of the facts of Shakespeare's career, achievement, and reputation" together with "verifiable references to all the original sources of information," avoiding "conjecture"), while allowing some of her personal reservations about him to come through.[8] She is here conscientiously the good student, reporting on both her research and her need to develop her "own opinion"—but her letter is also, manifestly, a request for intellectual companionship. She misses the sociability of their conversation about Shakespeare, which he now may be having instead with "Strachey etc."

The sonnets had long been a preoccupation of Victorian readers. Responding to Wordsworth's assertion that "with this key Shakespeare unlocked his heart,"

Robert Browning famously retorted in a poem of his own, "Did Shakespeare? Then, the less Shakespeare he!"[9] In 1889 Oscar Wilde published "The Portrait of Mr W.H." in which he identified the dedicatee of the sonnets "as Willie Hughes," a beautiful boy actor in Shakespeare's company.[10] Sidney Lee's book devotes four of its sixteen chapters, and an additional appendix of over seventy pages, to the sonnets—the topic that Virginia cites to Thoby.[11]

For the brother and sister, though, it seems to have been the *plays* of Shakespeare, rather than the sonnets or other poems, that excited their mutual interest. From the vantage point of "Sketch of the Past," written some thirty-six years after she assured Thoby that she would continue to "try her best with Shakespeare," Virginia Woolf remembered his passion:

> He had consumed Shakespeare, somehow or other, by himself. He had possessed himself of it, in his large clumsy way, and our first arguments . . . were about Shakespeare. He would sweep down upon me, with his assertion that everything was in Shakespeare. He let the whole mass that he held in his grasp descend in an avalanche on me. I revolted. But how could I oppose all that? Rather feebly; getting red and agitated. Still it was then my genuine feeling that a play was antipathetic to me. How did they begin? With some dull speech a hundred miles from anything interesting. To prove it I opened [*Twelfth Night*] and read "If music be the food of love, play on . . ." I was downed that time.[12] And he was ruthless; exasperating me; downing me, overwhelming me; with enough passion to make us both heated. So that my opposition cannot have been quite ineffectual. He made me feel his pride, it was like his pride in his friends, in Shakespeare—shuffling off Falstaff, he pointed out, without a sign of sympathy. That large natural inhumanity in Shakespeare delighted him. It was a tree's way of shedding its leaves. On the other hand, when Desdemona wakes again, he thought perhaps Shakespeare was "sentimental." These are the only particular criticisms I remember, for he was not, as I am, a breaker off of single words, or sentences, not a note taker. He was more casual, rough and ready and comprehensive. And so I did not get from him any minute comments, but felt rather that Shakespeare was to him his other world; the place where he got his measure of the daily world. He took his bearings there; and sized us up from that standard. I felt once that he was half thinking of Falstaff and Hal and Mother Quickly and the rest, in a third class smoker in the underground, when there was some squabble between drunken men; and he sat in the cor-

> ner, with his pipe in his mouth, looking over the edge of a newspaper; surveying them; unperturbed; equipped; as if placing it all. I felt (not only then) that he knew his own place; and relished his inheritance. I felt he scented the battle; was already, in anticipation, a law maker; proud of his station as a man; ready to play his part among men. Had he been put on, he would have proved most royally. The words Walter Lamb used of him were very fitting.
>
> So we argued; about Shakespeare; about many things; and often lost our tempers; but were attracted by some common admiration.[13]

The phrase "had he been put on," quoted by Walter Lamb, Thoby's Cambridge friend, is from Fortinbras's final speech in praise of the dead Hamlet: "Let four captains, / Bear Hamlet like a soldier to the stage, / For he was likely, had he been put on, / To have proved most royal" (5.2.379–82). It clearly struck a chord, since Woolf recurs to it two more times in the next paragraph: "He would have been, had he been put on, a judge certainly"; "He would have been a distinguished figure; but not prominent; for he was too melancholy, too independent, unconforming, to take any ready made mould. He would have been more of a character than a success, I suppose; had he been put on."[14]

The aptness of the phrase—and its pain—seems to have stuck with her, and came to mind when she read another story of brother-sister education, affection, and loss; in an essay for *Vogue* in 1924 she wrote of the poet John Keats—who had died at twenty-five, a scant year younger than Thoby—that "it was to his sister, whose education he supervised and whose character he formed, that he showed himself the man of all others who 'had he been put on would have proved most royally.'"[15]

Woolf's sense of herself as a stylistic and formalist critic, "a breaker off of single words, or sentences," as she describes it in the "Sketch," is evident in all her writing. But what is clearest and most moving is her pride in Thoby's pride in Shakespeare, "the place where he got his measure of the daily world." This she would learn and adapt and appropriate in her own daily diary entries and letters, as well as in her novels. Among her most indelible characters are those whom she endows with the same habit of finding their worlds through Shakespeare.

Some of her earliest written comments are responses to reading—and sometimes to seeing—the plays. She read *Romeo and Juliet* in November 1908 and wrote in her notes, "Who shall say anything of Romeo and Juliet? Do I dare—in private; it seems to me very immature work."[16] To Lytton Strachey, traveling in Europe, she reported that life in Bloomsbury was "a little pandemoniac" with guests, invitations, and the Friday Club, but that "in the intervals I try to read Romeo and Juliet!"[17] In 1908 and 1909 she read *Hamlet* and A. C. Bradley's analysis of it ("Bradley's chief points are that people who make Hamlet a weak sentimentalist are wrong"), *King Lear, Othello* ("This seems to me to be simpler than the other tragedies, because Othello & Desdemona stand out above all the rest, and draw all interest to them"), and *Macbeth* ("I hesitate to write of this play, because I read it in the train").[18]

Here, as in her correspondence with Thoby, she is still the good student. The next several years would bring many changes: the move to Bloomsbury, her marriage to Leonard, the acquisition of the Hogarth Press, the publication of her first two novels. Her diaries and letters reflect a new confidence in her own opinions and in her knowledge of—and admiration for—Shakespeare. Just as she would later say of her brother that Shakespeare was "the place where he got his measure of the daily world," so she too "took her bearings," and often her standards, from Shakespeare.

The classicist Janet Case, who had taught her Greek, preferred to read *Don Quixote* or *Paradise Lost* in the evenings rather than Shakespeare. "The coarseness of Shre I can see would distress her," Woolf reflects. "She would deal with it intellectually. All her generation use their brains too scrupulously upon books, seeking meaning rather than letting themselves run on for pleasure which is more or less my way."[19] Case's opinion leads her to look again at *Paradise Lost,* which confirms her own contrary view. Milton's poetry is so powerful that "even Shakespeare after this would seem a little troubled, personal, hot & imperfect," but he never—she thinks—deals with "the passions of the human heart. Has any great poem ever let in so little light upon ones own joys and sorrows?"[20] Although Milton's figures are "majestic," she finds them lacking in humanity: "There is nothing like Lady Macbeth's terror or Hamlet's cry, no pity or sympathy or intuition."[21] She knew her own mind and sensed her own forte. She was not especially interested in "sublimity."[22] It was for her a matter of scale.

Woolf often used Shakespeare as a yardstick when privately evaluating friends and acquaintances, or even people she didn't know. One reason she liked Katherine Mansfield, as she told a friend, was because she "has a passion for writing, so that we hold religious meetings together praising Shakespeare."[23] She was less fond of Mansfield's husband, John Middleton Murry, whose book on Shakespeare, published many years later, she initially refused to read, though ultimately she relented.[24] Of Rosalind Toynbee, the wife of Arnold Toynbee and the daughter of classics professor Gilbert Murray, Woolf noted in her diary: "She doesn't like King Lear. But, or perhaps therefore, I thought her rather distinguished, more so, at any rate, than the crop-heads of Bloomsbury."[25] Of Beatrice Webb: "Mrs Webb rapidly gave me her reasons for saying she had never met a great man, or woman, either. At most, she said, they possessed remarkable single qualities, but looked at as a whole there was no greatness in them. Shakespeare she did not appreciate, because a sister, who was a foolish woman, always quoted him wrong to her as a child."[26] The beautiful and socially prominent Lady Diana Manners is dismissed in an early diary entry as "one of those vaguely literary people who 'sometimes read Shakespeare.'"[27] And after an evening in London with Edith Sitwell, Eddie Playfair, Julian and Quentin Bell, and Ottoline Morrell, she notes succinctly, "Ottoline said you couldn't read Shre in India—too remote."[28] (The absence of commentary here is itself perhaps a sufficient comment.)

She wrote to friends and family members about Shakespeare in a spirit of discovery and delight, sharing even ordinary details with extraordinary pleasure. "I am re-binding all my Shakespeares—29 vols—in coloured paper, and think of then reading one of them," she explains to E. M. Forster. "But there are so many interruptions."[29] "Oh god what a good poem Venus and Adonis is," she wrote to T. S. Eliot in a letter inviting him to tea.[30] "I went to Hamlet the other night," she reported to her niece Angelica Bell, then age eleven. "I will take you there when you are in London; or any other play you choose. Hamlet is very exciting."[31] And after an evening at the theatre seeing *Romeo and Juliet* she asked her nephew Julian Bell, who was then teaching in China, "Do you appreciate Shakespeare? I think you used not to. To me he becomes so miraculous, I felt, sitting there . . . like the crowd who watch a rope go up into the air with a heavy basket on top. A thing one cant account for. Still acting it they spoil the poetry."[32] Those "acting it" on this occasion were John Gielgud, Laurence Olivier, Peggy Ashcroft, and Edith Evans in a much-lauded production at the New Theatre; Gielgud was especially praised for the way he spoke Shakespeare's verse, though Olivier was held to be a more persuasive lover.[33] (The two actors swapped the roles of Romeo and Mercutio five weeks into the run). As so often, Woolf preferred her own reading of the poetry, which she compares here to a magic trick.[34] For her Shakespeare was the real magician.

"Shre Surpasses Literature Altogether"

It is when her own writing reaches a height of intensity and power, though, that Woolf writes most vividly about her experience of reading Shakespeare. Few passages could be more compelling than this:

> I was reading Othello last night, & was impressed by the volley & volume & tumble of his words: too many, I should say, were I reviewing for the Times. He puts them in when tension was slack. In the great scenes, everything fits like a glove. The mind tumbles & splashes among words when it is not being urged on: I mean, the mind of a very great master of words who is writing with one hand. He abounds. The lesser writers stint. As usual, impressed by Shre.[35]

And there is this remarkable and brilliant description, part of which we briefly noted in the introduction. The full text expands to describe not only her reading experience but also her sense of Shakespeare as a working artist as well her own acute gifts as a critic:

> I read Shakespeare *directly* I have finished writing, when my mind is agape & red & hot. Then it is astonishing. I never yet knew how amazing his stretch & speed & word coining power is, until I felt it utterly outpace & outrace my own, seeming to start equal & then I see him draw ahead & do things I could not in my wildest tumult & utmost press of mind imagine. Even the less known & worser plays are written at a speed that is quicker than anybody else's quickest; & the words drop so fast one can't pick them up. Look at this, Upon a gather'd lily almost wither'd (that is a pure accident: I happen to light on it.) Evidently the pliancy of his mind was so complete that he could furbish out any train of thought; &, relaxing, lets fall a shower of such unregarded flowers. Why then should anyone else attempt to write. This is not "writing" at all. Indeed, I could say that Shre surpasses literature altogether, if I knew what I meant.[36]

The line she quotes here is from *Titus Andronicus* 3.1, a description of the tragically mutilated Lavinia, voiceless because her tongue has been cut out.[37] Though Woolf may have come upon it by "pure accident," it mirrors her own sense of incapacity compared to Shakespeare.

In fact it sorts with a comparison she has made before, in a diary entry headed "Returning Health": the return of physical and mental well-being "is shown by the power to make images; the suggestive power of every sight & word is enormously increased. Shakespeare must have had this to an extent which makes my normal state the state of a person blind, deaf, dumb, stone-stockish & fish-blooded."[38]

When John Lehmann showed her an admiring piece he had written on pattern and imagery in *The Waves,* she was quick to disavow a too-flattering comparison: "If you print it, as I hope you will, leave out Shakespeare, because I don't think anyone in their senses can have mentioned him in that connection. (I almost put a capital H, and that is rather my feeling)."[39]

Despite such self-deprecating comments, Woolf clearly found Shakespeare an inspiration—and sometimes a model—for her own writing. In a diary entry headed "An idea about Shre," she addresses the relationship between drama and fiction: "That the play demands coming to the surface—hence insists upon a reality wh. the novel need not have, but perhaps should have. Contact with the surface. Coming to the top. This is working out my theory of the different levels in writing, & how to combine them: for I begin to think the combination necessary. This particular relation with the surface is imposed on the dramatist of necessity: how far did it influence Shre? Idea that one cd. work out a theory of fiction &c on these lines: how many levels attempted, whether kept to or not."[40]

The question was one she wanted to pursue, especially with regard to dialogue. When Hugh Walpole dedicated to her his anthology of selections from the novels of Sir Walter Scott, she wrote a warm letter acknowledging his kindness: "As you know, the complete works of Sir Walter, in a fine large copy, in which my father used to read him to us, are lined up on my shelves," she noted, adding to her thanks a brief but tantalizing sketch for a future project. "One of the things I want to write about one day is the Shakespearean talk in Scott: the dialogues; surely that is the last appearance in England of the blank verse of Falstaff and so on! We have lost the art of the poetic speech—."[41] More than a year later she still had this idea in mind. In a letter to Dadie Rylands, the Shakespeare scholar and director, continuing a discussion they'd had on dialogue in novels and plays, she says, "I wish you'd read [Scott] and see whether you can't discover the last relics of Shakespeare's soliloquies in some of the old peasants speeches."[42] It was a project she herself would begin to undertake in her late, and unfinished, history of English literature, beginning with a chapter on "Anon."

"I Murder, as Usual, a Quotation"

Fragments of Shakespeare appear regularly in Woolf's letters, often unidentified—her assumption, like that of Lytton Strachey and others in Bloomsbury, is that the recipient will understand. Writing to her nephew Quentin, she asks about his romantic life: "Have you met anybody of such beauty that your eyes dance, as the waves danced, no, it was the stars; when Shakespeare's woman—Lord lord lord I've forgotten everything I knew—was born."[43] The quotation she is trying to remember is Beatrice in *Much Ado About Nothing* (2.1.293–94): "There was a star danced, and under that I was born," but she is probably mingling it in her memory with Florizel to Perdita: "When you do dance, I wish you / A wave o' th' sea, that you might ever do / Nothing but that" (*Winter's Tale* 4.4.140–42). Or, jokingly, she wrote to Vita Sackville-West about "old women" like Lady Oxford asking that she dedicate her next book to them: "What Poppy or Mandragora—no, its keep away I'm thinking of."[44] The Shakespeare reference is to drugs mentioned by Iago ("Not poppy nor mandragora / Nor all the drowsy syrups of the world / Shall ever medicine thee to that sweet sleep / Which thou owedst yesterday" [*Othello* 3.3.334–37]); the joke, from one dog owner to another, is that Keepaway was the brand name of a product designed to keep dogs away from bitches in heat. Quotes in passing such as this, as we've seen, function as a kind of secret handshake with like-minded Shakespearean friends.

Woolf also cites Shakespeare tags to herself, as if she were bantering with friends. After she finished *Orlando,* she wrote in her diary, "I think I am a little indifferent now to what anyone thinks. Joy's life is in the doing—I murder, as usual, a quotation. I mean it's the writing, not the being read that excites me."[45] The "murdered" quotation is from *Troilus and Cressida,* Cressida's all-too-apt observation about desire: "Women are angels, wooing; / Things won are done. Joy's soul lies in the doing. / That she beloved knows naught that knows not this:/ Men prize the thing ungained more than it is" (1.2.264–67). On a later occasion she alludes to sonnet 116: "I have promised to deliver The Years by 15th Feb. But if I want more time, I shall take it. I'm not time's fool—no."[46] On December 10, 1936, the day that King Edward VIII abdicated the throne—an event that she and her friends regretted—she met at Westminster with Ottoline Morrell and the poet and classicist R. G. Trevelyan. As Hermione Lee describes it, "These three exceptional upper-middle-class citizens, all of whom could remember Queen Victoria's Diamond Jubilee forty years before, walked down Whitehall with the crowd, talking about England."[47] That evening Woolf wrote in the margin of her diary, "Under wh. King, Bezonian? Speak or die?" quoting the words of Pistol in *Henry IV, Part 2* (5.3.105) after Henry V succeeds his father.[48]

With the Second World War there came a wave of despair that would ultimately contribute to Woolf's decision to take her own life. In February 1940 she found a brief respite through reading, in this case Stephen Spender's novel *The Backward Son,* which was to be published by the Hogarth Press later that year. "For some reason hope has revived," she writes. "Yes, Stephen gave me 3 hours of continuous illusion—& if one can get that still, there's a world—whats the quotation—There's a world outside? No. From Coriolanus."[49] The quotation she is seeking is from Shakespeare's tragedy *Coriolanus,* 3.3.131: "There is a world elsewhere"—the hero's defiant—and finally impossible—rejection of Rome, his family, and everything he has valued.

A few months later, in June, she mentions in the diary the German threat to Jews ("All Jews to be given up. Concentration camps") and the plan that she and Leonard had made to commit suicide together in their garage. But in the next paragraph she records "another reflection. I dont want to go to bed at midday. This refers to the garage."[50] But it also refers—though she does not need to say so—to the last words of the Fool in *King Lear:* "And I'll go to bed at noon" (3.6.78). Woolf at this point is determined not to leave the stage when the play is half over. In the diary in these weeks, reporting "nightly raids on the east coast" and "people killed nightly," she resigns herself to going forward ("And now dinner to cook. A role"), while she also thinks about the end of life: "I feel, if this is my last lap, oughtn't I to read Shakespeare? But cant."[51] Yet by early 1941, she suggests in a letter to Ethel Smyth that she had rethought this question and now imagines Shakespeare as part of her "last scene."[52]

Ethel Smyth was one of two correspondents with whom Woolf exchanged letters about Shakespeare extensively in the last two decades of her life. The other was Vita Sackville-West. A closer look at these two interchanges shows something of the way in which Shakespeare served to focus—and to enliven—her later relationships.

"The Home of All Your Tribe"

The correspondence between Virginia Woolf and Vita Sackville-West began—and continued—as a mode of flirtation, in which Shakespeare played a regular part. Vita's son Nigel Nicolson famously described *Orlando* as "the longest and most charming love-letter in literature," but the actual letters between the two women are, like the novel, interspersed with Shakespearean references.[53]

On July 5, 1924, Vita took Virginia to Knole, her family's ancestral home. That day Woolf wrote in her diary, "You perambulate miles of galleries; skip endless treasures—chairs that Shakespeare might have sat on—tapestries, pictures, floors made of the halves of oaks."[54] From that time Vita, descendant of the sixteenth-century statesman and dramatist Thomas Sackville (coauthor of *Gorboduc,* the first blank verse play in English) was in her mind an intriguing Elizabethan figure. She was also a poet at a time when poetry was of great interest to Woolf; in the same diary entry in which she wrote of having learned from

Vita Sackville-West, photograph by Howard Coster, ca. 1927

her brother Thoby to read Shakespeare for pleasure, she explicitly describes the plays as poems.[55] "I write prose, you write poetry," she wrote a year later to Vita, who replied, "What nonsense you talk. . . . There is 100% more poetry in one page of Mrs Dalloway (which you thought I didn't like) than in a whole section of my damned poem [*The Land*]." As for "the secret of poetry," how was it done; how did it, as Virginia had suggested, convey one thing by saying another? "Why should 'bare ruined choirs' sound so very twiggy?"[56] The quotation, from Shakespeare's Sonnet 73, is the only example she gives.

Sackville-West and her husband, Harold Nicolson, were departing for Persia—where he was to take up a diplomatic appointment—in late January 1926. Earlier in the month Vita wrote in a letter to Virginia, "Why does one ever read anybody but Shakespeare? He is coming to Persia with me,—complete works."[57]

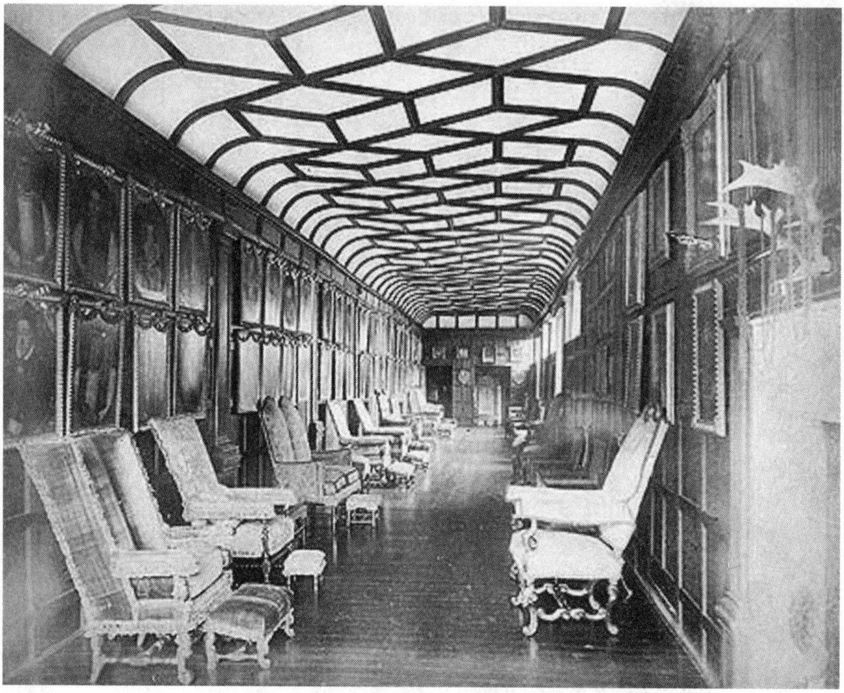

"Chairs that Shakespeare might have sat on" in the Brown Gallery, Knole

Certainly this was a sentiment that would find approval from the recipient (we may recall that Leonard Woolf took the complete works, a gift from Desmond MacCarthy, with him to Ceylon).

Back in England in June, and having seen the Woolfs at Rodmell, Vita "went to Knole and saw The Comedy of Errors played in the garden."[58] In the same letter she picks up again the discussion of the difference between prose and poetry. "I don't believe there is any."[59] In January she left again for Persia, having spent the morning of her departure alone with Virginia: "I treasure your sudden discourse on literature yesterday morning," she wrote en route from Germany: "a send-off to me, rather like Polonius to Laertes. It is quite true that you have had infinitely more influence on me intellectually than anyone, and for this alone I love you." Both women are likely to have enjoyed the analogy between Vita and the impulsive fencing champion Laertes; whether Virginia Woolf, ten years older, was really a Polonius has to be questioned, though Vita's tone is light and gently self-mocking. Woolf wrote back affectionately to clarify her "parting lecture," which she thought was probably not very coherent. "I was trying to get at something about the thing itself before its made into anything, the emotion, the idea. The danger for you with your sense of tradition and all those words—a gift of the Gods though—is that you help this too easily into existence."[60]

In 1928—the same year in which *Orlando* would be published—Radclyffe Hall's lesbian novel, *The Well of Loneliness,* was seized and withdrawn on a charge of obscenity by order of the home secretary, Sir William Joynson-Hicks. Virginia wrote to Vita, who was in Germany, to report that "Leonard and Morgan Forster began to get up a protest, and soon we were telephoning and interviewing and collecting signatures—not yours, for *your* proclivities are too well known." Forster then went to see Hall, who insisted that "she wont have any letter written about her book unless it mentions the fact that it is a work of artistic merit—even genius. And no one has read her book; or can read it; and now we've got to explain this to all the signed names—Arnold Bennett and so on. So our ardour in the cause of freedom of speech gradually cools, and instead of offering to reprint the masterpiece, we are already beginning to wish it unwritten."[61] Vita replied from Potsdam, "I feel very violently about The Well of Loneliness. Not on account of what you call my proclivities; not because I think it is a good book; but really on principle. (I think of writing to Jix suggesting that he should suppress Shakespeare's Sonnets.)"[62]

Vita quotes from the sonnets again after the one trip that they took together, a week's holiday to Burgundy in September 1928, just prior to the official publication date of *Orlando* on October 11. "Burgundy seems a dream. 'Before, a joy proposed; behind, a dream.' I was very happy. Were you?"[63] The line, from Sonnet 129, is here given as a freestanding thought, out of context. (The sonnet is the one that begins, "Th'expense of spirit in a waste of shame / Is lust in action"; the last four lines are: "A bliss in proof and proved, a very woe; / Before, a joy proposed; behind, a dream. / All this the world well knows; yet none knows well / To shun the heaven that lead men to this hell.")[64]

But the real Shakespeare connection for Virginia Woolf and Vita Sackville-West, as both of them acknowledged, was historical rather than literary: the link, partly proven, partly speculative, that bound Knole, the Sackvilles, and Shakespeare.

Woolf went to Stratford-upon-Avon in May 1934, and wrote a long, evocative account of the visit in her diary:

> All the flowers were out in Shre's garden. "That was where his study windows looked out when he wrote the Tempest," said the man. And perhaps it was true. Anyhow it was a great big house, looking straight at the large windows & the grey stone of the school chapel, & when the clock

> struck that was the sound Shre heard. I cannot without more labour than my roadrunning mind can compass describe the queer impression of sunny impersonality. Yes, everything seemed to say, this was Shakespeare's, [here] had he sat & walked; but you wont find me not exactly in the flesh. He is serenely absent-present; both at once; radiating round one; yes; in the flowers, in the old hall, in the garden; but never to be pinned down. And we went to the Church, & there was the florid foolish bust, but what I had not reckoned for was the worn simple slab, turned the wrong way, Kind Friend for Jesus' sake forbear—again he seemed to be all air & sun smiling serenely; & yet down there one foot from me lay the little bones that had spread over the world this vast illumination. Yes, & then we walked round the church, & all is simple & a little worn; the river slipping past the stone wall, with a red breadth in it from some flowering tree, & the edge of the turf unspoilt, soft & green & muddy, & two casual nonchalant swans. The church & the school & the house are all roomy spacious places, resonant, sunny today, & in & out [*illegible*]—yes, an impressive place; still living, & then the little bones lying there, which have created: to think of writing The Tempest looking out on that garden; what a rage & storm of thought to have gone over any mind; no doubt the solidity of the place was comfortable. No doubt he saw the cellars with serenity. And a few scented American girls, & a good deal of parrot prattle from old gramophone discs at the birthplace, one taking up the story from the other. . . . Now I think Shre was very happy in this, that there was no impediment of fame, but his genius flowed out of him, & he is still there, in Stratford.[65]

"You wont find me not exactly in the flesh." Ignoring the "florid foolish bust," moved by the "simple slab" and the "little bones," Woolf finds Shakespeare in Stratford "serenely absent-present; both at once; radiating round one . . . but never to be pinned down." In this description Shakespeare is a *genius loci* and his home a *locus amoenus.* Her apt phrase "absent-present," while it anticipates the theoretical speculations of poststructuralism, more immediately characterizes both Woolf's encounters with Shakespeare in her reading and the frequent but often fleeting glimpses of him in her fiction.[66]

To Vita she wrote, a few days later, "Yes, we're just back, arrived from Stratford on Avon last night. . . . Yes, you ought to go to Stratford, the home of all your tribe. I was tremendously impressed."[67] For Woolf, strongly attracted to Vita as a person, such historical associations were ancillary but in their own way erotic. (It's only an accidental plus that the play she saw performed on the day of her visit to Stratford was *As You Like It,* in which Rosalind dresses as the boy Ganymede to woo her tongue-tied beloved, Orlando.)

In 1922 Vita Sackville-West published *Knole and the Sackvilles.* A second edition was published in 1923, a third in 1947, and a fourth in 1958. "I often entertained wild dreams that some light might be thrown on the Shakespearean problem by a discovery of letters or documents at Knole," she wrote in a section added to the fourth edition. "What more fascinating or chimerical a speculation for a literary-minded child breathing and absorbing the atmosphere of that house? I used to tell myself stories of finding Shakespeare's manuscripts up in the attics, perhaps hidden away under the flooring somewhere, or in the Muniments Room where quite rightly I was forbidden to go and rummage. Yet, as I have since discovered, my imaginings weren't so chimerical as all that. There really are some possible connections between Shakespeare and Knole." Since "everything to do with Shakespeare, however slight, is of the deepest interest," she goes on to list four possibilities:

> 1: According to a suggestion in the *Times Literary Supplement* in 1929, Thomas Sackville may have been the model for Sir Toby Belch in *Twelfth Night* ("not a very complimentary character . . . but it is quite something to figure in a Shakespeare play at all"); 2: "the manor of Stratford-on-Avon came into the possession of the Sackvilles in 1674" (this was, of course, 58 years after Shakespeare's death); 3: William Henry Ireland refers to "two letters from the pen of Shakespeare discovered some time since at Knole in Kent," but "as William Henry Ireland was a well-known forger of Shakespeare plays his evidence may be rejected as of negligible value"; and 4: two lines from Sonnet 125, where the speaker says "Were't aught to me I bore the canopy. With my extern the outward honouring."

She connects this image, "taken by some commentators as a metaphor," to the occasion in 1604 when William Shakespeare, together with other actors from the King's Men, received a grant of red cloth from the king, and "with eleven other fellows waited in their red liveries." She conjectures ("is it not likely") that a canopy may have been held overhead and that Shakespeare's company held it. "In any case, the younger poet cannot have failed to gaze with interest on the old statesman who in his youth had practised the same craft of letters, and perhaps even took the opportunity to speak with him. Whatever the answer, we may safely say that Thomas Sackville and William Shakespeare once in their lives came face to face."[68]

Like many other biographical accounts of Shakespeare, this one, though brief, relies on frank speculation, and in Vita's case the collective suppositions somehow add up to a certainty ("is it not likely"; "cannot have failed to gaze with interest"; "perhaps even took the opportunity"; "we may safely say"). But what is also of interest here, of course, is the similarity to—or perhaps just the analogy with—Virginia Woolf's fictionalizing method in *Orlando* (subtitled *A Biography*), although Woolf's use of the speculative and hypothetical modes is always done with a knowing wink to the reader; there is far less of a sense in Vita's pages that she is anything but serious as she compiles this list of "possible connections" and "offer[s] them for what they are worth."[69]

Occasional mentions of Shakespeare and Shakespeare-related items appear in their later correspondence, some more consequential, some less so. By and large, however, their affectionate letters, which continued until Virginia's death, have less Shakespeare in them after the publication of *Orlando* than prior to it, almost as if *Orlando* itself had assumed that allusive function. The most playful and teasing of the letters date from the 1920s, when their affair was at its height, and when Shakespeare (and Knole, the Sackvilles, and the idea of Orlando) helped to carry messages of love between them.

"I Felt I Was Actually in Shakespeare"

Woolf's other extended correspondence on Shakespeare in these latter years was with Ethel Smyth, the composer, writer, and women's rights activist. Smyth, a generation older than Woolf, had gotten to know her late in life through their joint interest in women's suffrage and, at age seventy-one, fell in love with her. Initially amused and interested, Virginia grew impatient with Ethel as time went on, writing her a stern letter about her egotism, which she compared to that of Leslie Stephen in his old age. (The letter, typewritten, began without salutation, "Let me put it like this.")[70] A more attenuated friendship continued after some adjustments, though Virginia was often ironical and mocking about Ethel when speaking or writing to friends. Nonetheless, some of Woolf's letters show how much she continued to value Ethel's opinion in literary as in musical matters. It may be that a shared love for Shakespeare was a manageable replacement for the passion Ethel expressed for her, which she could not return. Whatever the reason, in the 1930s and especially after the death of Lytton Strachey, it was often in her letters with Ethel Smyth that Virginia Woolf discussed her own thoughts and questions about Shakespeare's plays.

"I'm reading a vast number of books," she wrote to Ethel in August 1933,

Dame Ethel Mary Smyth, photograph by Bassano Ltd., 1927

"Turgenev, Shakespeare's life, and huge masses of MSS. Do you know the difference between the Quarto's and the folios? I never did, till last night. Think of having spent a scholars life, correcting misprints!"[71] "Let me see, I wrote 2 hours this morning, walked by the river and saw a porpoise," she reported in July 1934, "and so home, and read Timon of Athens."[72] "I don't follow your flight about the heartlessness of Shakespeare," she wrote in response to a letter Ethel wrote her in March 1935. Did Ethel mean to compare him in this respect with Shelley and with Virginia Woolf? "Your grammar leaves me doubtful. However, Shelley is good enough company for me, much though I prefer Shre."[73] In November, as the Woolfs were going to see a production of *Romeo and Juliet,* she consulted Ethel about the psychology of Romeo's love at first sight.[74] After a party in February 1936, she wrote her, "You were divine the other night, and it is a side I admit I adore—Shre at his bawdiest, and also subtlest."[75] In September that year, in a postscript to a long letter, she asks, "Did you go to Stratford? I thought it almost, perhaps quite, the most moving emotion to be had anywhere—in any place."[76]

On April 23, 1938, Ethel's eightieth birthday—which was also Shakespeare's birthday—Woolf wrote to her, "Here's my health to you in ink, surely since it was with that liquid that Shakespeare wrote the sonnets; ah but you'll say, Shre had a heart; so have I; only not liquid; compact; congealed; stupid; solid however."[77] A few months later, while on a trip to Northumberland and Skye, she wrote, "oh me! The river running and the old Castle, and the grass path and the people—peasants, wandering along the bank, and talking to us, like something in the time of Elizabeth, so that I felt I was actually in Shakespeare, one of the northern ones."[78] In a letter in October she says, "I think I shall now read Troilus and Cressida. Its a roaring, raving evening, apples pelting down."[79] And after the war begins, she sends Ethel this energetic and spirited report: "To my infinite delight, they bombed our river. Cascades of water roared over the marsh—All the gulls came and rode the waves to the end of the field. It was, and still is, an island sea, of such indescribable beauty, almost always changing, day and night, sun and rain, that I cant take my eyes off it. Yesterday, thinking to explore, I fell headlong into a six foot hole, and came back dripping like a spaniel, or water rugg (thats Shakespeare)." As Hermione Lee observes, this letter, read in retrospect, strikes an ominous note, as Woolf describes her two-mile walk in the rain: "Oh dear, how I love this savage medieval water moved, all floating tree trunks and flocks of birds and a man in an old punt, and myself so eliminated of human feature you might take me for a stake walking." But she closes by saying that she is intoxicated with reading, writing fiction (the book that would be published as *Between the Acts*), and planning "oh such an amusing book on English literature"—and by exhorting Ethel to "write."[80]

Woolf's last letter to Smyth was written in February 1941, and in it, again, Shakespeare plays a central role. "Did I tell you I'm reading the whole of English literature through? By the time I've reached Shakespeare the bombs will be falling. So I've arranged a very nice last scene: reading Shakespeare, having forgotten my gas mask, I shall fade away, and quite forget." Her letter is far from despairing in tone. Rather, as she suggests by evoking Keats, it is about the consolations of literature in uncertain times. "Thank God, as you would say, one's fathers left one a taste for reading! Instead of thinking, by May we shall be—whatever it may be: I think, only 3 months to read Ben Jonson, Milton, Donne, and all the rest!"[81]

Virginia Woolf did not, of course, live till May. When she finally decided to take her own life, the letters she left for her husband and her sister were brief, urgent, and loving, devoid of quotation or citation. Nonetheless, we may perhaps take this imagined "last scene," of reading Shakespeare and fading far away on the wings of viewless Poesy—half in love with easeful Death, and longing to escape the weariness, the fever, and the fret—as an emblematic bracketing of a supremely literary life.[82]

ESSAYS AND REVIEWS

"If Shakespeare Were to Awake Now!"

Woolf's remarks about the plays and the playwright in her essays and reviews are often asides, comparisons, or associative thoughts. Except on special occasions—as when Lydia Lopokova appeared in *Twelfth Night*—she is not tasked by her editors with reviewing productions or books of literary criticism or literary history. The result, unsurprisingly, is to render her observations on Shakespeare in these pieces even more powerful, since they have come to mind when she is—at least ostensibly—thinking about something else.

As we should expect, Woolf's public voice in her essays and nonfiction writing is different from the more private, sometimes ecstatic, sometimes ruminative tone of her diary. There is very often the same sense of discovery as in the diary entries, but it is offered in a cooler and frequently a more didactic or epigrammatic style. These are sentences sculpted and honed to be read and remembered—perhaps to be quoted, cited, challenged. So deft is her writing that it often sounds spontaneous, though her notebooks make it clear that she weighed every word.

Consider, for example, this reflection on the lifelong interplay between Shakespeare and the reader: "To write down one's impressions of *Hamlet* as one reads it year after year, would be virtually to record one's own autobiography, for as we know more of life, so Shakespeare comments upon what we know."[83] The statement is superbly persuasive, both as a program for rereading and as an observation about the way Shakespeare reads *us,* informing how we think and feel, even perhaps who we *are.* It is also beautifully weighted and balanced, anticipating—for Woolf's essay was published in 1916—the rhetoric of T. S. Eliot's more acerbic comment in "Tradition and the Individual Talent." "Someone said: the dead writers are remote from us because we *know* so much more than they did. Precisely; and they are that which we know."[84] Woolf's tone is affirmative, Eliot's reproving, but the sentiments are linked.

Virginia Woolf, ca. 1933

Woolf's initial topic in this essay is Charlotte Brontë. Her aside about Shakespeare comes in the context of a description of a "real work of art" as that which changes every time we read it. But the force of Woolf's remark—a remark very much in the philosophical essayistic spirit of Montaigne—derives not only from its shapeliness but also from its truth. To record one's own autobiography by reading and rereading *Hamlet:* what could be more compelling or revealing as a practice, especially when every modern critic, from Coleridge to Freud, finds that he or she has a "smack of Hamlet myself." In a later essay she will again return to the experience of rereading *Hamlet*—which, unlike the "fat Victorian volumes" of Thackeray, Dickens, and George Eliot, can be read at a single sitting. "One reads *Hamlet* in the four hours between dinner and bedtime. It is not beyond human endurance to read it from first to last, in and out, and, so far as our faculties permit, as a whole. *Hamlet* may change; we know, indeed, that *Hamlet* will change; but tonight *Hamlet* is ours."[85]

Here is another example, also from 1916: "If Shakespeare had come to life again in the middle of the eighteenth century, he would very soon have understood his position; but if Shakespeare were to awake now! The thought of what he would see in the sky and on the earth is at once appalling and fascinating."[86] The book Woolf is reviewing concerns social life in England from 1750 to 1850—well after Shakespeare's time and before Woolf's. The great achievements of that hundred-year period included the industrial revolution, the rise of the middle class, and the Reform Bill. The skies of England would by 1850 have been darkened by smokestacks and coal fires; the earth, at least in many regions, would have borne the weight of factories and the scars of mining. Woolf is not very impressed with the book, a collection of lectures delivered to an American audience. Her review, unsigned, is circumspect and appropriately wry. That one sentence about Shakespeare, with its exclamation point—a mode of punctuation familiar from her diary but much less often found in the essays—stands out for its freshness and its sense of mental discovery. For that moment she is seeing the world through Shakespeare's eyes.

The review essays of 1916 are unsigned, but even had they been signed, the signature would not have signified beyond a certain circle of friends and family. The novels were to come in the next decades, and with them name recognition so great that the cultural shorthand for English literature surveys toward the end of the twentieth century was "From Beowulf to Virginia Woolf." (With a historical congruence Woolf could not have foretold, Miss Allan in *The Voyage Out* intends her primer of English literature to be called "Beowulf to Swinburne," but then decides to omit Swinburne: "Beowulf to Browning—I rather like the two B's myself. Beowulf to Browning," she repeated, "I rather think that is the kind of title which might catch one's eye on a railway bookstall."[87] Presumably Miss Allan would have liked the two "wulfs/woolfs" as well.)

"Nothing but Shakespeare and Oneself"

In "On Being Ill," published in the *New Criterion,* Woolf reflects again on reading Shakespeare and the paradoxical benefit of the sickbed—once again with a special emphasis on the uncanniness of *Hamlet,* a play in which "the critic sees something moving and vanishing . . . , as in a glass one sees the reflection of oneself."

> Rashness is one of the properties of illness—outlaws, that we are—and it is rashness that we chiefly need in reading Shakespeare. It is not that we should doff the intelligence in reading him, but that fully conscious and aware his fame intimidates us, and all the books of all the critics dull us in that thunderclap of conviction that nothing stands between us and him, which, if an illusion, is still so helpful an illusion, so prodigious a pleasure, so keen a stimulus in reading the great. Shakespeare is getting flyblown; a paternal government might well forbid writing about him, as they put his monument at Stratford beyond the reach of scribbling pencils. With all this buzz of criticism about, one may hazard one's conjectures privately, make one's notes in the margin; but knowing that someone has said it before, or said it better, the zest is gone. Illness in its kingly sublimity sweeps all that aside, leaves nothing but Shakespeare and oneself, and what with his overweening power, our overweening arrogance, the barriers go down, the knots run smooth, the brain rings and resounds with *Lear* or *Macbeth,* and even Coleridge himself squeaks like a distant mouse. Of all the plays and even of the sonnets this is true; it is *Hamlet* that is the exception. *Hamlet* one reads only once in one's life, between the ages of twenty and twenty-five. Then one is Hamlet, one is youth; as, to make a clean breast of it, Hamlet is Shakespeare, is youth. And how can one explain what one is? One can but be it. Thus forced always to look back or sidelong at his own past the critic sees something moving and vanishing in *Hamlet,* as in a glass one sees the reflection of oneself, and it is this which, while it gives an everlasting variety to the play, forbids us to feel, as with *Lear* or *Macbeth,* that the centre is solid and holds firm whatever our successive readings lay upon it.[88]

These are reflections on reading. But many of Woolf's essays concern writers and writing, and in those cases, too, Shakespeare is a benchmark. In "Poetry, Fiction, and the Future," published in 1927 in the *New York Herald Tribune,* she says that "Shakespeare's plays are not the work of a baffled and frustrated mind; they are the perfectly elastic envelope of his thought. Without a hitch he turns from philosophy to a drunken brawl; from love songs to an argument."[89] In the same article she observes that "the poet is always able to transcend the particularity of Hamlet's relation to Ophelia and to give us his questioning not of his own personal lot alone but of the state and being of all human life. In *Measure for Mea-*

sure, for example, passages of extreme psychological subtlety are mingled with profound reflections, tremendous imaginations."[90]

At other times Woolf explores the question of creativity and the roles of character and language in the literary imagination. Her "Letter to a Young Poet," addressed to—and solicited by—John Lehmann, asks rhetorically, "How can you learn to write if you write only about one single person? To take the obvious example. Can you doubt that the reason why Shakespeare knew every sound and syllable in the language and could do precisely what he liked with grammar and syntax, was that Hamlet, Falstaff, and Cleopatra rushed him into this knowledge; that the lords, officers, dependants, murderers and common soldiers of the plays insisted that he should say exactly what they felt in the words expressing their feelings? It was they who taught him how to write, not the begetter of the Sonnets."[91] And the "obvious example," whether for a young poet or a celebrated novelist of the past or present, is Shakespeare.

Virginia Woolf never worked as a professional theatre critic, but the Woolfs did go to the theatre, sometimes in London, at other times to see productions staged by the Marlowe Society. Through her friendships with Strachey, Dadie Rylands, Roger Fry, and Maynard Keynes, among others, she kept up with some of the questions facing modern actors and directors, even though her usual preference was to read a Shakespeare play rather than to see it ("Acting it they spoil the poetry," she would write in a letter to Julian Bell).[92] Reviewing a book about reviving early English drama on the London stage, she recalled Harley Granville Barker's influential productions of *A Midsummer Night's Dream* and other plays at the Savoy Theatre in 1913–14: "Mr Granville-Barker, while showing us how the play was probably staged in Shakespeare's time, deals with some of the problems which beset a producer at the present day. . . . To us, whose eyes and ears have grown used to a far more elaborate setting, simplicity may seem barrenness, reticence may appear starvation. To add the measure of exaggeration which is right in the circumstances, while keeping in mind that the play is a poetic play, and everything must serve, and nothing compete with, the poetry, is a highly ticklish undertaking."[93]

Woolf's interest in the biographical Shakespeare tends to remain at the level of the unabashedly speculative and fanciful, as in her thought about what would happen "if Shakespeare were to awake now!" or her response to the prose writers she called "the Strange Elizabethans": "If we rummage among these fragments [copies of letters, marginal notes, and so on] we shall, at any rate, leave the high-road and perhaps hear some roar of laughter from a tavern door, where poets are drinking; or meet humble people going about their milking and their lovemaking without a thought that this is the great Elizabethan age, or that Shakespeare is at this moment strolling down the Strand and might tell one, if one plucked him by the sleeve, to whom he wrote the sonnets, and what he meant by Hamlet."[94] In "The Art of Biography," published in 1939, several years after Lytton Strachey's death, she compared the Queen Elizabeth of his *Elizabeth and Essex* to the Queen Victoria of his 1921 biography: "Elizabeth never became real in the sense that Victoria had been real, yet she never became fictitious in the sense that Cleopatra or Falstaff is fictitious."[95]

Bearing in mind the fact that her father, Leslie Stephen, was the editor of the *Dictionary of National Biography,* and that his assistant, Sidney Lee, wrote a biography of Shakespeare, we might want as well to take note of this striking passage from an undated essay called "Personalities," published after her death:

> Directly Shakespeare is mentioned there comes to mind the popular opinion that he, of all great men, is the least familiar. Indeed very little is known of him biographically, but it is evident that most people have precisely that personal feeling for him which I think they have not for Aeschylus. There is never an essay upon Hamlet that does not make out with some confidence the author's view of what he calls "Shakespeare the man." Yet Shakespeare is a very queer case. Undoubtedly one has the certainty of knowing him; but it is as fleeting as it is intense. You think you have fixed him for ever; you look again; and something seems withheld. All your preconceptions are falsified. What was Shakespeare may, after all, have been Hamlet; or yourself; or poetry. These great artists who manage to infuse the whole of themselves into their works, yet contrive to universalise their identity so that, though we feel Shakespeare everywhere about, we cannot catch him at the moment in any particular spot.[96]

"Shakespeare the man" is a phrase from A. C. Bradley's book *Shakespearean Tragedy* (1904), where he *discounts* the importance of biography in a way very like Woolf's ("In these lectures, at any rate for the most part, we are to be content with the *dramatic* view, and are not to ask whether it corresponded exactly with his opinions or creed outside his poetry—the opinions or creed of the being whom we sometimes oddly call 'Shakespeare the man'").[97] One author who did, however, suggest the relevance of biography to the understanding of Shakespeare is—of course—Leslie Stephen who, as we have seen, published an essay called "Shakespeare as a Man."

"What was Shakespeare may, after all, have been Hamlet; or yourself; or poetry." "Though we feel Shakespeare everywhere about, we cannot catch him at the moment in any particular spot." This second observation is one that Woolf mischievously exploits in *Orlando:* "'He sat at Twitchett's table,' she mused, 'with a dirty ruff on. . . . Was it Sh—p—re?'"[98] But the first observation, "What was Shakespeare may, after all, have been Hamlet; or yourself; or poetry," is closer to her own feelings.

Several times in the last decade of her life Woolf considered writing "a whole book on English lit," a project that she in fact undertook while she was writing *Between the Acts.*[99] Sections of the unfinished work were painstakingly reconstructed from drafts by the scholar Brenda Silver and were then republished with further editorial interventions in the last volume of Woolf's *Essays.*[100] The witty section on the author known as "Anon," which begins in early medieval times and traverses the years to the time of the theatres built on the Bankside, comes to a close, not surprisingly, with Shakespeare. "But at some point there comes a break when anonymity withdraws. Does it come when the playwright had absorbed the contribution of the audience; and can return to them their own general life individualized in single and separate figures? There comes a point when the audience is no longer master of the playwright. . . . Yet he is not separate from them. A common life still unites them, but there are still moments of separation. Now, we say, he is speaking our own thoughts. Outside of Shakespeare, there is no complete unity. Now he is ourselves."[101] Here is yet another echo of the inside/outside conundrum: "What was Shakespeare may, after all, have been Hamlet; or yourself; or poetry." But "Anon" does not quite, after all, end with Shakespeare, though he reigns until the last five sentences.

> The curtain rises upon play after play. Each time it rises upon a more detached, a more matured drama. The individual on the stage becomes more and more differentiated; and the whole group is more closely related and less at the mercy of the plot. The curtain rises upon Henry the Sixth; and King John; upon Hamlet and Antony and Cleopatra and upon Macbeth. Finally it rises upon the Tempest. But the play has outgrown the uncovered theatre where the sun beats and the rain pours. That theatre must be replaced by the theatre of the brain. The playwright is replaced by the man who writes a book. The audience is replaced by the reader. Anon is dead.[102]

We might place this passage next to Roland Barthes's "The Death of the Author," published in 1967, with its invitation for the reader (or, in the case of drama, the spectator) to inhabit "the whole being of writing": "The reader is the very space in which are inscribed, without any being lost, all the citations a writing consists of; the unity of a text is not in its origin, it is in its destination; but this destination can no longer be personal . . . the birth of the reader must be ransomed by the death of the author."[103] In Barthes's version it is the author, and authorial intent, that is dead; biography and psychology as literary causation must give way to the multiple fissures and dialogues of the text. For Woolf something rather different seems to be taking place. For it is not the author but the theatre that in her vision must give way, and give way not only to the reader (of plays, of poems, of essays, of fiction) but also to the novelist. This is the argument of her second fragment, "The Reader":

> It was when the playhouses were shut presumably that the reader was born. The curious faculty of making houses and countries visible, and men and women and their emotions, from marks on a printed page was undeveloped so long as the play was dominant. The audience at the play house had to draw in the play with their eyes and ears. Without a book of the words they could not deepen and revise the impression left by the play, or ask those questions that are debated now in every newspaper. The lack of general reading accounts for the long pause between Shakespeare's death and the 18th century when the plays of Shakespeare hung suspended, unrealised.[104]

And again,

> Our own attempt when we read the early Elizabethan plays [to] supply the trumpets and the flags, the citizens and the apprentices is an effort to revert to an earlier stage. As time goes on the reader becomes distinct from the spectator. His sense of words and their associations develops.[105]

And yet again,

> We develop faculties that the play left dormant. Now the reader is completely in being. He can pause; he can ponder; he can compare. . . . He can read directly what is on the page, or, drawing aside, can read what is not written. There is a long drawn continuity in the book that the play has not. It gives a different pace to the mind. We are in a world in which nothing is concluded.[106]

This witty final turn—to a phrase from Johnson's *Rasselas* about which her father had written—marks the unconcluded stopping point of the fragment.[107]

Woolf's diaries and letters are full of her expressions of pleasure at the experience of reading and rereading Shakespeare. She almost always preferred the "book" version to the performance. But for a writer who freely admitted competitive feelings when it came to the work of a contemporary like Lytton Strachey, and who regularly expressed her inadequacy when compared to Shakespeare, the suggested timeline of Virginia Woolf's unfinished study of "English lit" makes another claim as well. The emergence of the reader and the book, developing "faculties that the play left dormant," implies that the inevitable literary successor to the Elizabethan playwright is the fiction writer, the novelist. Woolf could never, as she insisted, compete with "Shre,"—but now, through the processes of history and the evolution of genres, she would become his heir.[108]

Some modern commentators have seen Woolf's relationship with Shakespeare through the lens of Harold Bloom's theory about authors and "the anxiety of influence." Others have seen the relationship not as paternal/filial but as fraternal/sororal, pointing to the figure of "Shakespeare's sister" in *A Room of One's Own* and also to the literary "sibling rivalry" felt by the young Virginia Stephen toward her beloved brother Thoby. The cases they make are strong, and in many ways appealing. To look at her very last, unfinished project, the history of English literature, is to see how the change from the playhouse to the writer's desk, from the public theatre to the novel, positions Woolf as the successor, inheritrix, and lineal descendant of "Shre." As it did for Vita Sackville-West, the play of genders in *Orlando* addresses the question of entitlement and entailment, and the story of Judith Shakespeare, written so soon afterward, offers a cautionary parable about "looking back through our mothers" and "professions for women."

Much evidence exists in Virginia Woolf's writing—in her letters, diaries, essays, and drafts, as well as in the finished novels—that Woolf was comparing herself to Shakespeare, first as an admirer (in Bloom's terms, an "ephebe" to a "precursor"), later as one writer to another, and that she developed a strong interest over time in the relationship of poetry to prose, the coining of words, and the notion of the "scene" that established parameters for character and persona.

But the associations of the word *anxiety* need to be carefully calibrated, since there is always the risk of a slippage between the formal and the personal or the structure and the individual. "Anxiety" in Bloom's original formulation was a structural element, not a neurotic condition; in modern parlance, it was a feature, not a bug. His interest—and in the main the interest of those who followed his lead—or built on his argument, impelled by the same structure—was in understanding how literary history worked, and how great poets got to be great.[109] One of Bloom's key points is that the literary successor will find a way to "swerve" from the path of the predecessor, as Woolf does by writing fiction rather than drama (though "poetry" is a central value for her, and becomes manifest in a novel like *The Waves*). Yet of all her literary "rivals," the one Woolf feels least anxious about is Shakespeare. Although she does frequently compare her writing to his, in speed, pace, imagination, everything, the sensation she describes is exhilaration rather than anxiety.[110] She reads Shakespeare "*directly* I have finished writing"; she turns to him for passion and pleasure as well as for calm and solace.[111] His absent presence in Stratford is "sunny"; he "abides."

Woolf, of all writers, knew anxiety and its disabling, sometimes catastrophic, symptoms. And she also knew, and acknowledged in herself, profound feelings of professional competition and jealousy: with Lytton Strachey, with Maynard Keynes, with Katherine Mansfield, with T. S. Eliot, with Vita, with James Joyce. "One of my vile vices is jealousy, of other writers' fame," she wrote in her diary about Strachey's *Elizabeth and Essex,* which she thought a failure and was "secretly pleased." But she also says in the same diary entry, with equal self-awareness, "I have a mind that feeds perfectly dispassionately & apart from my vanities & jealousies upon literature: & that would have taken a masterpiece to itself."[112] Her relationship with Shakespeare was not fed by the envy she sometimes felt toward her contemporaries; it was consistently productive. Racing with him made her run faster.

FICTIONS

In her fiction Woolf was able to use all the "Shakespeares" she had developed in her private writing, and to add to these unerring brief portraits of people obsessed with, averse to, or splendidly ignorant of Shakespeare. Passages from the plays sometimes haunt or enchant her characters, as they did Woolf herself. Glimpses of the poet, again sometimes reverent and sometimes comical, flash in and out of her narratives: his eyes, his forehead, his name, the flowers on his grave. Always beneath the social comedies and social tragedies that Woolf made so indelibly her own is an acute awareness of Shakespeare's language, its rhythms and its words. Over time longer quotations—Clarissa Dalloway's memory of the dirge from *Cymbeline* that forms the plot line of her novel; Lady Bruton's imperial appropriation of the "this England" speech from *Richard II*—give way to what Woolf herself, quoting *Troilus and Cressida,* calls "scraps, orts and fragments." So complete is her knowledge and attunement that sometimes the most "Shakespearean" of her evocations are the ones that do not, on the surface, declare their lineage.

In these discussions of Woolf's "fictions" I have included not only her novels and her short story "The Mark on the Wall" but also her two long, separately published essays, *A Room of One's Own* and *Three Guineas,* each of which has a connection—the first extensive, the second brief—with Shakespeare.

"A Grand Fellow, Shakespeare": The Voyage Out *(1915)*

In Woolf's early novels, mentions of Shakespeare are often a kind of genre detail, like descriptions of clothing styles or paintings on the walls. In *The Voyage Out,* when the naïve Susan Warrington, who "had no love of language," listens to a parson reading a psalm "with the same kind of mechanical respect with which she heard many of Lear's speeches read aloud," or the vulgar Mrs. Flushing exclaims, "Shakespeare? I hate Shakespeare!" and her equally objectionable husband "admiringly" remarks, "I believe you're the only person who dares to say that, Alice," we know exactly who and what they are.[113] The lively and coquettish Clarissa Dalloway, as she is introduced in this, Woolf's first novel, engages the ship's steward, Mr. Grice, in a conversation that begins with her inspection of the "little glass jars" that contain his prized collection of sea specimens. "They have swum about among bones," she says with a sigh, and they are off:

> "You're thinking of Shakespeare," said Mr Grice, and taking down a copy from a shelf well lined with books, recited in an emphatic nasal voice:
>
> Full fathom five thy father lies,
>
> "A grand fellow, Shakespeare," he said, replacing the volume.
> Clarissa was so glad to hear him say so.
> "Which is your favorite play? I wonder if it's the same as mine?"
> "*Henry the Fifth,*" said Mr Grice.
> "Joy!" cried Clarissa. "It is!"

The interchange is amazingly deft—as well as wonderfully funny. Again we are left in little doubt as to the character of Clarissa or her well-developed social skills. We have no way of knowing what her favorite play actually is, or if she has one. But Mr. Grice is, predictably, charmed. "*Hamlet* was what you might call too introspective for Mr Grice, the sonnets too passionate. Henry the Fifth was to him the model of an English gentleman. . . . He was giving Mrs Dalloway his views upon the present state of England when the breakfast bell rung so imperiously that she had to tear herself away."[114] Technically this is a variant of what is called free indirect discourse. "Clarissa was so glad to hear him say so"; "she had to tear herself away." The interjected "what you might call" is Mr. Grice's phrase turned into the narrator's prose. The scene is a perfect drawing-room comedy in little, where Shakespeare is the ostensible subject and, at the same time, the perfect vehicle for exposing the personae of Woolf's characters. The initial poetic image from Ariel's song will recur obliquely, in a different key, later in the novel, when Terence Hewet tells Rachel Vinrace that when he first saw her, "I thought you were like a creature who'd lived all its life among pearls and old bones."[115] The fact that this is an allusion rather than an explicit citation or mention of Shakespeare changes the mode. Rachel may not catch the reference, but the reader will.

In the main, though, "Shakespeare" functions in *The Voyage Out* as a mode of social satire. The restless young Cambridge intellectual, St. John Hirst, asks Rachel Vinrace what books she has read. "Just Shakespeare and the Bible?" "I haven't read many classics," Rachel replies shyly, and he decides to lend her a copy of Gibbon.[116] The elderly Mrs. Thornberry, proud mother of many children, voices her romantic affection for people who live in the heart of the country. "There are the people, I feel, among whom Shakespeare will be born again if he is ever born again. In those old houses, up among the Downs—."[117] The inflection is gentler and more forgiving than T. S. Eliot's vision of the women who come and go talking of Michelangelo—these are not pretentious culture mavens—but the role of Shakespeare is similarly indicative and almost always comic, despite the powerful sense of loss at the heart of the novel.

That sense of loss is palpable, however, and all the more so when we consider that Terence's thoughts at the moment of Rachel's death are almost the same words that Virginia Woolf will use in her letter to Leonard more than twenty-five years later. Terence thinks to himself, "No two people have ever been so happy as we have been. No one has ever loved as we have loved." Virginia will write to Leonard, in a note she leaves for him before her suicide in March 1941, "I dont think two people could have been happier than we have been."[118]

"He Leant His Forehead on His Hand": "The Mark on the Wall" (1917)

At a key moment in Woolf's experimental short story "The Mark on the Wall," the daydreaming and free-associating narrator describes the process by which she is trying to focus her mind: "I want to sink deeper and deeper, away from the surface, with its hard separate facts. To steady myself, let me catch hold of the first idea that passes . . . Shakespeare . . . Well, he will do as well as another. A man who sat himself solidly in an arm-chair, and looked into the fire, so—A shower of ideas fell perpetually from some very high Heaven down through his mind. He leant his forehead on his hand, and people, looking in through the open door,—for this scene is supposed to take place on a summer's evening—. But how dull this is, this historical fiction! It doesn't interest me at all."[119]

E. M. Forster would later quote from "The Mark on the Wall" in *Aspects of the Novel,* characterizing its author as a fantasist, and Desmond MacCarthy, writing for the *New Statesman* in his persona as "Affable Hawk," comments, "Auras, in the sense of temporary and shifting integuments of dreams and thoughts we all carry with us while pursuing practical aims, are her subject matter."[120]

The image of a Shakespeare deep in thought will recur in *Orlando,* where the guileless hero speculates on what is, for him, an unexpected and enigmatic figure. ("Was this a poet?") The narrator of "The Mark on the Wall" knows quite well who Shakespeare is, and will shortly reflect on the ways in which his imagination prefigures that of "the novelists in future" rather than the realist novelists of the present. They will pursue mirror images, reflections, and "phantoms," while "leaving the description of reality more and more out of their stories, taking a knowledge of it for granted, as the Greeks did, and Shakespeare perhaps."[121] Even in this very early story Woolf is planting her flag, resisting the mere "description of reality" that—as she would continue to argue—had preoccupied and undermined the work of previous and current novelists. The narrative she begins—Shakespeare as a hard separate fact, seated "solidly" in his armchair on a summer's evening, peered at by people looking through the open door—is not what interests her.

Woolf later wrote to Ethel Smyth that she would never forget the day she wrote "The Mark on the Wall"—"all in a flash, as if flying, after being kept stone breaking for months."[122] The stone-breaking image refers both to her recent illness ("suffering every form of nightmare and extravagant intensity of perception") and to the discipline of writing *Night and Day* (1919), which she would later call her "exercise in the conventional style" of fiction writing.[123] During her convalescence, she told Smyth, she made herself "copy from plaster casts, partly to tranquillise, partly to learn anatomy."[124]

Both the "stone" and the "plaster casts" may return us, by association, to the image of Shakespeare, who "leant his forehand on his hand." Some statues of Shakespeare, notably the ones in Westminster Abbey and Trafalgar Square, picture Shakespeare not seated but leaning on a convenient plinth, resting his *chin* on his hand. The impression is of thought—or of *a* thought. The Roubiliac statue, commissioned by David Garrick for his Temple to Shakespeare, holds his left hand raised to his chin with the index finger extended along the jawline, as if—again—in thought. Both visual concepts are elegant and controlled. The playwright, clearly by this time successful in his craft, is stylishly dressed and carefully posed. Although the Roubiliac Shakespeare holds a pen in his other hand, he is not struggling to find the perfect phrase but rather displaying, for the admiration of viewers, the tools of his trade. By contrast, the Shakespeare imagined—and then discarded—in "The Mark on the Wall" is an actual writer at work, seated in a chair, a "shower of ideas" falling upon him, his forehead leaning on his hand. He is not demonstrating what the inspiration of a poet might look like—he is thinking. Though the dream image of Shakespeare will be shortly discarded by the narrator, who is not interested in creating "historical fiction," the vision of a writer sitting "solidly in his arm-chair" is the most vivid—as well as the most evocative—in the story.

Around 1912 Vanessa Bell painted two portraits of Virginia Woolf seated in an armchair in which "the face is deliberately blurred, although the effect, surprisingly, is not one of anonymity but of intimate presence." Perhaps, suggests Frances Spalding, "Bell is using indeterminacy to acknowledge that even those we know well are never entirely present to us, and can sometimes be more present when they are absent."[125] As we've seen, this sense of absent presence would be Virginia Woolf's experience of Shakespeare at Stratford when she finally visited there in 1934. In "The Mark on the Wall" the solidity of the armchair and its occupant are emphasized, while the face is shadowed. He is looking into the fire. Though Shakespeare is "the first idea that passes," and "will do as well as another," he is for her only one idea, and her restless imagination seeks the multiplicity of reflections that are found in his plays and in those of the Greeks—and in the "novelists in future."

At the story's close the narrator's reverie is interrupted by "someone standing over me" who announces, "I'm going out to buy a newspaper," although "Nothing ever happens. Curse this war. God damn this war." (It is this same casual realist who puts a sudden end to the narrator's creative fantasies, identifying the mysterious mark on the wall as a snail.) The harsh fact of the war and the disposable materiality of the daily paper occlude for the moment all the other, more visionary and permanent kinds of writing—Shakespeare's, the author's, and that of future novelists. Absent presence gives way to the demands of the present. Instead of the forehead of Shakespeare, the forehead of Zeus.

"I'm Dreaming of My *William":* Night and Day *(1919)*

Often described as a conventional novel, *Night and Day* makes its frequent use of "Shakespeare"—the man, the shrine, the pocket edition, and the text—a means of questioning convention while seeming to uphold or endorse it. While Katharine Hilbery tries to decide whether to marry the unexciting, wholly suitable poet William Rodney or the more intriguing and less polished Ralph Denham, her mother, herself the daughter of a celebrated poet, is quietly obsessed with Shakespeare.

> Even Katharine was slightly affected against her better judgment by her mother's enthusiasm. Not that her judgment could altogether acquiesce in the necessity for a study of Shakespeare's sonnets as a preliminary to the fifth chapter of her grandfather's biography. Beginning with a perfectly frivolous jest, Mrs Hilbery had evolved a theory that Anne Hathaway had a way, among other things, of writing Shakespeare's sonnets; the idea, struck out to enliven a party of professors, who forwarded a number of privately printed manuals within the next few days for her instruction, had submerged her in a flood of Elizabethan literature; she had come to believe in her joke, which was, she said, at least as good as other people's facts, and all her fancy for the time being centred upon Stratford-on-Avon. She had a plan, she told Katharine, when, rather later than usual, Katharine had come into the room after her walk by the river, for visiting Shakespeare's tomb. Any fact about the poet had become, for the moment, of far greater interest to her than the immediate present, and the certainty that there was existing in England a spot of ground where Shakespeare had undoubtedly stood, where his very bones lay directly beneath one's feet, was so absorbing to her on this particular occasion that she greeted her daughter with the exclamation:
>
> "D'you think he ever passed this house?"[126]

That these are parallel love stories, the daughter's and the mother's, is made explicit when Katharine, lost in her own daydream, mistakes Mrs. Hilbery's reference to "him":

> Mrs Hilbery burst out laughing.
>
> "My dear, I'm not talking about *your* William, though that's another reason for liking him. I'm talking, I'm thinking, I'm dreaming of *my* William—William Shakespeare, of course."[127]

To compound the irony, Woolf makes it clear that Katharine is not in fact dreaming of William but of Ralph. Mother and daughter continue to talk past one another, Mrs. Hilbery now rapt in her theme. "Isn't it odd," she says, that ordinary life goes on—"lawyers hurrying to their work, cabmen squabbling for their fares, little boys rolling their hoops, little girls throwing bread to the gulls, as if there weren't a Shakespeare in the world. I should like to stand at that crossing all day and say: 'People, read Shakespeare!'"[128] A moment later she has hatched a scheme to rectify this problem. "Katharine! I've hit upon a brilliant idea!" she says, "—to lay out, say, a hundred pounds or so on copies of Shakespeare, and give them to working men. Some of your clever friends who get up meetings might help us, Katharine. And that might lead to a playhouse, where we could all take parts. You'd be Rosalind—but you've a dash of the old nurse in you. Your father's Hamlet, come to years of discretion; and I'm—well, I'm a bit of them all; I'm quite a large bit of the fool, but the fools in Shakespeare say all the clever things. Now who shall William be? A hero? Hotspur? Henry the Fifth? No, William's got a touch of Hamlet in him too. I can fancy that William talks to himself when he is alone."[129] Katharine, mulling whether to confide in her mother about her own feelings, is unable to do so because of Mrs. Hilbery's single-minded fixation: "While she hesitated and sought for words not too direct, her mother had recourse to Shakespeare, and turned page after page, set upon finding some quotation that said all this about love far, far better than she could."[130]

William Rodney, to whom Katharine is first engaged, is not only a poet but also a scholar of the Elizabethan period. At one of the Wednesday evening gatherings hosted by the feminist social reformer Mary Datchet (modeled on Vanessa Bell's similar events in Bloomsbury), he is going to read a paper "upon the Elizabethan use of metaphor"—a "good solid paper, with plenty of quotations from the classics."[131] If he had his way, he says, "I could spend three hours every day reading Shakespeare." And he would write plays: "I've written three-quarters of a play already, and I'm only waiting for a holiday to finish it."[132]

Katharine tells William that she has never read Shakespeare, but when he begins to read to her from his verse drama the narrator reports, with an inflection worthy of Jane Austen, that "Katharine's ignorance of Shakespeare did not prevent her from feeling fairly certain that plays should not produce a sense of chill stupor in the audience, such as overcame her as the lines flowed on, sometimes long and sometimes short, but always delivered with the same lilt of voice, which seemed to nail each line firmly on to the same spot in the hearer's brain. Still, she reflected, these sorts of skills are almost exclusively masculine. . . . No one could doubt that William was a scholar."[133] (William's play, written in a style imitative of Shakespeare, probably also contains a private family joke. "Sylvano enters," he says, "accompanied by the rest of the gentlemen of Gratian's court."[134] "Gratian" was the name Vanessa Bell had initially given to her second son, born in 1910. Vanessa had expected a girl, whom she was planning to name Clarissa.

The baby "was hurriedly renamed Gratian," but "nobody seemed to like the name . . . and she began to think of alternatives," trying out Claudian but ultimately settling on Quentin.)[135]

In time William will suggest to Mary Datchet that the claim not to have read Shakespeare is "'one of Katharine's poses. . . . She pretends that she's never read Shakespeare. And why should she read Shakespeare, since she *is* Shakespeare—Rosalind, you know,' and he gave his queer little chuckle. Somehow this compliment appeared very old-fashioned, and almost in bad taste. Mary actually felt herself blush, as if he had said 'the sex' or 'the ladies.'"[136] Further support for William's suspicion that Katharine has indeed read Shakespeare comes in the scene we've already noticed, where Mrs. Hilbery laments her daughter's absence during the visit of the eminent man of letters: "I actually had to ask him the name of the lady Hamlet was in love with, since you were out."[137] William's appropriation of Shakespeare provokes Katharine's resistance, but it may not be, as he thinks it, merely a flirtatious ploy.

As for William's scholarship, it becomes a rehabilitating "masculine" defense mechanism when the confusions of his love life put him in a socially awkward position. To defuse the situation, Mrs. Hilbery adroitly asks her husband a question that, "from the ardour with which she announced it, had evidently been pressing for utterance for some time past": what was "the date of the first performance of *Hamlet*?" That this is a socially motivated query may be deduced from its result. "In order to answer her Mr Hilbery had to have recourse to the exact scholarship of William Rodney, and before he had given his excellent authorities for believing as he believed, Rodney felt himself admitted once more to the society of the civilized and sanctioned by the authority of no less a person than Shakespeare himself."[138] That modern social necessity "self-esteem" is here provided, in the nick of time, through the versatile recourse to Shakespeare.

Earlier in the novel Mrs. Hilbery had proposed a day trip to Blackfriars to "inspect the site of Shakespeare's theatre"; later she asks Katharine to find her the best train for Stratford-on-Avon.[139] Her note, delivered with early-morning tea, read, "I've been dreaming all night of you and Shakespeare, dearest Katharine."

> This was no momentary impulse. Mrs Hilbery had been dreaming of Shakespeare any time these six months, toying with the idea of an excursion to what she considered the heart of the civilized world. To stand six feet above Shakespeare's bones, to see the very stones worn by his feet, to reflect that the oldest man's oldest mother had very likely seen Shakespeare's daughter—such thoughts roused an emotion in her, which she

> expressed at unsuitable moments, and with a passion that would not have been unseemly in a pilgrim at a sacred shrine. The only strange thing was that she wished to go by herself. But, naturally enough, she was well provided with friends who lived in the neighbourhood of Shakespeare's tomb. . . . [S]he felt, she had always felt, that Shakespeare's command to leave his bones undisturbed applied only to odious curiosity-mongers—not to dear Sir John and herself.[140]

When she returns from Stratford, she brings with her armfuls of flowers which, as she drops them on the floor, she identifies as "From Shakespeare's tomb!"[141] Some contemporary reviewers took Woolf to task for situating the tomb outdoors instead of inside the church.[142] In fact, Woolf herself did not visit Stratford-upon-Avon until many years later, when she was struck by the same uncanny reverence she gently mocks in Mrs. Hilbery, writing to her friend Ethel Smyth, as we have seen, "I thought it almost, perhaps quite, the most moving emotion to be had anywhere—in any place."[143]

But the returning Mrs. Hilbery has, without knowing it, come back to a situation in which things have radically changed: William has fallen in love with Katharine's cousin Cassandra, and Katharine herself has come to acknowledge her feelings for Ralph. Mr. Hilbery, goaded by some elderly aunts, is furious at the situation and powerless to change it—though he takes refuge in insisting on reading aloud to Katharine from Sir Walter Scott (Leslie Stephen's favorite novelist). Receiving her mother's embrace, Katharine thinks it "amazingly appropriate" that she should have arrived at that moment and be "strewing the floor with flowers and leaves from Shakespeare's tomb."[144]

The word *strewing* is usually used in Shakespeare's plays to describe the decoration of a tomb (Juliet's, Ophelia's); the expression was so common that when in *The Winter's Tale* Perdita tells Florizel she wants flowers "to strew him o'er and o'er" he asks, teasingly, "What, like a corpse?" In this late romance, the "strewing" is fanciful; Perdita replies to her lover, "Not like a corpse—or, if, not to be buried, / But quick and in mine arms" (4.4.129–31). Woolf's novel, too, is a romance, and no one dies, or indeed is long bereft of love. But Ophelia, who makes two glancing appearances in the novel—once when Mrs. Hilbery forgets the name of "the lady Hamlet was in love with," and again in a casual mention of Millais's painting of her watery death—is Katharine's antitype, a submissive daughter with an overbearing father and a lover whose letters she is forced to return.[145]

Night and Day makes effective use of the same sort of Shakespeare "genre details" that we noted in *The Voyage Out*—details through which, as a kind of shorthand code, a character's persona is sketched. The clearest example is that of Katharine's Aunt Millicent—Mrs. Cosham—whom the narrator describes as having "the look of heightened, smoothed, incarnadined existence which is proper to elderly ladies paying calls in London."[146] (This description, apt enough in itself, also allows Woolf to deploy one of her favorite Latinate words from *Macbeth* [2.2.60], "the splendid word 'incarnadine.'")[147] Mrs. Cosham "carried her pocket Shakespeare about with her, and met life fortified by the words of the poets." Learning that Ralph Denham is a lawyer, she informs him that "they say, nowadays, that Shakespeare was a lawyer. They say that accounts for his knowledge of human nature."[148] A few minutes later she opens her pocket Shakespeare again to consult Ralph "upon an obscure passage in 'Measure for Measure.'" In the ensuing cross-talk, Woolf is able to make a mental leap from one suggestive part of the play to another:

> "I like rubies," he heard Katharine say.
>
> To be imprison'd in the viewless winds,
> And blown with restless violence round about
> The pendant world . . .
>
> Mrs Cosham intoned.[149]

Ralph is stuck listening to Mrs. Cosham; Katharine is part of another conversation. But Mrs. Cosham's quotation from Claudio's fearful account of death—a scene in which he urges his sister Isabella to save his life by sleeping with the deputy Angelo—is here tacitly juxtaposed, as Julia Briggs suggests, to a passage in the previous scene in Shakespeare's play. "Were I under the pains of death," the virginal Isabella tells Angelo, in a remarkable sadomasochistic image, "Th'impression of keen whips I'd wear as rubies, / And strip myself to death as to a bed / That longing hath been sick for, ere I'd yield / My body up to shame" (*Measure for Measure* 2.4.100–104).[150]

The association of the spoken and the unspoken lines offers a good insight into the scene's construction, underscoring both the passing irony of the social situation and the enduring irony of the novelist. Ralph feels "like death" in being separated from Katharine, especially after he learns, as he thinks, that she and William are engaged; the rubies mentioned are in a ring. When Katharine reflects at one point late in the novel that "all this talk about Shakespeare had acted as a soporific, or rather as an incantation," she is also describing the book's deliberate and contrasting modes of reference to Shakespeare, effectively juxtaposed through Woolf's careful art.[151]

"Plato's Brain and Shakespeare's": Jacob's Room *(1922)*

Woolf designed *Jacob's Room* as "a new form for a new novel," with "no scaffolding, scarcely a brick to be seen."[152] When it was finished, two years later, she reports that Leonard, perhaps her most exacting reader, "calls it a work of genius; he thinks it unlike any other novel; he says that the people are ghosts."[153] She was then forty years old. In a moment of self-assessment Jacob will reflect on his own comparative youth, envisaging his reading taste in the future. "At forty it might be a different matter."[154] Woolf's use of dramatic irony here is palpable and unerring, for Jacob—unlike his author—will not survive to reach that age.

There are three powerful ghosts in the novel: Jacob, Thoby Stephen, and Shakespeare. Jacob because he remains tantalizingly elusive and dies, offstage and off-page, before he can fulfill his promise. Thoby, to whom Woolf had thought of dedicating the novel with an epigram from Catullus. When she finished *Jacob's Room* in the summer of 1922, she wrote in her notebook, "Atque in perpetuum, frater, ave atque vale," and then "Julian Thoby Stephen (1881–1906)."[155] Thoby, like Jacob, died young, and was mourned by Cambridge classmates who admired him and took him as their model. And Shakespeare—variously the name, the book, and the poetry—who appears (and disappears, like a ghost) as both cultural standard and literary inspiration.

After an obligatory Sunday luncheon with a professor and his wife, Jacob deplores to his Cambridge friend Timmy Durrant the fact that senior dons waste their time on "Shaw and Wells and the serious sixpenny weeklies! What were they after, scrubbing and demolishing, these elderly people? Had they never read Homer, Shakespeare, the Elizabethans?"[156] This short list of the greatest of the greats and its Apostolic variant, "Plato and Shakespeare," will itself haunt the novel.

In the university vacation Jacob and Timmy Durrant set sail for Timmy's family home in the Scilly Isles. They have packed the boat with books and provisions, but the glory of the trip is itself a distraction. "What's the use of trying to read Shakespeare, especially in one of those little thin paper editions whose pages get ruffled, or stuck together with sea-water? Although the plays of Shakespeare had frequently been praised, even quoted, and placed higher than the Greek, never since they started had Jacob managed to read one through. Yet what an opportunity!"[157]

Inevitably, after this blissful start, the two young men quarrel. "Why the right way to open a tin of beef, with Shakespeare on board, under conditions of such splendour, should have turned them to sulky schoolboys, none can tell."[158] And before long, Shakespeare is no longer on board. After taking a swim Jacob gets back on board. "The seat in the boat was positively hot, and the sun warmed his back as he sat naked with a towel in his hand, looking at the Scilly Isles which—confound it! The sail flapped, Shakespeare was knocked overboard. There you could see him floating merrily away with all his pages ruffling innumerably; and then he went under."[159] "Merrily" is a nice touch, but "him" is even nicer. The personified copy of Shakespeare's plays, not an "it" or even a "them" but rather a "him," vanishes beneath the waves.[160]

After he leaves Cambridge, Jacob meets a number of women, and both he and the novel measure them, symptomatically, by their response to literature. Of Florinda, an artist's model, we hear that "Jacob took her word for it that she was chaste" and that he recommends that she should read Shelley. "To have at hand as sovereign specifics for all disorders of the soul Adonais and the plays of Shakespeare," he thinks, may allow him to develop "a comradeship all spirited on her side, protective on his."[161] ("Adonais," Shelley's elegy to Keats, predicts the genre of Woolf's novel, as the gifted Jacob will also die young.) When she takes it home to read in bed, Florinda finds Shelley boring ("What on earth was it *about?*"), preferring to eat chocolates, and the narrator tells us that over dinner Jacob begins to wonder "whether she had a mind." The description, whether intentionally or not, is unsparing to them both. Jacob tells another woman, a student at the Slade, that there is no point in reading anything but "Marlowe and Shakespeare, and Fielding if you must read novels." Predictably, she chooses Fielding and, equally predictably, finds *Tom Jones* "dull stuff."[162]

Woolf contrasts these mildly bohemian relationships to Jacob's behavior toward a "nice girl," Timmy Durrant's sister Clara. At an evening party designed to introduce marriageable girls to eligible men, Jacob stands next to Clara to listen to the evening's entertainment: a song from *The Two Gentlemen of Verona:*

> "Who is Silvia? what is she?
> That all our swains commend her?"
>
> sang Elsbeth Siddons.
>
> Every one stood where they were, or sat down if a chair was empty.
>
> "Ah," sighed Clara, who stood beside Jacob, half-way through.
>
> "Then to Silvia let us sing,
> That Silvia is excelling;
> She excels each mortal thing
> Upon the dull earth dwelling,
> To her let us garlands bring."

> sang Elsbeth Siddons.
>
> "Ah!" Clara exclaimed out loud, and clapped her gloved hands; and Jacob clapped his bare ones.[163]

In Shakespeare's play the song is sung by Proteus, the perfidious lover of Julia, who has developed a crush on his friend Valentine's beloved. It is thus a classic example of a quotation taken out of context, since the song itself is limpidly pure, while the singer's intention is corrupt. (In the Shakespeare section of Arthur Quiller-Couch's 1906 *Oxford Book of English Verse,* the poem is titled simply "Silvia," and it is not identified as coming from a play, so the ironic juxtaposition of song and singer is lost.)

There is no clear sense that Clara knows more about Shakespeare than Florinda does. And indeed we find out shortly that Clara will be the Proteus figure, the "unfaithful" one, since although Jacob invites her to go down to supper with him she instead joins another man whom her mother has wished her to meet ("'Mr Pilcher from New York—This is Miss Durrant.' 'Whom I have heard so much of,' said Mr Pilcher, bowing low. So Clara left him.")[164] Meantime, among the chaperones at the party, "old Lady Hibbert" is chatting with "Mr Salvin, who, owing to his lameness, was accommodated with a chair."

> "Never tell me that girls of ten are incapable of love! I had all Shakespeare by heart before I was in my teens, Mr Salvin!"
>
> "You don't say so," said Mr Salvin.
>
> "But I do," said Lady Hibbert.[165]

Random talk about Shakespeare in some of Woolf's early novels is a habit often associated with older women of a certain class. Thus, for example, one day when Jacob is reading and transcribing the works of Marlowe in the British Museum, another regular reader, Miss Marchmont, "in her old plush dress, and her wig of claret-coloured hair, with her gems and her chilblains," offers a disjointed running commentary about her philosophy of the soul, and how publishers are capitalists, "and Mr Asquith's Irish policy, and Shakespeare comes in," and then, with a mis-aimed gesture, she topples her pile of books onto the floor.[166] But Jacob's Shakespeare, although likewise contemplated in the British Museum, is designedly of a different order: abstract, timeless, classic, and classical. He does not "come in"; he looms. Jacob's Shakespeare is, in fact, the Shakespeare of the Cambridge Apostles, the young men who became the (male) foundation of the Bloomsbury Group.

In this same spirit Jacob thinks that "there is in the British Museum an enormous mind. Consider that Plato is there cheek by jowl with Aristotle; and Shakespeare with Marlowe."[167] In the space of a single page of Woolf's text, the pairing of "Plato and Shakespeare" appears five times:

> The vast mind was sheeted with stone; and each compartment in the depths of it was safe and dry. The night-watchmen, flashing their lanterns over the backs of Plato and Shakespeare, saw that on the twenty-second of February neither flame, rat, nor burglar was going to violate those treasures—poor, highly respectable men, with wives and families at Kentish Town, do their best for twenty years to protect Plato and Shakespeare, and then are buried at Highgate.
>
> Stone lies solid over the British Museum, as bone lies cool over the visions and heat of the brain. Only here the brain is Plato's brain and Shakespeare's; the brain has made pot and statues, great bulls and little jewels, and crossed the river of death this way and that incessantly, seeking some landing, now wrapping the body well for its long sleep; now laying a penny piece on the eyes; now turning the toes scrupulously to the East. Meanwhile Plato continues his dialogue; in spite of the rain; in spite of the cab whistles; in spite of the woman in the mews behind Great Ormond Street who has come home drunk and cries all night long, "Let me in! Let me in!"
>
> In the street below Jacob's room voices were raised.
>
> But he read on. For after all Plato continues imperturbably. And Hamlet utters his soliloquy. And there the Elgin Marbles lie, all night long, old Jones's lantern sometimes recalling Ulysses, or a horse's head; or sometimes a flash of gold, or a mummy's sunk yellow cheek. Plato and Shakespeare continue.[168]

"Plato's brain and Shakespeare's." "Plato and Shakespeare continue." Yet these are still abstractions. We heard a singer with a Shakespearean actress's name (Siddons) perform "Who Is Sylvia?" but it is not until the novel's scene shifts to Paris that we hear Jacob—or indeed anyone—recite lines from the plays. And when they do, the lines we hear are, once again, the first lines of Shakespeare that Virginia Woolf learned to love.

Jacob is in a café on his first trip abroad. ("Old Miss Birkbeck, his mother's cousin, had died last June and left him a hundred pounds"—here *Jacob's Room* anticipates *A Room of One's Own.*)[169] His drinking companions are painters, and they are discussing first art, and then literature. "'I'll tell you the three greatest things that were ever written in the whole of literature,' Cruttendon burst out. 'Hang there like fruit, my soul,' he began."

As we've seen, both the poet Tennyson and the young Virginia Stephen admired this same passage. Jacob, who is among other things an avatar of Thoby Stephen, is happy to concur.

> "That's Shakespeare, Cruttendon. I'm with you there. Shakespeare had more guts than all these damned frogs put together. 'Hang there like fruit my soul,'" he began quoting, in a musical, rhetorical voice, flourishing his wine-glass. "'The devil damn you black, you cream-faced loon!'" he exclaimed as the wine washed over the rim.
>
> "'Hang there like fruit my soul,'" Cruttendon and Jacob both began again at the same moment, and both burst out laughing.[170]

By juxtaposing Posthumus's tender phrase to Imogen with Macbeth's excoriation of his frightened servant (*Macbeth* 5.3.11), Jacob shifts the mood, allowing both men to "burst out laughing" when they chant together the lyric lines from *Cymbeline.* In this way Woolf can have her truth-telling moment about one of "the greatest things that were ever written in the whole of literature" (we never learn the other two) and retain, at the same time, the energy of this occasion among free-spirited young men.

Shakespeare will appear once more in the novel as a ghostly absence, when Jacob, now traveling in Greece, falls in love with a married woman, Sandra Wentworth Williams. Before they part, he gives her his copy of Donne's poems, which will ultimately wind up, we are told, on the shelf of the English country house where she lives with her husband ("There were ten or twelve little volumes already").[171] Jacob had already "marked the things he liked in Donne, and they were savage enough. However, you might place beside them passages of the purest poetry in Shakespeare."[172] Yet it is Donne he gives her, not Shakespeare. Shakespeare, we might say, he withholds, or retains. Till the tree die.

Jacob's Room, as critics have noted, is both an elegy and an aborted Bildungsroman. Like Thoby Stephen's, Jacob's life ends far too early, and there is a sense at the end of the novel that, like Hamlet and Thoby, he was likely "to have proved most royally" (*Hamlet* 5.2.341–42).[173] Only letters, bills, and an old pair of shoes are left in his room. We are not told what has become of his Shakespeare (for surely he had long ago replaced the one that floated away). It is not unlikely that it went to the war with him, somewhere in the gap between the last two chapters of the novel.

"Fear No More": Mrs. Dalloway *(1925)*

By the time she wrote *Mrs. Dalloway,* Virginia Woolf was fully in command of the kind of Shakespearean leitmotif that would come to characterize her fiction: the repeated iteration of a phrase, sometimes a quotation or part of a quotation, that would quickly and indelibly establish a persona and reflect a character's inner thought. Before her marriage she had visited Bayreuth several times with her brother Adrian and Saxon Sydney-Turner to hear Wagner's operas, and in an early article in the *Times* she twice compared Wagner's technique with Shakespeare's. "Like Shakespeare, Wagner seems to have attained in the end to such a mastery of technique that he could float and soar in regions where in the beginning he could scarcely breathe," she says.[174] A second comparison speaks directly to the question of motif while acknowledging "the difficulty of changing a musical impression into a literary one." "The more beautiful a phrase of music is the richer its burden of suggestion. . . . We are led on to connect the beautiful sound with some experience of our own, or to make it symbolise some conception of a general nature. . . . Something of the same effect is given by Shakespeare, when he makes an old nurse the type of all the old nurses in the world, while she keeps her identity as a particular old woman."[175]

Later Woolf came to dislike Wagner's music, finding what "used to carry me away" now full of "bawling sentimentality."[176] Leonard found Wagnerian opera monotonous, boring, and ultimately contributory to the barbarous ideas that led to the Second World War.[177] But the idea of connecting "a beautiful sound" with "some experience of our own," while also making it "symbolise some conception of a general nature" is a good description of the way she uses fragments of literary quotation in novels like *Mrs. Dalloway* and *To the Lighthouse.*

Two Shakespearean phrases are heard repeatedly in *Mrs. Dalloway:* "Fear no more," from the lovely lyric "Fear no more the heat o' the sun" in *Cymbeline,* and "If it were now to die, / 'Twere now to be most happy" from *Othello.* Both reflect on the question of death and joy. A third recurring reference is the title of a play, *Antony and Cleopatra,* linked in Septimus Smith's mind to his teacher, Miss Isabel Pole. That play, too, will take up the same question, playing extensively on the double meaning of "die" in the English Renaissance: to cease to be and to reach sexual climax.

Before we turn to the effect of these motifs, though, we should note that in *Mrs. Dalloway* Woolf continues to employ a more incidental kind of Shakespeare reference, as she had in earlier novels, to swiftly sum up a character—often a relatively minor character or one that is "flat" or unchanging. These short-takes, gently satirical in effect, can be measured against the more extended and more complex interweaving of Shakespeare phrases and references as they affect her two central figures, Clarissa Dalloway and Septimus Smith. Thus, for example, Clarissa's former suitor, Peter Walsh, shrewdly assesses her husband, Richard, by describing Richard's attitude toward the sonnets: "How could she let him hold forth about Shakespeare? Seriously and solemnly Richard Dalloway got on his hind legs and said that no decent man ought to read Shakespeare's sonnets because it was like listening at keyholes (besides, the relationship was not one that he approved)."[178] Likewise, the hyper-patriotic Lady Bruton, who invites Richard to lunch so he can advise her on writing a letter to the *Times,* is summed up by an allusion to John of Gaunt's famous deathbed speech in *Richard II:* "She never spoke of England, but this isle of men, this dear, dear land, it was in her blood (without reading Shakespeare). . . . She had the thought of Empire always at hand."[179]

Woolf's touch here is especially deft, since Gaunt does not mention the word *England* till halfway through this long speech, so sure is he that his listeners will understand his description:

> This royal throne of kings, this seat of Mars,
> This other Eden, demi-paradise,
> This fortress built by nature for herself
> Against infection and the hand of war,
> This happy breed of men, this little world,
> This precious stone set in the silver sea,
> Which serves it in the office of a wall,
> Or as a moat defensive to a house
> Against the envy of less happier lands;
> This blessed plot, this earth, this realm, this England,
> This nurse, this teeming womb of royal kings,
> Feared by their breed and famous by their birth,
> Renowned for their deeds as far from home
> For Christian service and true chivalry
> As is the sepulchre, in stubborn Jewry,
> Of the world's ransom, blessed Mary's son,
> This land of such dear souls, this dear dear land.
> (2.1.40–57)

The formidable Lady Bruton, with her "ramrod bearing" and "her robustness of demeanor" ("it was in her blood"—so she herself, in John of Gaunt's terms, is "feared by [her] breed"), voices an equal certainty.[180] She too "never spoke of England" but uses instead snatches of phrases she is sure her hearers would understand: "this isle of men, this dear, dear land." And since Gaunt's speech, a familiar set piece, would often have been quoted, half-quoted, anthologized, and otherwise widely known, she might well echo some of its phrases "without reading Shakespeare."

What Lady Bruton and Richard Dalloway have in common is not only a lack of aesthetic or poetic sensibility but the absence of any wish for one. They are political actors, believers in right sentiment and right politics, avoiding any relationships of which they do not approve. And they expect, like Richard Dalloway "on his hind legs," to be commended for their opinions, which they regard as self-evident truths.

Against this confident assurance, in each case tied by Woolf to a localized mention of Shakespeare, the novel will measure the doubts, passions, loves, and fears of its two central characters, Clarissa and Septimus. Again Shakespeare will be the vehicle, and the effect is in a real sense "dramatic," for although the lives of these two strangers cross only for a single moment, the same Shakespearean references will attach to them both.

In its context in *Cymbeline,* "Fear no more" is a dirge, sung over the body of "Fidele"—the play's heroine, Imogen, disguised as a boy. As soon becomes clear to the audience (though not yet to the mourners), Fidele is not really dead, but this harbinger of death—like the quotation from *Othello*—looms over the novel.

Woolf introduces the song early on: Clarissa Dalloway, we are told, is daydreaming when she looks into the window of Hatchards bookshop, and reads

> in the book spread open:
>
> Fear no more the heat o' the sun
> Nor the furious winter's rages.[181]

The book that catches her eye—though the novel does not identify it—is almost surely *Shakespeare's The Tragedie of Cymbeline: Printed from the Folio of 1623,* edited by Harley Granville Barker with illustrations by Albert Rutherston. Printed in two editions, one of 100 copies and another of 450, it was a "rare book" from the outset, and was published in 1923, three hundred years after the First Folio. With its large size, beautiful font, and colored illustrations by a well-known artist, it's just the kind of book that would have been "spread open" at a key passage to entice customers at a high-end establishment like Hatchards.[182]

Clarissa will remember this passage from *Cymbeline* three times more: once when she sees a note on her telephone pad indicating that Lady Bruton has asked Richard to lunch; a second time when she is mending a dress; and a third time when she hears that a young man has jumped to his death. "'Fear no more,' said Clarissa. Fear no more the heat o' the sun; for the shock of Lady Bruton asking Richard to lunch without her made the moment in which she had stood shiver, as a plant on the river-bed feels the shock of a passing oar and shivers: so she rocked: so she shivered."[183] Her distress is social, not, she assures herself, a matter of "vulgar jealousy": the invitation comes from "Millicent Bruton, whose lunch parties were said to be extraordinarily amusing." (As the reader will learn, this particular luncheon is really a business consultation and not especially amusing, although the food is good.) But Clarissa's momentary chill is related to her sense of "the dwindling of life," the shortening of expectations for the future, and it culminates in one of those lyric descriptions, so frequent in Woolf's novels, of going under the waves. Clarissa "felt often . . . an exquisite suspense, such as might stay a diver before plunging while the sea darkens and brightens beneath him, and the waves which threaten to break, but only gently split their surface, roll and conceal and encrust as they just turn over the weeds with pearl."[184] *Pearl* is the key word here, linking this image to another of Shakespeare's best-known and most beautiful lyrics, Ariel's song in the *Tempest*—another dirge, like "Fear no more," mourning a person wrongly believed to be dead: "Full fathom five thy father lies. . . . Those are pearls that were his eyes" (1.2.400–406).

The same conflation of "Fear no more" and the image of breaking waves will come to Clarissa's mind when she is mending a dress to wear to her party—a green dress, the same color dress in which Septimus remembers his Shakespeare teacher Miss Isabel Pole. Feeling calm and content as she draws the needle through the silk and gathers "the green folds," she thinks of how "on a summer's day, the waves collect, overbalance, and fall; collect, and fall, and the whole world seems to be saying, 'that is all' more and more ponderously, until even the heart in the body which lies in the sun on the beach says too, That is all. Fear no more, says the heart. Fear no more, says the heart, committing its burden to some sea, which sighs collectively for all sorrows, and renews, begins, collects, lets fall."[185]

As if he magically shares her thoughts, Septimus Smith will much later echo them. "Fear no more, says the heart in the body; fear no more. He was not afraid. At every moment Nature signified by some laughing hint . . . her determination to show . . . through Shakespeare's words, her meaning."[186] "Even the heart in the body" says, "Fear no more," thinks Clarissa; "Fear no more, says the heart to the body," thinks Septimus. At that moment, however different in circumstance, they are intermingled, identified.

When the self-satisfied society doctor Sir William Bradshaw and his wife, both of whom Clarissa "disliked" and found unsympathetic ("one wouldn't like Sir William to see one unhappy"), apologize for arriving "shockingly late" because a young man has killed himself, her first thought is the conventional response of a hostess. "Oh, thought Clarissa, in the middle of my party, here's death." "What business had the Bradshaws to talk of death at her party?"[187] (The reader knows, though Clarissa does not, that it is the complacent Sir William who, by threatening to confine Septimus to a rest home "without friends, without books, without messages," has driven him to his final desperate leap.)[188] Yet on reflection she thinks that "there was an embrace in death." By his suicide the unknown young man had preserved something valuable. "And the words came to her, Fear no more the heat of the sun." For a moment she feels "somehow very like him. . . . She felt glad that he had done it, thrown it away while they went on living"—and then she returns to her guests.[189]

In Woolf's elegant design, all lines will converge at the party. Inevitably, then, the news of Septimus's death also brings to Clarissa's mind the other Shakespeare quotation that has haunted her throughout the day, Othello's fateful greeting to Desdemona when he lands at Cyprus: "If it were now to die, / 'Twere now to be most happy" (2.1.186–87). "But this young man who had killed himself—had he plunged holding his treasure? 'If it were now to die, 'twere now to be most happy,' she had said to herself once, coming down in white."[190] The memory is that of her ecstatic youthful love for Sally Seton, which she also recalls much earlier in the novel: "Going downstairs, and feeling as she crossed the hall 'if it were now to die 'twere now to be most happy.' That was her feeling—Othello's feeling, and she felt it, she was convinced, as strongly as Shakespeare meant Othello to feel it, all because she was coming down to dinner in a white frock to meet Sally Seton!"[191]

But memories are, inevitably in this novel, not the same as present-day realities. Sally Seton appears at the party, uninvited, and is announced as "Lady Rosseter." She has married a wealthy man in Manchester and has "five enormous boys." Clarissa's Shakespearean epiphany on the terrace, when "the whole world might have turned upside down," had come when Sally picked a flower and kissed her on the lips.[192] Now "they kissed each other, first this cheek, then that, by the drawing room door," and Clarissa thinks that "she hadn't looked like *that*" all those years ago; now she was "older, happier, less lovely."[193]

She had anticipated for Sally a life (like Desdemona's? like Othello's?) that would "end in some awful tragedy; her death; her martyrdom; instead of which she had married, quite unexpectedly, a bald man with a large buttonhole who owned, it was said, cotton mills at Manchester."[194] For her part Sally confides to Peter Walsh that ("to be frank") Clarissa, despite her extraordinary charm, had always "lacked something."[195] How could she have married Richard Dalloway—or cared so much about society parties? (On the other hand, Lady Bruton thinks that it would have been better if Richard had married "a woman with less charm" who could have helped him in his work. "He had lost his chance of the Cabinet.")[196]

The quotation from *Othello,* as we have seen, was in Woolf's mind in April 1925, when she wrote in her diary after returning from a holiday in Cassis, "L. & I were too too happy, as they say; if it were now to die, &c. Nobody shall say of me that I have not known perfect happiness, but few could put their finger on the moment, or say who made it. Even I myself, stirring occasionally in the pool of content, could only say But this is all I want; could not think of anything better."[197] *Mrs. Dalloway* would be published in May of that year, and the only sense of fateful anticipation in the diary reflects this imminent event: "But, hush, hush—my books tremble on the verge of coming out, & my future is uncertain. As for forecasts—its *just* on the cards Mrs Dalloway is a success (Harcourt thinks it 'wonderful'), & sells 2,000—I dont expect it: I expect a slow silent increase of fame, such has come about, rather miraculously, since Js.R. was published."[198] Within *Mrs. Dalloway,* however, the full force of Othello's lines are felt: both the ecstasy of love and the danger of loss.

Losses in the novel take many forms, from war, madness, and violent death to banality and mediocrity. But love in its most enduring manifestation—or manifestations—ultimately attaches to the Septimus story rather than the story of Clarissa. And once again—as was the case in *Night and Day*—the vehicle of the love narrative is Shakespeare.

From 1905 to 1907 the young Virginia Stephen had taught evening classes for working women at Morley College, located in the Waterloo Road. We have seen that in 1923 she had a Shakespearean epiphany walking in the same area: "it was so lovely in the Waterloo Road that it struck me that we were writing Shakespeare; by which I meant that when live people, seemingly happy, produce an effect of beauty, & you dont have it offered as a work of art, but it seems a natural gift of theirs, then—what was I meaning?—somehow it affected me as I am affected by reading Shakespeare. No; its life; going on in these very beautiful surroundings."[199] In *Mrs. Dalloway* we learn that Septimus Smith, shy, stammering, and "anxious to improve himself," would "fall in love with Miss Isabel Pole, lecturing in the Waterloo Road upon Shakespeare." "Was he not like Keats? she asked; and reflected how she might give him a taste of *Antony and Cleopatra* and the rest; lent him books; wrote him scraps of letters; and lit in him such a fire as burns only once in a lifetime, without heat, flickering a red gold flame infinitely ethereal and insubstantial over Miss Pole; *Antony and Cleopatra;* and the Waterloo Road. He thought her beautiful, believed her impeccably wise; dreamed of her, wrote poems to her, which, ignoring the subject, she corrected in red ink; he saw her, one summer evening, walking in a green dress in a square."[200]

Antony and Cleopatra is one of the greatest love stories of all time, the dramatization of a peerless and legendary couple. Cleopatra, with her infinite variety, she whom age cannot wither, is the irresistible force; Antony, a soldier and a hero, willingly chooses to give all for love. (In her notebooks for 1924 and 1925, as she was writing *Mrs. Dalloway,* Woolf wrote, "There are obviously people like Cleopatra who stand for something in human nature, & so get built up by general consent," and—perhaps thinking of Shakespeare's Cleopatra versus Dryden's—"Of course, the first thing is the immensely greater richness of Cleo. In particular.")[201] One of the play's most famous passages is Enobarbus's description of how Antony fell instantly under Cleopatra's spell when he first saw her at Cydnus (2.2).

When war comes, we are told, "Septimus was one of the first to volunteer. He went to France to save an England which consisted almost entirely of Shakespeare's plays and Miss Isabel Pole in a green dress walking in a square."[202] But the war changes him, as it changed everyone. After the death on the eve of the Armistice of his best friend and soul mate, an officer named Evans, he found that "he could not feel." In a panic, he marries Lucrezia, a young Italian girl, the daughter of a hatmaker, and brings her with him back to England.

Rezia, as she is called, is explicitly modeled on Lydia Lopokova, the Russian ballet dancer whom Maynard Keynes would marry, and some of the tenderest moments in *Mrs. Dalloway* reflect Lydia's interest in studying Shakespeare and Maynard's eager tutelage. "Could she not read Shakespeare too? Was Shakespeare a difficult author?" Rezia asks Septimus, hoping to cheer him up by sharing one of his passions.[203] And again, "How serious he was, wanting her to read Shakespeare before she could even read a children's story in English!"[204]

Woolf could be ungenerous about Lydia in her private correspondence, writing to a friend: "Poor little wretch, trapped in Bloomsbury, what can she do but learn Shakespeare by heart? I assure you its tragic to see her sitting down to *King Lear.* Nobody can take her seriously."[205] But as Hermione Lee notes, "When Virginia drew on her for Rezia in *Mrs. Dalloway* (so closely that she caught herself calling Lydia 'Rezia') she made a touching, attractive character."[206] And Rezia's art form, her capacity to make hats and alter them to fit styles and moods, makes her the novel's embedded artist, the counterpart of figures in Woolf's later novels, like Lily Briscoe and Miss La Trobe.

Septimus's reading of Shakespeare becomes, for him and for the novel, a way of tracking his own feelings. The dream of Miss Isabel Pole in her green dress in the square has given way to the reality of his marriage in postwar London, and the anger and grief of a shell-shocked soldier. "He opened Shakespeare once more. That boy's business of the intoxication of language—*Antony and Cleopatra*—had shriveled utterly. How Shakespeare loathed humanity—the putting on of clothes, the getting of children, the sordidity of the mouth and the belly! This was now revealed to Septimus: the message hidden in the beauty of words."[207] And again, "Love between man and woman was repulsive to Shakespeare. The business of copulation was filth to him before the end. But, Rezia said, she must have children."[208]

Although they might seem at first an indication of his psychological instability, these observations accurately reflect major passages and characters in Shakespeare's plays: Hamlet, Thersites, King Lear, Timon, Lucius in *Measure for Measure,* Menenius's wry fable of the belly. The richness and diversity of Shakespeare's text, and the crucial fact that dramatic characters all speak for themselves and do not have a controlling narrative "author," make lines like "Nay, but to live / In the rank sweat of an enseamed bed, / Stewed in corruption, honeying and making love / Over the nasty sty" (*Hamlet* 3.4.51–54), and "Into her womb convey sterility! / Dry up in her the organs of increase" (*King Lear* 1.4.255–56) as authentically "Shakespearean" as the transcendent love scenes of *Antony and Cleopatra.* Reading Shakespeare, as Woolf knew, could encompass—and mirror and express—the whole of human experience.

After Septimus's physician, Dr. Holmes, advises him to "take up some hobby," it quickly becomes clear that to regard Shakespeare as a "hobby" will not do. "He opened Shakespeare—*Antony and Cleopatra;* pushed Shakespeare aside. Some hobby, said Dr. Holmes," who himself boasts that he restores old furniture as a way to "switch off from his patients."[209] It is Dr. Holmes who, sneering, advises the couple, "If they were rich people" ("looking ironically round the room") to "by all means go to Harley Street, if they had no confidence in him."[210] But the Smiths are not ironists; they make an appointment, forthwith, to see Sir William Bradshaw. All the pieces are now in place for the catastrophe. Sir William, in all his bland complacency, will tie the two plots together.

Meantime, at home with Rezia, Septimus's mood changes again, from terror to calm, and this is the point at which Woolf has him invoke the "Fear no more" passage we have previously associated only with Clarissa. "Fear no more, says the heart in the body; fear no more. He was not afraid. At every moment Nature signified by some laughing hint . . . her determination to show . . . through Shakespeare's words, her meaning."[211] He dictates some of his thoughts to Rezia, "telling her to write. The table drawer was full of those writings; about war; about Shakespeare; about great discoveries; how there is no death."[212] He hallucinates, imagining that Evans had come and was singing behind the screen. A few years before she wrote *Mrs. Dalloway,* Woolf had given a paper to the Memoir Club in which she recalled her own hallucinations during an early illness: "The birds were singing Greek choruses and . . . King Edward was using the foulest possible language among Ozzie Dickinson's azaleas."[213] Her description of Septimus's writings draws upon these memories; his papers include "how the dead sing behind rhododendron bushes; odes to Time; conversations with Shakespeare; Evans, Evans, Evans—his messages from the dead."[214]

Once "they found the girl who did the room reading one of these papers in fits of laughter . . . that made Septimus cry out about human cruelty. . . . 'Holmes is on us,' he would say, and he would invent stories about Holmes; Holmes eating porridge; Holmes reading Shakespeare—making himself roar with laughter or rage, for Dr. Holmes seemed to stand for something horrible to him. 'Human nature,' he called him."[215] So Rezia ties up the papers so no one can see them.

As the Septimus story draws toward its close, the patterns of Shakespearean allusion in the two plots converge, bringing the key phrases once more to the surface of Woolf's text, in all their accumulated ambiguity. Septimus had unconsciously echoed Clarissa's quotation from the dirge in *Cymbeline,* "Fear no more." Now Rezia will, likewise unconsciously, echo the foreboding lines Clarissa has said to herself from *Othello,* "If it were now to die, 'twere now to be most happy": "They were perfectly happy now, she said suddenly."[216] In a few moments Dr. Holmes—or "Human nature"—will come to the door.

But the novel does not end with Septimus's desperate leap for freedom. Its title is not *Mr. Smith* or *Septimus Smith* or even *Clarissa Dalloway.* It is as the wife of Richard Dalloway (even if Richard had "lost his chance at the Cabinet") that Clarissa gives her parties and experiences her current happiness. "Even now, quite often if Richard had not been there reading the Times . . . she must have perished. She had escaped. But that young man had killed himself."

> Odd, incredible: she had never been so happy. Nothing could be slow enough, nothing last too long.[217]

"She had never been so happy." Here is the *Othello* theme one last time, but devoid of its instantaneous and ominous ecstasy. Instead of a precipitous wish for death ("if it were now to die") Clarissa feels a pleasure precisely in the slower pleasures of middle age. "No pleasure could equal," she thinks, "this having done with the triumphs of youth, lost herself in the process of living, to find it, with a shock of delight, as the sun rose, as the day sank."[218] The American edition of *Mrs. Dalloway* makes the connection between her marriage and her feelings even clearer, reading: "It was due to Richard; she had never been so happy."[219]

Othello and *Antony and Cleopatra* are sometimes described as "love tragedies." Their protagonists love passionately and die with equal passion. But Clarissa is a survivor, a figure of romantic comedy, not a tragic heroine. As is so often the case in Virginia Woolf's novels, the last scene is given over to the feelings of an onlooker, in this case her old suitor Peter Walsh, who—alone—still harbors the feelings of Othello when he lands at Cyprus, or Antony when he first beholds Cleopatra at Cydnus:

> What is this terror? what is this ecstasy? He thought to himself. What is it that fills me with extraordinary excitement?
>
> It is Clarissa, he said.
>
> For there she was.[220]

"As with Your Shadow I with These Did Play": To the Lighthouse *(1927)*

Shakespearean references in *To the Lighthouse* begin with what seems like a rather inappropriate quotation, as Paul Rayley, having just proposed to Minta Doyle, sees the lights of the Ramsays' house in the distance and says to himself, "Lights, lights, lights." He and Minta are walking back from the shore, and "as they came out on the hill and saw the lights of the town beneath them, the lights coming out suddenly one by one seemed like things that were going to happen to him—his marriage, his children, his house."[221] Mrs. Ramsay had encouraged him to speak, and "directly they got back (he looked for the lights of the house above the bay) he would go to her and say, 'I've done it, Mrs Ramsay, thanks to you.'" "The house was all lit up, and the lights after the darkness made his eyes feel full, and he said to himself, childishly, as he walked up the drive, Lights, lights, lights, and repeated in a dazed way, Lights, lights, lights, as they came into the house, staring about him with his face quite stiff."[222]

In *Hamlet,* "Lights, lights, lights" is the cry that goes up after the disrupted play-within-a-play, *The Murder of Gonzago* (3.2.246). Speaking as chorus (or narrator), Hamlet has just explained the next stage in the plot: "You shall see anon how the murderer gets the love of Gonzago's wife." The king immediately rises to his feet and calls for light, bringing an end to the performance. "Give me some light! Away," he says, dismissing the courtiers and players. Claudius has been, in Hamlet's phrase, "frighted with false fire" (3.2.241–42, 247, 244). So "lights, lights, lights" is a response to the detection of adultery. Not an association one might expect from a happy prospective bridegroom.

Paul is neither a scholar nor, so far as we learn, a playgoer. His quotation—from the most famous of plays—is spontaneous and not thought out; in fact his next worry is that he will make a fool of himself at dinner. But many years and many pages later the reader will learn from Lily Briscoe that for the Rayleys "things had worked loose after the first year or so; the marriage had turned out rather badly."[223] And yet, "To go on with their story—they had got through the dangerous stage by now. . . . They were 'in love' no longer; no, he had taken up with another woman, a serious woman, with her hair in a plait and a case in her hand (Minta had described her gratefully, almost admiringly), who went to meetings and shared Paul's views. . . . Far from breaking up the marriage, that alliance had righted it. They were excellent friends, obviously."[224] Far from spelling the end of the marriage, the unconventional relationship—as was often the case among Woolf's friends—made the Rayleys' marriage work. Long after Mrs. Ramsay's death, Lily imagines that she "would feel a little triumphant" if she could tell her that the marriage had not been a success. Mrs. Ramsay had urged everyone to "marry, marry"; her ideas were "limited" and "old-fashioned." "One would have to say to her, It has all gone against your wishes."[225]

Hamlet had railed against marriage for quite different reasons, just as Paul Rayley would seem to be a most unlikely Claudius. But the brief and thoughtless interjection "lights, lights, lights" opens the way to these associations, with their surprisingly wry aptness. This is Woolf using Shakespeare in a new way. The ironic juxtaposition illuminates not the characters but the plot, and a view—at least Lily's view—of the modern world. At the same time Paul's "lights, lights, lights" inevitably reflects on the title of the novel. He and Minta saw "the lights of the town beneath them, the lights coming out suddenly one by one"; he "looked for the lights of the house above the bay"; the "house was all lit up." Mrs. Ramsay's house is a lighthouse for him and for others who shelter there. It welcomes and protects, but it can also warn of danger if its signals are seen and understood.

Later Lily will ask Andrew and Prue, the two eldest Ramsay children, whether a light should be left burning.

"No," said Prue, "not if everyone's in."

"Andrew," she called back, "'just put out the light in the hall."

"One by one the lights were all extinguished," Woolf writes, and while this describes nightfall at the Ramsay house, it also clearly echoes, and is meant to echo, the words of the British foreign secretary Sir Edward Grey on the eve of the war: "The lights are going out all over Europe; we shall not see them lit again in our lifetime."[226] Andrew will die in the war. Prue will die in childbirth. Whether there is a glancing reference here to Othello pondering the death of Desdemona is not clear, but the passage is similar enough to deserve mention:

> Put out the light, and then put out the light.
> If I quench thee, thou flaming minister,
> I can again thy former light restore
> Should I repent me; but once put out thy light,
> Thou cunning'st pattern of excelling nature,
> I know not where is that Promethean heat
> That can thy light relume.
> (*Othello* 5.2.7–13)

Mr. Ramsay, for his part, has a different idea about light; he associates it with fame, in particular with his own fame as a scholar and philosopher—or his lack of it. (Here Woolf is drawing on Leslie Stephen's own regrets as expressed in his *Mausoleum Book:* "The sense in which I do take myself to be a failure is this: I have scattered myself too much. I think that I had it in me to make something like a real contribution to philosophical or ethical thought. . . . I do feel that if, for example, the history of English thought in the nineteenth century should ever be written, my name will only be mentioned in small type and footnotes" rather than "the honour of a paragraph in full sized type or even a section in a chapter all to myself.")[227]

Woolf's language, projecting Mr. Ramsay's thoughts, is heroic, or rather mock-heroic. Only one man in a generation reaches the top:

> Is he to be blamed then if he is not that one? provided he has toiled honestly, given to the best of his power, till he has no more left to give? And his fame lasts how long? It is permissible even for a dying hero to think before he dies how men will speak of him hereafter. His fame lasts perhaps two thousand years. And what are two thousand years? (asked Mr Ramsay ironically, staring at the hedge). What, indeed, if you look from a mountain-top down the long wastes of the ages? The very stone one kicks

> with one's boot will outlast Shakespeare. His own little light would shine, not very brightly, for a year or two, and would then be merged in some bigger light, and that into a bigger still. (He looked into the darkness.)[228]

"The very stone one kicks with one's boot will outlast Shakespeare." Mr. Ramsay is paraphrasing, though probably not consciously on his part, the famous story Boswell tells about Dr. Johnson: "After we came out of the church, we stood talking for some time together of Bishop Berkeley's ingenious sophistry to prove the non-existence of matter, and that every thing in the universe is merely ideal. I observed, that though we are satisfied his doctrine is not true, it is impossible to refute it. I never shall forget the alacrity with which Johnson answered, striking his foot with mighty force against a large stone, till he rebounded from it, 'I refute it *thus.*'"[229] Woolf has Mr. Ramsay say "kicks with one's *boot*"—not, as in Boswell, "foot"—anticipating the moment later in the novel, when Lily, at her wits' end to find a compliment to cheer up Mr. Ramsay, praises his "beautiful boots" and finds to her surprise that this does the trick.[230] And in case we have forgotten the passing mention of Shakespeare, Woolf will remind us later in Mr. Ramsay's reverie that the "hero" (that is, Mr. Ramsay's alter ego) "now perceives by some pricking in his toes that he lives, and does not on the whole object to live, but requires sympathy, and whisky, and someone to tell the story of his suffering to."[231] The "pricking of my thumbs" heralds for one of the witches in *Macbeth* the fateful approach of the hero: "Something wicked this way comes" (4.1.61–62). Mr. Ramsay's sensation of "pricking in his toes" (is he still wearing his boots?) is by contrast wonderfully bathetic without being entirely unsympathetic—as is the entire episode.

Like Leslie Stephen, Mr. Ramsay is partial to the novels of Walter Scott and is fond of declaiming poetry out loud, preferring the more bellicose, and often the more laychrymose, of verses (Tennyson, Cowper). Mrs. Ramsay, by contrast, reads quietly and to herself. The most extended reference to Shakespeare in *To the Lighthouse*—although the poet's name is never mentioned—comes in the scene of reading at the end of the novel's first section, "The Window," when Mrs. Ramsay reaches for a book on the table and begins "reading here and there at random," while her husband watches her: "He looked at her reading. She looked very peaceful, reading."[232]

> Nor praise the deep vermilion in the rose,

> she read, and so reading she was ascending, she felt, on to the top, on to the summit. . . . Her mind felt swept, felt clean. And then there it was,

> suddenly entirely shaped in her hands, beautiful and reasonable, clear and complete, the essence sucked out of life and held rounded her—the sonnet.[233]

Mr. Ramsay

> wondered what she was reading, and exaggerated her ignorance, her simplicity, for he liked to think that she was not clever, not book-learned at all.
>
> He wondered if she understood what she was reading. Probably not, he thought. She was astonishingly beautiful. Her beauty seemed to him, if that were possible, to increase.
>
> Yet seem'd it winter still, and you away,
> As with your shadow I with these did play,
>
> she finished.
>
> "Well?" she said, echoing his smile dreamily, looking up from her book.
>
> As with your shadow I with these did play,
>
> she murmured, putting the book on the table.[234]

Whether or not Mrs. Ramsay understands what she is reading—or whether Mr. Ramsay would understand if he read over her shoulder—Woolf clearly does. The sonnet—Shakespeare's Sonnet 98—is a time bomb, predicting the future. It's a sonnet that begins with "absence" and ends with "winter."

> From you have I been absent in the spring
> When proud-pied April dressed in all his trim
> Hath put a spirit of youth in every thing,
> That heavy Saturn laughed and leaped with him.
> Yet nor the lays of birds nor the sweet smell
> Of different flowers in odour and in hue
> Could make me any summer's story tell,
> Or from their proud lap pluck them where they grew;
> Nor did I wonder at the lily's white,
> Nor praise the deep vermilion in the rose;
> They were but sweet, but figures of delight,
> Drawn after you, you pattern of all those.

Yet seemed it winter still, and, you away,
As with your shadow I with these did play.

Mrs. Ramsay's eye may have fallen on a beautiful descriptive passage, but the symptomatic rhetoric of the poem is in the conditional and in the negative ("nor the lays," "nor the sweet smell," "nor did I wonder," "nor praise," "They were but . . . figures," and so on). In the book's next section, the poetic and elegiac "Time Passes," the hypothetical becomes actual, and phrases like "from you I have been absent" and "you away" and "seemed it winter still" are no longer figures of speech. The death of Mrs. Ramsay, her absence from the rest of the novel, is foretold here, in this most peaceful of domestic scenes.

As it was in *Mrs. Dalloway,* so in *To the Lighthouse* these citations of Shakespeare, however brief, are strongly indicative, and if the characters miss something of their relevance, Woolf makes sure that the reader will not. Three lines before the end of the first section Mrs. Ramsay thinks to herself, "Nothing on earth can equal this happiness."[235] It is a reprise of Clarissa Dalloway, a reprise of Othello at Cyprus: "If it were now to die, / 'Twere now to be most happy." The next time we encounter Mrs. Ramsay, she will be an absence and a memory or, in the terms of Sonnet 98, a "pattern" and a "shadow." Perhaps it is only an accident that, in the two sections still to come in *To the Lighthouse*—even though Mr. Ramsay makes an expedition to an island with his young children—no one else will quote or remember Shakespeare.

"He Sat at Twitchett's Table": Orlando *(1928)*

Orlando, famously described by Vita Sackville-West's son Nigel Nicolson as "the longest and most charming love-letter in literature," is also, as it declares itself on the title page, "A Biography," the purported life story of the novel's aristocratic, gender-fluid, and often hilariously naïve protagonist.[236] Accordingly, Woolf, the daughter of one famous biographer and the friend and literary rival of another, furnishes her fictional biography with that hallmark of serious nonfiction, an index. She must have taken a good deal of amusement in compiling it, from the first entry "A., Lord," together with his alphabetical colleagues, "C., Marquis of," "M., Mr," and "R., Countess of"—distinguished from "R., Lady," separately listed—to the last, "Wren, Christopher"; thus, as she does throughout the novel, combining the fictional and the "real."

Under "S" in the index, between Sir Adrian Scrope and Marmaduke Bonthrop Shelmerdine, appears the name of William Shakespeare. But the reader seeking for that name in the text will be disappointed. Only in the last of the three references given in the index is a name attached to the person described on the page, and even there it is only an abbreviation (or a hieroglyph or a rebus): "Sh—p—re," a version of Woolf's usual abbreviation in her diaries, "Shre." The mysterious shabby poet, unprepossessing (except for his eyes), becomes in effect the Alfred Hitchcock of the novel, making cameo appearances that call for a double take.

In fact there are in *Orlando* four appearances of this figure, not three. In chapter 1, set in the Elizabethan age, Orlando, rushing through the halls of Knole (for he is late to dinner) takes a shortcut through the back quarters of the great house.

> There, sitting at the servants' dinner table with a tankard beside him and paper in front of him, sat a rather fat, rather shabby man, whose ruff was a thought dirty, and whose clothes were of hodden brown. He held a pen in his hand, but he was not writing. He seemed in the act of rolling some thought up and down, to and fro in his mind till it gathered shape or momentum to his liking. His eyes, globed and clouded like some green stone of curious texture, were fixed. He did not see Orlando. For all his hurry, Orlando stopped dead. Was this a poet? Was he writing poetry? "Tell me," he wanted to say, "everything in the whole world"—for he had the wildest, most absurd, extravagant ideas about poets and poetry—but how speak to a man who does not see you? who sees ogres, satyrs, perhaps the depths of the sea instead? So Orlando stood gazing while the man turned his pen in his fingers, this way and that way; and gazed and mused; and then, very quickly, wrote half-a-dozen lines and looked up. Whereupon Orlando, overcome with shyness, darted off.[237]

In chapter 2, we hear of Orlando's own prowess as a writer: "There had been written, before he was turned twenty-five, some forty-seven plays, histories, romances, poems; some in prose, some in verse; some in French, some in Italian; all romantic, and all long. One he had had printed by John Ball of the Feathers and Coronet opposite St. Paul's Cross, Cheapside; but though the sight of it gave him extreme delight, he had never dared to show it even to his mother, since to write, much more to publish, was, he knew, for a nobleman an inexpiable disgrace."[238] This is the rationale by which some people, then and now, have claimed that the real authors of Shakespeare's plays—Francis Bacon, the Earl of Oxford, Queen Elizabeth—were required to conceal their true identities, using Shakespeare's name as what we would now call a "front."[239] "Dipping his pen in ink," Orlando pauses, remembering a face:

> But whose was it, he asked himself? And he had to wait, perhaps half a minute, looking at the new picture which lay on top of the old, as one lantern slide is half seen through the next, before he could say to himself, "This is the face of that rather fat, shabby man who sat in Twitchett's room ever so many years ago when Old Queen Bess came here to dine; and I saw him," Orlando continued, . . . "sitting at the table, as I peeped in on my way downstairs, and he had the most amazing eyes," said Orlando, "that ever were, but who the devil was he?" Orlando asked, for here Memory added to the forehead and eyes, first, a coarse, grease-stained ruffle, then a brown doublet, and finally a pair of thick boots such as citizens wear in Cheapside. "Not a Nobleman; not one of us," said Orlando . . . "a poet, I dare say."[240]

"Not one of us" is another private joke; the phrase was the title of a review Woolf published as she was in the midst of writing *Orlando.*[241] ("Not one of us" was what Mary Shelley had said of her husband the poet, meaning to praise his transcendent persona. Orlando uses it instead to indicate that Shakespeare was "not a nobleman." Woolf's comic irony is clear: Shelley, though not the heir to a vast ancestral property like Knole, was the son of a baronet.) The social disparity seems to add fervor to Orlando's ambition. As he remembers the "image of a shabby man with big, bright eyes," he finds himself newly inspired. "Standing upright in the solitude of his room, he vowed that he would be the first poet of his race and bring immortal lustre on his name."[242]

In chapter 4, Orlando, now a woman, sails back to England after a long absence and is struck by something "like a dome of smooth, white marble"—St. Paul's Cathedral, rebuilt by Christopher Wren after the Great Fire of 1666.

> The form of it, by the hazard of fancy, recalled that earliest, most persistent memory—the man with the big forehead in Twitchett's sitting-room, the man who sat writing, or rather looking, but certainly not at her, for he never seemed to see her poised there in all her finery, lovely boy though she must have been. . . . She thought now only of the glory of poetry, and the great lines of Marlowe, Shakespeare, Ben Jonson, Milton, began booming and reverberating. . . . The truth was that the image of the marble dome which her eyes had first discovered so faintly that it suggested a poet's forehead . . . was no figment but a reality . . . nothing

less than the dome of a vast cathedral rising among a fretwork of white spires.[243]

Finally, in chapter 6, set in the present day, as Orlando is driving her car and thinking of poetry and fame (she has just won a prize for her poem "The Oak Tree"), she suddenly "stopped short, and looked ahead of her intently at the bonnet of her car in profound meditation. 'He sat at Twitchett's table,' she mused, 'with a dirty ruff on. . . . Was it old Mr Baker come to measure the timber? Or was it Sh—p—re?' (for when we speak names we deeply reverence to ourselves we never speak them whole)."[244] The insistence on "Sh—p—re"'s dirty ruff and generally shabby look ("not one of us") speaks in part to the familiar theme about great writers unrecognized in their own time, and also to the questions raised by the Shakespeare-isn't-Shakespeare crowd. But it also engages with the various speculations made by artists and critics about the historical Shakespeare's appearance.

Sidney Lee's biography, which Woolf had read, quotes the gossipy—and not always reliable—Elizabethan biographer John Aubrey, who "reported that Shakespeare was 'a handsome, well-shap't man.'"[245] However, Lee is quick to caution the reader, contemporary visual evidence is equivocal at best. "Only two of the extant portraits," he wrote, "are positively known to have been produced within a short period after his death. These are the bust in Stratford Church and the frontispiece to the folio of 1623. Each is an inartistic attempt at a posthumous likeness. There is considerable discrepancy between the two; their main points of resemblance are the baldness on the top of the head and the fulness of the hair about the ears."[246] Moreover, neither image inspires confidence as an image of genius. About the Stratford bust, Lee remarks, "The round face and eyes present a heavy, unintellectual expression."[247] (As for the Droeshout engraving in the First Folio, the "expression of countenance" lacks "artistic sentiment.")[248]

Following Orlando's lead, I have here identified the poet with the high forehead and the amazing eyes according to his conjecture—was this "Sh—p—re?"—not only because of the reverence that both Orlando in the novel and Virginia Woolf in her diaries pay to the sacred name, but also because there is another character in the novel, far less mysterious, who goes by the name of "Shakespeare."

This Shakespeare, whose name is always spelled out, is a popular playwright, an habitué of taverns, one of Orlando's "heroes," but, according to the louche rival poet Nicholas Greene, merely a profit-seeking writer taking advantage of a booming market.[249] "The great age of literature is past," Greene tells the impressionable (and impressed) Orlando. "Now all great writers were in the pay of the booksellers and poured out any trash that would sell. Shakespeare was the chief offender in this way and Shakespeare was already paying the penalty."[250] Fascinated, Orlando listens to Greene's stories "as the talk now got on the lives and characters of Shakespeare, Ben Jonson, and the rest": "These, then, were his gods! Half were drunken and all were amorous. Most of them quarreled with their wives; not one of them was above a lie or an intrigue of the most paltry kind. Their poetry was scribbled down on the backs of washing bills held to the heads of printer's devils at the street door. Thus Hamlet went to press; thus Lear; thus Othello. No wonder, as Greene said, that these plays show the faults that they do."[251] The poet whom Nicholas Greene familiarly calls "Kit Marlowe" was even more familiar—according to Greene—when addressing his friend Shakespeare.

> "Stap my vitals, Bill" (this was to Shakespeare), "there's a great wave coming and you're on the top of it," by which he meant, Greene explained, that they were trembling on the verge of a great age in English literature, and that Shakespeare was to be a poet of some importance. Happily for himself, he was killed two nights later in a drunken brawl, and so did not live to see how this prediction turned out.[252]

The comical anachronism of Marlowe calling Shakespeare "Bill" reflects Woolf's opinion of such unwonted (and unhistorical) familiarity when used by a popular university lecturer on Shakespeare, the first holder of the chair of English literature at Oxford, Sir Walter Raleigh. "The Professor of English literature could scarcely open his lips without dropping into slang," she wrote in a review of Raleigh's letters. "He could never mention Bill Blake or Bill Shakespeare or old Bill Wordsworth without seeming to apologize for bringing books into the talk at all. Yet there is no doubt, Walter Raleigh was one of the best Professors of Literature of our time; he did brilliantly whatever it is that Professors are supposed to do."[253] At the same time she wrote privately to Vita Sackville-West: "And, Vita, answer me this: why are all professors of English literature ashamed of English literature? Walter Raleigh calls Shakespeare 'Billy Shax'—Blake, 'Bill'—a good poem 'a bit of all right.' This shocks me. I've been reading his letters."[254]

"Sh—p—re," the disheveled poet with the high forehead and the "amazing eyes," sitting in the servants' hall, seems like a very different kind of character from the drunken, amorous, and opportunistic "Shakespeare" pouring out trash at the behest of greedy booksellers. To complicate matters further, there is (perhaps) yet another figure with a similar name in *Orlando,* one whom Virginia Woolf had encountered even before her novel was written, when she first made her way down the grand hallways and corridors at Knole.

The "chairs that Shakespeare might have sat on" do not appear as such in Orlando's inventory of the furnishings in Knole's 365 rooms, although he does mention the lacquered cabinet that he bought from "a Moor in Venice."[255] But the chairs—briefly glimpsed, vividly recalled—evoke the image of a perambulating ghost in the great house, a figure never encountered, always just missed, having perhaps only a few moments earlier risen from his chair. This is the Shakespeare whom Orlando continues to revere when he thinks to himself, "Shakespeare must have written like that, and the church builders written like that, anonymously, needing no thanking or naming," or—echoing his earlier thoughts about poetry as the highest calling—"A silly song of Shakespeare's has done more for the poor and the wicked than all the preachers and philanthropists in the world."[256]

When an eighteenth-century Orlando remembers "how she had loved sound as a boy, and thought the volley of tumultuous syllables from the lips the finest of all poetry," her thoughts and words again resemble those of Virginia Woolf, who wrote in her diary on April 24, 1928, the day after Shakespeare's birthday, "I was reading Othello last night, & was impressed by the volley & volume & tumble of his words."[257] *Orlando,* with its "volley of tumultuous syllables" and its cabinet purchased from a Moor in Venice, would be published six months later.

"Sh—p—re" the poet, Shakespeare the popular dramatist, Shakespeare the literary legend, enhanced by the spectral contiguity of the empty chairs at Knole. In none of these configurations, we should note, does a single line of Shakespearean verse appear. We hear of play titles (*Hamlet, Lear, Othello*) and of a "silly song of Shakespeare's," but no passage of blank verse, no couplet from a sonnet, no striking phrase. Even the "Sh—p—re" who gazes, thinks, and puts pen to paper does not reveal the words he writes.

Despite this absence, however, *Orlando* as a novel is full of references to the Shakespearean text. The Shakespeare citations—and there are many, some obvious, some oblique—are transactions between the narrator and the reader with, perhaps, the idea of one particular reader, Vita Sackville-West, making them coded allusions. Each offers the narrator a chance to play with Shakespeare, to make some affectionately mocking observations about the character of Orlando and, from time to time, to send a wink in Vita's direction.

Early in the novel, Orlando and the princess come upon what they perceive as "some kind of theatrical performance," compared by the narrator to "our Punch and Judy show," and stop to watch: "A black man was waving his arms and vociferating. There was a woman in white laid upon a bed. Rough though the staging was, the actors running up and down a pair of steps and sometimes tripping, and the crowd stamping their feet and whistling, or, when they were bored, tossing a piece of orange peel onto the ice which a dog would scramble for, still the astonishing, sinuous melody of the words stirred Orlando like music.... The frenzy of the Moor seemed to him his own frenzy, and when the Moor suffocated the woman in her bed it was Sasha he killed with his own hands."[258] Afterward, as tears stream down his face, Orlando recalls some lines from the play he has just seen: "Methinks it should be now a huge eclipse / Of sun and moon, and that the affrighted globe / Should yawn" (*Othello* 5.2.108–10).[259] We are not told the title of the theatrical performance or the names of any of the characters. In the index, however, and keyed to this page, there appears the word "Othello." It is not italicized, as are other titles of published works, like *Gulliver's Travels* or *Lock, Rape of the.* And no explicit connection is made here, or elsewhere, between the play and the indexed name of "William Shakespeare." But it is of course clear to the reader what play is being performed. And the lines Orlando quotes about the "huge eclipse / Of sun and moon" would have had special meaning for Vita.

In June 1927, Virginia and Leonard had traveled with Quentin Bell and the Nicolsons to North Yorkshire to see the first total eclipse of the sun visible in Britain for over two hundred years. As Woolf wrote the next day in her diary, "Rapidly, very very quickly, all the colours faded; it became darker & darker as at the beginning of a violent storm; the light sank & sank: we kept saying this is the shadow; & we thought now it is over—this is the shadow when suddenly the sun went out. We had fallen. It was extinct. There was no colour. The earth was dead. That was the astonishing moment."[260] Orlando might have quoted any lines from *Othello*—including, for example, the lines that reverberate in *Mrs. Dalloway,* "If it were now to die / 'Twere now to be most happy"—and still be moved to tears. By selecting the "eclipse" passage Woolf is able to triangulate her effect: Orlando is moved but does not recognize the work as "Shakespeare"; the reader readily identifies this famous passage; and the novel's dedicatee may see, if she likes, a personal reference, like one of Shakespeare's periodic inset compliments to Queen Elizabeth, in the midst of the ongoing narrative.[261]

In another early episode, this one deliberately modeled on *Hamlet* (as well as on that other Bloomsbury favorite, the Jacobean "skull beneath the skin" playwright John Webster). Orlando descends into the family crypt, thinking of "how all pomp is built upon corruption, how the skeleton lies beneath the flesh; how we that dance and sing above must lie below." He muses about his ancestors and, like Hamlet in the graveyard, on the fleetingness of life and fame. ("Why might that not be the skull of a lawyer? Where be his quiddities now...?"

[5.1.90–91].) "'Nothing remains of all these Princes,' Orlando would say, indulging in some pardonable exaggeration of their rank, 'except one digit,' and he would take a skeleton hand in his and bend the joints this way and that. 'Whose hand was it?' he went on to ask. 'The right or the left? The hand of man or woman, of age or youth? Had it urged the war-horse, or plied the needle? Had it plucked the rose, or grasped cold steel? Had it—' but here either his invention failed him, or, what is more likely, provided him with so many instances of what a hand can do that he shrank, as his wont was, from the cardinal labour of composition, which is excision."[262] Woolf the indefatigable self-critic and self-editor here does the working of cutting, or at least of cutting off, for the verbose and undisciplined Orlando. Yet despite the editorial intervention, there will shortly be a reprise of this scene. After he recalls to mind "the image of a shabby man with big, bright eyes" Orlando finds himself thinking once more about fame and death: of his ancestors, the great warriors and hunters and eaters and drinkers, "what remained? A skull; a finger." Their deeds were "dust and ashes." But a great writer's words "were immortal."[263]

The ornate family crypt, so unlike the graveyard in *Hamlet* or the modest Stratford church, also calls to mind John Milton's famous poem:

> What needs my Shakespeare for his honoured bones,
> The labor of an age in pilèd stones,
> Or that his hallowed relics should be hid
> Under a star-y pointing pyramid?
> Dear son of Memory, great heir of fame,
> What need'st thou such weak witness of thy name?
> Thou in our wonder and astonishment
> Hast built thyself a live-long monument.
> For whilst to th' shame of slow-endeavouring art,
> Thy easy numbers flow, and that each heart
> Hath from the leaves of thy unvalued book
> Those Delphic lines with deep impression took,
> Then thou, our fancy of itself bereaving,
> Dost make us marble with too much conceiving;
> And so sepúlchred in such pomp dost lie,
> That kings for such a tomb would wish to die.

Orlando will not know this poem. But both the author and the privileged reader surely do.

A particularly rich opportunity for Woolf to complicate an allusion, allowing for a layering of readerly responses, is provided by Orlando's return voyage to England after an absence of many years. As they near land, the ship's captain informs her that they are approaching the cliffs of Dover, pointing to the site. As "the chalky cliffs loomed nearer," she is able to see their details more clearly. "Closer and closer they drew, till the samphire gatherers, hanging halfway down the cliff, were plain to the naked eye."[264]

The Shakespearean reference, though it passes quickly, is both deft and complex. The "samphire gatherers" on the cliffs of Dover are mentioned by Edgar in *King Lear:*

How fearful
And dizzy 'tis, to cast one's eyes so low.
The crows and choughs that wing the midway air
Show scarce so gross as beetles. Halfway down
Hangs one that gathers samphire, dreadful trade!
Methinks he seems no bigger than his head.
(4.6.16–21)

But in Shakespeare's play Edgar is disguised as a countryman, he is addressing Gloucester, his blinded father, and they are nowhere near the cliffs of Dover. The entire scene is imaginary, meant to make Gloucester believe he is teetering on the edge of a precipice when he is actually safe on flat ground. Woolf's/Orlando's phrase "plain to the naked eye" underscores both the reference and its conversion, in her novel, from high tragedy to comic fiction. Likewise, Orlando's shipboard vision of the gleaming white St. Paul's as a poet's forehead flashes back to the first sight of the unnamed poet, but also nods to the "victorious brow" of Matthew Arnold's Shakespeare sonnet. There is always another layer.

Woolf's novel is an *Orlando* without a Rosalind or a Ganymede; instead the protagonist gets to play all the parts. As the narrator explains, Orlando "found it convenient . . . to change frequently from one set of clothes to another. Thus she often occurs in contemporary memoirs as 'Lord' So-and-so, who was in fact her cousin; her bounty is ascribed to him, and it is he who is said to have written the poems that were really hers. She had, it seems, no difficulty in sustaining the different parts, for her sex changed far more frequently than those who have worn only one set of clothing can conceive; nor can there be any doubt that she reaped a two-fold harvest by this device; the pleasures of life were increased and its experiences multiplied. For the probity of breeches she exchanged the seductiveness of petticoats and enjoyed the love of both sexes equally."[265] Nor, perhaps, should we forget that in *As You Like It* Orlando is a notably *bad* poet whose love poems, though earnest enough, are readily mocked and parodied by Touchstone the fool.

One device Woolf often used in her early novels was to introduce, sometimes briefly, sometimes in a more extended fashion, a character or characters who had appeared in one of her previous books. Thus the Dalloways are introduced in *The Voyage Out,* and Mrs. Hilbery, that energetic and passionate Shakespeare buff encountered in *Night and Day,* reappears, albeit older and less assertive, at Clarissa Dalloway's party. In a similar way Hatchards, the bookshop where Clarissa sees *Cymbeline* open to "Fear no more the heat o' th' sun" at the beginning of *Mrs. Dalloway,* will make a cameo appearance in *Orlando.* Although the establishment is not cited by name, it is clearly identified as "a shop where they sold books" located around the corner from St. James's Street (where indeed it can still be found today).[266] Orlando's time-traveling discovery of this new kind of commerce offers both author and reader yet another "Shakespeare" moment:

> All her life long Orlando had known manuscripts; she had held in her hands the rough brown sheets on which Spenser had written in his little crabbed hand; she had seen Shakespeare's script and Milton's. She owned, indeed, a fair number of quartos and folios, often with a sonnet in her praise in them and sometimes a lock of hair. But these innumerable little volumes, bright, identical, ephemeral, for they seemed bound in cardboard and printed on tissue paper, surprised her infinitely. The whole works of Shakespeare cost half a crown and could be put in your pocket. One could hardly read them, indeed, the print was so small, but it was a marvel, none the less.[267]

The personal memory in this case is probably linked to a much earlier moment when Leonard Woolf, taking ship for Ceylon after graduating from Cambridge, was presented by Desmond MacCarthy with just such a set: "the Oxford Press miniature edition of Shakespeare and Milton in four volumes which have accompanied me everywhere ever since."[268] Leonard went to Ceylon in 1904; the Oxford edition was published the previous year. Orlando, browsing in the bookshop, may not be looking at the same edition—miniature "Shakespeares" were highly popular in the early years of the twentieth century, and "innumerable" certainly suggests a number greater than three—but the episode allows again for a graceful private gesture. (In *Night and Day,* as we've seen, Mrs. Cosham carries a "pocket Shakespeare," though in her case it is likely to be a single-volume anthology rather than a set.)

At the beginning of chapter 2 of *Orlando,* writing in the ironic high style she affects for much of the novel, Woolf announces, "The biographer is now faced with a difficulty which it is better perhaps to confess than to gloss over"—namely, that although in the previous chapter "documents, both private and historical, have made it possible to fulfill the first duty of a biographer, which is to plod without looking to right or left, in the indelible footprints of truth," the next episode in Orlando's life is "dark, mysterious, and undocumented," so that the reader will need to "make of them what he may."[269]

In October 1927, just as she was starting to write this chapter, Woolf had published "The New Biography" in the *New York Herald Tribune.* The essay began with a quotation from Sir Sidney Lee who—as editor of the *Dictionary of National Biography*—"had perhaps read and written more lives than any man of his time."[270] "The aim of biography," as she quotes him, "is the truthful transmission of personality."[271] Lee's intended distinction, as he explains in his *Principles of Biography,* was in fact between "moral edification" and "personality," but Woolf has a different distinction in mind, that between "personality" and "truth." "Truth of fact and truth of fiction are incompatible," she maintains, since "the life which is increasingly real to us is the fictitious life; it dwells in the personality rather than in the act. Each of us is more Hamlet, Prince of Denmark, than he is John Smith, of the Corn Exchange."

But at the same time she offers a warning: "The biographer's imagination is always being stimulated to use the novelist's art of arrangement, suggestion, dramatic effect to expound the private life. Yet if he carries the use of fiction too far, so that he disregards the truth, or can only introduce it with incongruity, he loses both worlds; he has neither the freedom of fiction nor the substance of fact." Whether "the world of brick and pavement; of birth, marriage and death; of Acts of Parliament; of Pitt and Burke and Sir Joshua Reynolds" is "a more real world than the world of Bohemia and Hamlet and Macbeth we doubt, but the mixture of the two is abhorrent."[272]

"Abhorrent," that is to say, for the seeker after "truth of fact," the reader of a certain kind of biography. The occasion for this essay on a "new" biography was a book recently published by Harold Nicolson, the husband of Vita Sackville-West, whom she credits with pointing "in a possible direction"—a direction already marked out by the innovative writing of Lytton Strachey.[273] She takes aim at Sidney Lee ("Sir Sidney's life of Shakespeare is dull") and praises Strachey ("He chooses; he synthesizes; in short he has ceased to be the chronicler; he has become an artist"), while contending that we cannot yet name "the biographer whose art is subtle and bold enough to present that queer amalgamation of dream and reality, that perpetual marriage of granite and rainbow. His method still remains to be discovered."[274] (The phrase "rainbow and granite" will appear in *Orlando* as a figure for uncanny contradiction: the essay and the novel are in many ways closely tied.)[275]

"*His* method." Given the topic of *Orlando,* it may be appropriate here to reflect on the question of gender. Was "the biographer"—the hypothetical ideal biographer—inevitably male? ("The biographer," Woolf writes at one point in the novel, "must confine himself to one simple statement"—though elsewhere she will finesse the question by moving from "he" to "we.")[276] Her use of the male pronoun in "The New Biography" is partly convention, partly a reflection of the gender of the biographers she discusses, but almost surely also ironic, especially as it appears in a stand-alone sentence ("His method still remains to be discovered") that deliberately calls attention to gender. We might compare it to the opening words of *Orlando:* "He—for there could be no doubt of his sex, though the fashion of the time did something to disguise it."[277]

The issue will be taken up far more substantially in *A Room of One's Own,* published a year later, in 1929, but it is of interest to find it linking the text of *Orlando* and the question of a "new [kind of] biography." For "his method"—the method of the subtle and bold biographer who can present a queer amalgam of dream and reality—was, in fact, hers.

"The Plays of Shakespeare Are Not by You": A Room of One's Own *(1929)*

"Young women," the speaker of *A Room of One's Own* says to her audience, "the plays of Shakespeare are not by you. . . . What is your excuse?"[278] She is speaking both in jest and in earnest; her objective is to encourage them to pursue their dreams—especially those who (like Woolf, like Shakespeare) aspire to become writers.

Although it is probably most famous for its portrait of the fictional Judith Shakespeare, Virginia Woolf's *A Room of One's Own* is at least as full of references to that other Shakespeare—always called only Shakespeare—whose plays are on Woolf's shelves. The book started its life in the form of two invited lectures delivered to students at Newnham and Girton, the women's colleges at Cambridge. The set topic was "Women and Fiction." The published version, which Woolf wrote and rewrote meticulously, uses as a frame the narrator's comparison of the lives of men and women, in Shakespeare's time and in the present, as they seek independence, a livable income, and the chance to make their mark in the world.

Early in the book the semi-autobiographical narrator, curious about the history of women, goes to the British Museum seeking books on women and poverty. Like Orlando glimpsing the dome of St. Paul's, she describes the "vast dome" of the museum as a "huge bald forehead" and conceives of herself as a "thought" within that forehead.[279] Once inside the reading room she creates a kind of index of the topics that concern her about women, including "Condition in the Middle Ages of," "Offered as sacrifice," "Less hair on the body of," "Greater length of life of," "Higher education of," and "Shakespeare's opinion of"—this last followed by the opinions of various other authorities, like Lord Birkenhead, Dean Inge, La Bruyère, Dr. Johnson, and Mr. Oscar Browning.[280] (Few of these, as her readers would know, were proponents of women's education or learning.)

The faux naïve tone Woolf had perfected in *Orlando* serves her well here, as she wonders to herself "under what conditions women lived in England, say in the time of Elizabeth. For it is a perennial puzzle why no woman wrote a word of that extraordinary literature when every other man, it seemed, was capable of song or sonnet."[281] She "went, therefore, to the shelf where the histories stand and took down one of the latest, Professor Trevelyan's *History of England.* Once more I looked up women, found 'position of,' and turned to the pages indicated. 'Wife-beating,' I read, 'was a recognized right of man, and was practiced without shame by high as well as low. . . . Similarly,' the historian goes on, 'the daughter who refused to marry the gentleman of her parents' choice was liable to be locked up, beaten, and flung about the room, without any shock being inflicted on public opinion.'"[282]

> That was about 1470, soon after Chaucer's time. The next reference to the position of women is some two hundred years later, in the time of the Stuarts. "It was still the exception for women of the upper and middle class to choose their own husbands, and when the husband had been assigned, he was lord and master, so far at least as law and custom could make him. Yet even so," Professor Trevelyan concludes, "neither Shakespeare's women nor those of authentic seventeenth century memoirs, like the Verneys and the Hutchinsons, seem wanting in personality and character." Certainly, if we consider it, Cleopatra must have had a way with her; Lady Macbeth, one would suppose, had a will of her own; Rosalind, one might conclude, was an attractive girl. Professor Trevelyan is speaking no more than the truth when he remarks that Shakespeare's women do not seem wanting in personality and character. Not being a historian, one might go even further and say that women have burnt like beacons in

> all the works of all the poets from the beginning of time—Clytemnestra, Antigone, Cleopatra, Lady Macbeth, Phèdre, Cressida, Rosalind, Desdemona, the Duchess of Malfi, among the dramatists; then among the prose writers.[283]

George Macauley Trevelyan, a distinguished historian and later master of Trinity College, Cambridge, was an Apostle of the generation just previous to that of Strachey, Keynes, and Woolf. His *History of England* had been published in 1926. Trevelyan and his friends were often criticized by those who would form the nucleus of the Bloomsbury Group for their attitudes to literature and the arts, as well as for their "Whiggish" politics. In 1902, as a Trinity undergraduate, Leonard Woolf had written to Strachey about Trevelyan's dislike of the tragedies of John Webster, whom the Cambridge play-reading X Society much admired. "They don't know what literature is of course. They read a novel for the story and poetry for 'a criticism of life' & they only recognize what they call style when it shouts at them."[284]

To her own critique of Trevelyan Woolf adds, in the published version of *A Room of One's Own,* a footnote to a recent Hogarth Press book on tragedy by F. L. ("Peter") Lucas, a Cambridge don, an Apostle, a colleague of Dadie Rylands, and a friend of the Woolfs and of others in Bloomsbury: "The paradox of this world where in real life a respectable woman could hardly show her face alone in the street, and yet on the stage woman equals or surpasses man, has never been satisfactorily explained. . . . A very cursory survey of Shakespeare's work . . . suffices to reveal how this dominance, this initiative of women, persists from Rosalind to Lady Macbeth."[285]

Woolf reviews the challenges to women in Shakespeare's time and some of the questions that later historians of women would need to answer: how women in the Elizabethan age were educated, whether they were taught to write, how many had children before they were twenty-one, how young they were when they married. Bearing these questions, and their possible answers, in mind, she "could not help thinking," as she looked at "the works of Shakespeare on the shelf," whether it would not in fact "have been impossible, completely and entirely, for any woman to have written the plays of Shakespeare in the age of Shakespeare."[286] It is at this point that she embarks upon the saga of Judith Shakespeare: "Let me imagine, since facts are so hard to come by, what would have happened had Shakespeare had a wonderfully gifted sister, called Judith, let us say."[287]

Woolf's Judith may have been named after the protagonist of William

Black's eponymous 1884 novel, which had been serialized in *Harper's.* Black was a popular novelist of the day who had also briefly appeared in mute Shakespearean roles on the stage. Judith was also the name of William Shakespeare's second daughter, the twin of his son Hamnet, who had died in 1599. (The historical Shakespeare did have a sister, but her name was Joan, not Judith.) In a brief fantasia reminiscent of *Orlando,* Woolf imagines her Judith Shakespeare in the situation described by Trevelyan. Beaten by her father when she resisted a betrothal that was "hateful to her," inspired by "her own gift" as a writer ("her genius was for fiction"), she left home at sixteen and first sought a role as an actress—forbidden for women in the public theatre at the time. Then "Nick Greene the actor-manager" (a figure also familiar, though in a slightly different role, to readers of *Orlando*) takes her up. When she finds herself pregnant she kills herself and is buried, as was the custom with suicides, at a crossroads—in this case, with Woolf's deliberate descent from pathos to bathos, "where omnibuses now stop outside the Elephant and Castle."[288]

As the narrator resumes her own voice ("That, more or less, is how the story would run, I think, if a woman in Shakespeare's day had had Shakespeare's genius"), the difficulties facing a gifted woman of this kind are reiterated and enumerated—mockery, violence, shunning, sexual predation—and the "woman born with a great gift" begins to sound like a projection: "To have lived a free life in London in the sixteenth century would have meant for a woman who was poet and playwright a nervous stress and dilemma which might well have killed her."[289]

Despite its relative brevity, Judith's story has, over the years since Woolf wrote it, captured the imagination of many critics and readers. The narrative ("Let me imagine . . . what would have happened") takes up only about three pages of *A Room of One's Own,* and then reappears very briefly in the essay's inspirational peroration: "She lives in you and in me. . . . The dead poet who was Shakespeare's sister will put on the body which she has so often laid down."[290] Yet however appealing it may be, Woolf's relatively brief excursus into the fictional life of Shakespeare's sister should not overshadow the consistent and searching interest she manifests throughout in that other Shakespeare, the one whose plays she can recite by heart. Judith Shakespeare was one hypothetical idea. Another hypothesis, perhaps equally intriguing in its own way, is suggested when Woolf invites us to "suppose, for instance, that men were only represented in literature as the lovers of women, and were never the friends of men, soldiers, thinkers, dreamers"—just as women have often been seen only as the lovers or love objects of men. In such a situation, she says, "how few parts in the plays of Shakespeare could be allotted to them; how literature would suffer! We might perhaps have most of Othello; and a good deal of Antony; but no Caesar, no Brutus, no Hamlet, no Lear, no Jaques—literature would be incredibly impoverished."[291]

"What is the state of mind that is most propitious to the act of creation?" Woolf asks rhetorically, and at this point, significantly, she introduces one of the "stage directions" that are often to be found in her memoirs and semi-autobiographical writings. "Here I opened the volume containing the Tragedies of Shakespeare. What was Shakespeare's state of mind, for instance, when he wrote *Lear* and *Antony and Cleopatra*? It was certainly the most favourable to poetry that there has ever existed. But Shakespeare himself said nothing about it."[292] In a few pages she will return to this question, thinking it through not on the level of biography or historical anecdote or gossip but in terms of creativity and imagination. For where with the fictional Judith the emphasis had, of necessity, to be on the writer's personal history, here Woolf admits, and celebrates, the relative unimportance of mere biographical data. The information she seeks is, instead, fully present in the plays themselves.

> The mind of an artist, in order to achieve the prodigious effort of freeing whole and entire the work that is in him, must be incandescent, like Shakespeare's mind, I conjectured, looking at the book that lay open at *Antony and Cleopatra.* There must be no obstacle in it, no foreign matter unconsumed.
>
> For though we say that we know nothing about Shakespeare's state of mind, even as we say that, we are saying something about Shakespeare's state of mind. The reason perhaps why we know so little of Shakespeare—compared with Donne or Ben Jonson or Milton—is that his grudges and spites and antipathies are hidden from us. We are not held up by some "revelation" which reminds us of the writer. All desire to protest, to preach, to proclaim an injury, to pay off a score, to make the world the witness of some hardship or grievance was fired out of him and consumed. Therefore his poetry flows from him free and unimpeded. If ever a human being got his work expressed completely, it was Shakespeare. If ever a mind was incandescent, unimpeded, I thought, turning again to the bookcase, it was Shakespeare's mind.[293]

This is the second time in *A Room of One's Own* that Woolf has produced *Antony and Cleopatra* as, in effect, a theatrical prop. She has previously referred in passing to its title characters—Cleopatra as a woman who "must have had a way with her," Antony as one of the few male characters who would survive if the plays considered men only as subjects or objects of love. But the mention of *Antony and Cleopatra* as a play has, I want to suggest, another relevance to the larger argument she is making, one that only becomes visible as she delves deeper into her speculations about Shakespeare's "incandescent" mind.

The play will be cited a third time at the beginning of the last chapter (chapter 6) when the narrator looks out of her window "to see what London was doing on the morning of the twenty-sixth of October 1928. And what was London doing? Nobody, it seemed, was reading *Antony and Cleopatra.* London was wholly indifferent, it appeared, to Shakespeare's plays."[294] She had earlier imagined Shakespeare as very much a part of London street life: "the women at the street corners with their arms akimbo . . . talking with a gesticulation like the swing of Shakespeare's words."[295] Still—why think now of *Antony and Cleopatra*? Why should this particular play be cited by name and gestured toward as a prop? Perhaps the reason is as simple as that Woolf happened to be reading the play at the time. We can't ever really know "why" a writer includes something in her work; we can only look at the effect such a mention produces.

But there is another strong associational pull here, and that is between *Antony and Cleopatra* and the question of mental androgyny. For the glance out the London window is the preamble to an extended discussion of "whether there are two sexes in the mind corresponding to the two sexes in the body." The "ordinary sight of two people getting into a cab" is said to be what provokes this thought, but Woolf moves quickly on from the street scene to Samuel Taylor Coleridge, whose "notes on Shakespeare," she had once written, are "the only criticisms which bear reading with the sound of the play still in one's ears."[296] She pondered what Coleridge might have meant when he said that "a great mind must be androgynous."[297] The same words that she had used in her previous discussion of Shakespeare's mind—"incandescent, unimpeded"—appear again in this analysis: "He meant, perhaps, that the androgynous mind is resonant and porous; that it transmits emotion without impediment; that it is naturally creative, incandescent, and undivided. In fact one goes back to Shakespeare's mind as the type of the androgynous, of the man-womanly mind."[298]

We might note that Coleridge does not directly mention Shakespeare in this connection; his example of an individual with an androgynous "great mind" is Emanuel Swedenborg. But the womanly man and the manly woman had been part of the story of *Orlando,* and the question becomes explicit when that novel describes the relationship of Orlando and her husband, Marmaduke Bonthrop Shelmerdine. "'Are you positive you aren't a man?' he would ask anxiously, and she would echo, 'Can it be possible that you're not a woman?' and then they must put it to the proof without more ado. For each was so surprised at the quickness of each other's sympathy, and it was to each such a revelation that a woman could be as tolerant and free-spoken as a man, and a man as strange and subtle as a woman."[299] Furthermore, in this image of "the man-womanly mind" and its relationship to transcendence and to poetry, there is direct relevance not only to *Orlando* but also to *Antony and Cleopatra*.

In the first act of Shakespeare's play Octavius Caesar, the puritanical Roman, deplores what he sees as the fall of a great hero in Antony's all-consuming love for Cleopatra:

> From Alexandria,
> This is the news: he fishes, drinks, and wastes
> The lamps of night in revel; is not more manlike
> Than Cleopatra, nor the Queen of Ptolemy
> More womanly than he.
> (1.4.3–7)

To Octavius, his own mind set on war and empire, the exchange of qualities is a loss, not a gain.

Previously, in a scene set in Egypt, the audience had been privy to a quick but telling exchange between Antony's friend Enobarbus and Charmian, Cleopatra's attendant—an exchange that makes a similar point.

> ENOBARBUS: Hush, here comes Antony.
> CHARMIAN: Not he, the Queen.
> (1.2.81–82)

The mistake—if it is a mistake—is symptomatic. In Egypt roles have been reversed. Enobarbus, though he loves Antony, is concerned. And later in the play, when Antony allows Cleopatra to decide about the site of a battle, choosing—against his own best judgment—to fight by sea rather than by land, and allowing her to appear at the head of her forces, his followers feel that he has capitulated to her completely:

> ENOBARBUS: Your presence needs must puzzle Antony,
> Take from his heart, take from his brain, from's time
> What should not then be spared. He is already
> Traduced for levity, and 'tis said in Rome
> That Photinus, an eunuch, and your maids
> Manage this war.

CLEOPATRA: Sink Rome, and their tongues rot
That speak against us! A charge we bear i' th' war,
And, as the president of my kingdom will
Appear there for a man. Speak not against it!
I will not stay behind.
(3.7.10–19)

The battle plan is, predictably, doomed to fail, and it does. But the last two acts of the play, and the poetry throughout, make it clear that the love of what Antony early on calls "such a mutual pair" (1.1.38) will transcend mere war and politics, and even life and death.

None of these passages is quoted or alluded to in *A Room of One's Own,* nor, indeed, are any lines from this (or any) play. The book is rich and full without them, telling many stories, moving swiftly from one detail to another while remaining true to its central topic. But Woolf is an exceptionally skilled writer, and she knows her Shakespeare. With Judith Shakespeare in mind she could have mentioned *As You Like It, Cymbeline,* or *Twelfth Night,* three popular plays, each with a resourceful woman who tries to make her way in a man's world. There is no reference to any of these in her lecture to the women of Girton and Newnham. But the play she mentions—three times—is *Antony and Cleopatra,* a play about Shakespeare's most transgressive female figure, one who breaks all rules, knows no boundaries, and earns enduring fame.

In her memoirs Ottoline Morrell remembers her excitement at going to an Artists Revels at the Botanical Gardens in the early years with the Bells and Virginia Stephen, but she disapproved of their costume choices. "Virginia was hardly suited to pose as Cleopatra, whose qualities, as I had imagined them, were just those that Cleopatra did not possess."[300] Arguably, Lady Ottoline's Cleopatra would have been quite different from the Cleopatras of both the young Virginia Stephen and the mature Virginia Woolf. The "infinite variety" of that legendary figure—the dream role for the elderly Mrs. Swithin in *Between the Acts* as well as for the youthful Lytton Strachey—has seldom been more adaptable than in Bloomsbury and its environs.

"The Marriage of True Minds": The Waves *(1931)*

In a diary entry about the novel that would become *The Waves,* Virginia Woolf wrote that she intended for it to be "an abstract mystical eyeless book: a playpoem."[301] *Playpoem* is Woolf's coinage, and an apt one, for what became in practice a novel built of passages of dialogue alternating with italicized prose poems. But the term *playpoem* could also appropriately be used to describe the form of early modern drama. Certainly Woolf and her friends thought of Shakespeare's plays as poetry. "It is poetry that I want now, long poems," Woolf wrote, looking forward to an evening finishing *King John* and thinking eagerly about then moving on to *Richard II.*[302] By the time she was, by her own report, "at page 100" in the writing of *The Waves,* Woolf saw it very clearly as "a series of dramatic soliloquies," adding, "The thing is to keep them running homogenously in & out, in the rhythm of the waves."[303]

To mark the speakers of these intertwined "soliloquies" Woolf uses the neutral phrase "said X" ("said Jinny," "said Louis," "said Rhoda") in the same way that a playscript uses a speech prefix (Hamlet; King; 1 Murderer). When a play is performed, these speech prefixes are not spoken since the character is there onstage. When the play is read rather than seen, the reader needs the prefix to know who is speaking. In *The Waves* this deliberately formulaic phrase is inserted after a speech has begun so as to orient, or reorient, the reader without coloring the utterance. ("If I could believe," said Rhoda, "that I should grow old . . .").[304] The phrase never varies. The name and verb are never inverted (it is never "Rhoda said"—always "said Rhoda"). No character "argues," "cries," "growls," "announces," or performs any of the other familiar kinds of novelistic stage directions. How they say what they say is a matter for the reader to decide.

The characters—Bernard, Neville, Louis, Jinny, Susan, Rhoda—speak in their "own" voices in that they have distinct "personalities" and obsessions and fears and temperaments and social backgrounds—but they are all, at the same time, arguably various "selves," or avatars, of a single consciousness or speaker. The self that is flirtatious, the self that is loquacious, the self that is shy, the self that is ambitious, the self that wants solitude, the self that fears failure or exposure, and so on. As a result, when Bernard and Neville begin to reflect on the question of the "self" or when, late in the novel, Bernard—taking it upon himself "to sum up"—becomes the only speaker, what happens is the conversion of the "playpoem" into a novel. "And now I ask, 'Who am I?' I have been talking of Bernard, Neville, Jinny, Susan, Rhoda and Louis. Am I all of them? And I one and distinct? I do not know."[305] The process that Woolf intuitively understood as a matter of literary history, that the early modern playwright (like Shakespeare) would be succeeded, in due time, by the modern novelist (like Woolf), is performed in her own experimental work of fiction.

The title *The Waves* and its italicized "interludes" or inter-chapters may well have been inspired by Shakespeare's Sonnet 60, to which, in any case, the design of the novel bears a strong sequential resemblance.

> Like as the waves make towards the pebbled shore,
> So do our minutes hasten to their end,
> Each changing place with that which goes before,
> In sequent toil all forwards do contend.
> Nativity, once in the main of light,
> Crawls to maturity, wherewith being crowned,
> Crooked eclipses 'gainst his glory fight,
> And time that gave doth now his gift confound.
> Time doth transfix the flourish set on youth,
> And delves the parallels in beauty's brow,
> Feeds on the rarities of nature's truth,
> And nothing stands but for his scythe to mow.
> And yet to times in hope my verse shall stand,
> Raising thy worth, despite his cruel hand.

The sonnet first posits and then develops the foundational analogy between the waves and the passage of human life that will also structure the novel. By Woolf's own report, the recursive pattern of the waves ("each changing place with that which goes before") was matched by her process of composition: "Unlike all my other books in every way, it is unlike them in this, that I begin to re-write it, & conceive it again with ardour, directly I have done. . . . One wave after another."[306] The powerful "eternizing" pledge of the sonnet's concluding couplet ("And yet to times in hope my verse shall stand, / Raising thy worth, despite his cruel hand") has its counterpart in Bernard's final lines in *The Waves*—lines that Leonard Woolf chose as the inscription on Virginia's memorial tablet: "Against you I will fling myself, unvanquished and unyielding, O Death!"[307]

In addition to Sonnet 60, there is another "waves" passage in Shakespeare that can also be usefully juxtaposed with Woolf's novel, one perhaps less well known but equally germane. The passage occurs in the late romance *The Winter's Tale* when Florizel, a prince disguised as a shepherd, expresses his love for Perdita, a shepherdess who will turn out to be a princess. Florizel's lines, too, capture the visual illusion of waves that, in their repetition, seem eternal.

> When you do dance, I wish you
> A wave o' th' sea, that you might ever do

Nothing but that, move still, still so
And own no other function.
(4.4.140–43)

The marvelously compact phrase "move still, still so" articulates the paradox of move/still while also doubling the meaning of "still" (unmoving; always). It would be interesting, and I suspect gratifying, to know Bernard's assessment of it—or perhaps the poet Neville's.

As many critics have noted, the characters in *The Waves* also align with various personalities within the Bloomsbury Group.[308] The "we" to whom Bernard begins frequently to refer at the end of the novel, especially in his praise of the supreme value of friendship, extends across the fictional/biographical boundary. Underscoring this connection, Woolf gives to Neville, who has many affinities with Lytton Strachey, a thought about the Bloomsbury Apostles' favorite pairing: "We spin round us infinitely fine filaments and construct a system. Plato and Shakespeare are included."[309]

Shakespearean references in *The Waves* range, in a way that is by now familiar in Woolf's fiction, from mentions of characters in the plays to quotations and allusions and, in one significant instance, to a direct discussion of the impact of Shakespeare on the characters' friendship. It is probably not surprising, since the novel centers on young men and women who are finding themselves in a complex world and have the habit of soliloquizing about it, that the play most directly mentioned is *Hamlet.* Bernard initially identifies himself with a rather Romantic version of Hamlet (before he decides he is more like Shelley or the hero of a novel by Dostoyevsky or, ultimately, Byron).[310] "Let's discuss Hamlet" is Neville's instrument in the "symphony" Bernard imagines being played by his friends, each on "his own tune, fiddle, flute, trumpet, [or] drum."[311] Even in their early childhood *Hamlet* underwrites their conversation, as the schoolboy Neville asks that Bernard tell them stories while "soft white clouds" scud across the sky, and Bernard obliges with images: "'Like a camel,' . . . 'a vulture,'" echoing the dialogue between Hamlet and Polonius ("Do you see yonder cloud that's almost in shape of a camel?" [3.2.345–51]).[312] Neville's invitation "And now . . . let Bernard begin" will be balanced at the end of the book by Bernard himself ("Now, to sum up"), and in the course of his last ruminations as "an elderly man, a heavy man with grey hair" who is, or ought to be, "done with phrases," he revisits, for a while, his inner Polonius.[313] After the news of Percival's death, Rhoda picks violets and binds them together, describing them as "my tribute to Percival, withered violets, blackened violets."[314] They are only withered in her mind, which has remembered the words of the mad Ophelia: "I would give you some violets, but they all withered when my father died" (*Hamlet* 4.5.180–81).

Other works of Shakespeare also recur with some frequency. The youthful Bernard emulates, if only in his imagination, the behavior of an enraptured lover: "He has left me his poem. O friendship, I too will press flowers between the pages of Shakespeare's sonnets!"[315] The elderly Bernard is not only a Polonius but also a Lear: "So now, taking upon me the mystery of things, I could go like a spy without leaving this place, without stirring from my chair."[316] It is also likely that Bernard is recalling one of Woolf's favorite songs from *Cymbeline* when he says that they might "better be like Susan and love or hate the heat of the sun."[317]

Neville "reads" Shakespeare in the activities of passersby as he walks down Shaftesbury Avenue, not coincidentally the location of many London theatres. . . . "Here's the fool, here's the villain, here in a car comes Cleopatra, burning on her barge. . . . This is poetry if we do not write it. . . . They act their parts infallibly, and almost before they open their lips I know what they are going to say, and wait the divine moment when they speak the word that must have been written. If it were only for the sake of the play, I could walk Shaftsbury Avenue for ever."[318]

On his own walks Bernard cites songs and lines from Shakespeare together with nursery rhymes: "So into the street again, swinging my stick. . . . Murmuring Pillicock sat on Pillicock hill, or Hark hark, the dogs do bark, or The World's great age begins anew, or Come away, come away, death—mingling nonsense and poetry, floating in the stream."[319] Some of the same rhymes—and another Shakespeare sonnet—come to his mind when he deplores the lockstep process of biographers: "They compel us to walk in step like civilised people with the slow and measured tread of policemen though one may be humming any nonsense under one's breath at the same time—'Hark, hark, the dogs do bark,' 'Come away, come away death,' 'Let me not to the marriage of true minds,' and so on."[320] Bernard's description of these chanted verses as "nonsense" is, in a way, a diversionary tactic; certainly his Shakespeare choices—"Come away death" and "the marriage of true minds"—are highly pertinent to his entire group of friends and their mutual history.

The most extended discussion of Shakespeare per se in *The Waves*—as contrasted with the characters and language of his plays—occurs in Bernard's reflection on his lifelong friendship with Neville. Their intimacy was based at least in part on "certain plays and poems, certain favourites of ours" discussed as they met or walked together, cementing not only their relationship with one another but also with books and reading.

> If I have to wait, I read; if I wake in the night, I feel along the shelves for a book. Swelling perpetually augmented, there is a vast accumulation of unrecorded matter in my head. Now and then I break off a lump, Shakespeare it may be, or it may be some old woman called Peck; and say to myself, smoking a cigarette in bed, "That's Shakespeare. That's Peck."—with a certainty of recognition and a shock of knowledge which is endlessly delightful, though not to be imparted. So we shared our Pecks, our Shakespeares; compared each other's insight to set our own Peck or Shakespeare in a better light; and then sank into one of those silences which are now and again broken by a few words.[321]

At this point in the novel Bernard's soliloquy sounds very much like the voice of Virginia Woolf in her private diaries, reflecting on the intense pleasures of reading and discussing Shakespeare. The mention of "some old woman called Peck"—intended by Bernard as a comic alternative to the eminence of Shakespeare—stirs some memories of the "Mrs. Brown" of Woolf's essay "Character in Fiction," though "Peck" is identified as a published author and Mrs. Brown, though a ubiquitous figure essential to the writer, is certainly not a writer herself.[322]

What is most striking, though—and the more so for the informal tone of this personal anecdote—is the centrality of Shakespeare to the very idea of friendship. The narrative strategy of the book's final section, which takes the form of a soliloquy so long it resembles a diary entry, allows for an unusually direct method of commentary, especially when it is linked to a mode of collective biography in which thoughts and emotions are held in common. Bernard's phrase—"a certainty of recognition and a shock of knowledge which is endlessly delightful"—is a compelling description of the effect that shared passages from Shakespeare could, and did, evoke among intimate and loving friends, whether the friends are those depicted in *The Waves* or their close relations and models, the members of the Bloomsbury Group.

"But Shakespeare Did Not Pause": Flush *(1933)*

In the wake of a novel titled *Orlando: A Biography* and an essay called "The New Biography" came *Flush,* Virginia Woolf's eponymous biography of Elizabeth Barrett Browning's English cocker spaniel. In this gem of a book, by turns comic and moving, Woolf turns once more to the twinned problems of biographical writing and authorial imagination. Unsurprisingly, the question is raised—if not entirely resolved—by recourse to the example of Shakespeare.

> Here, then, the biographer must perforce come to a pause. Where two or three thousand words are insufficient for what we see . . . there are no more than two words and one half for what we smell. The human nose is practically non-existent. The greatest poets in the world have smelt nothing but roses on the one hand, and dung on the other. The infinite gradations that lie between are unrecorded. Yet it was in the world of smell that Flush mostly lived. Love was chiefly smell; form and colour were smell; music and architecture, law, politics and science were smell. To him religion itself was smell. To describe his simplest experience with the daily chop or biscuit is beyond our power. Not even Mr Swinburne could have said what the smell of Wimpole Street meant to Flush on a hot afternoon in June. As for describing the smell of a spaniel mixed with the smell of torches, laurels, incense, banners, wax candles and a garland of rose leaves crushed by a satin heel that has been laid up in camphor, perhaps Shakespeare, had he paused in the middle of writing *Antony and Cleopatra*—But Shakespeare did not pause. Confessing our inadequacy, then, we can but note that to Flush Italy, in these the fullest, the freest, the happiest years of his life, meant mainly a succession of smells.[323]

With this elegant coupling of Shakespeare and the inexpressibility topos, Woolf the biographer rests her case.

Shakespeare and the "Educated Man's Daughter": Three Guineas *(1938)*

Shakespeare plays a very minor role in *Three Guineas,* Woolf's polemic about men, war, and the situation of the "educated man's daughter."[324] There are a few passing allusions to *Hamlet,* including "the criticism that Ben Jonson gave Shakespeare at the Mermaid" about blotting some of his lines ("There is no reason to suppose, with Hamlet as evidence, that literature suffered in consequence") and a more pointed reference, in one of her footnotes, to the Victorian era's insistence on "chastity, both of mind and body" and the way "the grip of its white if skeleton fingers" was invoked "to prevent [women] from reading Shakespeare."[325]

Nonetheless, a brief mention of Shakespeare in the context of *Three Guineas* is warranted in the light of Q. D. Leavis's scorching review in *Scrutiny,* which appeared under the title "Caterpillars of the Commonwealth Unite!," and Woolf's extended remarks, in *Three Guineas* and elsewhere, on the question of the teaching of English literature in the universities.

By her own account Woolf was not unduly bothered by Leavis's review, though she confesses that she "didnt read it through": "But I read eno' to see that it was all personal—about Queenie's own grievances & retorts to my snubs." She added, "Why I dont care more for praise or wigging I dont know. Yet its true."[326] (Unless, of course, the praise or wigging came from her Bloomsbury friends, in which case she cared a good deal.)[327] Leavis clearly saw herself and her own achievements as a university teacher occluded or erased by *Three Guineas,* and her attack, though full of facts, details, and sociological recommendations—Woolf, she thought, should read Margaret Mead to get a better sense of the comparative roles of women in society—was certainly also "personal." But it is the title of Leavis's review that brings Shakespeare into the picture. The "caterpillars of the commonwealth" (*Richard II* 2.3.166) were Richard II's hangers-on, useless and destructive, construed in Shakespeare's play as the enemies of a strong and healthy England ("swarming with caterpillars" [4.48]). The phrase "Caterpillars of the Commonwealth Unite!," ironically modeled on its Marxist original, was the equivalent of the modern "poor you"—mocking the supposed plight of those born to upper-middle-class privilege. The title may have occurred to Leavis's mind by association—Woolf twice mentions "caterpillars" in *Three Guineas,* though in very different connections from Shakespeare's.[328]

Woolf was unsympathetic to the teaching of English literature in the universities, although the history of English literature was a topic on which she had begun to plan her own book. She herself, the paradigmatic "educated man's daughter," had not been sent to school or to university. She studied the books in her father's library; she read literature with his guidance, and then on her own. Her passion for Shakespeare, as we have seen, was inspired and fostered by her brother Thoby who, although a Cambridge student, had "consumed Shakespeare" as a reader, not in the classroom. "The reduction of English Literature to an examination subject," she wrote in a long footnote to *Three Guineas,* "must be viewed with suspicion by all who have firsthand knowledge of the difficulty of the art, and therefore the very superficial value of an examiner's approval or disapproval."

In a remark that Q. D. Leavis and her husband F. R. Leavis may well have regarded as directed at them, Woolf observes that "the violence with which one school of literature is now opposed to another, the rapidity with which one school of taste succeeds another, may not unreasonably be traced to the power which a mature mind lecturing immature minds has to infect them with strong, if passing, opinions, and to tinge those opinions with personal bias." In fact the "demand from lectures upon English literature steadily increases . . . from the very class that should have learnt to read at home—the educated." She is willing to excuse those "whose homes are deficient in books. If the working class finds it easier to assimilate English literature by word of mouth they have a perfect right to ask the educated class to help them thus. But for the sons and daughters of that class after the age of eighteen to continue to sip English literature through a straw, is a habit that seems to deserve the terms vain and vicious; which terms can justly be applied with greater force to those who pander to them."[329]

These are harsh words to which Leavis understandably takes strong exception, pointing out among other things that Woolf seems to conflate education with indoctrination. ("The effective method of teaching literature does not tell young men and women what to approve or disapprove of" but rather "develops in them individual sensibility—a capacity for discovering what is of value in art.")[330] This is a long-running debate and dispute among what Leavis calls "educationalists," and it will not be resolved here. But in particular she objects to Woolf's resistance to English literature as one of a university's "disciplined specialist studies."[331] Woolf wants, says Leavis, "to penalize specialists in the interests of amateurs." The result would "only be a breeding-ground for boudoir scholarship (a term I once heard applied to the learning of one of Mrs Woolf's group) and belletrism."[332]

"One of Mrs Woolf's group"—together with "boudoir" and "belletrism"—identifies what Leavis clearly thinks is the real problem: Bloomsbury. Not that Lytton Strachey, had he been alive to read Leavis's review, would have necessarily objected to these terms (and presumably he is the target, since F. R. Leavis had long waged his own critical war against Strachey's style, success, and admirers). "Boudoir" and Woolf are a more difficult pairing to imagine. Queenie Leavis is offended that Woolf should demean her professionalism in an essay that is, in part, about opening the professions to women. Woolf, on her part, seems to claim that English literature differs in fundamental ways from those subjects that "can only be taught with diagrams and personal demonstration," noting that university lectures on English follow "an obsolete practice dating from the Middle Ages when books were scarce."[333] If "boudoir" and "belletrism" are Leavis's terms of disparagement, "vanity" and "the desire to impose authority" are Woolf's.

It is worth recalling that the English department at Cambridge, the university Woolf knew best, had been founded only in 1919, and that unlike Oxford—which had had an English department since 1894—and other British universities, Cambridge did not require its students to study philology and Anglo-Saxon. Instead some of its earliest professors of English, like George ("Dadie") Rylands and F. L. ("Peter") Lucas, preferred to relate English poetry to Greek and Latin literature. Both had been undergraduates at King's College, both were Apostles, and both had published books with the Hogarth Press that discussed Shakespeare's plays. "The first dons in the faculty," wrote Noel Annan—also an Apostle and also at King's—"were determined to meet the jibes of Bloomsbury and other writers that the last thing professors of literature ever asked themselves was why poems and novels touched the heart." Furthermore, "the founding fathers also took another notion from Bloomsbury. Why not examine what a writer is doing, what makes him tick, rather than pontificating about him?"[334]

In a letter to her nephew Julian Bell, then teaching English at a Chinese university, Woolf wrote half-jokingly about the limits of university teaching when it comes to English literature: "I hope you wont follow Dadies example; I see in the paper hes been made [Cambridge] University Lecturer in English for three years. But why teach English? As you say, all one can do is to herd books into groups, and then these submissive young, who are far too frightened and callow to have a bone in their backs, swallow it down; and tie it up; and thus we get English literature into ABC; one, two, three; and lose all sense of what its about." "Nobody reads with open eyes," she adds. "All are mere catalogue makers."[335] Woolf's dismissive tone may be teasingly designed to provoke a reply from Julian, but she did not think "English" or "English literature" or Shakespeare should be primarily the province of scholars, or, indeed, of universities. It is doubtful that she would have changed her mind once her own work had become, by the 1960s, an essential addition to English department offerings.

"A Scene from Shakespeare . . . I Forget Which": The Years *(1939)*

Toward the end of *The Years* Eleanor Pargiter arrives for her annual visit to the house in Dorsetshire where her brother Morris and his wife Celia are staying. It is August and very hot. "Every summer she came to visit Morris at his mother-in-law's house." There had been a fête that day to raise money for a new church steeple: the event featured "Lady St. Austell and the Bishop, coconut shies and a pig." Celia fans herself with a sheet of paper. "It's been a great success, she tells Eleanor.

> "We had the bazaar in the garden. They acted." It was a programme with which she was fanning herself.
>
> "A play?" said Eleanor.
>
> "Yes, a scene from Shakespeare," said Celia, "*Midsummer Night*? *As You Like It*? I forget which. Miss Green got it up. Happily it was fine. Last year it poured."[336]

This play in the countryside foreshadows the pageant in *Between the Acts,* as Miss Green will be transformed into the admirable and self-critical Miss La Trobe, and the fine weather, when "last year it poured," will also be imported to Woolf's final novel. But where Miss La Trobe is the author as well as the director of her pageant, Miss Green has "got up" what Celia describes as "a scene from Shakespeare." Which scene? From which play? The two plays she mentions, with their woodsy settings and their light-hearted love stories, are both staples of outdoor summer Shakespeare performance. But they are hardly indistinguishable, except to someone for whom "a scene from Shakespeare" ranks with the pig and the bishop as standard fare for a village fête.

Against this happy insouciance *The Years* will balance the brief and often enigmatic quotations from Shakespeare associated with Sara Pargiter, the novel's artist and onlooker, a fey and dreamy figure whose observations tend to begin with facts and then sometimes slide without warning into fantasy. Sara has a slight physical deformity—she was dropped as a child and one shoulder is higher than the other—that underscores her "outsider" status (some critics have compared her to a Shakespearean fool). In the last sections of the novel Sara is joined periodically in conversation by her younger cousin North ("Captain Partiger"), a soldier with whom she had corresponded while he was ranching in Africa after the war.

A few examples will illustrate Woolf's technique as she deftly inserts small bits of Shakespeare into the ongoing narrative. In the section called "1911," Sara spends a day in London with her aunt Rose. When her sister Maggie asks what they did together, she replies, "Stood on the bridge and looked into the water.... Running water; flowing water. May my bones turn to coral, and fish light their lanthorns; fish light their lanthorns in my eyes."[337] The practical Maggie disregards this response and merely repeats her question: "You went out with Rose.... Where to?" It takes a while to get the unremarkable story of the day's outing. But the reader has, in the meantime, had the chance to note Sara's glancing allusions to Ariel's song in *The Tempest* ("Of his bones are coral made / Those are pearls that were his eyes" [1.2.401–2]) and its terrifying tragic equivalent, Clarence's dream in *Richard III:*

> Methoughts I saw a thousand fearful wrecks,
> A thousand men that fishes gnawed upon;
> ....
> Inestimable stones, unvalued jewels,
> All scattered in the bottom of the sea.
> Some lay in dead men's skulls, and in those holes

> Where eyes did once inhabit, there were crept—
> As 'twere in scorn of eyes—reflecting gems.
> (1.4.24–25, 27–31)

Throughout the conversation Sara's affect is calm, even abstracted; she is anything but terrified. She hums to a tune she has been playing on the piano; her mind drifts to a garden. If she is thinking of Shakespeare at all, it is only as words and sounds, not as scenes and plots.

Clarence's dream will be quoted again much later, in the "Present Day" section of the novel when North Partiger comes to visit Sara in her cheap lodging house, and is temporarily left alone in her room. And again the context of the quotation will be elided. "He took up a book and read a sentence: 'A shadow like an angel with bright hair.'" The "shadow" is the shade or ghost of the murdered Prince of Wales; the next line of the passage makes it clear that his "bright hair" is "dabbled in blood" (*Richard III* 1.4.53–54).

But the story behind the words is masked by the excerpted quotation. North has read the classics, he recognizes the verse and can see the whole page, not just this phrase (which is not even a full "sentence"). Yet on the surface of Woolf's text the line floats free. It could be a vision rather than a nightmare. This is Shakespearean quotation against the grain. Manifestly the novelist knows the scene and the play, but we can assume that North does, too—and so does Sara, since she has earlier shown her familiarity with this same passage. But blood, murder, death by drowning—in both Ariel's song and Clarence's dream, all these remain unvoiced, unspoken. Tragedy is elided.

Here is another, very brief, example, from "1917." Eleanor has come to dine with her niece Maggie and Maggie's French husband René, known to their English friends and family as Renny. They are joined by Sara and by Nicholas, the urbane, serious gay man ("Russian? Polish? Jewish?" wonders Eleanor) who is Sara's close friend. Admiring Maggie's dress—silver with gold threads—Eleanor asks her where she got it.

> "In Constantinople, from a Turk," said Maggie.
> "A turbaned and fantastic Turk," Sara murmured.[338]

The (mis)quoted line is from the very end of *Othello,* when Othello recalls that he once killed a Turk who had "traduced the state." But the phrase Othello uses to describe this traitor to Venice—to whom he now implicitly compares himself—is "a malignant and a turbaned Turk" (5.2.363). In her letters and diaries Woolf often ruefully remarks that she misquotes Shakespeare when she is writing quickly

("I murder, as usual, a quotation"), and this may of course be such an instance.[339] Yet Woolf the novelist, unlike Woolf the diarist and correspondent, was a meticulous, even obsessional, editor and reviser of her own work. And the change is significant.

The word *Turk* seems to provoke Sara's intervention. (Perhaps there is a memory here of "Vita stalking in her Turkish dress" at Knole; the Nicolsons had in the first years of their marriage been stationed in Constantinople.)[340] The scansion is correct, but Sara's substituted phrase is purged of menace and becomes, instead, simply exotic—and indeed, in the context, "fantastic." Like the bones turning to coral, like the angel with bright hair, a reference that if pursued would lead to a thought of death is here passed over, in the dinner-table conversation, as a typically fanciful irrelevance from the odd but engaging Sara. The reader may sense it; the guests (excepting perhaps Nicholas) do not.

A third Shakespearean example will return us to Sara and North, who are expected to attend the party that Eleanor is giving, an event that will bring together all the novel's surviving characters for a final time. Sara, who doesn't enjoy such large gatherings, is delaying. North has twice already told her that she should get ready to go.

> Sara did not answer. She had pulled a book toward her and pretended to read it.
>
> "He's killed the king," she said. "So what'll he do next?" She held her fingers between the pages of the book and looked up at him; a device, he knew, to put off the moment of action. He did not want to go either. Still, if Eleanor wanted them to go—he hesitated, looking at his watch.
>
> "What'll he do next?" she repeated.
>
> "Comedy," he said briefly. "Contrast," he said, remembering something he had read. "The only form of continuity," he added at a venture.
>
> "Well, go on reading," she said, handing him the book.
>
> He opened it at random.
>
> "The scene is a rocky island in the middle of the sea," he said. He paused.
>
> Always before reading he had to arrange the scene; to let this sink; that come forward. A rocky island in the middle of the sea, he said to himself—there were green pools, tufts of silver grass, sand, and far away the soft sigh of waves breaking. He opened his mouth to read.[341]

The "he" who has "killed the king" seems to be Macbeth, and the "book," therefore, a volume of Shakespeare's plays. But surely Sara knows—doesn't she?—

what Macbeth does next. Perhaps she is putting herself in the place of an audience watching the play unfold. Or perhaps "he" is Shakespeare, and the question one of artistic design, not of dramatic plot. In any case North's response to "what'll he do next" addresses the playwright, not a character in the play.

There is, of course, no footnote in *The Years* to identify the "something" North had read, and he does not elaborate. But there *is* a footnote to a relevant critical work in *A Room of One's Own*—Woolf's friend F. L. Lucas's book *Tragedy,* published by the Hogarth Press—and what it says is relevant. "The greatest Elizabethan tragedy is half the child of comedy," writes Lucas. "Polonius and Macbeth's Porter and Lear's Fool produced some of the most striking scenes in their plays."[342]

As for the "rocky island," if it is indeed in the same book that Sara hands to North, it must be the scene of *The Tempest.* Stage directions in Shakespeare's play do not include this description—or any description—of the island, but Caliban complains to Prospero that he has been forced to remain in "this hard rock," his cave, and Prospero retorts that he was "deservedly confined into this rock" for attempting to violate Miranda (1.2.346). Woolf may be inventing the passage or paraphrasing a prose synopsis like those in the Lambs' *Tales from Shakespeare.* Whether borrowed or invented, the description shows us how much North, the soldier-farmer, resembles Sara, for he too begins to place himself within the scene, to elaborate it in his mind before he "opened his mouth to read." And as he does so, before he can read further, there is an interruption. Renny and Maggie arrive. They have been to "a very bad play."

> "Were you reading?" said Renny, looking at the book which had fallen on the floor.
>
> "We were on a rocky island in the middle of the sea," said Sara.[343]

The contrast between the unnamed "very bad play" and the book from which North and Sara are reading does not need further emphasis. But Sara's response—"We were on a rocky island"—indicates the completeness of their transposition into the imagined scene.

North, in fact, is Sara's inheritor in this novel of a family and its generations. The point is again made through the briefest of Shakespearean references after they have arrived at Eleanor's party. "Spinners and sitters in the sun," North thought, "taking their ease when the day's work is over," as he watches Eleanor and her brother Edward, the Oxford don, chatting easily together.[344] The phrase is from *Twelfth Night,* Orsino's request that Feste sing "Come away death." (The song, one of Woolf's favorites, had been twice evoked by the aging Bernard in

The Waves.) In *The Years* we do not hear the song itself, nor yet its full description, only a fragment of a line. But it may be worth looking at the context. "O fellow, come, the song we had last night," says Orsino.

> Mark it, Cesario, it is old and plain.
> The spinsters, and the knitters in the sun,
> And the free maids that weave their thread with bones,
> Do use to chant it. It is silly sooth,
> And dallies with the innocence of love,
> Like the old age.
>
> (2.4.41–47)

Shakespeare says "spinster," not "spinner," though the words in his time would have meant the same. The legal meaning of "spinster" as an unmarried woman begins in the late sixteenth or early seventeenth century, and by the eighteenth century began to carry the sense of a woman beyond the usual age of marriage, that is, literally an "old maid," since a maid was an unmarried woman. It's not clear whether it is North or Woolf who changes "spinster" to "spinner," nor whether the change is a simple error or a polite emendation; in any case, Eleanor Pargiter is a spinster in the legal and social sense, and glad to be one. North (or Woolf) also changes Shakespeare's "knitters" to "sitters," a word more appropriate to a different social class and an evening party, but also shifting from an active to a passive image: a "sitter in the sun" may be lolling, but a "knitter in the sun" is hard at work.

Neither Eleanor nor Edward, who is still an active scholar, would concur that their "day's work was over." (North, indeed, eagerly seeks out his uncle Edward for further conversation about "the past and poetry": "I'd like to brush up my classics," he tells him, and they make a date for the following autumn.)[345] Orsino's reference to the "old age" means the golden age, the innocent time of the past; again the modern sense of "elderly" flicks briefly over this phrase, and may have put the passage into North's—or Woolf's—mind. But although Shakespeare's spinsters and knitters in the sun may have been accustomed to chant "Come away death" (a title that means not "go away" but "hurry here"), for them it is a work song, not a harbinger.

There is no extended Shakespearean counterplot in *The Years,* juxtaposing those who know Shakespeare well with those who don't, or who don't much care. Celia's indifference to the choice of a scene from a pastoral play is treated kindly; she has other things on her mind. Sara's associations of events in "real life" with phrases from Shakespeare are often out of joint, but no one is troubled by them, and those who love her, like Nicholas and Maggie and North, seem to regard her Shakespearisms with a mix of toleration and pleasure. The fact that many of these quoted fragments lead, if pursued, to images of death is available to the reader, but it offers not so much a counterplot as an underplot.

What Sara regards in the final pages of the novel as "the old brothers and sisters," what Morris will call "us old fogies," look forward to the summer. Woolf, who has by now perfected the art of the last word in her novels ("For there she was"), points in the direction of the future: "And now?" Eleanor asks Morris. "'And now?' she asked, holding out her hands to him."[346] The technique, once again, calls to mind that of Shakespeare, whose plays always point forward to a future "act 6" beyond the present moment: "Cesario, come— / For so you shall be while you are a man; / But when in other habits you are seen, / Orsino's mistress, and his fancy's queen" (*Twelfth Night* 5.1.372–75); "This and what needful else / That calls upon us, by the grace of grace / We will perform in measure, time, and place" (*Macbeth* 5.11.37–39); "Lead us from hence, where we may leisurely / Each one demand and answer to his part" (*Winter's Tale* 5.3.153–54). The time that Woolf calls in *The Years*—and in *Orlando* and *Between the Acts*—the "Present Day" is always at the same time "present" and about to be superseded.

"Scraps, Orts, and Fragments": Between the Acts *(1941)*

In the spring of 1940 Virginia Woolf was asked by the Rodmell Women's Institute—of which she was an active member—to "write a play for the villagers to act. And to produce it myself. I should like to if I could," she told a friend. "Oh dear how full of doings villages are—and of violent quarrels and incessant intrigues."[347] The Rodmell play was never written, but the pageant in *Between the Acts* gives some sense of the "doings," "quarrels," "intrigues," and complex emotions that such a play could elicit.

Woolf's last novel, published in 1941 after her death, is a feast of Shakespearean references, direct and indirect, poignant, witty, and sly. From the "village idiot" who is cast as the "hindquarters of [a] donkey" to Mrs. Swithin, the elderly widow who realizes after watching the pageant that she "could have played . . . Cleopatra," every citation, or absence of citation, tells a Shakespeare-inflected story.[348]

"The Barn," we are told at the beginning of the novel, "was as old as the church itself, and built of the same stone. . . . The roof was weathered red-orange, and inside it was a hollow hall, sun-shafted. . . . If it rained, the actors were to act in the Barn; planks had been laid together at one end to form a stage."[349] Both the barn and the pageant's producer, the commanding and self-doubting Miss La Trobe, were clearly inspired, at least in part, by the Barn Theatre Society, founded by Edy Craig, the daughter of Ellen Terry and sister of Edward Gordon Craig. After Terry's death Edy, assisted by her partner, Christopher St. John, and their friend Tony (Clare Atwood), converted the thatched Elizabethan barn near her mother's cottage at Smallhythe to a theatre, to be supported by subscriptions. A Shakespeare performance was given every year to commemorate the anniversary of Ellen Terry's death, and in the summer months Edy produced plays and pageants. "The actors dressed in the cottage, walked across the garden and spoke Shakespeare's lines on the intimate stage."[350] Michael Holroyd's description of productions in the Barn, "with nosegays hanging from the rafters, rushes spread across the floor, the red fire buckets lined against the walls, swallows and swifts circling and swooping overhead," shows how close the scene was to that of Virginia Woolf's village pageant. Smallhythe, in Kent, was a few miles from Sissinghurst, where Vita Sackville-West lived. Vita performed her poem "The Land" there, and Vita and Virginia were invited to lunch by Craig and St. John. In 1933 Woolf expressed an interest in becoming a subscriber—although a later letter from Vita suggests that she had not as yet done so.[351]

Miss La Trobe's pageant resembles the kind of event held annually on Empire Day, then a national holiday celebrating the breadth of a British Empire that spanned almost a quarter of the globe. On a date marking the birthday of the late Queen Victoria, who had been crowned Empress of India, schoolchildren and their families gathered to sing songs like "Jerusalem" and "God Save the King" and to commemorate the deeds of British national heroes with concerts, tableaux, and festivals. Miss La Trobe's audience expects—although it will not get—a "Grand Ensemble, round the Union Jack," and at the end of the pageant a retired colonel muses, "Why leave out the Army? What's history without the Army?"[352] Among all the national heroes, from Clive of India to Gordon of Khartoum, one was of course uniquely appropriate for a day given over to local plays and pageants—William Shakespeare, "blest Genius of the Isle," the poet who was one of the symbols of British national identity.[353]

The word *pageant* in this context meant "historical pageant," a play depicting scenes from history, national or local, usually performed outdoors and featuring elaborate, colorful costumes. For most of the novel that is exactly what it means. "I've been nailing the placard on the Barn . . . for the pageant," announces Mrs. Swithin, as she enters carrying a hammer, and the unflappable Mrs. Manresa asks for information about "this pageant, into which we've gone and butted."[354] But at the end of the day, when all the guests have gone, we learn of Isa "sitting in the shell of the room [as] she watched the pageant fade."[355]

A "faded" pageant, needless to say, is central to one of the most famous of all set pieces in Shakespeare, Prospero's abrupt conclusion to the masque of marriage and fertility in *The Tempest:*

> Our revels now are ended. These our actors,
> As I foretold you, were all spirits, and
> Are melted into air, into thin air;
> And like the baseless fabric of this vision,
> The solemn temples, the great globe itself,
> Yea, all which it inherit, shall dissolve;
> And, like this insubstantial pageant faded,
> Leave not a rack behind.
>
> (5.1.148–56)

This passage is neither read nor performed in *Between the Acts,* but nonetheless it is suggestively present. The phrase "the great globe" embeds the name of Shakespeare's public playhouse, which does make an appearance in Miss La Trobe's pageant. "Were they about to act a play in the presence of Queen Elizabeth? Was this, perhaps, the Globe theatre?" the audience wonders, as helpers enclose the queen's throne with screens papered to represent walls.[356] At the same time, "the great globe" is also the worldwide scope of the British Empire, happy and glorious—even as planes, bombs, and sirens began to invade the island of Britain.

Other pertinent moments from *The Tempest* are likewise hinted at throughout the novel. "Dispersed are we," wails the gramophone in Miss La Trobe's pageant. "Dispersed are we." As the Neapolitans come to shore after the shipwreck, Ariel tells Prospero that, in accordance with his instructions, "in troops I have dispersed them 'bout the isle" (1.2.220–21). This stratagem allows Ferdinand to be separated from the others and thus to be persuaded—when he hears Ariel's mysterious and haunting song—that his father the king is dead: "Sea nymphs hourly ring his bell. / Hark now I hear them, ding dong bell" (1.2.406–8).

In *Between the Acts* church bells at the end of the pageant make the same sound, calling worshippers to the evening service. "That's the bell. Ding dong. Ding . . . Rather a cracked old bell." The church bells continue to sound, punctuating conversation as the audience departs—"Are machines the devil, or do they introduce a discord . . . Ding, dong, ding . . . by means of which we reach the final . . . Ding dong . . . Here's the car"—though that modern convenience, the telephone bell, bids finally to replace them as a mode of social community: "Ring us up. Next time we're down don't forget."[357]

As she was engaged in writing the novel, Woolf complained in her diary about the way the incessant church bells in Rodmell interrupted her work. "Sunday is the devils own day at M[onks]H[ouse]. Dogs, children, bells . . . there they go for evensong." And again, "Ding dong bell . . . ding dong—why did we settle in a village?"[358] The tonal dissonance between this private reflection and the poetry of Ariel's song is characteristic of her method throughout, juxtaposing "high" and "low" for both comic and serious effect, allowing readers who know Shakespeare to find extra layers in her already layered text.

Disconnection and dispersal are closely linked to fragmentation—"scraps, orts, and fragments"—another pervasive Shakespearean theme. Instead of the social body, it is the physical body that, in this image, is separated from itself. The key words are all taken from *Troilus and Cressida,* a play Woolf had chosen to read again on a "roaring, raving evening" in 1938, "apples pelting down" in the garden at Monks House.[359] She is quoting Troilus's disillusioned judgment of the woman he has loved and idealized, and about whom he now despairingly concludes, "This is and is not Cressid" (5.2.146). Unsupported by her father, compelled by her circumstance as a prisoner of the Greeks, Cressida has turned to the Greek Diomedes for succor and protection. Troilus describes his lover's faithlessness, as he sees it, in images of table scraps and leftovers:

> The bonds of heaven are slipped, dissolved, and loosed,
> And with another knot, five-finger-tied,
> The fractions of her faith, orts of her love,
> The fragments, scraps, the bit and greasy relics
> Of her o'er-eaten faith, are bound to Diomed.
> (5.2.155–60)

Again, there are no footnotes or "aha" moments in the novel to identify this passage, which is never quoted in full. But the key words are constantly repeated, like a refrain, and pass from one speaker or consciousness to another. Isa thinks about the vulgar and seductive Mrs. Manresa: "Her hat, her rings, her finger nails red as roses, smooth as shells, were there for all to see. But not her life history. That was only scraps and fragments to all of them."[360] When the audience members began to talk with one another, "scraps and fragments reached Miss La Trobe where she stood, script in hand, behind the tree."[361] After the children leap out of the bushes holding their pieces of mirror, a loudspeaker voice ("the anonymous bray of the infernal megaphone") taunts the spectators: *"Look at our-*

selves, ladies and gentlemen! Then at the wall; and ask, how's this wall, the great wall, which we call, perhaps miscall, civilization, to be built by (here the mirrors flicked and flashed) *orts, scraps and fragments, like ourselves?"* And again: *"What? You can't descry it? All you can see of yourselves is scraps, orts and fragments?"*[362]

In his closing remarks after the pageant, the vicar tries to interpret this scene: "'I caught myself reflected, as it happened in my own mirror . . .' (Laughter). 'Scraps, orts and fragments! Surely we should unite?'"[363] And when Mrs. Swithin asks Isa whether she agrees with the vicar that "we act different parts but are the same," Isa's feelings are divided. "'Yes,' Isa answered. 'No,' she added. . . . 'Orts, scraps and fragments,' she quoted what she remembered of the vanishing play."[364]

Meantime Miss La Trobe, shy and distrustful of praise, paraphrases to herself another line from *Troilus and Cressida* as she thinks about the response of the audience: "It was in the giving that the triumph was. . . . If they had understood her meaning . . . it would have been a better gift."[365] "Things won are done; joy's soul lies in the doing," Cressida says wryly, describing a woman's vulnerability to the fickleness of men (1.2.265). As we've seen, Woolf had also quoted a version of this passage to herself in her diary after she finished *Orlando:* "Joy's life is in the doing—I murder, as usual, a quotation. I mean it's the writing, not the being read that excites me"—a sentiment nearer to Miss La Trobe's than to Cressida's.[366]

"Orts, scraps, and fragments" is also a fair enough description of the pageant itself. A Renaissance play-within-the-play is performed before "great Eliza"—Mrs. Clark of the village shop, resplendent in a cape "made of cloth of silver—in fact, swabs used to scour saucepans."[367] The plot, a pastiche of Shakespearean and other romances, including a false duke, a princess disguised as a boy, a noble daughter lost in a cave, a boy put into a basket as a baby, and an aged beldame who lives long enough to recognize him by marks on his body: "the crone, who saved the rightful heir," explains one audience member to another, peering at the program on a "blurred carbon sheet" through her lorgnette. Shakespearean phrases are scattered throughout, occasionally mixed with bits of the Romantic poets. The "beldame" is a figure borrowed from Keats, and her "skinny forearm" suggests both the Ancient Mariner and the witches in *Macbeth;* when she says, "There is little blood in my arm," the play may also glance at Lady Macbeth's sleepwalking remembrance of the dead Duncan: "Who would have thought the old man to have had so much blood in him?" (5.1.33–34).[368]

Isa, thinking about a scene of "love embodied," associates it with two images from *Romeo and Juliet* ("The nightingale's song? The pearl in night's black ear"? [3.5.2; 1.5.42–43]).[369] The newfound prince cries, "*Look where she comes!*" when he sees his beloved approaching—a variant of a line in *Antony and Cleopatra* that Woolf had cited several times in *The Waves.*[370] The death of the aged crone is greeted by the crowd with a line adapted from *King Lear:* "Peace, let her pass. She to whom all's one now, summer or winter."[371] And the priest's final blessing—"Let Heaven rain benediction! / Haste ere the envying sun / Night's curtains have undone"—is a mashup of phrases from *Twelfth Night* and *Romeo and Juliet.*[372] After a disruption, "great Eliza" invokes Falstaff commanding Prince Hal to "play out the play" (*Henry IV, Part 1* 2.4.471).[373]

More scraps are on display when the actors come onstage together for a final bow. "Queen Bess; Queen Anne; and the girl in the Mall; and the Age of Reason; and Budge the policeman. . . . They all appeared. What's more, each declaimed some phrase or fragment from their parts." In this cacophony Shakespeare is again both represented and tweaked: a slightly misquoted line from Sonnet 66, a slightly misquoted version of "Is this a dagger that I see before me?" and a line from *King Lear* ("I fear I am not in my perfect mind" [4.7.72]) that is not, in fact, from the pageant at all, but instead comes to Giles Oliver's mind when he hears Mrs. Manresa "trolloping out" the words of a song.[374] Audience and actors are again intermingled and conflated. ("Scraps, orts and fragments! Surely we should unite?") Meantime the swallows that so fascinate Mrs. Swithin, returning to the same location every year, skimming in and out of the trees during the performance, are associated—in the mind of some unidentified audience member or the collective audience—with a half-remembered phrase: "The swallows—or martins were they?—the temple haunting martins, who come, have always come. . . . Yes, perched on the wall, they seemed to foretell what after all the *Times* was saying yesterday: Homes will be built. Each flat with its own refrigerator." A martin is a kind of swallow, and house martins are common in England. But Banquo's praise of the "temple-haunting martlet" that nests in every "jutty, frieze, [and] buttress" of Macbeth's castle is followed immediately by the entry of Lady Macbeth, "our honored hostess," and King Duncan is welcomed to the place that will be his death (1.6.1–10). The irony, if pursued, is high and low: the castle's "pleasant seat" and the modern flats, each with its own refrigerator; the back pages of the *Times* and Shakespeare's dark tragedy of vaulting ambition; "Homes will be built" and Lady Macbeth's duplicitous cry, "What, in our house?" But no one pursues it: the slightly misremembered tag "temple-haunting martins" is simply a familiar phrase, devoid of anything but pleasure.

Other than "great Eliza"'s bawled assertion that "for me Shakespeare sang," Shakespeare is mentioned by name only at two moments in the novel, and both, it is fascinating to note, involve the distinctly unbookish Mrs. Manresa. The first is Bartholomew Oliver's courtly, old-world compliment. Why, he wonders aloud, are most English people "so incurious, irresponsible, and insensitive" to the arts, "whereas Mrs Manresa, if she'll allow me my old man's liberty, has her Shakespeare by heart?"

> "Shakespeare by heart!" Mrs Manresa protested. She struck an attitude. "To be or not to be, that is the question. Whether 'tis nobler . . . Go on!" she nudged Giles, who sat next to her.
>
> "Fade far away and quite forget what thou amongst the leaves hast never known . . ." Isa supplied the first words that came into her head by way of helping her husband out of his difficulty.
>
> "The weariness, the torture, and the fret . . ." William Dodge added, burying the end of his cigarette in a grave between two stones.
>
> "There!" Bartholomew exclaimed, cocking his forefinger aloft. "That proves it! What spring's touched, what secret drawer displays its treasures."[375]

Isa's associative suggestion of a passage from Keats's "Ode to a Nightingale" is neatly capped by William, who offers the next line of the poem, but no one—and certainly not Giles—picks up Mrs. Manresa's challenge to be Hamlet. Whether Mrs. Manresa herself knows any more of the soliloquy is left to the imagination.

The other time Shakespeare's name comes up in conversation is after the Victorian scene in the pageant when Mrs. Swithin asks the others in her group, "D'you get her meaning . . . Miss La Trobe's?"

> Isa, whose eyes had been wandering, shook her head.
>
> "But you might say the same of Shakespeare," said Mrs Swithin.
>
> "Shakespeare and the musical glasses!" Mrs Manresa intervened. "Dear, what a barbarian you all make me feel!"
>
> She turned to Giles. She invoked his help against this attack upon the jolly human heart.
>
> "Tosh," Giles muttered.[376]

"Shakespeare and the musical glasses" is a phrase from *The Vicar of Wakefield* that had been picked up by Aldous Huxley in his 1928 novel, *Point Counter Point* (and was the title of an early unpublished fragment of an essay by Lytton Strachey).[377] In Goldsmith, it is part of the supercilious conversation of two rather questionably bred young ladies, "richly drest," introduced as "women of very great distinction and fashion from town," who overshadowed the local residents at an evening of country dancing, "for they would talk of nothing but high life, and high-lived company; with other fashionable topics, such as pictures, taste, Shakespeare, and the musical glasses." (They also shocked the company by occasionally "slipping out an oath.") Huxley puts the phrase in the mouth of Everard Webley, the charismatic leader of a proto-fascist group called the Brotherhood of British Freemen who is irritated that Elinor Quarles won't decide whether to have an affair with him: "Shall we talk about Shakespeare? . . . Or the musical glasses?"[378] Mrs. Manresa is more likely to have read the "modern" Huxley than the "classic" Oliver Goldsmith, but in neither case is she certain to have seen the entire relevance of the quotation. (In a metafictional world we might want to ask her a version of Mrs. Swithin's query, "D'you get her meaning . . . Mrs Woolf's?")

In this novel, so brilliantly threaded with Shakespearean *quotations,* direct and slant, it may seem that there are surprisingly few named or personated Shakespearean *characters.* Even when lines are easily recognizable as belonging to one or another familiar dramatic persona (Hamlet, Lear, even Cressida), they are often voiced by persons who seem peculiarly unlike their Shakespearean counterparts. The one figure who does express a direct kinship with a character in the plays is Mrs. Swithin, and her identification with Cleopatra seems likewise spectacularly unfitting, though tinged with admirable resolve.

Nonetheless, if we pause for a moment to think about it, this episode, disarming and moving in itself, can also be seen to provide a pertinent clue. Mrs. Swithin offers her impulsive revelation as a compliment to the pageant's producer, but it also reflects upon her own character. "What a small part I've had to play. But you've made me feel I could have played . . . Cleopatra!" she tells Miss La Trobe during an interval. The villagers, overhearing, think Mrs. Swithin is being "Batty" (one of her local nicknames), but Miss La Trobe understands. "'You've twitched the invisible strings,' was what the old lady meant; and revealed—of all people—Cleopatra! Glory possessed her."[379]

The pageant had been constructed around the reigns of three queens, Elizabeth, Anne, and Victoria. The mention of Cleopatra adds a fourth queen, famously ageless and alluring, though also flawed and self-absorbed. Such a figure is discernible in *Between the Acts.* But the novelist has cast someone else for the role. For despite Mrs. Swithin's wistful longing for the part, it is Mrs. Manresa who emerges instead as the novel's unlikely Cleopatra. Tasteless, shameless, vain, and self-confident, with a dubious past and an absent husband, she arrives in her "great silver-plated car" with its initials twisted "so as to look at a distance like a coronet," with William Dodge cast, however reluctantly, in the part of one of the "pretty dimpled boys" who propel Cleopatra's barge.

Inevitably, Mrs. Manresa attracts the attention not only of Bartholomew Oliver but also of his son Giles, married to Isa—though Giles mutters "lust" to himself when he thinks of "Manresa" (and "coward" when he thinks of himself).[380] Still, watching her belt out the lyrics of a popular song playing on the gramophone, his mind is full of words like "vulgar," "abandonment," and indeed "trolloped." He thinks she is a "good sort," worth far more than the "half-breeds" like William Dodge whom she "brings . . . in her trail."[381] Age cannot wither her. She pours cream "luxuriously" into her coffee, and adds a "shovel full of brown sugar candy." "May I help myself? I know it's wrong. But I've reached the age—and the figure—when I do what I like."[382] When during an interval she looks around and sees Giles, she "caught his eye; and swept him in, beckoning. He came. . . . Taking him in tow, she felt: I am the Queen, he my hero, my sulky hero."[383] And in the scene of the flashing mirror fragments, when everyone else has a startlingly frank and disconcerting glance at "ourselves," Mrs. Manresa, "facing herself in the glass, used it as a glass; had out her mirror; powdered her nose; and moved one curl, disturbed by the breeze, to its place. 'Magnificent!' cried old Bartholomew."[384]

In his description of Cleopatra, Shakespeare's Enobarbus emphasized not only her magnificence ("The barge she sat in, like a burnished throne, / Burned on the water" [*Antony and Cleopatra* 2.2.197–99]) but also her flaws.

I saw her once
Hop forty paces through the public street,
And having lost her breath, she spoke and panted,
That she did make defect perfection,
And breathless, pour breath forth.
(2.2.234–38)

The petty vanities of Cleopatra, her allure, and the way she makes defect perfection are all on display in Woolf's portrait of Mrs. Manresa: a gamesome, flawed, and infuriatingly seductive woman whose name begins with "Man."

We noticed in discussing *The Years* that Woolf's novels often end with what I called "act 6"—the indication in a final sentence that something is yet to come. *Between the Acts* presents two such moments, one for Miss La Trobe and the other for Isa. Both concern creation: artistic in one case and biological in the other. About Miss La Trobe, musing on her next theatrical work, we are told,

"She heard the first words."[385] About Isa and Giles, left alone together after a troubling day, we hear that "before they slept, they must fight; after they had fought, they would embrace. From that embrace another life might be born." The two kinds of "acts," theatrical and sexual, are here juxtaposed. The last sentences of the novel, still describing the young Olivers, continue this juxtaposition of art and life: "Then the curtain rose. They spoke."[386] What words Isa and Giles spoke, what words Miss La Trobe heard, are left unwritten, unspoken. Between the acts.

One final point, certainly speculative and arguably trivial, about the presence and absence of Shakespeare in Woolf's final novel. Shortly after the arrival of their unexpected guests, Mrs. Swithin offers to show them the house, an invitation meant for and accepted by William Dodge—who had been introduced by Mrs. Manresa as "an artist," though he corrects her: "I'm a clerk in an office."[387]

"'Here are the poets from whom we descend by way of the mind, Mr . . . ' she murmured. She had forgotten his name. Yet she had singled him out." A few minutes later, indicating the bed where she was born, she returns to the theme of descent and heritage. "'We have other lives, I think, I hope,' she murmured. 'We live in others, Mr . . . We live in things.'" He thinks to himself, "She had forgotten his name. Twice she had said 'Mr' and stopped." And then, "Could he say 'I'm William'? He wished to."[388] At the top of the house they pause to watch the audience assembling for the pageant ("but they, looking down from the window, were truants, detached") and here Mrs. Swithin addresses him once more. "'Mr . . . ' she began. 'I'm William,' he interrupted. At that she smiled a ravishing girl's smile."[389]

"I'm William." He says it again when he seeks her out after the pageant to say good-bye. ("Who was it? Dear me, the young man whose name she had forgotten; not Jones; nor Hodge. . . .) 'I'm William,' he said. At that she revived, like a girl in a garden in white, among roses, who came running to meet him—an unacted part."[390]

Mrs. Manresa prefers to call him Bill ("Jump in, Bill," she instructs him peremptorily, as her car is poised to depart at the end of the day.)[391] Isa sees him as "the lip reader, her semblable, her conspirator, a seeker like her after hidden faces."[392] Mrs. Swithin, though happy to use the familiar name ("I took you . . . away from your friends, William"), had three times employed, instead, a title inseparable from its ellipsis: "Mr . . ." And then had again forgotten his name.[393]

As we have noted, in a review of the letters of the popular English professor Sir Walter Raleigh, Woolf had criticized him for referring to Shakespeare as Bill, a practice that she found disrespectful and aimed at crowd-pleasing. "Walter Raleigh calls Shakespeare 'Billy Shax.' . . . This shocks me."[394] (In her diary she described Raleigh as a "self-conscious poseur.")[395] "Mr . . . " sorts well with the supposed lacunae in Shakespeare's biography, as well as with the more literary and philosophical inaccessibility implied in works like Borges's "Everyone and No One." Isa's idea that Dodge is a version of herself, that he somehow asks the same kinds of questions and thinks the same kind of thoughts, is what almost every percipient reader of Shakespeare has sensed at one time or another. Whether "I'm William" is a joke, a clue, an instance of critical overreading—or all three of these—it is an audible and legible refrain in the novel, disappearing as its speaker disappears. "The play's over," he says to Mrs. Swithin. "The actors have departed." As he presses her hand and turns to go, the narratorial voice intervenes, seeming to shut the door—or close the curtain—against another version of act 6: "Putting one thing with another, it was unlikely that they would ever meet again."[396]

CHAPTER 4

Shakespeare Among the Apostles

When the young men who would become part of Bloomsbury were up at Cambridge, several joined the Shakespeare Society of Trinity College, whose members met weekly to read the plays aloud. A delightfully solemn photograph of the Shakespeare Society, taken around 1901, includes, seated at one end of a bench, Lytton Strachey with a mustache; seated at the other end, Leonard Woolf in a straw hat; and, standing in the second row, a robust, confident Thoby Stephen with his chest thrown out and his hands in his pockets.[1]

But it was another, more celebrated society at Cambridge that would bind many of them together for life. Of the ten men associated with what became known as Old Bloomsbury, as Leonard Woolf noted, seven were members of the Cambridge Conversazione Society, often called simply the society or the Apostles. Six of them—Desmond MacCarthy, Lytton Strachey, Saxon Sydney-Turner, E. M. Forster, Maynard Keynes, and Woolf—had been up at Cambridge in the same or overlapping years and had been strongly influenced by (or, as Woolf says, "permanently inoculated with") the ideas and values of the philosopher G. E. Moore. Roger Fry, an Apostle who was older than Moore and tended to be critical of his philosophy, was nonetheless closely allied to the group. The other members of Old Bloomsbury—Vanessa Bell and Virginia Woolf, Clive Bell and Duncan Grant—were introduced to these ideas by their friends and by reading Moore's *Principia Ethica.* In his biography of Keynes, Robert Skidelsky

The Shakespeare Society, Trinity College, Cambridge, 1901

writes of "that London extension of Apostolic Cambridge known as the Bloomsbury Group."[2]

While they were at Cambridge several of the Apostles also became interested in a new undergraduate theatre group, the Marlowe Dramatic Society, founded in 1906, which focused on Shakespeare's language rather than on the elaborate staging settings and formal gestures of the previous century. An Apostle of the next generation, the director and King's College lecturer George "Dadie" Rylands, elected to the society in 1922, became one of Britain's most influential interpreters of drama and Shakespeare.

The Saturday evening meetings of the Apostles—whose informal name derived from the fact that there were twelve elected members—involved the delivery of papers and responses, and a vote on some aspect of the topic under discussion. Leonard Woolf quotes from, and concurs with, a passage from the memoir of Henry Sidgwick describing the special quality of these meetings. The society featured, Sidgwick wrote, "the spirit of the pursuit of truth with absolute devotion and unreserve by a group of intimate friends, who were perfectly frank with each other, and indulged in any amount of humorous sarcasm and playful banter, and yet each respects the other, and when he discourses tries to learn from him and see what he sees. Absolute candour was the only duty that the tradition of the society enforced. . . . It was rather a point of the apostolic mind to understand how much suggestion and instruction may be derived from what is in form a jest—even in dealing with the gravest matters."[3]

This credo, if it may be so described, was fundamental to the interchanges of Bloomsbury, and would be echoed in the plan for the Memoir Club when it was founded in 1920: absolute candor, frank exchanges among friends, wit, and privacy. The first invitations to the Memoir Club were sent by Molly MacCarthy (the daughter of one Apostle and the wife of another) to twelve potential members, following the apostolic number, although, unlike the Cambridge Apostles, this group notably included women. Leonard Woolf—who remembers the original number as thirteen—describes the rules of the Memoir Club very much as he did those of the society: "It was agreed that we should be absolutely frank in what we wrote and read"—though he adds that "absolute frankness, even among the most intimate, tends to be relative frankness" and that "absolute truth was sometimes filtered through some discretion and reticence."[4] The passage of years and the growing celebrity of the members had ingrained some caution. Yet Maynard Keynes, addressing the Memoir Club in 1938 at the age of fifty-five, could look back to Cambridge and the Apostles as what continued to distinguish these friendships from others: "The habits of feeling formed then still persist in a recognisable degree. It is those habits of feeling, influencing the majority of us, which make this Club a collectivity and separate us from the rest."[5]

Not all of the Bloomsbury Apostles contributed directly to the group's Shakespearean heritage. Saxon Sydney-Turner's work did not bring him further in touch with Bloomsbury or the arts. His conversations with Virginia are all the record we have of his thoughts about Shakespeare. E. M. Forster said and wrote little about Shakespeare directly; he is perhaps most eloquent on the topic when he writes about the ideas of earlier Apostle and Bloomsbury friend G. L. Dickinson.[6] Rupert Brooke, who was an Apostle and an early leader of the Marlowe Dramatic Society, began as a friend of the other Bloomsbury Apostles but then turned vehemently against them. On the other hand Clive Bell, though not himself elected to the Apostles, had a crucial role in founding two early play-reading groups at Cambridge to which many of them belonged, and he was certainly a central member of Bloomsbury from the outset. His observations about Shakespeare will be discussed in chapter 6. Nonetheless, the beliefs, opinions, and intellectual intimacies that the Apostles shared while at Cambridge were foundational in "what came to be called Bloomsbury," and their ideas about Shakespeare were among the most vivid—and enduring—of their views.[7] As will be evident from what follows, these ideas inspired and affected work in a remarkable range of fields across the humanities, the social sciences, and the arts.

THE BIOGRAPHER: LYTTON STRACHEY

"Before we are aware of it, we all of us find that we are talking about Shakespeare," wrote Lytton Strachey in his introduction to George Rylands's *Words and Poetry*. By "all of us," he explains, he means "every English writer on English literature."[8]

Although Strachey is best known as an innovative biographer and essayist, both his professional and his personal lives were almost always engaged with Shakespeare. He was the first drama critic of the *Spectator,* for which he wrote theatre reviews under the pen name Ignotus. He regularly attended performances of Shakespeare plays at the Amateur Dramatic Club in Cambridge as well as in London and Paris. Even if he were ill or out of town, he would often write to ask for news about a production. "Throughout his life," says Charles Richard Sanders, "Strachey was extraordinarily fond of plays—of seeing them, of writing them, of acting in them. He never missed a chance to participate in the amateur theatricals in which his family and friends were constantly engaging."[9]

Strachey liked to read Shakespeare's plays aloud, both in reading groups at Cambridge and in Bloomsbury, and privately with friends like the painter Carrington (Dora de Houghton Carrington), with whom he lived for much of his later life. His correspondence and conversation were full of Shakespeare references. His article "Shakespeare's Final Period," published when he was an undergraduate, remains today a remarkable intervention, and his three major biographies, *Eminent Victorians, Queen Victoria,* and *Elizabeth and Essex,* are testament to his absorption in and understanding of Shakespeare's poems and plays.

"Had Shakespeare Any Character?"

As a child Strachey was sent to study with a man named Henry Forde, who took a few boys for private teaching at his home in Dorset. There Strachey performed in school plays, including tableaux drawn from Shakespeare. He was Romeo in one, Othello ("with my face blackened") in another.[10] When he moved to the New School, Abbotsholme, in December 1893, he appeared as Hippolyta, queen of Amazons, in a production of *A Midsummer Night's Dream,* wearing what he described in a letter to his mother as a "lovely" dress and a "beautiful

Lytton Strachey, photograph possibly by
Dora Carrington, mid-1920s

yellow wig."[11] The headmaster of Abbotsholme, the educational reformer Cecil Reddie, wrote much later to Strachey—by now a famous author—that he remembered him "very well" and still had a photograph of the cast, with Lytton as a "fascinating female."[12] (Reddie, who was opposed to coeducation, "proposed," Robert Skidelsky suggests, "to conquer lust with love" among the school's students. In one of his lectures he asked rhetorically, "Is it not natural for boys to love each other? Is it not a fact that the very best types in every school naturally tend to this?" It was, he said, "an enthusiasm even of the age of Shakespeare.")[13]

Despite his success at Abbotsholme, however, Strachey's time there was unsatisfactory and brief; after two terms he moved to another, more conventional, public school, where he became a school prefect and head of house. Still too young—thought his mother—to go directly to Oxford or Cambridge, he was instead sent in 1897 to Liverpool University College, where Walter Raleigh, a distant relation by marriage, was King Alfred Professor of English literature. Raleigh's lectures on Elizabethan literature and on Shakespeare were popular, and Strachey attended some of them.

In March 1898, in an entry dated two days after his eighteenth birthday, Strachey began a new diary, noting that the "chief interest" of such a diary is to be able to reread it in the future, "when the feelings and thoughts resulting therefrom are dim and faint in the memory"—although the act of writing might also serve as "a safety-valve" to his "morbidity." "My character is not crystalized," he says, "so there will be little recorded here that is not transitory." In fact, he adds—much in the later spirit of Jorge Luis Borges—he himself "perhaps after all [may] not exist but in my own phantasy." Yet, "not to be modest (for this is a private confession)" there might be a useful prototype. Perhaps "character," in the sense of decided opinions and personality, was inimical to a certain creative plenitude.

> —Had Shakespeare any character? Of his own, that is to say? Was he not a mere shadow, a mere receptacle for phrases, for faces, for minds, for hearts? All passing away to give place to the next batch? Could he ever have propounded a gospel of his own believing? Did he believe in anything? No, certainly not. Not even, I think, in Right as opposed to Wrong. He was a sceptic, a cynic in his inmost of hearts, swept over and domineered by passions of love; beauty; justice; honour; horror; unutterable woe; calm contentedness. He could never have been a leader of men—mentally, or spiritually, for he was a sceptic, and a sceptic is nought. Better so, perhaps; in fact necessarily so. And there are quite sufficient of the other sort.[14]

This is a quite remarkable piece of speculation about art and art-making. "Better so" may be a remembered, or half-remembered, quotation from Matthew Arnold's sonnet "Shakespeare," which described, in a way the young Strachey might well have felt about himself, the poet's initial obscurity: "Thou . . . Self-school'd, self-scann'd, self-honour'd, self-secure, / Didst tread on earth unguess'd at.—Better so!" But the idea that Shakespeare had no character "of his own" but was instead "a mere receptacle for phrases, for faces, for minds, for hearts," accords with John Keats's observation "Men of Genius . . . have not any individuality, any determined Character."[15] This was a view that Keats would develop and tie explicitly to Shakespeare in his theory of "negative capability": "At once it struck me, what quality went to form a Man of Achievement especially in Literature & which Shakespeare possessed so enormously—I mean Negative Capability, that is, when man is capable of being in uncertainties, Mysteries, doubts, without any irritable reaching after fact & reason."[16]

Midnight at Cambridge

Early in his time at Cambridge, Strachey became a member of the Midnight Society, a group of six undergraduates who met in Clive Bell's rooms in Trinity College at midnight on Saturday to read plays aloud. (Another such group, the X Society, to which he also belonged, met earlier on Saturday evening.) The members of the Midnight Society included several men who were to be essential to what later became known as Bloomsbury: Bell, Leonard Woolf, Saxon Sydney-Turner, and Thoby Stephen (whose death in 1906 was one of many catalysts that bound the group together). The Midnight Society read works like Shelley's *Prometheus Unbound* and *The Cenci,* Milton's *Comus,* and Ben Jonson's *Bartholomew Fair.*

It's worth recalling that none of these literary classics would have been encountered in their university classwork. The Cambridge University English department was not founded until 1917. The study of Shakespeare, like that of Jonson, Milton, and Shelley, was what we would now call an extracurricular activity, pursued on evenings and weekends. Clive Bell remembered that "as often as not it was dawn by the time we had done; and sometimes we would issue forth to perambulate the courts and cloisters, halting on Hall steps to spout passages of familiar verse, each following his fancy as memory served."[17]

The pleasure of such play-reading groups would be carried into their adult lives, when women joined the men. The Bloomsbury Play Reading Society was founded in December 1907; among its earliest choices was *Troilus and Cressida.*[18] During the war years Vanessa Bell wrote to a friend that one of their collective entertainments was "reading plays, which is a very good way of spending an evening."[19]

John Sheppard, Strachey's close friend at Cambridge and later the provost of King's College, told the biographer Michael Holroyd a story about a meeting of the Decemviri, a Cambridge undergraduate debating society. The motion proposed on one occasion, strongly advocated by an Alpine climber, was "that this house would rather be Drake than Shakespeare." At the end of the proposer's speech in favor of "the life of action and adventure," Sheppard told Holroyd, "a pair of heavy curtains, concealing a window-seat, were drawn open, and Lytton's falsetto voice cried out: 'Utterly ridiculous!' The tall, frail figure spoke of the supreme value of Shakespeare. It was a performance Sheppard never forgot."[20]

Transmigrations of Cleopatra

On January 9, 1901, when the Midnight Society read *Antony and Cleopatra,* Lytton took the leading female role. At a key moment near the end of the play, the Egyptian queen determines to take her own life rather than be brought in captivity to Rome, where, as she tells her attendants, "I shall see / Some squeaking Cleopatra boy my greatness / I' th' posture of a whore" (5.2.215–17). The famous "Strachey voice," which could rise to falsetto at unexpected moments, would seem to be an all-too-perfect fit here, but as Clive Bell reports in his account of the Midnight Society proceedings, "Lytton read well; and seemed to have those squeaky notes, to which his voice rose sometimes but by no means generally in conversation, under control."[21]

Cleopatra—both history's and Shakespeare's, the two often conflated—was a favorite figure for Lytton, one that he would remember and allude to all his life. When he wrote to Leonard Woolf about the death of Thoby Stephen, he cited the words of Cleopatra after the death of Antony: "There is nothing left remarkable / Beneath the visiting moon" (4.16.69–70).[22] But not all his references to her are tragic. Some are admiring, some companionable, and a few frankly comic.

At the end of 1900, as he told Leonard Woolf, he had had a discussion with "an Oxford person, who teaches little boys, and in the intervals writes poems for the *Spectator*" about "people we should like to meet." Strachey had "mentioned Cleopatra." The solemn "Oxford person" said he "should rather see Our Lord."[23]

Cleopatra was also on his mind when he wrote "Conversation and Conversations," a paper read to the Sunday Essay Society in November 1901. No art would be more characteristic of what would later be called Bloomsbury than conversation, and in his paper Strachey rejoices in the fact that "we all of us have this much in common with Shakespeare, that we mouth, every day of our lives, the very syllables which he did." In particular, Strachey idealizes "the conversation of lovers," imagining "Antony swoon[ing] in the arms of Cleopatra."[24] "Sex in conversation is the spice which makes it commonly bearable," he observes, noting that "tragedy itself must bow before the wit of Cleopatra."[25] Declaring—in a striking phrase that shows the influence of Walter Pater—"Drama is conversation treated architecturally," he takes a moment to mention Sophocles and to reflect on "the overwhelming conversations of King Lear," but his Shakespearean benchmark and lodestar does not change: "Phèdre lived again in Racine; Cleopatra in Shakespeare." These are "noble instances of transmigratory perpetuation," and "to converse is the unique privilege of souls which we inalienably inherit."[26]

Strachey would later return to the idea of conversations with Cleopatra and "transmigratory perpetuation" in two of his imaginary dialogues, one between Cleopatra and the Victorian novelist Mrs. Humphry Ward, the other between Cleopatra and William Henry Salter, an acquaintance of Strachey's from Cambridge, subsequently active in the Society for Psychical Research.[27] Needless to say, Strachey's Cleopatra gets the better of each of them. In one dialogue Cleopatra pretends to mistake Mrs. Ward for the livelier fiction writer Marie Corelli (who spent her last years in Stratford-upon-Avon and raised funds for the conservation of buildings and gardens associated with Shakespeare). In the other dialogue, set in "the Infernal Regions," a bored Cleopatra, missing Antony, briefly pretends a sexual interest in Salter, portrayed there as a clueless Englishman. Salter was married to Helen Verrall, the daughter of classics professor and Cambridge Apostle A. W. Verrall, a fellow of Trinity; all were interested in spiritualism, and Verrall's wife and daughter were "mediums." The connection with spiritualism is probably what led Strachey to cast Salter in his dialogue.[28]

In the first paper Strachey read to the Cambridge Apostles, "Ought the Father to Grow a Beard?" (May 10, 1902), he begins by quoting a famous passage from *Antony and Cleopatra:*

> CLEOPATRA: If it be love indeed, tell me how much.
> ANTONY: There's beggary in the love that can be reckoned.
> CLEOPATRA: I'll set a bourn how far to be beloved.
> ANTONY: Then must thou needs find out new heaven, new earth.
> (1.1.14–17)

In the course of his argument, this exchange becomes the basis for a discussion between Life and Art on whether there is anything that art cannot, or should not, represent.[29] Strachey's Apostolic debut is probably best remembered for its lèse-majesté fantasy, only a year after Queen Victoria's death, of a classically naked Prince Albert: the solemn "central figure of the Albert Memorial" rises to its feet overnight, dressed only "in the garb of nature" ("Imagine the indignant rush up those sacred steps. . . . But to consider our late beloved Prince in such a situation is too painful. I draw a shuddering veil.")[30] But Shakespeare features in almost every other example in the paper: the sexual organs ("Can we say to Antony, 'you may enjoy the limbs and the head and the breast of Cleopatra as much as you like, but there are some parts of her which you shall never enjoy; for with these you have nothing whatever to do?'"); unpoetic language, exemplified by Shakespeare's use of words like *knife* and *blanket* at a key moment in *Macbeth*—a passage ridiculed by eighteenth-century editors; the act of defecation ("The thought of every member of the human race—the human race which has produced Shakespeare, and weighed the stars—retiring every day to give silent and memorable proof of his matinal mould is to me fraught with an unutterable significance. There, in truth, is the one touch of Nature which makes the whole world kin! There is enough to give the Idealist perpetual pause!").[31]

From Antony to Macbeth to Ulysses, this series of Shakespearean allusions is deftly and wittily deployed to show Shakespeare as the poet of Art and Nature, "the Artist who works not by rules but by genius and an invisible flame within him."[32] If this sounds "romantic" rather than iconoclastic, it is worth considering that both attitudes are vividly present in the young Strachey—and arguably in the older Strachey as well. In another Apostolic paper, "Christ or Caliban" (October 25, 1902), Strachey briefly imagines going back in time to "be doorkeeper at the Globe," closing his argument by citing "the wild triumphant cry of Caliban.—Freedom, hey-day! Hey-day, freedom!" to personate, and personalize, the tension—as he saw it—between Victorian repression and modern rebellion.[33] But *Antony and Cleopatra* seems to have occupied a special place in his memory and imagination.

As early as 1904, in one of his first published reviews in the *Spectator,* Strachey noted that the reason "*Antony and Cleopatra,* in spite of the unsurpassed wealth of its characterizations, has never been a popular play" is that its "brilliance and universal complexity" are "almost too amazing to follow. There is really nothing amid all this bewildering exuberance which can satisfy the craving of 'the man in the street' for something which he can easily understand, and he has quietly relegated to an obscure corner of his Pantheon the play which ranks among the half-dozen most stupendous achievements of Shakespeare's genius."[34]

The appeal of Shakespeare's play and of the transcendent relationship between the lovers extended as well to the last of his major biographies. As we'll see, several contemporary reviewers would compare *Elizabeth and Essex* to *Antony and Cleopatra,* as does biographer Michael Holroyd. But lines from the play would leap to Strachey's mind even on trivial occasions. One example may suggest the mode: in 1927, when he and Carrington were living in the country setting of Ham Spray House, an airplane suddenly circled the area three times and landed nearby. Virtually everyone in or near the house—including Lytton, the farmhands, the housemaids, and the cats—rushed toward it in excitement, he wrote to a friend, "and Carrington was left solitary on her bed, like Antony 'whistling to the air.'"[35] The allusion is to the famous scene, reported in the play by Enobarbus, when Antony first met Cleopatra at Cydnus: "The city cast / Her people out upon her, and Antony, / Enthron'd i' th' marketplace, did sit alone, / Whistling to th'air, which but for vacancy / Had gone to gaze on Cleopatra too, / And made a gap in nature" (2.2.219–24). Cleopatra's beauty is such that it almost transgresses the physical law about nature abhorring a vacuum. The airplane, an unaccustomed sight in that time and place, causes a similar thrilling disruption. The comic inappropriateness of the comparison is part of its wit, which depends on his correspondent recognizing this very familiar quotation. Such references mark the not-so-secret handshake of an educated class. But this throwaway line is also a good example of the way Strachey, like Virginia Woolf in her letters and diaries, tended to see the world, instinctively, through and with Shakespeare.

Perplexities of King Lear

Like *Antony and Cleopatra, King Lear* remained a lifelong favorite with Strachey, both as a dramatic achievement and as a perception of life. In two early pieces for the *Spectator* Strachey addressed the play and its power, noting especially the way the play reflected or refracted emotion across diverse characters and situations. In *King Lear* "we have [Shakespeare's] most elemental situation reflected to us in a thousand complications from the agonies of his profoundest mind," he wrote in 1904.[36] And a few years later: "*King Lear,* more than any other play ever written, arouses feelings of vastness and universality; it is something more than the history of an individual—it is a history of a world, and of a world in which, like our own, the issues are not only vital and tremendous, but multitudinous and perplexed."[37]

This description of the "impression of immense and complicated movement, which forms, as it were, the setting of the whole drama," written when Strachey was still in his twenties, is strikingly similar to what W. B. Yeats had called the play's "emotion of multitude."[38] "We think of *King Lear* less as the history of one man and his sorrows than as the history of a whole evil time," says Yeats. "Lear's shadow is in Gloster, who also has ungrateful children, and the mind goes on imagining other shadows, shadow beyond shadow till it has pictured the world."[39] Like Yeats, Strachey considered the horrific blinding of Gloucester—

criticized by Coleridge and others as excessive—essential to the dramatic effect: "Without the experience of Gloucester's suffering we should have lacked a measure for the suffering of Lear," Strachey argues, suggesting that "the profundities of the spirit stretch infinitely beyond the pains of the body."[40]

It was also *King Lear* that he instanced as a young writer when he objected to the fashion for bracketed stage directions prescribing how characters should feel. If Shakespeare had been influenced by Shaw or Harley Granville Barker, Strachey scoffed, he might have written "Lear (*angrily*); Blow, winds, and crack your cheeks."[41] Shakespeare's text itself was sufficient; it told the actors all they needed to know. Comparing the styles of French and English dramatists, he commented in 1905 on a "literal translation of *King Lear*" that was "drawing full houses at the Théâtre Antoine," noting that Shakespeare remains a "living, and a growing, force," whereas "our interest in the dramas of Voltaire is solely an antiquarian interest."[42] On a journey to France when he had only one day in Paris, he spent part of it at the Odéon watching *Lear* in "a bad translation, feebly acted, that filled the audience with amazement."[43] And when his friend Dadie Rylands produced the play at the Marlowe Dramatic Society in Cambridge, he offered, after seeing a rehearsal, his highest praise: "The play is allowed to express itself, and there are absolutely no theatrical horrors."[44]

"Shakespeare's Final Period"

What would become Lytton Strachey's most cited essay on Shakespeare was published when he was still an undergraduate. "Shakespeare's Final Period," a spirited takedown of the pieties of regnant Shakespeare scholars that might well have been titled "Eminent Shakespeareans," was read before the Sunday Essay Society on November 29, 1903, and appeared in the August 1904 number of the *Independent Review;* it was later republished in Strachey's essay collection *Books and Characters.*[45] He would, much later, revisit some of its ideas in his introduction to George Rylands's *Words and Poetry.*

Like the papers Strachey read to the Apostles, it is written in a spirit of deliberately provocative iconoclasm (Gordon McMullan calls it "relishable shamelessness").[46] One of its goals is to unsettle the complacent notion that at the end of his life Shakespeare retired in a happy mood that rounded out his career. The other is to demonstrate that the eminent are not always so wise. They will find comforting truth in manifest falsehood—and insist upon it—only if they refuse to look at the evidence before them.

Thus the "ordinary doctrine of Shakespeare's mental development" as set forth by "modern writers" like F. J. Furnivall, Edward Dowden, Sir Israel Gollancz, Bernhard Ten Brink, and Sir Sidney Lee argues that the chronology of the plays can chart the chronology of Shakespeare's mood and state of mind. Thus the scholars infer his personal progression, from the gaiety of the early comedies to the "gloomy middle age" of the tragedies to an ultimate "state of quiet serenity" in which Shakespeare, now retired from London to Stratford and returned to the bosom of his family, enjoys the company of his daughters and the pleasures of country life.[47] This, Strachey notes, is "the universal opinion." But it is not his. He twits in particular the captions given by Dowden to the last two periods of Shakespeare's writing life, from the despair of "In the Depths" to the triumphantly serene culmination "On the Heights," pointing to Dowden's assertion that "in these latest plays the beautiful pathetic light is always present."[48] He then proceeds, methodically and devastatingly, to puncture this fantasy.

Is the Isabella of *Measure for Measure* not as pure and lovely as Perdita and Miranda? Is her success not as complete? Why then should the "happy" ending of *Measure* seem futile, while the conclusions of *The Winter's Tale* and *The Tempest* are said to show virtue triumphant? "Why does it sometimes matter to us a great deal, and sometimes not at all, whether virtue is rewarded or not?" Strachey's answer is that nearly every play before *Coriolanus* is "essentially realistic. The characters are real men and women, and what happens to them upon the stage has all the effect of what happens to real men and women in actual life. Their goodness appears to be real goodness, their wickedness real wickedness; and, if their sufferings are terrible enough, we regret the fact, even though in the end they triumph, just as we regret the real sufferings of our friends."[49] (This is the true Strachey note: "the sufferings of our friends" would always, for him, have a particular power and poignancy; friendship, from the Apostles, from Moore's *Principia Ethica,* from Bloomsbury and its satellites, was among the highest of values, if not the highest.)

In the plays of the final period, though, "all this has changed; we are no longer in the real world, but in a world of enchantment, of mystery, of wonder, a world of shifting visions, a world of hopeless anachronisms." The characters of the plays are now (merely) fairy-tale creatures, either more or less than human: "fortunate princes and wicked step-mothers"; "goblins and spirits"; "lost princesses and insufferable kings." The happy endings of such tales, Strachey contends, "cannot be taken as evidences of serene tranquility on the part of their maker; they merely show that he knew, as well as anyone else, how such stories ought to end."[50] Moreover, the language of many characters in the last plays is shocking in its violence, its "brutality of phrase," its "coarseness," its "hideous rage," whether the speaker is Caliban, Cloten, Iachimo, or the outraged Paulina of *The Winter's Tale.*[51] How does this comport with "serenity"? "Nowhere, indeed, is Shakespeare's violence of expression more constantly displayed than in the 'gentle utterances' of his last period."[52] "Is it fair to say that Shakespeare was in a 'gentle, lofty spirit, a peaceful, tranquil mood,' when he was creating the Queen in *Cymbeline,* or writing the first two acts of *The Winter's Tale*?"[53]

The essay's most famous pronouncement, and one suitably "Apostolic" in its studied deflation, was that Shakespeare "was getting bored." He was "bored with people, bored with real life, bored with drama, bored, in fact, with everything except poetry and poetical dreams. He is no longer interested, one often feels, in what happens, or who says what, so long as he can find a place for a faultless lyric, or a new, unimagined rhythmical effect, or a grand and mystic speech." *Bored* is Strachey's brilliantly chosen word; had he said *wearied* or some other more "poetical" word, the sense (however fleeting) of an insult to the greatest of poets would not have been so acutely registered. "Is it not thus, then, that we should imagine him in the last years of his life? Half enchanted by visions of beauty and loveliness, and half bored to death; on the one side inspired by a soaring fancy to the singing of ethereal songs, and on the other urged by a general disgust to burst occasionally through his torpor into bitter and violent speech? If we are to learn anything of his mind from his late works, it is surely this."[54]

It was the word *bored* that would in coming years especially irritate his readers, often blinding them to the logic of his argument.[55] As Russ McDonald notes, this became a "notorious passage, usually cited so that the critic can ridicule and dismiss it."[56] Arguably it is a young man's word, rather than an old man's, and yet it served its role as a trigger; Strachey was, McDonald suggests, "impatient with the supposed spiritual wisdom of the palsied eld."[57] And they were often glad to return the favor.

One thing in particular that Strachey refused to countenance was the sentimental view, still popular in some quarters today, that Prospero, the protagonist and major mouthpiece of Shakespeare's best-known late play, is a Portrait of the Artist as an Old Man. "Prospero is the central figure of *The Tempest;* and it has often been wildly asserted that he is a portrait of the author—an embodiment of that spirit of wise benevolence which is supposed to have thrown a halo over Shakespeare's later life. But, on close inspection, the portrait seems to be as imaginary as the original. To an irreverent eye, the ex-Duke of Milan would perhaps appear as an unpleasantly crusty personage, in which a twelve years' monopoly of the conversation had developed an inordinate propensity for talking."[58] He suggests that Ariel, of all those with whom Prospero talks (and talks and talks), might well have shared this critical view, but perhaps feared, were he to express it, that he would be imprisoned once again in the "knotty entrails of an oak tree." Prospero, in fact, comes across in Strachey's description as a particularly tiresome kind of don: "It is sufficient to point out that, if Prospero is wise, he is also self-opinionated and sour, that his gravity is also another name for pedantic severity, and that there is no character in the play to whom, during some part of it, he is not studiously disagreeable."[59] As for the other characters, the shipwrecked noblemen are not even disagreeable but "simply dull." Caliban is a great creation but a terrifying one, "moving us mysteriously to pity and to terror, eluding us forever in fearful allegories, and strange coils of disgusted laughter and phantasmagorical tears."[60] Caliban's passionate outcry to Prospero, "You taught me language, and my profit on't / Is, I know how to curse," sounds, says Strachey, much like Job addressing God. In any case, he concludes, "it is not serene, nor benign, nor pastoral, nor 'On the Heights.'"[61]

When Lytton Strachey published this essay in the *Independent* he was twenty-four years old. The confident and persuasive tone of the piece is striking, and so is the authorial persona. It's understandable that some readers, finding it in an anthology of essays on Shakespeare's final plays, might mistakenly believe that it was written much later, after some of Strachey's other works had already earned him a place and a voice. Its most remarkable element, beyond the effective dismantling of the bardic pieties of an earlier generation of critics, is the close attention paid to Shakespeare's language. His interest, we might say, is micro rather than macro; he locates speeches and characters that seem to cut against the grain.

Subsequent critics have held the last plays in higher esteem; they are not bored but intrigued. What Strachey sees as flaws they often see as transformative elements emblematic of Shakespeare's artistic versatility even, or especially, in his later years—as well as a canny adjustment to changing public taste. But the point here is not whether Strachey is "right" or "wrong" to judge the last plays as he does; it is that the evidence he marshals to make his argument is based on close reading, whether what he is reading is the bland and celebratory language of scholars or the acerbic, angry, and manifestly "disagreeable" language of some of Shakespeare's most admired dramatic characters. (That the tiresomely loquacious Prospero who loves to monopolize conversations may have reminded him of some of the learned scholars he sends up in his article is, perhaps, an additional motive for his animus.)

Nonetheless, as scholars like G. E. Bentley, Sam Schoenbaum, and Gordon McMullan have shown, Strachey does not really argue against the idea that the state of mind of the author corresponds to the spirit and content of the work. "Bored" is a mood, like "serene." Schoenbaum notes that "Strachey set a high value on boredom, a condition from which he frequently suffered himself," adding that "even the boredom may be a cynic's version of serenity."[62]

Strachey was a polemicist by nature, and his experience with the Cambridge Apostles as well as his later life in Bloomsbury (and indeed his earlier life as a younger child in his outspoken family) confirmed him in this taste for verbal jousting. Moreover, he was—or would become—a skilled biographer, attuned to tone and nuance in the writings of his subjects. Although he detected and ridiculed a mode of romantic idealization in Dowden and his other Victorian adversaries, he could also, when reading the works, argue forcefully in favor of Shakespeare's emotional involvement, strongly resisting the idea that they should be largely considered as evidence of technical mastery. Unsurprisingly, perhaps, this was most evident in his reading of the sonnets.

Art and Authenticity: Emotion in Shakespeare's Sonnets

Shakespeare's sonnets in those years were at the center of a critical controversy that has not abated. Oscar Wilde and others had celebrated them as powerful documents of same-sex passion. Strachey, who had engaged with Maynard Keynes and other Apostles in discussions of the "Higher Sodomy," was infuriated by scholars like Sidney Lee who read the sonnets as skilled literary exercises in a familiar genre rather than eloquent records of lived experience. In fact, as Alan Bell and Katherine Duncan-Jones note, this point of view marked a major shift from Lee's earlier claim in the first (London) edition of the *Dictionary of National Biography* (1897) that "Shakespeare's relations with men and women of the court involved him at the outset in emotional conflicts, which form the subject-matter of his sonnets." Bell and Duncan-Jones suggest that the "literary exercises" claim might have been a delayed response to the trial and imprisonment of Oscar Wilde. "The vehement prolixity with which Lee promoted his last, 'impersonal' reading of the *Sonnets* in many later writings may reflect continued discomfort on the matter," they argue, adding that "his ensuing study of French and Italian Renaissance poetry, especially the sonnet, seems to have been informed by an almost desperate determination to discover models there for Shakespeare's 'purely literary' devotion to a young male patron."[63]

In late December 1904—the same year in which he excoriated Lee and others for their biographical claims about Shakespeare's mind and art—Lytton Strachey wrote to Leonard Woolf, who was then in Ceylon, about a discussion he had had with his mother, the redoubtable Jane Maria Grant Strachey. He had agreed to write a review for the *Spectator* about Shakespeare's sonnets and promised to send it to Woolf when it was printed, though "I'm afraid it may be boring, pedantic, pompous, involved, and sentimental." He also took a swipe at "Dr Furnivall—the old Shakespearean donkey" who had advocated admitting "girls" to the workingmen's college, before returning later in the letter to the topic of the review. "I have had a rather wonderful conversation with my mother on the subject of the Sonnets," he reported.[64]

Lady Strachey was not only a powerful personality but also a strong literary influence upon Lytton as a young man. Her friends included Robert Browning, George Eliot, the Carlyles, Darwin, Galton, and Huxley. She enjoyed reading aloud and was, writes Charles Richard Sanders, "in great demand for both public and private readings.[65] Virginia Woolf said that she was "by far the best reader I have ever heard," and that she read for two and a half hours without stopping, "acting every part."[66] Her reading tastes encompassed French literature and Elizabethan drama as well as Donne, Milton, Scott, and Henry James. As a child Lytton kept a commonplace book in which he copied lyrics from Shakespeare, Marlowe, Blake, and other poems she taught him.[67]

Michael Holroyd notes that although Lady Strachey's sons and daughters "remained uninstructed, and, in the case of the daughters, unenlightened regarding the facts of life, she read them the bawdiest Elizabethan dramatists" as well as *Tom Jones*.[68] Lytton seems, apparently, to have mentioned the assigned review, and perhaps to have consulted her opinion. As Strachey wrote to Woolf,

> She sent my younger sister out of the room, and then began—Saying that Sydney [*sic*] Lee presented the dilemma of (1) their being addressed to a patron or (2) to a catamite—or words to that effect. I think this is true, and of course absurd. It's quite clear in my mind that one *can* be in love with a man without having sexual feelings about him. I gather that my mother is certain that this was the case. But do you altogether believe that? There are lines in Sonnet 20 which look suspicious—
>
> And for a woman wert thou first created
> Till Nature, as she wrought thee, fell a-doting,
> And by addition me of thee defeated,
> By adding one thing to my purpose nothing.
>
> My mother admits that this passage has to be "got over," but urges a good many reasons in favour of Shakespeare's "purity"—no! she didn't use the

> word—especially the great no. 129 on lust in action. I think that only shows he was perfectly aware of the degradations and horrors. But that he didn't feel them with W.H.? . . . I can't see it. And, good lord, what does it matter? It really does seem the apex of idiocy to make everything turn on the wretched physical movements of our unhappy bodies—but this is the only point of the anti-sodomy movement, *I* was too discreet to *say* this. But my rage is so great that I want to smash that fiend Sydney Lee, who—whatever Shakespeare may have been—is certainly a bugger. I think of reviewing Beeching in the Independent. And I believe I can do it without hurting susceptibilities—other people's or my own. This I believe can be done by refraining from use of the word "unnatural," which is the root of all evil, muddling, and tomfoolery.[69]

"Beeching" was the Reverend Henry Charles Beeching, a poet and clergyman. His 1904 edition of the sonnets was one of two books that Strachey reviewed in the *Spectator* (not the monthly *Independent Review,* in which Strachey had previously published several essays) in February of the following year. "Canon Beeching's introduction to his edition," wrote Strachey, "contains a counterblast to a theory of the sonnets which has lately obtained wide acceptance, and has gained strong support by the advocacy of Mr Sidney Lee. That the sonnets were not the outcome of deep emotion; that they were written, not to a friend, but to a patron; and that that patron was probably the Earl of Southampton—these are the main articles in the creed of Mr Lee and his followers."[70] Beeching rebuts the idea that Southampton was "Mr W.H." ("It is difficult to believe," Strachey asserts, "that an unbiased reader of Canon Beeching's pages will fail to see that a case of such strength has been made out against Mr Sidney Lee's position that this theory is now no longer tenable") and offers some evidence, though not a firm conclusion, in support of William Herbert, Earl of Pembroke.[71] But to Strachey—and, as he suggests, to Beeching—the "essential thing" is not the identity of "Mr W.H." but the power of Shakespeare's poetry.[72]

"No one who has read the sonnets in this spirit will ever believe that they are nothing more than literary exercises, or that they were merely written as propitiatory addresses to a patron," he writes, smoothing over the "rage" he had expressed in his letter to Woolf with something of the cool assurance that would in time come to characterize his essayistic voice. "These theories belong to the artificialities of criticism." Moreover, how could it be that "the very poems which Mr Sidney Lee has declared to be devoid of any emotion whatever" have been attacked by others for their "excessive" and "misplaced" affection? Surely there is a middle course available, he argues. That this is still a very young Lytton Strachey writing under deadline one of his first pieces for his cousin St. Loe Strachey's journal may be seen in the fact that he cites in support of this idea not, as one might expect, a passage from Shakespeare's sonnets but instead lines from a particularly bleak and bloody scene in *Titus Andronicus:* "O brother, speak with possibilities, / And do not break into these deep extremes." The citation is wildly taken out of context and may be the result of a hasty search for the word "extreme" or "extremes" in a concordance.[73] Strachey's review—which, like all reviews in the *Spectator* at that time, was published anonymously—concludes with an appropriate rhetorical flourish. "What need is there," he asks, "to deny that the greatest of poets felt any emotion at all?"[74]

This is what Strachey had protested in his letter to Woolf. But it was not precisely what Sidney Lee had proposed. Rather, he undertook to explain why a vogue for sonnet writing could produce both imitation and innovation. "Most of Shakespeare's sonnets were produced in 1594," Lee says, "under the incitement of that freakish rage for sonnetteering which, taking its rise in Italy and sweeping over France on its way to England, absorbed for some half-dozen years in this country a greater volume of literary energy than has been applied to sonnetteering within the same space of time here or elsewhere before or since." The thousands of sonnets written in England in those years "were of every literary quality, from sublimity to inanity, and they illustrated in form and topic every known phase of sonnetteering activity." Shakespeare's sonnets came late in this temporal sequence and used, or rather reused, many of the same themes. "He borrows very many of his competitors' words and thoughts, but he so fused them with his fancy as often to transfigure them." And now comes the declaration that Strachey found so objectionable. "Genuine emotion or the writer's personal experience very rarely inspired the Elizabethan sonnet, and Shakespeare's sonnets proved no exception to the rule. A personal note may have escaped him involuntarily in the sonnets in which he gives voice to a sense of melancholy and self-remorse, but his dramatic instinct never slept, and there is no proof that he is doing more in these sonnets than produce dramatically the illusion of a personal confession."[75]

Shakespeare, in other words, was above all a playwright, a talented dramatist who could, and did, meld his gift for characterization into a lyric form that mimed individual passion and sincerity. Or, as Lee's "summary of conclusions respecting the sonnets" declared, "The processes of construction which are discernible in Shakespeare's sonnets are thus seen to be identical with those that are discernible in the rest of his literary work." With "his marvelous genius and skill in adapting and transmuting for his own purposes the labours of other workers in the field that for the moment engaged his attention," Shakespeare transformed the sonnet as he had transformed Elizabethan comedy and history, and would soon transform tragedy.[76] This is a professional account of a professional writer at work.

Lee further describes Shakespeare's need for patronage, again a commonplace of the period: "The sole biographical inference deducible from the sonnets is that at one time in his career Shakespeare disdained no weapon of flattery in an endeavour to monopolise the bountiful patronage of a young man of rank."[77] Nine years after Oscar Wilde's "Portrait of Mr W.H." and decades after Wordsworth's "Scorn not the sonnet" and its rousing claim, "With this key / Shakespeare unlocked his heart," Sidney Lee is trying to rebalance the equation, to restore art to the place where biographical speculation had come to stand. Strachey's complaint that Lee denies that the "greatest of poets" felt "any emotion at all" is a loose translation at best. What Lee claims instead is that the "greatest of poets" was also the greatest of playwrights, and that the emotions shown in the sonnets, like the emotions shown in the plays, could be understood as brilliant projections into the mind, and the thoughts and language, of his poetic speakers. But for Strachey—or at least the Strachey who took energy from his "wonderful conversation" with his mother and wrote so ardently to Leonard Woolf about it—Sidney Lee's dispassion seems to have read as the denial of authentic passion. What he dismisses in Lee as "the artificialities of criticism" might equally be understood as the critic's praise of art.

Both "Shakespeare's Final Period" and Strachey's review of commentaries on the sonnets are infused with strong critical feeling, what we might, in the modern way, call "attitude." Arguably, a distinction might be made between sonnets and poems, on the one hand, and plays on the other; the lyric "I" might be thought of as more personal, if not more autobiographical, than the voices of a wide range of characters, each with his or her own dramatic persona. (Indeed, that is how Strachey sometimes uses the sonnets in his own correspondence, as when he wrote sympathizing with Maynard Keynes on the end of Keynes's affair with Duncan Grant: "Love's the very devil. But it *is* Time's fool.")[78] But this is not a formal distinction that Lytton Strachey emphasizes in his critique. Rather, he takes issue with the scholars' dependence on external narratives, whether in the supposed aleatory biography or the history of Elizabethan sonneteering. The "right method of interpreting [Shakespeare's] poetry—in spite of all the inkpots of all the commentators," lies in the poems themselves.[79]

Strachey(s) at the Spectator

The Stracheys were a reviewing family—and a family of Shakespeare enthusiasts. St. Loe Strachey was the longtime editor of the *Spectator,* and Lytton's younger brother James worked for him as his private secretary for six years, as well as reviewing two Shakespeare productions at the Savoy.[80] Marjorie Strachey published a review of "*King Lear* at the Théâtre Antoine" in the *Independent Review,* and Mrs. St. Loe Strachey contributed a review of the "Shakespeare Ball Souvenir" to the *Spectator.*[81] (Lytton's sister Dorothy, though not herself a reviewer, taught Shakespeare at the Allenwood School before her marriage.)

The younger Stracheys disagreed with some of their cousin St. Loe's views. He was an admirer of Tennyson's poetry and a friend of Sir Evelyn Baring, Lord Cromer, whom he praised as "the greatest of living Imperialists."[82] (Lytton Strachey would later eviscerate Lord Cromer in *Eminent Victorians,* but they regarded him, as James would write, as "the kindest of friends and a most entertaining companion," possessed of "a highly romantic admiration for the Strachey family and a quite special affection for my mother, his Aunt Janie.")[83] The opportunity to write for the *Spectator* gave Lytton a chance to develop his style and opened the door to other opportunities. St. Loe, for his part, would come to regard Lytton and Lord Cromer as his best reviewers. He himself published a few articles on Shakespeare and toward the end of his time at the *Spectator* he spoke at a luncheon of the English-Speaking Union on Shakespeare Day, 1925, telling a congenial audience that Shakespeare is "the real patron saint of the English-speaking race," reminding them that "Carlyle, writing for our race as a whole, whether dwelling within these islands, the British Empire, or the United States of America," had declared that "we are all subjects of King Shakespeare."[84]

Lytton Strachey's article on Shakespeare's sonnets was one of his earliest pieces for the *Spectator.* From the autumn of 1907 through the spring of 1909 he wrote weekly reviews: the literary reviews were, according to *Spectator* policy, unsigned, but the theatre reviews—an innovation that some thought might worry the "vicarages" that were among the paper's most faithful readers—were signed Ignotus, so as—in James Strachey's phrase—"to insulate them from editorial responsibility."[85] Lytton ultimately tired of the weekly deadlines and turned his attention to longer essays and then to the writing of books. But the *Spectator* reviews give a good sense of his maturing style and of his continued interest in Shakespeare.

"Shakespeare's First Editors" praises Thomas Lounsbury's study of Alexander Pope and Lewis Theobald as "a book which deserves the attention of everyone interested in the history of English literature."[86] Strachey, a lifelong fan of Pope ("the greatest man of letters of two hundred years ago"), has no difficulty in condemning him as a terrible Shakespeare editor: "As one turns over the pages of his Shakespeare it is impossible not to be appalled by the mass of ignorance, stupidity, and bad taste which it contains."[87] By contrast, Theobald, famously ridiculed and maligned in Pope's *Dunciad,* should properly be regarded as "the greatest of Shakespearian scholars" who "revolutionized the study of Shakespeare" and "introduced the methods of science into literary criticism."[88] Pope's technique was to use his own taste as the unit of measurement; if he disliked a phrase he changed or cut it. Strachey, citing a passage that would become a touchstone of Shakespearean brilliance for Virginia Woolf, quotes Macbeth's

> This my hand will rather
> The multitudinous seas incarnadine,
> Making the green one red

and reports—following Lounsbury—that Pope "found the language turgid, and discarded the second line to a footnote." Since Pope objected to the metaphor in "Sleep, that knits up the raveled sleeve of care," he removed the line from the text. Equally problematic was the fact that he "made no serious effort to collate the various editions of Shakespeare."[89] Pope, indeed, was not interested in "editing" in any modern sense.

In this he differs sharply, and to his detriment, with Theobald, who not only collated previous editions but also made it his business to study earlier literature so as to understand what Shakespeare might have read and known. But he was not merely diligent and learned. Theobald's "genius," Strachey avers, his "flashing insight," is to be seen in his "brilliant and profound emendations" that "restored to the world, in a multitude of passages, the true meaning of Shakespeare." Here he cites a number of well-known cases from Lounsbury's book that have been accepted by subsequent scholars, pointing out that in more than one instance "if Theobald had never made the alteration the sense of the passage would have been entirely lost to many generations of readers."[90] These are all achievements worth commending; manifestly the Shakespeare we known today is indebted to Theobald, just as it had been deformed by Pope. But what provokes Strachey's very evident passion in this controversy? In part his feelings are marshaled against complacency and injustice. "The story is one of the least creditable in the annals of English scholarship." The "general chorus of obloquy and scorn" so heedlessly perpetuated by later eighteenth-century editors outrages him. Moreover, it is still to be heard in "our own day," he says, in a gratuitous insult voiced by the editor of the "latest and most complete" edition of Pope's works.[91] The insult is quoted; the editor's name is not.

The "calumnies of two hundred years" are Strachey's target as well as Lounsbury's. The ironic tone of this early review—especially noticeable when it addresses Pope's editorial practice ("Words which are to us neither obscure, nor in some cases even antiquated, appeared to Pope to be full of mystery. . . . He gravely informs his readers that 'eld' means old age, and 'gyves' shackles")—anticipates the unmasking of pretentiousness that would become a hallmark of Strachey's later biographies.[92] But in the essay's praise of Theobald's editorial brilliance and insight there is as well a particular concern about Shakespeare's language. Example after example illustrates the way Theobald's learned emendations would be borne out by modern scholarship. The Shakespeare that emerges from this short piece is a poet whose deftly chosen words are rescued by Theobald from the "footrule" and "compasses" of "literary surveyors."[93]

And it is also Shakespeare as poet that Strachey celebrates in his review of Walter Raleigh's *Johnson on Shakespeare,* published in the *Spectator* under the splendidly postmodern title "Shakespeare on Johnson." "Johnson was not, in essence, a critic of literature; he was a critic of life," says Strachey, "and it is this fact that accounts alike for the merits and the defects of his treatment of Shakespeare."[94] The merits derive from Johnson's common sense, his knowledge of humanity, and the fact that "he refuses to be dazzled by his author."[95] The defects arise from his resistance to Shakespeare's "bold and imaginative use of words." Johnson objected to Shakespeare's use of the words *knife, peep,* and *blanket* in a famous speech in *Macbeth,* dismissing them as "mean expressions."[96] He judged that Ariel's songs in *The Tempest,* though "seasonable and efficacious," nonetheless "express nothing great, nor reveal anything above mortal discovery." Strachey, who would become well known (and in some quarters notorious) for his criticisms of Shakespeare's late plays, here is astonished into a rebuke: "Do [the songs] not reveal a power of evoking enchanting imaginations by means of exquisite melody which has been discovered by very few mortals indeed, before or since? But such a question would have conveyed very little to Dr Johnson."[97]

Strachey concedes the power of Johnson's editorial exclamations about the heartrending conclusions of the tragedies (on the final scene of *Othello:* "I am glad that I have ended my revisal of this dreadful scene. It is not to be endured"; on the end of *King Lear:* "I might relate that I was many years ago so shocked by Cordelia's death, that I know not whether I ever endured to read again the last scenes of the play till I undertook to revise them as an editor"), but he is clear-eyed about what is at stake for Johnson in such scenes: "These appalling climaxes of passion and horror," he notes, "moved him through their humanity and not their poetry." In short, he declares in a sentence of singularly devastating critique, "It is hardly an exaggeration to say that Johnson's criticisms are such as might have been made by a foreigner of great ability and immense experience who was acquainted with Shakespeare solely in a prose translation."[98] Again it is Shakespeare as poet, Shakespeare's creative and often unconventional (that is, imaginative) use of language, that Strachey is defending against Johnson: "He could not see that it was in the very expressions to which he objected that the whole force and mystery of Macbeth's invocation lay; he completely failed, in fact, to realize the nature of the object which he believed himself to be discussing."[99] The proleptic postmodernism of the essay's title is here effectively fulfilled in a sentence of literary analysis that would seem at home in the most trenchant of deconstructive readings.

But Strachey, as we have seen, was not only a book reviewer for the *Spectator* but also its first theatre critic. In this role, under the byline Ignotus, he observed in "Shakespeare on the Stage" that while he understood the attitude of those who, like Charles Lamb, "refuse to see Shakespeare acted"—as well as those, like Lytton Strachey himself, who found a special "charm" in "the silent utterance of the poet to oneself alone"—it was nonetheless the case that the plays continued to be performed and were indeed "at the present moment," in April 1908, playing to full houses at the Lyceum (Matheson Lang's *Romeo and Juliet*) and His Majesty's (Herbert Beerbohm Tree's *The Merchant of Venice*). "It is impossible to blink the fact that, after three hundred years, Shakespeare's drama remains a living force upon the stage," he wrote. "And since this is so, it can only be regretted that literary critics persist in applying their powers exclusively to the literary side of Shakespeare's work and ignore altogether its relation to the art of acting."[100]

What Strachey had in mind, it soon became clear, was a wholesale critique of contemporary acting and directing, with their "histrionic" motives designed to produce "a series of well-marked climaxes, each climax being followed immediately by the fall of the curtain."[101] In Shakespeare's time there had been no front curtain, so changes in the action were indicated by changes in tone and mood. But in these West End productions transitional speeches were summarily cut so as to produce applause lines for the major actors. Commenting on a tonal shift at the end of the courtroom scene in *The Merchant of Venice,* when—after Shylock's exit—the minutiae of life goes on as usual, Strachey asks, "Could there be a more poignant summary of the relentless indifference with which the world looks upon a tragedy, and passes on? But actors will have none of this, because, being actors, it is only natural that they should prefer what is stagy to the image of life itself."[102]

Worse (even) than these directorial decisions was the actors' delivery of their lines. "Their object seems to be to buoy up the meaning of the words they utter by all the stage devices at their command—by exaggerated gesture and ceaseless movement, by forced laughter and preposterous sighings and undercurrents of incidental music, by an intolerable slowness of enunciation, and by an intonation of the blank verse more barbarous than can be described. These," says Strachey, "are merely the refuges of weakness, like the attempts of a bad writers to obtain emphasis by underlinings and italic type."[103] And as for the interpretation of characters, "Why is it that while in modern plays ladies and gentlemen are acted as ladies and gentlemen, in plays by Shakespeare they must be acted as minxes and buffoons? There seems to be a convention upon the stage that what is 'Shakespeare' cannot be natural," he laments. Instead it must be "propped up and decorated and explained."[104] Again the short-essay format of the *Spectator* allows Strachey an epigrammatic ending of a kind that he would continue to deploy in his later work: until theatres begin to recognize "the simple fact" that Shakespeare, if "truly great," will need no trickery, "we must be prepared to face the absurd anomaly of the greatest dramatist in the world being acted as if he were the worst."[105] The publication date of Ignotus's review was April 25—possibly as close as the weekly *Spectator* could get to the annual commemoration of Shakespeare Day (and St. George's Day), April 23.

The Marlowe Dramatic Society

In objecting to the dominance of old-style theatre managers and to a histrionic, actor-centric mode of performance, Strachey was expressing a point of view held by many of his friends in Bloomsbury and Cambridge and directly espoused by the organizers of the Marlowe Dramatic Society. The society was founded by Justin Brooke at King's College, Cambridge, in 1906, and he was soon joined by another undergraduate with the same surname, Rupert Brooke. Rupert had been at school with James Strachey, and James had told his brother Lytton about Rupert; Geoffrey Keynes had likewise alerted his older brother Maynard. Rupert had other connections, too, to Duncan Grant and the Stephen family, so that, as Tim Cribb points out in his history of the Marlowe Society, "even before he had set foot in King's the stage was well set for Rupert to bring the two groups together."[106] The Marlowe also attracted strong support among Cambridge scholars, including Francis Cornford at Trinity, John Sheppard at King's, and the distinguished founder of the Cambridge school of anthropology, Jane Ellen Harrison at Newnham. One of its earliest efforts was

Milton's masque *Comus,* with Rupert Brooke in the role of the Attendant Spirit. Following the guidelines of the society, no players were named in the program.

The Marlowe Society's initial plan was to perform plays by Shakespeare's contemporaries—as with the Midnight Society for play reading, the idea was to retrieve neglected works of the past. But this was soon expanded to include little-known Shakespeare plays and then to Shakespeare in general. Since, as Cribb observes, there had been no undergraduate production of Shakespeare at Cambridge since 1886, "in that respect he was as neglected as his contemporaries."[107] An early plan to produce *The Two Gentlemen of Verona* did not come off, but the society staged *Richard II* in February 1910, *Henry IV, Part 1* in June 1919, and *Troilus and Cressida* in March 1922. The war years had led to a hiatus, but after 1918 there was a burst of theatrical energy. What were called "bisexual" performances—that is, performances in which women as well as men were cast—were initially permitted by the vice chancellor only as unofficial events staged during the vacation.[108] (This ban was later reversed, and in the 1960s the future novelist Margaret Drabble, then a Cambridge undergraduate and later the first woman to become a member of the society's committee, starred as Imogen in a Rylands production of *Cymbeline.*)

Lytton Strachey's anonymous review of *Comus* for the *Spectator* in July 1908 focuses—after a characteristic jab at Milton's sententious "priggishness" ("Comus is a play of prigs. The Lady is a prig, and so is the Elder Brother, and so is the Attendant Spirit")—on the undergraduate actors' exceptional command of language. "How infinitely rarely does one hear, in any theatre, the beauty that is in blank verse! From this point of view, the performance at Cambridge was indeed memorable." The verse of Milton, declares Strachey, is more difficult than any in English to recite well, "with the exception of that of Shakespeare's latest manner"—a claim that he had also made in "Shakespeare's Final Period." And here he adds an indictment of current acting on the professional stage of a kind that would become familiar in Bloomsbury critiques: "The hideous and barbaric utterance with which, in our ordinary theatres, actors attempt to reproduce the poetry of Shakespeare is nothing short of a disgrace." In the absence of any training schools or tradition in England for the recitation of "one of the chief glories of the language—its dramatic verse," occasional failures are to be expected: some monotony, some inaudibility. But the "declamation of the company at Cambridge," with its enthusiastic love of poetry, is "at least an augury of better things."[109] In short, since the professionals were hopeless, it was with the amateurs that, for the moment, hope lay.

A little more than ten years later, in the aftermath of the war, "the company at Cambridge" received Strachey's even more enthusiastic endorsement for its production of *Henry IV, Part 1.* He begins by rejoicing in the return of peacetime energy to the universities. "The Marlowe Society is an undergraduate body, full of the spirit of youth; and it was primarily as a spontaneous expression of both the high purposes of youth and of youthful delight in beauty that its rendering of *Henry IV* must have struck the more mature among the audience. That young men should have come together, so soon and so eagerly, to enjoy themselves thus—with candour, with painstaking, with geniality—was surely an admirable thing."[110]

But this compliment to the resilience of the young was only the prolegomenon to the critic's assessment of the performance, and in the rest of his review—published in the *Athenaeum*—he had more good news to report, not only about the rising generation but also about the art and craft of Shakespearean acting.

> The first instantaneous impression was one of relief. The King was speaking. The *blasé* critic might well prick up his ears. How very rarely has a King been heard to speak on any stage! Yet that was what this King, unmistakably, was doing. He was neither mouthing, nor gesticulating, nor rolling his eyes, nor singing, nor chopping his words into mincemeat, nor dragging them out in slow torment up and down the diatonic scale; he was simply speaking; and as he spoke one became conscious of a singular satisfaction—of soothing harmonies, of lovely language flowing in fine cadences, of beautiful images unwinding beautifully, of the subtle union of thought and sound. He ceased, and another speaker followed, and yet another; and the charm remained unbroken. This, then, was the first surprise—the delight of hearing the blank verse of Shakespeare spoken unaffectedly and with the intonation of civilised English; the next was the perception of the fact that, given a good delivery of the verse, the interest of drama and character automatically followed.[111]

The problem with the professional acting of Shakespeare, in Strachey's view, was that it so little resembled the "instinctive" style of the amateur. What was needed was a "new tradition" in which the young actor could be taught that "he must preserve at all costs his natural enunciation, his economy of gesture, his sobriety of emotional expression, that it is his business, not to 'interpret' Shakespeare's words, but to speak them, that the first rule for acting Shakespeare is to trust him."[112] The production's director—unmentioned in the review—was Strachey's friend and fellow Apostle, John Sheppard.

The enormous success of *Eminent Victorians* in 1918 and then of *Queen Vic-*

toria in 1921 made it possible for Strachey to leave reviewing and to focus on the kind of writing that most interested him. But so long as his health permitted, Lytton continued to attend plays as well as to read them. He and Carrington planned to go together to see Frank Birch's production of *Coriolanus* at the Amateur Dramatic Club in Cambridge in the spring of 1928, but Lytton fell ill and could not go. (Carrington thought the lead actor "lovely, very proud and cruel with a tiger face.")[113] On other occasions they did go together, especially if the director was Lytton's friend Dadie Rylands. When the young John Gielgud, age twenty-seven, played Lear at the Old Vic in the spring of 1931, Strachey wrote to Roger Senhouse, "I am longing to hear about *King Lear.* All the reviews I've seen have been very favourable but one can't judge much from them. From what they said it sounded as if he'd got the hang of the part—for one thing not making Lear a decrepit and already half-cracked vieillard, as the actors generally do, thereby making nonsense of the whole thing; but I doubt whether his physique would have been equal to it—though I suppose with sufficient eminence one might get round this."[114]

The Biographer's Shakespeare

As they traveled together by train in June 1923, Strachey and Virginia Woolf "talked all the way," and one of their chief topics was Shakespeare. Lytton said "he wanted to write about Shre as a dramatist; not as a philosopher or poet," she noted. "He wanted to discuss his contrasts. The scene with Emilia in Othello for instance. And he may write on Lear from this point of view."[115] Strachey died before the Shakespeare book could be written, leaving only an unfinished piece on *Othello.* But his lifelong reading of Shakespeare allowed him to incorporate dramatic elements into his major work. Shakespeare in Strachey's three innovative biographies plays a range of roles, from offstage voice to canonical author to hidden architect of the plot. Each biography, in a different and distinctive way, not only links Shakespeare and Strachey but also offers a shrewd understanding of psychology, language, and the power of literary allusion.

SHAKESPEAREAN IRONY: *EMINENT VICTORIANS* (1918)

Strachey's habit of using Shakespearean citations as commentary on recent events, familiar from his letters and correspondence, carries over into the witty and ironic text of *Eminent Victorians.* Many of his quotations would have been recognizable to his readers, but he also seems to use them, in part, as a kind of conversation with himself.

Lytton Strachey and Virginia Woolf, photograph by Lady Ottoline Morrell, 1923

A typical example occurs in the chapter on Cardinal Manning, in which the Oxford religious zealot Hurrell Froude, described as a "clever young man to whom had fallen a rather larger share of self-assurance and intolerance than even clever young men usually possess," determines to convince his friend John Henry Newman of the preferable truth of Catholicism. Strachey has recourse here to one of his favorite literary devices, free indirect discourse, channeling Froude's thoughts: "All Oxford, all England, should know the truth. The time was out of joint, and he was only too delighted to have been born to set it right."[116] The uncertainty and self-doubt of Hamlet are neatly turned inside out. Of Newman's argument in his famous Tract 90 that the Thirty-Nine Articles of the Anglican faith were not incompatible with Roman Catholic belief, Strachey writes, "A man may be of a scrupulous and impeccable honesty, and yet his respect for the truth—it cannot be denied—may be insufficient. He may be, like the lunatic, the lover, and the poet, 'of imagination all compact'; he may be blessed, or cursed, with one of those 'seething brains,' one of those 'shaping fantasies,' that 'apprehend more than cool reason ever comprehends,' he may be by nature incapable of sifting evidence, or by predilection simply indisposed to do so."[117]

Theseus's indulgent dismissal of the fantasies of poets in *A Midsummer Night's Dream* is seamlessly juxtaposed with Newman's report, after his conversion to Catholicism, of seeing the liquefaction of St. Januarius's blood when he visited Naples. In the same chapter Strachey observes in passing that those cardinals who supported the doctrine of infallibility but insisted that it reposed in the Church and not in the bishop of Rome failed to realize that "the Catholic Church without the absolute dominion of the Pope might resemble the play of *Hamlet* without the Prince of Denmark."[118] The phrase, by this time a cliché, was nonetheless all too apt in this sometimes acerbic discussion in which Pius IX's internal debates are often noted, though as shrewdly political rather than earnestly self-questioning.

Strachey often cites Shakespeare obliquely to bring out an ironic point. Of the commanding power of Florence Nightingale, despite her demure appearance, he writes that "as for her voice, it was true of it, even more than of her countenance, that it 'had that in it that one must fain call master.'" The citation here is from the first act of *King Lear,* in which the banished Kent returns in disguise to offer his services to the king. The Shakespearean phrase is in quotation marks; catch it if you can. But Miss Nightingale, a young woman rather than an old man, is far more perceptive than Lear, and far more effective in managing her troops: "When she had spoken," without ever raising her voice, "it seemed as if nothing could follow but obedience."[119]

Familiar quotations are not always marked. Of an ill-fated Egyptian colonel mentioned in "The End of General Gordon," Strachey writes, "A new order was indeed upon the point of appearing: but it was of a kind undreamt of in Arábi's philosophy."[120] But when he comes to discuss the complex character of Prime Minister Gladstone the scare quotes reappear. "It was easy," he writes, "to detest him as a hypocrite, to despise him as a demagogue, and to dread him as a crafty manipulator. . . . 'The elements' were 'so mixed' in Mr Gladstone that his bitterest enemies (and his enemies were never mild) and his warmest friends (and his friends were never tepid) could justify, with equal plausibility, their denunciations or their praises."[121] The tell-tale quotation marks are the tipoff, if we need one, that some kind of literary analogy is afoot: the reference, presumably well known to Strachey's intended readers, is Brutus—the dead Brutus eulogized by Antony at the end of *Julius Caesar* as "the noblest Roman of them all."

> His life was gentle, and the elements
> So mixed in him that nature might stand up
> And say to all the world, "This was a man."
> (5.5.72–74)

Mark Antony's eulogy for Brutus is unqualified praise. His phrase "so mixed" means superbly balanced, the four humors perfectly in harmony with one another, no one predominating. But applied to Strachey's Gladstone the citation hints at the opposite; mixed means undigested, at odds; first one, then another temperament would take over. "Man is more various than nature; was Mr Gladstone perhaps a chimera of the spirit? Did his very essence lie in the confusion of incompatibles?"[122] This is the special Strachey genius. Little is lost if one does not catch the fleeting allusion; but a great deal is gained if one does. It is the very familiarity of these brief quotations, and the fame of the literary characters to whom they are linked, that enables the wit.

Later in the "General Gordon" chapter the narrator intervenes in his own voice, quoting from Shakespeare's Sonnet 94 to explain the ambition and dispassionate cruelty of Gordon's nemesis, Sir Evelyn Baring, the British consul general of Egypt:

> The greatest of poets, in a bitter mood, has described the characteristics of a certain class of persons, whom he did not like. "They," he says,
>
> that have power to hurt and will do none,
> That do not do the things they most do show,
> Who, moving others, are themselves as stone,
> Unmoved, cold, and to temptation slow,
> They rightly do inherit heaven's graces,
> And husband nature's riches from expense;
> They are the lords and owners of their faces. . . .
>
> The words might have been written for Sir Evelyn Baring.[123]

In this case Strachey's weapon is not wit but scorn—scorn and poetry. Baring, who, as Strachey notes, "had been careful to keep up his classics," spoke six languages, and looked forward to "a pleasant retirement" with "some literary recreations," had never bothered to learn Arabic, the language of the common Egyptian people.[124] This long chapter, the last in *Eminent Victorians,* ends with a blandly ironic sentence, a projection of the supposed general view: "At any rate, it had all ended very happily—in a glorious slaughter of 20,000 Arabs, a vast addition to the British Empire, and a step in the Peerage for Sir Evelyn Baring."[125]

By using the words of Shakespeare to frame the ultimate critique of men like Baring (later Lord Cromer), the privileged aristocrats who made the British Empire at the cost of human life and human feelings, Strachey is able to undercut the pretensions of this born-to-rule class by hoisting them on the petard of their own national poet. Cromer died in 1917; Strachey's book was published the following year. Like the last speeches in many of Shakespeare's history plays—

perhaps especially the epilogue to *Henry V,* in which the audience is reminded that everything Henry won was lost in the next generation, this move brings the narrative with startling force into the present moment.

SHAKESPEAREAN EDUCATION: *QUEEN VICTORIA* (1921)

Eminent Victorians made Lytton Strachey a best-selling author. Three years later he repeated his success with *Queen Victoria,* an unexpectedly affectionate—though also ironic—biographical portrait of the woman who gave her name to an era. And in this book, too, Shakespeare played a crucial cameo role.

Victoria became queen of England at the age of eighteen. She had not had much experience of the world's pleasures, but after her accession, as Strachey reports in the deadpan style he had made his signature,

> Occasionally, there were little diversions: the evening might be spent at the opera or at the play. Next morning, the royal critic was careful to note down her impressions:
>
> > It was Shakespeare's tragedy of *Hamlet*, and we came in at the beginning of it. Mr Charles Kean (son of old Kean) acted the part of Hamlet, and I must say beautifully. His conception of this very difficult, and I may almost say incomprehensible, character is admirable; his delivery of all the fine long speeches quite beautiful; he is excessively graceful and all his actions and attitudes are good, though not at all good-looking in face. . . . I came away just as *Hamlet* was over.
>
> Later on, she went to see Macready in *King Lear*. The story was new to her; she knew nothing about it, and at first she took very little interest in what was passing on the stage; she preferred to chatter and laugh with the Lord Chamberlain. But as the play went on, her mood changed; her attention was fixed, and then she laughed no more. Yet she was puzzled; it seemed a strange, a horrible business. What did Lord M. [Melbourne] think? Lord M. thought it was a very fine play, but, to be sure, a "rough, coarse play, written for those times, with exaggerated characters." "I'm glad you've seen it," he added. But, undoubtedly, the evenings which she enjoyed most were those on which there was dancing.[126]

In this little snapshot—what the eighteenth century might have called a "character"—the reader has all the information that will later be reiterated throughout the book. Hamlet as a persona is "difficult," indeed perhaps "incomprehensible"—to a strong-willed girl who would become a strong-willed queen; philosophical hesitation and existential doubt were unfamiliar, unrecognizable traits. She had never heard of *King Lear* and found the opening court scenes—and the warring daughters—without much interest. Her own father had died long before she came to the throne; she was an only child, brought up by women. But as the play progressed, she became more engaged. She learned enough from it to be disturbed by its events—or, as Strachey has it, "puzzled" by them.

The celebrated actor William Macready had been responsible for the restoration of Shakespeare's original text of *King Lear* to the stage in his 1838 production at the Covent Garden Theatre. (For the previous 150 years, theatre audiences in England had only seen Nahum Tate's happy-ending version, the 1681 *History of King Lear,* in which Cordelia lives and marries Edgar, and from which the part of the Fool had been excised as indecorous.) Lord Melbourne had doubtless seen Tate's *Lear,* but Macready's restored version would have been new to him, though he had surely read the play. His response as described by Strachey—a "rough, coarse play" but "I'm glad you've seen it"—nicely encapsulates his complex role: adviser, mentor, guide, father substitute, and loyal subject. There is no sense here or later in Strachey's biography that Victoria was moved to read *King Lear* herself or to engage further in her education with the works of Shakespeare. Lord M.'s "written for those times" might well have seemed to suggest that it was not relevant to hers.

Indeed, during her extended period of mourning, Victoria eschewed all theatrical pleasures. Only "after an interval of thirty years" did she resume "the custom of commanding dramatic companies from London to perform before the Court at Windsor." And even then her taste was not necessarily for the classics. "She loved acting; she loved a good plot; above all she loved a farce," Strachey says. "Engrossed by everything that passed upon the stage she would follow, with childlike innocence, the unwinding of the story; or she would assume an air of knowing superiority and exclaim in triumph, 'There! You didn't expect *that,* did you?' when the *dénouement* came. Her sense of humour was of a vigorous though primitive kind."[127]

Other Shakespearean touches in *Queen Victoria* are few and momentary, though each adds to the portrait. Disraeli's famous pet name for Victoria, "the Faery," was drawn from Spenser's *Faerie Queene,* but on at least one occasion he had called her "Titania." He alludes to the "enchanted Isle," and at one point the queen, infuriated by her old enemies, the Russians, during the conflict between Russia and Turkey, writes to him in a phrase that—although she surely did not know it—echoes the frustrated words of Beatrice in *Much Ado About Nothing:* "Oh," Victoria exclaims in her letter to Disraeli, "if the Queen were a man, she would like to go and give those Russians, whose word one cannot believe, such a beating!"[128] (Beatrice, appalled by Claudio's slandering her cousin Hero, had exclaimed, "O God that I were a man! I would eat his heart in the market place" *Much Ado About Nothing* [4.1.302–3].)

There is, interestingly, no mention in Strachey's biography of how important Shakespeare was to Prince Albert. As a young man in Coburg he was taught English vocabulary by his tutor through the painstaking exercise of glossing the words in *Hamlet:* "to befit," "self-slaughter," "jelly," "fowl," "melt," "thaw," and so on. His political mentors, Count Stockmar chief among them, were already planning for him to marry the heiress to the English throne. When Albert's own children were born he made sure that they, too, were exposed to Shakespeare. "Vicky [the Princess Royal] recited the whole scene of Shylock before the court in *The Merchant of Venice,*" he wrote proudly to his old tutor.[129] His eldest son, Bertie—always to be a disappointment to his parents—"was called upon to recite the all-too-apt scene in *Henry IV Part One* in which, supposing his father to be dead, Prince Hal placed the crown on his own head."[130] The materials containing these details are now in the Royal Archives at Windsor. It is fascinating to think what Strachey might have made of them.

SHAKESPEAREAN APOTHEOSIS: *ELIZABETH AND ESSEX* (1928)

Strachey's third great historical biography is clearly linked to Shakespeare and Elizabethan drama in its subject matter and also in its form. "The age," Strachey tells us in the opening pages, "was that of Marlowe and Spenser, of the early Shakespeare and the Francis Bacon of the Essays." Thus characterized, it "needs no description: everybody knows its outward appearances and the literary expressions of its heart." Yet the period seemed to him nonetheless "remote" from present-day sensibilities. "With very few exceptions—possibly with the single exception of Shakespeare," he writes, "the creatures in it meet us without intimacy; they are exterior visions, which we know, but do not truly understand."[131]

T. S. Eliot, reviewing Strachey's book in the *Times Literary Supplement,* immediately identified its affinities with Shakespeare. *Elizabeth and Essex,* wrote Eliot,

> is a "tragic history"; and it is not only of dramatic material, but is treated with dramatic skill. So dramatic is it that we forget at times that it is history at all. Yet it has its perfectly correct historical face. Dialogue is restricted to a minimum—only words actually reported, and quotations of letters skillfully embroidered into the text. It is only occasionally, with

> one of Mr Strachey's characteristic devices—one which is dangerous for him, and fatal for anyone else—the reverie, the thoughts and dreams which some person may be supposed to have indulged at some critical moment, as of death, that we are reminded that this is drama, of a peculiar kind, more than history.[132]

Eliot has his eye on the Shakespearean parallels throughout. Robert Cecil is a figure "always kept behind the arras."[133] (Strachey had called it a "curtain," but "behind the arras" immediately invokes Polonius concealed in *his* queen's closet.) He describes Francis Bacon, Strachey's Machiavellian villain, as "a dramatic figure, flashing and glittering before us."[134] And his review closes with a summation that insists upon both "drama" and "Shakespeare":

> It is part of [Strachey's] dramatic gift to be able to give us the feeling, and the impatience, of intolerable delays and shifts and changes, and the rush of sudden events as well. For this reason we want to read the book at a sitting; we could no more insert a bookmark until tomorrow than we could see a play by going to a different act each night. The account of the tumult in the city is as exciting as the brawl of a Shakespearian mob, and instills the sense of the destiny and doom of Essex. And the last paragraph of the book, after Elizabeth has expired, reads like the chorus at the end of a tragedy. The last figure on the stage is that of Robert Cecil, first Earl of Salisbury.[135]

Other contemporary readers also recognized the connection between *Elizabeth and Essex* and *Antony and Cleopatra.* Francis Birrell, a friend since Cambridge, noted in an appreciation written for a French journal shortly after Strachey's death that *Elizabeth and Essex* resembled a dramatic composition in both form and plot, and pointed out its many correspondences with Shakespeare's play. Desmond MacCarthy cited Birrell, translating his key paragraph directly, in his own memorial essay on Strachey, published in 1934:

> The long meditations attributed to Elizabeth, to Essex, to Bacon, and Cecil, are monologues inspired by those of the Elizabethan drama, where the protagonist often occupies the stage alone, delivering in poetry the passions and perplexities which divide his soul. Like Antony, Essex leaves and returns to his Queen; like Antony he dies a violent death. The passage, so carefully weighed, with which the book ends, where Cecil is seen at his writing table, brooding over the future of England and the destiny of his own house, is also an invention borrowed from the Elizabethan

> stage. Does not *Antony and Cleopatra* close with the triumph of Octavius, *Hamlet* with the crowning of Fortinbras?[136]

Some years later Strachey's biographer Michael Holroyd offered a similar comparison, declaring that "*Elizabeth and Essex* is his *Antony and Cleopatra*" and noting the book's relation to Strachey's early blank verse play, *Essex: A Tragedy.*[137] Citing Strachey's review of a book on Roman history, Holroyd suggested that "passion" was the supreme motive in *Elizabeth and Essex.*[138] "There is only one thing which could have blinded a man in Antony's position so completely as we now know he actually was blinded," Strachey had argued, "and that thing is passion. It was not the sophisms but the charms of Cleopatra which led Antony to his ruin. The world might be lost if he fled to Egypt, but it would be well lost; it would be lost with Cleopatra. Is not that the only possible explanation of what occurred?"[139] *Passion,* in fact, was a word with a special significance for Strachey, both in literature and in life. Bertrand Russell recalled a conversation with him during which they debated "what literature should aim at." After Strachey rejected one possibility after another, Russell asked him directly, "'Well, Lytton, what should it aim at?' And he replied in one word—'Passion.'"[140]

T. S. Eliot's review had emphasized not only Strachey's dramatic achievement but also his historical insight into character. "The author's presentation of his chief figures"—Essex, Bacon, and Queen Elizabeth—was, Eliot thought, "as near to the right historical judgment as posterity can ever arrive."[141] In this opinion, though for quite different reasons, Eliot was in accord with another shrewd reader of Shakespeare, Strachey, and human character—Sigmund Freud.

Freud, who admired all of Lytton Strachey's books, wrote him after reading *Elizabeth and Essex*, "This time you have moved me deeply, for you yourself have reached greater depths." As a historian "steeped in the spirit of psychoanalysis," Freud said, "you have approached one of the most remarkable figures in your country's history, you have known how to trace back her character to the impressions of her childhood, you have touched upon her most hidden motives with equal boldness and discretion, and it is very possible that you have succeeded in making a correct reconstruction of what actually occurred."[142] In his letter Freud took the occasion to offer some thoughts of his own on Shakespeare and Elizabeth:

> My opinion is that it was Elizabeth—the childless woman—who suggested to Shakespeare the character of his Lady Macbeth, about whom he found so little in historical sources. When in Act V, scene 5, the cry goes up, "The queen is dead," the Londoner of that time may have been

> reminded of how recently he had heard the same news, so that the identification of the two queens was brought home to him. Reports of Elizabeth's depression and remorse after Essex's execution might have given the poet material for the portrayal of Lady Macbeth's tortured conscience. Indeed, Elizabeth had also put to death a guest who trusted her (Mary Stuart), and this murder might have made him think of Essex. It is just possible, I thought, that contemporary history is visible to this degree through the elaboration of legendary material. Shakespeare was compelled to distribute Elizabeth's character between two persons, Macbeth and his Lady, but they complement each other and thereby show that they are actually only one human being. In the two Macbeths, Elizabeth's indecisiveness is portrayed along with her harshness and remorse. If she really was a hysteric, as Lytton Strachey diagnoses her, perhaps the great psychologist was not incorrect when he split her up into two persons.[143]

The "great psychologist" in the last line is—needless to say—Freud's characterization of Shakespeare. In an early essay, "Some Character-Types Met with in Psycho-Analytic Work" (1916), Freud had offered his own perceptive analysis of Lady Macbeth, in which the argument for the "split . . . into two persons" is clearly set forth.[144] There may be two "great psychologists" to be detected here, as well as two Elizabeths and two Macbeths.

The English historian and Cambridge Apostle George Trevelyan, with whom Strachey had often jousted in the past, congratulated him on *Elizabeth and Essex,* which he thought "much your greatest work," adding that it had been written "about people to whom you are spiritually akin—far more akin than to the Victorians. And it is not a piece of satire but a piece of life."[145] Virginia Woolf and others had reservations (Woolf thought it "meretricious" and a "bad book"; the things Freud praised were among those that irritated or disconcerted her).[146] But the book was enormously popular both in Britain and the United States, selling 110,000 hardback copies in the former and 150,000 hardback copies in the latter.[147]

It may be worth pausing for a moment on Woolf's objections, which in part, as she acknowledged, stemmed from professional rivalry: "Though I am (& I think we all are) secretly pleased to find Lytton's book is a bad one, I also feel depressed. If I were to analyse, the truth I think is that the pleasure is mean, & therefore not deep or satisfying; one would, in the depths, have got real pleasure, though superficial pain, had E & E been a masterpiece. . . . It is so feeble, and so shallow; & yet Lytton in himself is neither. . . . And Dadie & Pernel &

Janie Bussy & Dorothy [Bussy] all declared with emotion that this book was his best!"[148] Pernel and Dorothy were Lytton's sisters; Janie was his niece.

This diary entry was written on November 28, 1928, which Woolf notes is "Father's birthday." In fact, this is the famous entry in which Woolf observes that if Leslie Stephen had lived "his life would have entirely ended mine."[149] She would have written no books, would not have become herself. Might a reader, whether psychoanalytically inclined or not, observe that *Elizabeth and Essex* is also a book about the complex relationship between a father and a daughter? Strachey's Elizabeth remembers her father's magnificence, his pride in her, his obtrusive masculinity—and also his murder of her mother.[150] She is also conscious of her sense of competition with Essex for public favor and her pleasure at her renewed and heightened popularity after his death.[151]

When Woolf did sit down with Strachey to tell him her criticisms of his book ("His suppression of irony; his being tied by the story; the difficulty of using reality imaginatively; a wrong subject for him; could only be treated exactly")—many of which she would revisit in an essay on the future of biography—she experienced not only a certain schadenfreude ("I felt, among the discreditable feelings, how I had no longer anything to envy him for; & how, dashing off Orlando I had done better than he had done") but also a victory for Bloomsbury ("and this is what I liked—that though his surrounders—Carrington, Dadie & the rest—all praised, he himself felt, he was not pleased unless we Bloomsbury, praised too. What we said mattered.").[152] "Surrounders" here are courtiers, if not flatterers. "We Bloomsbury" are something else: history? family? intellectual aristocracy? enduring quality and "the good"? ("For the first time I think he thought of me as a writer, with some envy.")[153] If Virginia is Elizabeth-the-daughter to Leslie Stephen's Henry VIII in one diary entry, she is also Elizabeth-the-queen to Strachey's Essex in another.

To read *Elizabeth and Essex* as "Strachey's *Antony and Cleopatra*" is to read psychoanalytically, allegorically, and transferentially. "You seem, on the whole, to imagine yourself as Elizabeth, " Maynard Keynes wrote perceptively to Strachey in 1928 when the book was published, "but I see from the pictures that it is Essex whom you have got up as yourself."[154] A glance at the portraits reproduced in the original 1928 Chatto and Windus edition suggests that each has a touch of Strachey: the tall, slim, elegant, and bearded Essex and the watchful queen, a flower held in her long, thin fingers.[155] Both Elizabeth and Essex, the old shrewd queen and the handsome, impetuous boy, were aspects of Strachey's persona, just as his young lover Roger Senhouse might be seen as an Essex.

Notably, in this last of his great triad of biographies Strachey does not allude to any work of Shakespeare, nor does he quote him, though he does mention his name, together with those of Spenser and Marlowe, in describing the great writers of the era. In *Orlando,* a book published in the same year and often compared to *Elizabeth and Essex,* Virginia Woolf has "Sh—p—re" make a number of Hitchcock-like cameo appearances. This would have been easy for Strachey to do, but he does not. Instead his great author figure is the book's other absorbing "enigma," Robert Cecil.[156] For although Holroyd's view of Cecil as an Octavius Caesar fits the analogy between the biography and Shakespeare's play, there is another role for Cecil here as well.

In the closing moments of the book, as "anxious courtiers" offstage bend over "the haggard husk" of a sleeping form, "all that was left of Queen Elizabeth," narrative attention reverts at the last to a scene of writing and to Robert Cecil:

> But meanwhile, in an inner chamber, at his table, alone, the Secretary sat writing.
>
> All eventualities had been foreseen, everything was arranged, only the last soft touches remained to be given. The momentous transition would come now with exquisite facility. As the hand moved, the mind moved too, ranging sadly over the vicissitudes of mortal beings, reflecting upon the revolutions of kingdoms, and dreaming, with quiet clarity, of what the hours, even then, were bringing—the union of two nations—the triumph of the new rulers—success, power, and riches—a name in after ages—a noble lineage—a great House.[157]

Cecil, with his crooked posture and his brilliant mind, of whom we had earlier been told that he was "not cynical—he was not aloof enough for that—but sad," is here revealed as the author of all that has gone before.[158] His circumstances may remind us of Strachey himself, once caricatured for his physical appearance, now at the height of his own success, power, and riches, yet still an onlooker, the biographer "ranging sadly over the vicissitudes of mortal beings" as his hand moves over the pages he has written. At the same time the image might perhaps bring to mind the Escher-like closing moments of Peter Greenaway's *Prospero's Books* (1991), when the manuscript that Prospero (John Gielgud) has been writing throughout the film is revealed to be *The Tempest.* Strachey's Cecil, like Gielgud's Prospero, emerges at the end of the work as the mastermind who has arranged the story before our eyes and made its progress seem inevitable.

Strachey's Final Period

In December 1931, Virginia Woolf wrote Strachey a cheerfully affectionate letter: "I'm recumbent, lazy, content, reading book after book. And what are you doing? Reading Shakespeare I hope and occasionally making a note very neatly in a very beautiful book. By the way I read As you like it the other day and was almost sending you a wire to ask what is the truth about Jacques [*sic*]—What is it? His last speech reads so very odd."[159]

At the end of *As You Like It,* the witty and ironical Jaques—often described in the play as "melancholy"—announces that he will absent himself from the marriage celebrations and the dance that traditionally end dramatic comedy: "To your pleasures," he tells his friends. "I am for other than for dancing measures." The "last speech" to which Woolf alludes, "To see no pastime, I; What you would have / I'll stay to know at your abandoned cave" (5.4.184–85) reflects Jaques's decision to remain as a contemplative in the woods with the converted Duke Frederick rather than rejoin the lively society of the court. In hindsight the passage reads with some unintended pathos, given Strachey's worsening condition. But Woolf had no idea when she wrote that he was so ill, though she would soon hear. Her vision of him reading Shakespeare and making occasional notes "very neatly in a very beautiful book" is at the same time idealized and plausible; it reflects both her love for him and her sense of his taste and style.

Strachey briefly rallied at the very end of December, after his friends had given up hope. Encouraged by the (temporary) good news passed on by Vanessa, Virginia Woolf wrote in her diary on December 27, "I am therefore freely imagining a future with my old serpent to talk to, to laugh at, to abuse: I shall read his book on Shre; I shall stay at Ham Spray; I shall tell him how L. and I sobbed on Christmas Eve."[160] The book on Shakespeare was Lytton's projected collection of essays, to begin with a piece on *Othello.*[161] The "old serpent" could be any old serpent with a sharp tongue and a flickering wit, but I like to think it referred, at least glancingly, to Antony's affectionate name for Cleopatra as she quotes him at the beginning of the play: "Where's my serpent of old Nile?" (1.2.25).

Strachey died the following month, on January 21, 1932. A devastated Carrington found herself occupied in answering letters from kind friends, giving away Lytton's clothes and other keepsakes, and facing the fact that she would never see him again. A few weeks later the Woolfs went down to Ham Spray to see her. "He was going to write about Shakespeare," Carrington said to them. "It was ironical, his dying, wasnt it. He thought he was getting better. He said things like Lear when he was ill."[162] The next day she shot herself. Virginia reported this conversation in her diary on March 12, the day after Carrington's suicide.

THE ECONOMIST: MAYNARD KEYNES

When Roger Fry had lunch with his old friend Maynard Keynes at King's College, Cambridge, in May 1930, he found him "very charming" and "full of his own ideas about financial history which are rather fascinating. He thinks he can show exactly how much inflation of currency is necessary to produce an outburst of artistic creation. He says that if Shakespeare had been born fifty years earlier England couldn't have afforded him."[163]

Keynes's mention of Shakespeare in connection with England's primacy in the arts was not merely a casual reference. Once he had achieved wealth and power as an economist he worked actively to create—and often to fund—institutions conducive to the support of art, theatre, and performance. His early admiration for Shakespeare's work would inform both his writing and his professional and personal life.

John Maynard Keynes spent his childhood in Cambridge. His father, John Neville Keynes, an economist and university administrator, was "addicted to Theatre at all levels," wrote Dadie Rylands, "and the family were inveterate playgoers." His parents often took him to see productions at the New Theatre, founded in 1896 by Herbert Beerbohm Tree.[164] Keynes's mother, Florence, a social reformer, credited these early experiences of performances like the plays produced by F. R. Benson's touring Shakespeare Company with inspiring "that love of drama which developed throughout his life and led to his building the Arts Theatre as a gift to the Borough of Cambridge."[165] "Keynes admired artists above all others," says his biographer Robert Skidelsky. He "had well-developed aesthetic tastes of his own, especially for poetry, Shakespeare in particular." And "he loved the dramatic arts best of all."[166]

At Eton, when he was not winning prizes in mathematics or divinity—or, as his fond mother reports, "blossom[ing] out into a fancy waistcoat" as a member of the elite Eton Society known as Pop—Keynes was a member of the Shakespeare Society.[167] At the Fourth of June celebration in 1902 he took the part of Dogberry in *Much Ado About Nothing;* the bumbling constable Dogberry with his famous malapropisms was, whether intended or not, the antitype of the eloquent young Keynes. When he moved on to the University of Cambridge and became president of the Cambridge Union, he wrote to his friend

John Maynard Keynes, photograph by Walter Stoneman, 1930

Bernard Swithinbank, "I find my chief comfort more and more in Messrs. Plato and Shakespeare. Why is it so difficult to find a true combination of passion and intellect? My heroes must feel and feel passionately—but they must see too, everything and more than everything."[168]

Another of Keynes's heroes was the philosopher G. E. Moore, whom he also grouped with Shakespeare: Moore "lives with Socrates, Shakespeare, and Tomlinson—the trinity of our holy faith," he wrote to Lytton Strachey.[169] "Tomlinson" was George Tomlinson, who founded the Cambridge Conversazione Society, aka the Apostles, in 1820; Moore, like Keynes and Strachey, was a leading figure in the society at the beginning of the twentieth century and the author of their key text, the *Principia Ethica.* ("Socrates and Shakespeare" is a variant of the "Plato and Shakespeare" pairing that headed the ranked list compiled by Strachey, Leonard Woolf, and Saxon Sydney-Turner.)

In 1906 Keynes read a paper to the Apostles, titled "Egoism," in which he rhetorically speculated on how the world might judge someone who "elected to sup with Plato and Shakespeare in Paradise" rather than to suffer on earth "through eternity" to assist others who were in need.[170] A few weeks previously, just before Christmas, he had bought the "most beautiful" forty volumes of Shakespeare's complete works.[171] He was "a collector who *read,*" said Dadie Rylands. "Noting that performances of *Hamlet* at Cambridge and Oxford are recorded in the introduction to the First Folio," Keynes asked him, "What Elizabethan play had the greatest number of editions before 1640?" On another occasion, his question was "Do I think Drayton's *Idea* influenced Shakespeare's Sonnets?"[172]

Plato and Shakespeare; Socrates, Shakespeare, Tomlinson, and Moore. Throughout his life, Keynes returned again and again to Shakespeare as the measuring stick for passion and intellect—and the chief example of the value of his own economic theory. His friend Virginia Woolf would compare him to Shakespeare in his quickness of thought: "When he gave me some pages of his new book [on monetary reform] to read," she wrote in her diary, "the process of mind there displayed is as far ahead of me as Shakespeare's."[173]

Shakespeare the Economist

"Shakespeare, like Newton and Darwin, died rich," wrote Keynes in *The Applied Theory of Money* (1930). "His active career chanced to fall at the date of dates, when any level-headed person in England disposed to make money could hardly help doing so. 1575 to 1620 were the palmy days of profit—one of the greatest 'bull' movements ever known until modern days in the United States (with some bad years, of course, due to harvests, plague, commercial crises and chances of war—1587, 1596, 1603)—Shakespeare being eleven years old in 1575 and dying in 1616. I offer it as a thesis for examination by those who like rash generalisations, that by far the larger proportion of the world's greatest writers and artists have flourished in the atmosphere of buoyancy, exhilaration and the freedom from economic cares felt by the governing class, which is engendered by profit inflations."[174] In fact, Keynes remarked, since England had fortunately escaped the depression in prices that afflicted both Spain and France at the beginning of the seventeenth century, "We were just in a financial position to afford Shakespeare at the moment that he presented himself."[175]

This is the Keynes who would ten years later found the Committee for the Encouragement of Arts and Music, taking its chair in 1942. The connection between creativity and economic prosperity remained important to him throughout his life and marked his own later career. That Shakespeare was his chosen example here may be in part a sign of the times, but he was clearly fond of this particular grouping, repeating it in his essay on Newton: "Newton died rich as well as famous—like Shakespeare, Darwin, and Shaw."[176] A century later, it is hard to know which is more surprising: that a top economist would think through and with Shakespeare, or that he would expect his readers to recognize his references.

Equivocation and the Primrose Path

In *The Economic Consequences of the Peace* (1919), written in white-hot anger and deep despair after what he saw as the disastrous "peace" treaty with Germany, Keynes invoked the spirit of Shakespeare, specifically the language of *Macbeth*. "The word was issued to the witches of all Paris," he wrote,

> Fair is foul, and foul is fair,
> Hover through the fog and filthy air.

In order to satisfy the vain "self-deception" of President Woodrow Wilson, the participants "began the weaving of that web of sophistry and Jesuitical exegesis that was finally to clothe with insincerity the language and substance of the whole Treaty," Keynes declared.[177] Another name for "Jesuitical exegesis" in the Jacobean period was "equivocation," a key word in *Macbeth*—not only in the witches' lines above, but also in the porter's performance as keeper of hell gate ("come in, equivocator") and in Macbeth's despairing recognition of the "equivocation of the fiend that lies like truth" (5.5.42–43). The Gunpowder Plot conspirator Father Henry Garnet had written the *Treatise of Equivocation* in which he advocated the practice of "mental reservation," speaking in ambiguous terms to others while knowing a different truth in one's heart; Garnet was executed in 1606 for his part in the conspiracy. Through such citations, direct and indirect, Keynes indicts the signers of the treaty.

Nor was he finished with them, or with *Macbeth*. In 1922, reviewing Keynes's book *A Revision of the Treaty* in the *New York Times Book Review*, the American lawyer David Hunter Miller—who had been the U.S. adviser at the 1918 Peace Conference and had harshly attacked *The Economic Consequences of the Peace*—took a sarcastic swipe at what he felt to be the infelicity of the economist author's literary style. "Mr Keynes," he wrote, "goes so far as to speak of Mr Lloyd George handing us 'down the primrose path,' and then putting out the bonfire. We do not have primrose paths in America, but I should think that the sight of one with a bonfire down it would be rather queer even in England. Politics makes strange metaphors."[178]

Keynes quoted this passage in his own letter to the editor of the *Times Book Review,* adding gleefully:

> No! Not politics, poetry. Even in his literary cavillings Mr Miller has no luck. For, as there are no primrose paths in America, how was he to know that I was echoing the words of a porter (or *commissionaire*) who in a play *Macbeth,* by an author well known in England, speaks of those "that go the primrose way to the everlasting bonfire"? (In writing "*path*" instead of "*way,*" I was vaguely influenced, through the mixed complex of associations which makes the atmosphere of a word, by another passage where Ophelia describes the moralist who
>
> Himself the primrose path of dalliance treads
> And recks not his own rede.
>
> What explanations, in these days, a poor author has to make! And what waste of words it is!

He concluded his letter by observing, "I am not quite sure that there may not be, after all, some 'primrose paths in America'—and bonfires down them."[179] Whether by accident or not, Keynes's letter was dated April 23—the traditional date of Shakespeare's birthday. As Martin Harries notes, Keynes implies that Miller's "failure to recognize the Shakespearean provenance of his phrase" is equivalent to "other sorts of interpretative failures, political as well as poetic."[180]

Miller, offered a chance to reply—and not having learned his lesson—returned to this question, seeking to have the last word: "In its relation to the Treaty of Versailles, any question of Shakespearean learning is of little importance. In my review I smiled at the idea of Mr Lloyd George putting out the bonfire, an idea which hardly seems to me to echo the metaphor of the 'everlasting bonfire' but I shall not waste time on literary differences or distinctions which in a discussion of grave issues are trifles light as air."[181] It is hard to believe that Miller did not realize that he was quoting Iago here. But it is equally hard to believe that he did.

The inverse snobbism of "We don't have primrose paths here in America," neatly met and countered by Keynes's mention of "an author well known in England," all too easily encapsulates the debate, which—despite Miller's claim—is not trivial. A lawyerly approach that regards literary discussion and allusion as a waste of time will inevitably raise questions about the weight and meaning of words in other documents and the degree to which they are fully understood.

The glancing mention of Ophelia's advice to Laertes cautioning him as he goes off to France to avoid the hypocrisy of "Do as I say, not as I do" is also presumably lost on Keynes's interlocutor, deftly couched as it is in the form of an apologia for a minor misquotation.

Macbeth was the play that haunted Keynes above all others, at least when it came to politics and the dangerous foibles of politicians. Much later, on the brink of the Second World War, he published a scathing critique of Prime Minister Neville Chamberlain in the *New Statesman and Nation:* "He is not escaping the risks of war. He is only making sure that, when it comes, we shall have no friends and no common cause. He is forgetting the imponderables of the world, the power of courageous bearing, the majesty of right action, the comfort and stiffening to our friends of faithful words and counsel. He is leaving all the imponderables to the other side, allowing them to exploit the foreseen and the inevitable for purposes of terror and prestige. Yet what a response an act of constructive statesmanship would evoke! Is it impossible to build a bridge between 'I dare not' and 'I would'"?"[182]

Malthusian Shakespeare

A far more playful piece of Shakespearean badinage came Keynes's way courtesy of C. R. (Charles Ryle) Fay, an economic historian who had been his contemporary at King's College and was a professor of economics at Toronto; he would later return to Cambridge as a Reader.

In the fall of 1923 Keynes had been embroiled in a controversy with Sir William Beveridge, the new director of the London School of Economics, about the question of population growth and its relation to the economy. Keynes, at that time and for some years afterward a neo-Malthusian, had argued that "the problem of unemployment is . . . in part a problem of population," and that living standards could rise only if the rate of population growth were to slow down.[183] (In a laudatory essay on Malthus, delivered in its earliest form in 1914 under the title "Is the Problem of Population a Pressing and Important One Now?" and then revised and expanded in 1922 and 1924 before its publication in 1933, Keynes had hailed him as "the first of the Cambridge economists" and "a great pioneer.")[184] But Beveridge, in his Presidential Address to the LSE, maintained that what was needed was not birth control but free trade.

On March 27, 1924, Fay—himself an advocate of cooperation, women's rights, and workers' rights—sent the following letter to Keynes:

Dear Malthus,

For more than a century you have been worrying about it and all the while the answer was in Shakespeare's *Tempest,* Act II, Sc. 1.

> *Gonzalo.* Had I plantation of this isle, my lord—
> . . .
> All things in common nature should produce
> Without sweat or endeavour . . .
> nature should bring forth
> Of its own kind, all foison, all abundance,
> To feed my innocent people.
> *Sebastian.* No marrying 'mong his subjects?
> *Antonio.* None, man; *all idle; whores and knaves.*

In other words, leave the wheat crop alone. Concentrate on human beings. 10 years of Labour government will turn the unskilled labourers into idle knaves. 10 years of life in factories and in the streets will turn the females into the social equivalent of whores, i.e., copulators without issue.

It was you and your school who from 1798 onward exalted work and childbearing into virtues and so disturbed nature's balance.

But you will say, I have always opposed population. No, you have encouraged it. If men work, women will labour. If men are idle, women will be idle too. Paris knows this, Paris lives up to it. But Paris is frightened, because London and Berlin and the Pope will not follow suit. So [?] in your next Summer School, men & women in equal numbers; take as your subject all play and no work, & see that the women understand their part in it: and "thus by contraries execute all things."

No charge for this instruction.

Yrs.,
C. R. FAY[185]

Keynes's Shakespearean Economists

The assessment of Malthus appeared in the first edition of Keynes's *Essays in Biography* in 1933. A revised and expanded version of the book was published in 1951, after his death. Among the works were "Sketches of Politicians," essays on Newton and Einstein, two memoirs (including his famous presentation to the

Bloomsbury Memoir Club, "My Early Beliefs"), accounts of some friends from King's College, and a section called "Lives of Economists," many of which began as obituary notices in the *Economic Journal,* of which Keynes was editor. With the possible exception of the pieces on Newton and Einstein—and I would not really except even those—it is arguable that all of these categories and individuals served either as models or as cautionary warnings for Keynes over the course of his varied and storied career. It's of some interest, then, that Shakespeare makes several appearances in these pages.

Keynes's highly praised essay on the economist William Stanley Jevons (1835–82), for example, includes an excerpt from Jevons's journal from 1863 lamenting the fact that his pamphlet *Gold* had attracted little attention—except from his sister. Although it would later receive more notice, *Gold* sold only seventy-four copies. Jevons muses on ways he could have built up an admiring audience for his work: "Get friends, and impress them with your cleverness. Send them about to advertise your cleverness, get their testimonials like so many levers to force yourself where you wish to go." At this point he adds in his journal entry, written only for his own perusal, "How well did Shakespeare see through all these things when he wrote his sixty-sixth sonnet."[186] Acknowledging that "the praise or admiration" of friends and acquaintances "must be sweet," Jevons vowed in his journal, "I must go upon a different tack," and set about to make his book *The Coal Question* a best seller.[187] What intrigues me here is the casual mention of a Shakespeare sonnet, perhaps not one of his most famous, as the natural association in a nineteenth-century economist's private thought. Keynes could easily have cut this reference when he quoted from Jevons's journal—it's not directly relevant to the story he is telling. But he lets it stand, and it seems to me therefore to function as a sign, both to Keynes and to his audience: economists, great economists, read literature, read poetry, read Shakespeare—and can apply what they learn there to the business at hand.

Jevons died the year before Maynard Keynes was born—and the year after Malthus's death. But Keynes notes in the opening paragraph of his account that Jevons had "examined my father in the Moral Sciences Tripos of 1875, his name being known to me from my early years as, in my father's mind, the pattern of what an economist and logician should be."[188] Keynes is fond of these small personal details, part of what he called in his 1933 preface to *Essays in Biography* "the solidarity and historical continuity of the Higher Intelligentsia of England."[189] He likewise notes in his essay on Malthus that Malthus's house in Haileybury, where he lived for thirty years until his death, later became the home of Sir James Stephen, the last holder of Malthus's chair and the father of Leslie

Stephen.[190] Keynes's term "the Higher Intelligentsia" is, I think, the equivalent, and perhaps the forerunner, of Noel Annan's later coinage, the "Intellectual Aristocracy."[191] As Robert Skidelsky points out, Keynes's idea of civilization, centered on the model of King's, was "an endowed aristocracy of learning and the arts, with a strong sense of duty."[192]

Although Keynes had not known Stanley Jevons, he definitely knew Alfred Marshall (1842–1924), with whom he had studied at Cambridge. His feelings about Marshall were ambivalent, but in his obituary profile he includes, as he did with Jevons, a statement by the renowned economist of his methods of work. "When I went to Cambridge and became full master of myself," Marshall wrote in 1917, "I resolved never to read a mathematical book for more than a quarter of an hour at a time without a break. I had some light literature always by my side, and in the breaks I read through more than once the whole of Shakespeare, Boswell's *Life of Johnson,* the *Agamemnon* of Aeschylus (the only Greek play I could read without effort), a great part of Lucretius, and so on."[193]

It's not wholly clear whether the entirety of Shakespeare and the *Agamemnon* in Greek would have constituted "light literature" for Alfred Marshall, or whether he had a collection of detective stories on hand as well. (I suspect the former.) In any case, reading literature for pleasure was a practice that Keynes both admired and emulated. Mary Paley Marshall, Alfred's wife and another—wholly affectionate—subject of Keynes's "Lives of Economists," reported that her home schooling included nightly readings aloud by her clergyman father ("*The Arabian Nights, Gulliver's Travels,* the *Iliad* and *Odyssey,* translations of the Greek dramatists, Shakespeare's plays, and, most beloved of all, Scott's novels"). Her conservative father also agreed to send his daughter to university at Cambridge, which—as she notes—was "in those days, an outrageous proceeding."[194]

Also included in the *Essays in Biography* is a review of Trotsky's book on England in which Keynes compares the attitude of the author to that of Bottom in *A Midsummer Night's Dream* ("If only it was so easy! If only one could accomplish by roaring, whether roaring like a lion or like any sucking dove!" [1.2.67–68]) and a brief sketch of Einstein, written in 1926, in which Keynes suggests that the best description of the brilliant and "impish" physicist would be "Charlie Chaplin with the forehead of Shakespeare."[195]

Theatre in Postwar Cambridge

The Cambridge to which Keynes returned after the war and the peace negotiations was a place engaged as much with theatre and poetry as with politics and economics. At King's were J. T. Sheppard, Donald Beves, Frank Birch and, before long, Dadie Rylands, appointed as a fellow in 1927. Birch, educated at Eton and King's, had been a lieutenant commander with the Royal Navy Volunteer Reserve, serving in the Atlantic, the Channel, and the Dardanelles before he joined an intelligence division as a cryptographer for the remainder of the war. He returned to Cambridge as a fellow and a history don, becoming also a dramatic producer with a broader, more comic, and more emphatic style than the one that would later be favored by Lytton Strachey and Dadie Rylands.

At the Marlowe Society Birch directed both *Troilus and Cressida* (1922) and *Coriolanus* (1928), productions that were thought, at least in part, to reflect his response to the war in which he and many of his undergraduate cast members had fought. Among the returned veterans were Dennis Arundell (Ulysses), Dennis Robertson (Pandarus), and Joe Ackerley (Achilles). *Troilus and Cressida* had seldom been seen onstage; between 1734 and 1898 there were no recorded performances. As Tim Cribb notes, when the Marlowe chose to put it on, two years after the publication of Keynes's *The Economic Consequences of the Peace,* "it was the post-war reaction which made certain that the play was heard."[196] The *Manchester Guardian* explicitly drew the comparison: "The futility and waste of war, the barrenness of much that passes for honour, the disillusionment of a young soldier—all these are lessons that the world of 1922 is ready to receive."[197] Critics were impressed, and the production made money. In June 1922 there was a revival at the Everyman Theatre in Hampstead, for which the society's rules—since the building was off college grounds—permitted women in the cast.

In the 1928 production of *Coriolanus* Dadie Rylands played Volumnia, and Keynes's fellow economist and sometime collaborator Dennis Robertson, the wily Pandarus of *Troilus and Cressida,* took on the role of the equally wily Roman councilor Menenius. After *Coriolanus* Frank Birch left Cambridge to pursue a career as an actor, performing in theatre, film, pantomime (he was a memorable Widow Twankey in a West End production of *Aladdin*), and even on the new medium of television. In 1939 he joined the Naval Section at Bletchley Park and became head of the German Team working on the Enigma code.[198]

Lydia's Shakespeare

Keynes was a lifelong Shakespeare enthusiast, but his interest sharpened further when he fell in love with the Russian ballet star Lydia Lopokova. As a child in Russia Lydia had performed small speaking parts in Shakespeare's plays: Mamillius in *The Winter's Tale,* Peaseblossom in *A Midsummer Night's Dream.*

John Maynard Keynes and Lydia Lopokova, ca. 1922–23

(When Lydia asked Keynes in a letter in August 1922, "Why did you choose *Winter's Tale* for me to read?" her earlier experience with the play might have been one of his reasons.)[199]

In the 1920s, living at 41 Gordon Square amid the Bloomsbury crowd and waiting for her divorce from Randolfo Barocchi to become final—while Maynard spent much of his time at Cambridge—Lydia read Shakespeare's sonnets for pleasure and to improve her English. "Sonnets are repeated for the first part of to-day," she wrote him. "In my head I would like to learn them all, but when in tongue it requires perseverance."[200] But she liked to think and talk about them, too. When Maynard was in Cambridge writing an article for the *Nation,* she wrote, "Perhaps I shall meet it in your eyes like Shakespeare did in his sonnet 14."[201] When she was worried or concerned about something, or found the day stretching before her without a plan, she resolved that "I shall find my peace in Shakespeare reading."[202] Sometimes a friend, like the musician Basil Stephen Maine, would drop by in the evening, and "we read *Twelfth Night.* Lovely passages! I execute Viola and Olivia (positive and negative)."[203] A few years later she would play Olivia in a production of the play, occasioning both "positive and negative" reviews.

From King's College, where he was at work, Maynard wrote to Lydia, "I send you separately four little Shakespeares (in the same edition as your favorite sonnets) which you can take into the bathroom or carry in your bag or on the bus. I saw them on the bookstall in the marketplace and thought of you."[204] The edition seems to have been leather bound, since Lydia replied praising the handsome covers: "The little red objects are such comfort, and their skin is of such well shaved order. I thank you."[205] Later in the year he bought a Second Folio of Shakespeare for himself, confessing to Lydia that it was an extravagance; when it arrived he worried that although it was a "very good copy," too much of it was in facsimile. A previous purchase, similarly flawed, he reminds her, he had sent back to the shop.[206]

Maynard's friend Dadie Rylands—later to have such a transformative effect upon the Royal Shakespeare Company—was the best undergraduate actor of his time at Cambridge, a skilled performer in female parts. In February 1924 Maynard wrote Lydia to ask her to come see Dadie in *The Duchess of Malfi* at the Marlowe Society. A week later she replied jauntily, "I read a little of the *Duchess of Malfi,* there is intensity in characters [*sic*]. Dadie should appear pregnant, in one of the first scenes, may I apply for the part as I had apricocks jam for lunch very near from apricocks of the Duchess?"[207] (In an early scene the duchess's enemy Bosola tempts her with a dish of apricots, thus proving—according to the lore of the period—that she is secretly pregnant.)

Lydia embarked on a study of *A Midsummer Night's Dream* (the other play in which she had performed as a child), first reporting that she was "learning *Midsummer Night's Dream,* but without sticking" and, a few weeks afterward, that she was learning "my gentle Puck." Puck was not her own choice of role, however. When Maynard mentioned that he had been discussing the founding of a theatre with another Cambridge economist, Dennis Holme Robertson, she wrote back to say that "if ever your and his idea about a theatre succeeds, in *Midsummer Night's Dream* you must engage me as Oberon, the 'fairy lord' who would not be satisfied unless his Puck is Dennis."[208] In March 1925 she reported her experience of seeing John Barrymore in *Hamlet* at the Haymarket Theatre: "*Hamlet* was very interesting, respectably performed, and some of the scenes by the way of speech very beatiful [*sic*], but the play is too long. Hamlet is inteligent [*sic*], not an ideal Hamlet, but then was he? I loved the end what a right dimension for all of them to die. I was so glad. Ophelia [as] Fay Compton charming, the Queen mother good, but yet undetachable from 'our betters' and the ghost father made one think of spiritualism and Sir Oliver Lodge. I applauded for the noble exposition of the play."[209]

Lydia and Maynard were married on August 4, 1925, as soon as her divorce was finalized. His Bloomsbury friends were not entirely enthusiastic. Some—like Virginia Woolf and Vanessa Bell—thought Lydia bird-brained ("parakeet" and "canary" were favorite terms, though Woolf also compared her mind to "a lark soaring; a sort of glorified instinct"); they lamented the loss of their previous intimacy with the shrewd, witty—and homosexual—Cambridge Apostle Maynard Keynes.[210] What they criticized, however, was for him part of her appeal. "A great part of Lydia's charm for Maynard," writes Robert Skidelsky, "was her extremely individual use of the English language, or what Keynes called 'Lydiaspeak.' Her emphases, pronunciation and unerring choice of words and phrases were a constant joy." He was protective of her vulnerability among the intellectuals of Bloomsbury, and—says Skidelsky—"regarded her utterance as privileged, beyond rational criticism."[211] Cambridge friends like Dadie Rylands enjoyed her freewheeling company, though, and with his help Maynard now determined on a new phase for Lydia's career. She would appear in a program at the ADC Theatre—a triple bill in which she would dance in Stravinsky's ballet *A Soldier's Tale* and appear as the forsaken maiden in Shakespeare's poem *A Lover's Complaint* opposite the young actor Michael Redgrave, then a Cambridge undergraduate, who played her seducer. The director, Dennis Arundell, acted the part of the poet and composed the music. The mime-dancer Hedley Briggs took the nonspeaking part of the "reverend" old man, Duncan Grant designed the sets and costumes, and Maynard guaranteed the show against financial loss.

A LOVER'S COMPLAINT

Despite the fact that she had long lived in Britain, Lopokova's English was still Russian-inflected. Her Russian Os still sounded like "oahs," and in the run-up to the ADC performance Keynes coached her by letter from Cambridge, where he was working: "Sorrow, borrowed, owed. Can you hear me pronouncing them?"[212] Dennis Arundell found her initial reading of the poetic verse "ultra-

Michael Redgrave, Lydia Lopokova Keynes, and Dadie Rylands in Shakespeare's *A Lover's Complaint,* photograph by Cecil Beaton, ca. 1930

regular," "as unvaried as the ticking of a clock," and was surprised when Keynes insisted that she was merely being true to the poem's scansion.[213] ("My dear Dennis," Keynes said to him about Lydia's idiosyncratic pronunciation, "it doesn't matter, they haven't heard the piece before.")[214] Arundell was soon taken by her "unpretentious" enthusiasm and found the rehearsals "most happy."[215]

The performances took place in early November 1928. *A Lover's Complaint* was an unfamiliar work (it had never been previously staged) and reviewers found it "rather dull" and "better left in the book."[216] Francis Birrell, however, writing in the *Nation* (which was owned by Keynes) wrote appreciatively, "The Shakespeare poem seemed to be neither acted nor read aloud but presented from another angle in another medium," with decorations by the Bloomsbury artist Duncan Grant. He emphasized that "Madame Lopokova showed genuine dramatic talent, and her accent was no more foreign than that of the Elizabethans might have been."[217]

In 1930 Lydia appeared in a new staging of *A Lover's Complaint* at the Arts Theatre Club in London as part of a presentation called *Beauty, Truth, and Rarity: A Masque of Music and Dancing* that played for a week between December 10 and December 16. (Despite the quotation in the title, it is not clear whether Shakespeare's poem "The Phoenix and Turtle" was on the program.) Lydia danced in a ballet based on a poem by Thomas Campion and played the lady in a version of *Comus* that ended in a dance; the choreographer was her friend Frederick Ashton. In *A Lover's Complaint* she again took the part of the "afflicted fancy," with Redgrave as the perfidious lover, but Dadie Rylands, who directed, played the poet, and Donald Beves, another accomplished actor from King's, was the "reverend man." Reviewers concurred on the grace of her dancing and miming but once again differed as to whether her "faint foreign accent" (to quote the *Times*) or "very broken accent" (the *Evening Standard)* was a liability or—according to Birrell—an asset: "Mr Rylands and Mr Redgrave," his article in the *Nation* declared, "struggled to triumph over the extraordinary difficulties of the remote and inspissated diction, while Madame Lopokova's still slightly foreign accent positively helped to carry the unearthly Masque into a still more remote and faery region." The professionals, in short, had something to learn from the newcomer. "In her voice," observed another critic in the *Evening Standard,* "mingle the clipped consonants of Bloomsbury and the liquid labials of her native land."[218]

MADAME LOPOKOVA'S OLIVIA

Lydia's next Shakespearean role—and her last, except for a reprise of the *Lover's Complaint*—was Olivia in Tyrone Guthrie's production of *Twelfth Night* in September 1933. For this appearance, which the Keyneses thought especially important for Lydia's future as an actress, they sought a favor from Virginia Woolf—would she review the play? Woolf was skeptical about the project. At the end of July she had written to Ethel Smyth that the "Keynes's [her spelling] came and stayed till after 8 and the dinner was burnt but they were very very charming. Maynard prancing all over the world and saying outrageous things.... [We] were very fond of each other, too—Lydia is now going on the stage, as Rosalind or Ophelia: though she speaks English like a parrokeet."[219] On September 3 she wrote to Francis Birrell that she and Leonard were going to Tilton, the Keyneses' home in Sussex, where she imagined the men would argue about politics "while Lydia sits mumbling the part of Olivia in 12th night which she is set to do at the old Vic."[220] A week later, on September 10, she wrote in her diary, "I must read 12th night for Lydia's extortion (an article on her appearance)."[221] In a letter to Ethel Smyth on September 14 she wrote, "Wednesday we go up to Lydia's play; then my horror is that I must write an article on it; all because my friends love me; and again must see Keynes' etc."[222]

Then on September 19, a day before she and Leonard drove to London from Rodmell to see the play, she read W. A. Darlington's review in the *Daily Telegraph*. "Lydia Lopokova makes her bow . . . as the most humourless female in literature," it said. "What possessed anybody to give the part of Olivia to her?"[223] Woolf wrote that day to her nephew Quentin Bell: "Have you read the mornings paper on Lydia? The D.T. is scathing. My god; what shall I say? I think the only possible line to take is how very exciting it is to see Shakespr mauled; of course one might make play with the idea that the Elizabethans were just as unintelligible; and throw in a hint about opposites being the same thing as equalities—if you take my meaning. Either the worst, or the best—that sort of remark. Well. Pity me."[224]

Other London newspapers were divided in their views of Lopokova's performance. The *Times,* which liked the production, agreed with Darlington that she was miscast: "What to say of Olivia one hardly knows, Madame Lopokova speaking Shakespearean English with so strong an Illyrian accent that much of its sense and all its music vanish."[225] But the *Daily Express* treated her appearance and interpretation as a triumph. "Great Dancer Turns Actress. Lopokova's Superb Olivia. Audience of 2,500 Spellbound," proclaimed the headline, and the review declared, "All preconceived ideas of Olivia the haughty beauty, she brushed aside at the outset by the magic expressiveness of her hands. They acted for her. The audience was fascinated. The immortal words twisted her tongue, but Mme. Lopokova only regarded them as guide-posts for her sensitive, full-blooded acting."[226]

Part of Darlington's objection was that the "humourless" Olivia was a bad fit for Lopokova's persona. Judith Mackrell, in her biography, reports the response of some of Lydia's friends and supporters to Guthrie's offer of the part. "That any director could envisage her as this most stately and solemn of Shakespeare's women seemed incomprehensible and a campaign was launched to dissuade her from accepting. Walter Sickert told Lydia she would be putting her entire reputation in jeopardy, and Dadie Rylands begged her instead to ask for Maria, Olivia's quick-tongued lady-in-waiting."[227] But Lopokova was determined to be Olivia, whose "fine poetry" she admired, and whom she imagined playing—she wrote to Keynes—as "haughty and princess like," with special attention to her "clothes, speech, ankles and wrists."[228]

When Virginia Woolf finally sat down to write her review—which she described in her diary as "that horrid tough little article on 12th night"—she paid special attention to such physical qualities, derived from a lifetime of dancing.[229] "Madame Lopokova," she wrote, "has only to float on to the stage and everything round her suffers, not a sea change, but a change into light." But the general strategy Woolf adopted—very deftly—was to compare the experience of reading *Twelfth Night* on one's own to the experience of seeing the Guthrie production at the Old Vic.

The homework she had set herself, to reread the play, produces some brilliant observations on its poetry. She notes the number of "queer jingles" like "that live in her; when liver, brain and heart," and "a foolish knight that you brought in one night," asking "whether it was from them that was born the lovely, 'And what should I do in Illyria? My brother he is in Elysium.'" These are side notes of surpassing interest; another critic might have made them the focus of an entire article. But Woolf's goal, and her task, is to review the performance, and she sets this up by comparing the personal reading with the production, the reading in a garden from the viewing in a theatre, permitting herself to ask how her own ideas about the characters might differ from the way they are presented. Two more elements of this well-thought-out strategy may also be noted as ways that Woolf is able to address Lopokova's performance without undermining it: first, she uses the plural "we" rather than the personal "I" to designate the reader's view ("let us compare the two versions"), referring to "our Malvolio" and "our Olivia," rather than "mine" (much less "Shakespeare's"). And second, in marking the difference between the character-as-read and the character-as-performed, she opts first to describe Malvolio and only after that to move on to Olivia.

"We make Mr Quartermaine's Malvolio stand beside our Malvolio," she writes. "And to tell the truth, wherever the fault may lie, they have very little in common." Leon Quartermaine's Malvolio was "a splendid gentleman, courteous, considerate, well bred; a man of parts and humour who has no quarrel with the world." But "our Malvolio, on the other hand, was a fantastic, complex creature, twitching with vanity, tortured by ambition."[230] After setting upon the contrast, Woolf is able to move to the more difficult comparison. "Then there is Olivia."

"Madame Lopokova," she says, has "that rare quality . . . the genius of personality." When she appears onstage "the air rings with melody and human beings dance toward one another on the tips of their toes possessed of an exquisite friendliness, sympathy and delight." So far it is all praise before Woolf introduces

Lydia Lopokova Keynes (*far right*) with the cast of *Twelfth Night,* photograph from *The Times,* September 18, 1933

what seems, in her careful crafting, merely a matter of choice. "But our Olivia was a stately lady; of sombre complexion, slow moving, and of few sympathies. She could not love the Duke nor change her feeling. Madame Lopokova loves everybody. She is always changing. Her hands, her face, her feet, the whole of her body, are always quivering in sympathy with the moment. She could make the moment, as she proved when she walked down the stairs with Sebastian, one of intense and moving beauty, but she was not our Olivia." And Woolf then immediately adds, underlining an issue without calling attention to it, "Compared with her the comic group, Sir Toby, Sir Andrew, Maria, the fool were more than ordinarily English."[231] Unlike the other reviewers, she does not say anything explicit about Lopokova's accent or her pronunciation of Shakespeare's lines. She does not have to; it is here, tacitly and tactfully, in the comparison.

Woolf's article ends with a cheerful and nonjudgmental assessment. The production, she says, "has served its purpose. It has made us compare our Malvolio with Mr Quartermaine's; our Olivia with Madame Lopokova's; our reading of the whole play with Mr Guthrie's; and since they all differ, back we must go to Shakespeare. We must read *Twelfth Night* again."[232]

The Woolfs had dined with the Keyneses on September 23 before a meeting of the Memoir Club; that day she wrote in her diary, "I shall read my memoir tonight, send off my article on Monday morning, & so consider myself quit of all duties to my friends."[233] Her review, "'Twelfth Night' at the Old Vic," was published in the *New Statesman and Nation* on September 30.

A week later Woolf wrote to Ottoline Morrell reprising a phrase she had used in her diary: "Oh how I hated writing that tough little article! Poor dear Lydia asked me to do it—she attached great value to her acting—she wants to be an actress—and the whole thing was a dismal farce, and she is out of the Cherry Orchard in consequence. But never will I write about a friend again. They may wear the stones out on their knees before I go through that agony."[234] (The allusion here is probably to *The Winter's Tale* [3.3.208–12]: "A thousand knees / Ten thousand years together, naked, fasting, / Upon a barren mountain, and still winter / In storm perpetual, could not move the gods / To look the way thou wert.")

The Keyneses "liked my article on her, so that's all right," Woolf later reported—with relief—to Quentin Bell, though "they were both in the depths of gloom."[235] Tyrone Guthrie had proposed a series of roles for Lopokova, and Woolf's review had closed by looking forward to future Old Vic productions of *The Cherry Orchard, Henry VIII,* and *Measure for Measure.* But the negative press reviews foreclosed some opportunities, and it was another theatre company that a few months later offered her a role in which she would triumph (even in Woolf's opinion): Nora in Ibsen's *A Doll's House.*[236] Although she appeared in several other stage plays, Olivia was Lydia's last Shakespearean part.

A New Theatre in Cambridge

His commitment to Lydia's acting career was influential in Keynes's decision to support the construction of a purpose-built theatre in Cambridge. In November 1933, two months after the *Twelfth Night* production, he wrote to her that he was "thinking out a plan to build a small, very smart, modern theatre for the College. Will you agree to appear in the first production of it if it comes off?" He was firmly engaged from the start. "The project fascinates me," he told her, "and I already begin to draw up plans of my own for it."[237] As Robert Skidelsky notes, "The building project at Cambridge, together with his writing, was to be Maynard's main preoccupation over the next two years."[238] The Cambridge Arts Theatre opened in 1936. Keynes himself had loaned about half the money necessary for construction, but within ten years, with his careful management, all the loans had been repaid out of theatre profits.[239]

When he fell ill in 1937, Keynes was constrained to bed for some weeks; he spent his time listening to the radio. With his usual wide-ranging energy, he sent a letter to Sir Stephen Tallents, the controller of public relations at the BBC, to report his experiences. He deplored the fact that a Schubert symphony had been interrupted for ten minutes to give the public the latest news from Wimbledon. ("Anything more boring and tiresome than descriptions of tennis you cannot see cannot be imagined.") He recommended a practice long enjoyed by previous generations and highly valued by his friends in Bloomsbury: "I feel that there is an immense field for really good reading out loud. This is something on which so many of us were brought up and is one of the best things to be communicated to the greater public." Plays performed by a troupe of actors, were, by contrast, extremely hard for a listener to follow. "They still seem to me a complete failure. The only exception, so far as they are concerned, is where I know the play thoroughly already. For example, I enjoyed 'As You Like It' done by the Stratford-on-Avon players. But that was because I know the play by heart. If I had had to pick it up afresh, I could never have had the concentration and patience to do so."[240]

Having moved, for reasons partly personal, into the realm of arts management, Keynes was called upon when war came to become chairman of CEMA, the Council for the Encouragement of Music and the Arts. CEMA had been set up in 1940; Keynes took over its leadership in 1942 and set about trying to shift the organization's emphasis from village concerts and amateur choral singing to professional arts productions. As Kenneth Clark noted, Keynes "was not the man for wandering minstrels and amateur theatricals. He believed in excellence. In four years he transformed CEMA, the social service, into a universal provider for the arts."[241] In 1945, under a new title, the Arts Council of Great Britain became a permanent entity with annual funding from the Ministry of Education, tasked with increasing the public's access to the arts and improving the quality of artistic production.

For Keynes's enduring influence on Shakespeare performance and interpretation, however, we should look not so much to the Arts Council as to his beloved personal project, the Cambridge Arts Theatre. It could be said, in fact, that Lydia Lopokova's critically judged performance as Olivia in *Twelfth Night* brought about a new and exciting moment for what might be called Bloomsbury Shakespeare. Converted by Keynes from a shareholders' company into an educational charity trust, the Arts Theatre became the home of the Marlowe Society and, in consequence, the site of numerous inventive Shakespeare productions produced and directed by Dadie Rylands. Remembering his friend, Rylands stressed their shared enthusiasms: "I do not recollect the word 'economics' ever passing our lips. A friendship of twenty-five years was cemented by mutual devotion to Theatre, English Literature, and King's."[242]

THE ARTIST: ROGER FRY

Roger Fry, born in 1866, was among the oldest members of the Bloomsbury Group—and also, in his energy, imagination, and vitality, among the most youthful. Like so many other men of what would come to be called Bloomsbury, he was a graduate of King's College and was elected to the Cambridge Conversazione Society, otherwise known as the Apostles. Brought up in a wealthy Quaker family and trained as a scientist—he was awarded first-class honors in the Natural Science Tripos—he became a painter, a vastly influential art critic, curator of paintings at the Museum of Modern Art in London, the organizer of the first and second Post-Impressionist exhibitions in London, and the founder of the Omega Workshops. For recreation and pleasure, he translated the poems of Mallarmé. (Frances Partridge recalled in her memoir that "among his wilder beliefs were that Shakespeare's Sonnets were just as good in French as in En-

Roger Fry, photograph by Alvin Langdon Coburn, 1913

glish.")[243] In 1933 Fry was appointed the Slade Professor of Art at Cambridge. He died in 1934.

What role did Shakespeare play in a life so dedicated to the visual arts? And how did Fry's visual imagination—and his aesthetic theory—influence ideas about Shakespeare?

Two contrasting performances of *Antony and Cleopatra*—one in London, the other in Rome—offer a good sense of Fry's theatrical taste. The chief attraction in each case was a famous female star. "One night he went to see Mrs Langtry act in *Antony and Cleopatra,*" Woolf reports in her biography of Fry, quoting his account: "Mrs Langtry really is very grand, quite worth going to see and acts really tolerably well, but anything more hopelessly absurd than the rest of the show it is hard to conceive. If you can imagine a number of respectable cheesemongers who have retired to Bedlam ranting and strutting about not invariably accompanied by the prescribed number of H's, you will have some idea of the ridiculousness of the whole thing."[244]

Lillie Langtry's production of the play ran at the Princess's Theatre from November 1890 to February 1891. But by February Fry was in Rome—"Rome at last," he wrote exultantly to his friend Goldsworthy Lowes Dickinson ("My dear old Goldie").[245] In March he wrote again to report, among other things, that he had been to the theatre:

> Last night I went to hear *Anthony and Cleopatra* [*sic*]—I had read it first in Italian. The translation is vile, e.g. "the tears live in an onion that should water this sorrow" becomes "One must indeed have great riches of tears to be able to bewail so slight a grief" (forget the Italian). Cleopatra was done by the great Duse of whom I had heard even in England. She is called the Italian Sarah Bernhardt and she is really magnificent. I've never seen anything near it—she made one understand how she could chain Anthony. . . . What was curious about her interpretation of the character was that she emphasized the witch or gipsy-like side of the character rather than the grand queen and yet kept it full of dignity. She is not exactly beautiful but has the most marvelous play of expression and is very lithe and serpentine. The whole play was done in perfect taste and excellently shortened; it was incomparably finer than Mrs Langtry.[246]

Like many other theatregoers at the time, Fry seems to have been especially struck by the performance of star actresses in Shakespearean roles. "I went yesterday with your sisters to see *As You Like It,*" he wrote to Dickinson in November 1891. "Ada Rehan was splendid. I think nearly perfect and can't find any touch of vulgarity or hardly any. Anyhow it was just as full-blooded and full of verve and go as it could be and that's something *almost* everything for Rosalind. What a splendid play it is. All the witty conversation is just like what one would say if one were only clever enough and decent enough. Jacques [*sic*] was well done—he is one of the modernest, most suggestively complex of all Shakespeare's characters."[247]

Fry's pleasure in the play's witty exchanges and his response to the modernism of "the melancholy Jaques" reflect interests that would remain significant for him. The Apostles, described by Virginia Woolf as "the society of equals, enjoying each other's foibles, criticising each other's characters, and questioning everything with complete freedom," were the center of his life in Cambridge, and the same unbridled elements of wit, criticism, and moral seriousness were carried over into the world of Bloomsbury.[248]

In another letter to Dickinson Fry praised an 1877 play by Henrik Ibsen, *The Pillars of Society,* which he was then reading: "It is simply wonderful, quite Shakespearian in the way in which three sentences give you a character and so concentrated (to the verge of exaggeration I think), exactly the reverse of what one expects from a laborious photographic realist. It is no more realistic than Shakespeare is—like him he deals with the men and women and circumstances of every day life and like him he interests and intensifies."[249] This preference for the emblematic over "photographic realis[m]" would also mark his later aesthetic theory. It is striking to see it here articulated so firmly and anchored from the start to a critical understanding of Shakespeare. "No more realistic than Shakespeare" is a gauntlet thrown gracefully down, praising Shakespeare for his *lack* of mere mimesis. The "Shakespearian" quality Fry discerns and praises—the powerful brief sketch of character set forth in a few telling lines—is very much the same quality he would later identify in Rembrandt, and would, again, compare to Shakespeare.

"Smothered in Scenery"

One of the most consistent faults that Bloomsbury critics found with the previous generation of professional Shakespeare productions is well summed up in Desmond MacCarthy's phrase "smothered in scenery."[250] Even Sir Sidney Lee—no Bloomsburyite—had deplored the crowded stages, invented scenes, and elaborate flights of visual and aural fantasy that replaced Shakespeare's own imaginative language. Roger Fry, as both a painter and an art critic, was among the strongest of voices calling for change.

After the death of the Victorian artist Lawrence Alma Tadema, Fry published an article in the *Nation* that became a flash point for conservative outrage. Alma Tadema, Fry claimed, was in essence a salesman of a certain kind of Victorian culture: his "products" are "typical of the purely commercial ideals of the age in which he grew up." His art "demands almost nothing from the spectator beyond the almost unavoidable knowledge that there was such a thing as the Roman Empire, whose people were very rich, very luxurious, and, in retrospect at least, agreeably wicked." The paintings that had inspired his stage designs for Shakespeare's Roman plays suggest "that all the people of that interesting and remote period, all their furniture, clothes, even their splendid marble divans, were made of highly scented soap." His realism was that of "the Kodak Company." He "gave his pictures the expensive quality of shop-finish"; his work "is like very good, pure, wholesome margarine, and for all we know, Sir Lawrence put it forward as such, and never had an opportunity of correcting the little misunderstanding on the part of the public which insisted on calling it butter."[251]

Shop-finish, soap, and margarine—nothing could be further from the Bloomsbury aesthetic. Fry's brief, scathing, and witty polemic took special aim at the artist's receipt of the Order of Merit, a new honor, inaugurated in 1902, that had first been awarded to G. F. Watts. It's not Fry's style to tag his argument, as Lytton Strachey might well have done, with "O Hamlet, what a falling off was there," but the sense of loss and outrage is manifest, and the essay ends with a direct hit at the "honors" presented to the artist: "How long will it take to disinfect the Order of Merit of Tadema's scented soap?"[252]

Fry, who had gained fame in some quarters and notoriety in others by organizing two major Post-Impressionist exhibitions in London, was already persona non grata among many conservative English artists, and the lions of the Royal Academy took this occasion to roar. In her biography of Fry, published in 1940, Virginia Woolf, observing that "since times have changed and Alma-Tadema's marble is no longer as solid as it seemed, a few phrases are worth resurrecting," proceeds to describe the scene: "Sir Philip Burne-Jones began the attack. 'Fortunately at this date,' he wrote, 'the work of Alma-Tadema needs no sort of defence. It rests in the security of a practically unanimous European reputation.' But since Mr Fry had attacked it, and expressed no contrition when called to order, lovers of art must protest."[253] Another Academician, Sir William Richmond, suggested that Fry "'must not be surprised if he is boycotted by decent society.'"[254] The general view of the Academy, as Woolf summarizes it, was that the man who could champion the works of the Post-Impressionists was capable of anything. Yet even he must realize that "'his malignant sneers at a great artist only just dead did no good but great harm.'"[255] "Roger Fry," Woolf reports, "was delighted. He would quote Sir William's boycott with great appreciation."[256]

"The Malign Influence of the Theatre on Drama"

Not only in painting but also in the art and theory of set design there had been a significant shift into modernism in the first years of the twentieth century. In 1911 the Leicester Galleries in London held the first one-man exhibition for the artist and scene designer Edward Gordon Craig. Among the items on display were Craig's designs for *Macbeth, Hamlet, Henry V, The Tempest, Julius Caesar,* and *Romeo and Juliet.*[257] Two months later, on September 16, Fry published an article called "Mr Gordon Craig's Stage Designs" in the *Nation.*

The article began with a remarkable sentence, as striking for its wit as for its justice: "The malign influence of the theatre on drama has been long apparent." Fry supported his claim by reviewing the recent history of Shakespearean stage design, offering an argument that was congruent with that of the Marlowe Society and would be implied in his postmortem assessment of Alma Tadema. "The expensive and much-advertised setting which was habitually arranged for Shakespearean drama, with its realistic and archaeological rendering of actual scenes, infected even the most demonstrative of actor-managers with its own unreality."[258]

The director William Poel, who had founded the Elizabethan Stage Society and was committed to the bare-stage concept of performance, had shown "that merely to get rid of scenery altogether was a great assistance." But Edward Gordon Craig's contribution, Fry thought, was of a different order: "He it was who had the brilliant idea . . . that it might be possible to design scenery to express the idea of a play instead of contradicting it." During his time in Europe, Craig had "perfected and simplified his methods to an extraordinary degree," Fry wrote. "His designs are now purified of any trace of the old picturesque conceptions of scenery."[259]

Craig's commitment to designing for "poetic drama" was especially important. The "emotional pitch" of comedy is low, so it can get "its due effect" from the imitation of "actual scenes of modern life." But, Fry believed, "the poetic drama needs something other than this." "Mr Gordon Craig shows that a few elementary rectangular masses, placed in certain relations to one another and illuminated by a natural light, will stir the mind to the highest pitch of anticipation, will inspire already the mood of high tragedy. Such a scene clears the mind of all accidental and irrelevant notions, and leaves it free to be filled with the tragic theme."[260] Looking at Craig's models, Fry reports that he feels "an almost impatient anticipation." "One waits, hoping to see the slow-moving figure emerge from behind one of the monolithic masses, or descend slowly one of the convergent stairways which lead from the mysterious depths of gloom. One knows that the moment the figure moves into sight we shall be in the midst of fatal memorable deeds."[261]

This, indeed, sounds as if the spectator is present in the audience for a performance, perhaps of *Macbeth* (for which Craig drew designs in 1906 and 1908) or *Hamlet* (for which his designs were used onstage in 1912 at the Moscow Art Theatre). But after one brief mention in the opening paragraph ("the expensive and much-advertised setting which was habitually arranged for Shakespearean drama") and a fleeting offhand allusion to "a palace at Verona," there is no further citation of Shakespeare or any other dramatist until, near the end of the article, Fry offers a comment on the power of Craig's "thrilling scenes." "I understand," he writes," that some actors complain of their perfection, and dread that there will not be room for them to make their particular personal effect. As Mr Craig wittily remarks in the notes to his catalogue, they might as well complain that Shakespeare's verses left them very little to do."[262]

It is important to emphasize here that Roger Fry is reviewing small constructed stage models, not a live theatrical performance. Indeed it is not clear that Fry, or any of his Bloomsbury friends, ever saw a stage production designed by Edward Gordon Craig. But the designs and models appealed powerfully to his imagination, according with both his aesthetic theory and its relation to the emotions. And once again Shakespeare—a Shakespeare whose plays Craig would continue to claim were "unactable" even as he designed stage sets for them—is Fry's template and his index of value, as well as his frame.[263]

As for Craig, the son of actress Ellen Terry, his assertion about the "unactable" plays may be indebted not only to Romantic critics like Hazlitt, but also to a more recent one: Lytton Strachey. "I am more thoroughly convinced than ever that the plays of Shakespeare are unactable—that they are a bore when acted," he wrote in 1912.[264] The boredom of Strachey's Shakespeare is here transmuted into the boredom of Craig the spectator. Had Craig read Strachey's essay "Shakespeare's Final Period," published only a few years before and imbued with an iconoclastic spirit very congenial to him?

Much later, in a book on *The Tempest* (1924), he used a phrase from the essay as an epigraph, describing Strachey as "a wise reader and a fine writer" before venturing to say that he was "wondering now whether Mr Strachey is quite right."[265] The phrase ("the dreary puns and interminable conspiracies of Alonso and Gonzalo and Sebastian and Antonio and Adrian and Francisco and other shipwrecked noblemen") is credited only to "Lytton Strachey," with no specific citation to any text; we might infer that a reader would be expected to recognize it or at least to understand that it was meant to be recognized. By that time Strachey's essay, which had so effectively tweaked Shakespeare criticism, was available for a gentle tweak of its own. "I am wondering," writes Craig, "whether there would be great harm done for an inventive yet reverential stage manager to exert some of his cunning"; and, of the characters named in Strachey's list, "Were it not that one of these six men is bored I might be bored too—but while Sebastian swings his foot, 'sblood, I cannot close an eye."[266]

"Stage manager" is the period term for what we would today call a director. The cunning, reverential—but above all inventive—figure here is, of course, Craig himself.

Shakespeare and Rembrandt

The Cambridge Apostles of Roger Fry's generation were mainly interested in politics and philosophy. With only one or two exceptions there was, as Virginia Woolf suggests, little evidence that they ever "looked at pictures or debated the theory of aesthetics." Instead, "Art was for them the art of literature."[267] It is not surprising, then, that when Fry became chief art critic of the leading literary periodical the *Athenaeum* in 1901, he initially drew on the language of literary criticism and "often called in Shakespeare to help him out with a quotation."[268]

In an article he wrote on Claude Lorrain in 1907 for the *Burlington Magazine* Fry included a suggestive observation about Shakespeare's art of language. He begins by citing the poet Robert Bridges, a friend with whom he often corresponded about prosody and art. "In his essay on Keats," Fry suggests, Bridges "very aptly describes for literature the kind of beauty which we find in Shakespeare: 'the power of concentrating all the far-reaching resources of language on one point, so that a single and apparently effortless expression rejoices the aesthetic imagination at the moment when it is most expectant and exacting.'" This observation, he thinks, "applies admirably to certain kinds of design. It corresponds to the nervous touch of a Pollaiuolo or a Rembrandt."[269]

The Shakespeare/Rembrandt comparison marks for Fry a particular kind of aesthetic effect to which he would return. In a lecture given late in his life, published posthumously, he begins, "Rembrandt has been called the Shakespeare of painting," and then—before heads can start wagging in easy assent—he deftly explains the problem with this claim. "One approaches Rembrandt with some of those mixed feelings that disturb the critics of each. One approaches a shrine already overlaid with offerings, many of them of doubtful taste, and one's view of the divinity is slightly troubled and obscured by the traces of so many previous worshippers." But, says Fry, "the worst of it is" that the comparison "has some truth."[270]

The quality Rembrandt shares with Shakespeare (and only very few others), he says, is "an imagination of that high order that seizes at once on the essentials and reveals them without any apparatus or adornment with such simplicity that they come upon us at once with a delightful shock of surprise and a sense of their entire naturalness and inevitability."[271] Moreover, "Both Rembrandt and Shakespeare have the almost miraculous power of creating and placing before us in all their fulness and solidity, credible living beings . . . and of doing this with an unparalleled economy of words or pen strokes. Shakespeare gives us what we call a character by a reply of half a line—Rembrandt by three strokes which indicate the turn of a head or the thrust of a hand. Both do this by a kind of creation from within, that is to say, by a method of intuitive sympathy rather than by external observation."[272] The connection between these later observations and the insight Fry gained from Robert Bridges is clear. "Seizes at once"; "delightful shock of surprise"; "unparalleled economy"; "intuitive sympathy." Bridges was comparing Shakespeare and Keats; Fry compares Shakespeare and Rembrandt.

But Fry will take his argument one step further, linking the two artists not only with poetic imagination but with *drama*. The quality of Rembrandt's invention, he says, "is proof of the highest kind of dramatic insight and imagination." "This art of drama, whether in words or in images, moves, as does the cinematograph, by calling up the passions and emotions of actual life. Its effect shares something of this poignancy. When it is in the hands of great creators like Shakespeare and Rembrandt, it also interprets and classifies these emotions. But the aesthetic emotion as such is not concerned with the passions of actual life. It takes us into a region of more contemplative delight."[273]

"The aesthetic emotion as such is not concerned with the passions of actual life" is Fry's core argument in his landmark "Essay in Aesthetics" (1909), where the analogy of the "cinematograph" also appears. "Morality," he says there, "appreciates emotion by the standard of resultant action. Art appreciates emotion in and for itself."[274] And again, "The graphic arts are the expression of the imaginative life rather than a copy of actual life."[275] In her biography Virginia Woolf emphasized the importance of this distinction for him, both as a critic and as an artist. "Often in later life," Woolf wrote, "Roger Fry was to deplore the extraordinary indifference of the English to the visual arts, and their determination to harness all art to moral problems."[276]

After the uproar caused by the Post-Impressionist exhibitions of 1910–11 and 1912–13 and the controversy that exploded after his article criticizing the work of "the late Sir Lawrence Alma Tadema O.M.," he wrote to Dickinson, "I'm continuing my aesthetic theories and I have been attacking poetry to understand painting. I want to find out what the function of content is, and am developing a theory . . . that it is merely directive of form and that all the essential aesthetic quality has to do with pure form. . . . I think that in proportion as poetry becomes more intense the content is entirely remade by the form and has no separate value at all. . . . The emotions of music and pure painting and poetry when it approaches purity are really free abstract and universal. Do you see this and do you hate it? The odd thing is that apparently it is dangerous for an artist to know about this."[277]

The ideas Fry expresses in this letter—"As poetry becomes more intense the content is entirely remade by the form and has no separate value at all"; "The emotions of music and pure painting and poetry when it approaches purity are really free abstract and universal"—are strikingly similar to arguments that would be made years later—with specific reference to Shakespeare—by Dadie Rylands as well as by Lytton Strachey: "In the last period of all, the characters and the plot are sacrificed to the reckless power of expression; that is, to the poetry," Rylands would write in *Words and Poetry*.[278] In his introduction to Rylands's book, Strachey underscored this claim: "In Shakespeare's later works character has grown unindividual and unreal; drama has become conventional and operatic; the words remain more tremendously, more exquisitely, more thrillingly alive than ever—the excuse and the explanation of the rest."[279] But where Strachey—as perhaps befits his profession as a biographer—imagines Shakespeare in terms of teleology ("At last, it was simply for style that Shakespeare lived"), Fry, a formalist and theorist, sees it possible to separate "the emotions aroused by certain formal relations from the emotions aroused by the events of life."[280]

"The Mêlée *of Aesthetic Discussion"*

In 1914 Clive Bell, Fry's friend and acolyte, published a book with the simple (and grandiose) one-word title *Art,* a book that made popular the phrase "significant form"—a term that the Oxford professor A. C. Bradley had first used to describe poetry, but that Bell associated with the visual arts.[281]

Much of the argument in *Art* was indebted to Fry's ideas and writing, but the tone is breezier and more journalistic, less scholarly and philosophical. Bell's formalism is more absolute than Fry's and less nuanced. His book was accessible, bold, and brief, and "the literary contingent in Bloomsbury," as Frances Spalding notes, was now able to share in "the *mêlée* of aesthetic discussion."[282] In public Fry was generous about the book, which he reviewed in the *Nation* under the title "A New Theory of Art." In private he was less pleased; when Virginia Woolf was writing her biography of him, she came upon some letters in which he expressed "irritation" at Bell's borrowing of his ideas and "his lack of understanding of art."[283] (None of these opinions made it into her book, one of many reasons why she found it a challenge to write.)

In his review Fry—who had been corresponding with Dickinson on the question of analogies among the arts—expresses the wish that Bell "had extended his theory, and taken literature (in so far as it is an art) into fuller consideration, for I feel confident that great poetry arouses aesthetic emotions of a similar kind to painting and architecture. And to make his theory complete, it would have been Mr Bell's task to show that the human emotions of 'King Lear' and 'The Wild Duck' were also accessory, and not the fundamental and essential qualities of these works."[284] As he had done in an early letter, he again pairs Shakespeare and Ibsen as outstanding practitioners of dramatic art.

Later he will again raise this question about the "essential" versus the "accessory" emotions evoked by a work of art, this time using as his example Shakespeare's "Winter Song" from *Love's Labour's Lost.*[285] When he asked his friend the historian George Trevelyan what he liked about the "Winter Song," Trevelyan replied, "The thought that Shakespeare saw these things going on—milk coming home in pail, etc.—that that was actually part of the life of Elizabethan England."[286]

Fry's response, though not one he passed along to George Trevelyan, was that such feelings were secondary, indeed "trivial": "I've no objection to a person feeling that historical thrill, though I think he might have it by a little reflection without help from Shakespeare, but I maintain that it's a trivial kind of emotion compared to what a person sensitive to pure poetry gets from that particular sequence of images."[287] What Fry is here gesturing toward is a mode of "significant form" in poetry. We've already noted that A. C. Bradley, in his 1901 Oxford lecture "Poetry for Poetry's Sake," had used the term ("The style is here expressive also of a particular meaning, or rather is one aspect of that unity whose other aspect is meaning. So that what you apprehend may be called indifferently an expressed meaning or a significant form."). There is no reason to think that Fry—or indeed Clive Bell—is thinking of Bradley, but the coincidence of ideas is suggestive. In the early twentieth century formalism was shaping modern criticism in both literature and the visual arts.

"I've always been after this question of the irreducible essence of the work of art," Fry reflected. "I do also quite definitely think that the quality of emotion which that arouses is more universal and more profound than the accessory emotions."[288] Shakespeare's "Winter" lyric is here both example and proof text. Not *what* was being described but *how* it was described; not the "accessory" responses (nostalgia, social realism, anecdote, history) but the "essential" ones. "No doubt literature is conspicuously *impure* art," he wrote to Dickinson. "But I do think there is a pure or nearly pure art of words, and that that comes into my aesthetic."[289]

Artists and Writers

Shakespeare continued to be a touchstone for Fry in comparisons of visual art and literature, exemplified in a pair of exchanges he had with Virginia Woolf and Vanessa Bell. Woolf reports a conversation with him about aesthetics and form in which she spoke for fiction and he for painting: "Roger asked me if I founded my writing upon texture or upon structure; I connected structure with plot, and therefore said 'texture.' Then we discussed the meaning of structure & texture in painting and in writing. Then we discussed Shakespeare, & Roger said Giotto excited him just as much."[290]

Vanessa enjoyed such debates—familiar from the old Thursday Evenings and Friday Club days in Gordon Square—entering into them as an artist committed to "form" over content or "human interest." During the war, when Fry was in France, she wrote him describing a visit from Lytton Strachey and the mathematician H. T. J. ("Harry") Norton, another Cambridge friend and Apostle.

> We have had long discussions in the old style about art, about literature especially, though Lytton really thinks me too much without sense of what it's all about, I think, to be able to argue [with me] without in the end getting very cross. We quarreled over [King] Lear as I said it was of no interest as a story—in fact a rather mechanical and stilted affair with quite unreal relationships and feelings—and that I thought the human

> interest was of no value. But of course it's quite impossible to describe what it is that one does think of value. Lytton thought I had no appreciation of it and that it was really of great importance, even, that it should actually be like life. However it sounds very dull written down, I'm afraid. But Lytton admitted in the end that he had very little sense of anything but the human interest in painting. He is very suspicious of our attitude about art and thinks we don't understand our own feelings and are trying to prove a theory. I, on the other hand, think him almost entirely dramatic in his appreciations. I mean I believe he only feels character and relationships of character and has no conception of the form it's all being made into.[291]

In her account of this discussion Vanessa espouses form over (mere) "relationships of character," underscoring the difference, as she sees it, between Strachey's literary, or dramatic, response, and "our attitude about art." Conversely, Strachey, who had in his "Final Period" essay described Shakespeare's late romances as, to use Vanessa's phrase, "rather mechanical and stilted affair[s] with quite unreal relationships and feelings," strongly supports the human interest of *King Lear,* maintaining that it was "of great importance . . . that it should actually be like life." Vanessa is not a theorist—"our attitude" reflects Fry's influence on her, as well as her bond with him as a fellow painter. But at the same time it is intriguing to see that the story of the demanding old father and his three daughters strikes Vanessa, who suffered with Virginia and their stepsister Stella the occasional rages of the widowed Leslie Stephen, as wholly unrealistic and of "no interest." Form, we might conjecture—and as Fry would acknowledge—is sometimes a refuge from content as well as an abstraction of it.

Thine Own Self

Like many of his friends, Fry often casually quoted Shakespeare without attribution, confident that the implicit reference would be understood. Thus, for example, in a letter to his partner Helen Anrep, he says that after a visit from Goldie Dickinson he had become aware of how much his own thinking had evolved over time. "There are such thousands of things that I seem to understand that are outside his philosophy," he reports, casting himself as Hamlet and Dickinson as Horatio. "It just showed me how much I'd joined a younger generation."[292] Fry, feeling youthful, was then sixty-two years old, Dickinson only four years his senior.

Sometime after that, however, Fry produced a comical version of himself as Polonius in an undated and unfinished letter addressed to "Reginald" that may, as Denys Sutton suggests, be a draft for the Woolfs' fictional *Hogarth Letters* series.[293] The letter writer is an older man ("approaching the onset of decrepitude") whom a brash young correspondent has pressed for wise counsel. "It is of course extremely flattering," writes Fry, tongue firmly in cheek, "to be asked for advice by the young. That is one of the signs of how much life has changed since I was young myself. We were all taught an exaggerated respect for the old. We knew that we must listen without any awkward sign of impatience to their long-winded pomposity, their vain and garrulous self-display." Nonetheless he will "rise to the bait" because this gives him the opportunity to exhibit his own "pet prejudices" while commenting acerbically on English food, tailors, and imported razors. But the upshot comes when the author, "driven back to talk about [his] general philosophy of life," identifies the position as that of Polonius: "'This above all—' Good heavens! what advice! Of course Polonius didn't know in the least what he was talking about, but Shakespeare, though he was laughing at him, seems to me to have a little relished the fine phrase even while he was grinning—and even Shakespeare didn't know all the monstrosity of such advice." The world needed to wait for "our dear Doctor Freud" to reveal "the strange menagerie we keep inside" and to "show us how many of our true selves" were better kept hidden.[294]

In casting himself as Polonius—elderly, garrulous, all the things "we" once thought of the old before "we" were old ourselves—Fry is able to both reject and accept the role. He likes the idea that Shakespeare, while he laughed at Polonius, might also have "relished the fine phrase," the completion of "This above all—" by the other half of the famous truism. But what was one's "own self" to the dramatist who created so many living characters?[295] In this unfinished letter to the inquisitive and fictional "Reginald" it is neither arts nor politics but the "self," or rather the possibility of many and conflicting "true selves," that brings Shakespeare so aptly to Roger Fry's mind.

THE PUBLISHER: LEONARD WOOLF

In her Memoir Club talk "Old Bloomsbury," Virginia Woolf recalled that her brother Thoby had described his friends from school, and later from Cambridge, "as if they were characters in Shakespeare" and that one of these friends, "a man who trembled all over" and was "a Jew," was Leonard Woolf. Addressing the gathering, which included her husband, she quipped that she was "of course

Leonard Woolf, photograph by Alfred Harris, 1927

inspired with the deepest interest in that violent trembling misanthropic Jew who had already shaken his fist at civilisation."[296]

Leonard Woolf was not a misanthrope, but he did shake his fist—and his pen—at civilization whenever he felt the world needed improvement. Given the times in which he lived, this was, needless to say, very often. Choosing any one term to describe Woolf requires that many of his other major roles—as political theorist, editor, novelist, and literary executor, just to name a few—are unmentioned, but all were essential to his long and productive career. It will come as no surprise to learn that Shakespeare played an important part in his life's work, both public and personal.

We have already noted that as first-year students at Trinity College, Cambridge, Leonard Woolf, Lytton Strachey, and Saxon Sydney-Turner invented a game that ranked writers through the ages according to how they should stand in a hypothetical Cambridge Tripos, placing Plato and Shakespeare at the top.[297] In the Easter vacation in 1901 Strachey sent Woolf a handsome copy of the book of Job that he had found in a bookshop. Woolf wrote to thank him, urging him to add Job to the fellowship list: "The more I read it, the more certain I feel that it is above the first class, that it is absolute perfection & *can only* rank with Plato & Shakespeare."[298]

A year later Lytton and Leonard corresponded about *Le Père Goriot,* discussing whether or not it compared to *King Lear.* Strachey thought Balzac's novel "less universal," though "they both say nearly the same thing."[299] Woolf replied to "My dear Strache" to say that he resisted the comparison: "Balzac never attempts to do what Shakespeare does, & *Le Père Goriot* never even shimmers on the transcendental."[300] In the same letter Woolf comments acerbically on the resistance of the older Cambridge Apostles of the pre-Bloomsbury generation, G. W. Trevelyan and his friends, to the works of the Elizabethan dramatist John Webster: "They don't really know what literature is of course. They read a novel for the story & poetry for 'a criticism of life.' . . . They know they don't understand it & that it bores them unless there's something indecent in it to tickle their pruriency or something 'good' to tickle their lickerish sense of moral responsibility."[301] The debate between the Trevelyan Apostles and the Strachey-Keynes Apostles on this kind of question would occupy a good deal of their attention in the next few years, especially after G. E. Moore's *Principia Ethica* was published in 1903.

"What literature is," and how it could be understood through Shakespeare, became for them a key rallying point, a central difference between old and new, nineteenth and twentieth century, Victorian and modern. Woolf's talk to the Apostles, "Othello or Lord Byron?," delivered on October 31, 1903, and directly reflecting the influence of Moore, contrasted the true pathos of Shakespeare's tragedy with the false sentiment exhibited in the poems of Byron.[302] To expend emotion on objects unworthy of such feelings was inappropriate, he contended. Othello's emotion, however tragic its outcome, belonged to the realm of the appropriate, Byron's to the mawkish. It was a distinction that would matter to Leonard Woolf throughout his life.

Like Strachey, Woolf began writing for publication while he was still an undergraduate. In November 1904, he published an unsigned review in the *Spectator* of two books on Shakespeare, John Churton Collins's *Studies in Shakespeare* and Richard Moulton's *The Moral System of Shakespeare.* From the first sentence he establishes a tone of quiet authority: "Of the making of books relating to the works of Shakespeare there is no end, and much of the learning devoted to this perennial subject is certainly a weariness of the flesh." His style is already both mature and personable—Collins's essay on Shakespeare's text and prosody "will be read with real pleasure by all scholars who feel the fascination of the delightful art of text-mending"—and he is again critical of those who look to Shakespeare primarily for moral instruction: "The great human poet is not first of all a moralist; to be didactic is his last conception."[303] Woolf was twenty-four years old at the time.

The following year he set out for Ceylon to take up his position as a colonial administrator. This was the occasion on which Desmond MacCarthy gave him that treasured gift as a farewell present, "the Oxford miniature edition of Shakespeare and Milton in four volumes," which would immediately—and thereafter—become an essential companion and vade mecum.[304] Soon after his arrival he wrote to MacCarthy to thank him, reporting that "the books you gave me were a godsend at once. I had to travel for two nights & a day in a bullock waggon through the jungle in order to reach this place. For discomfort it was simply hell. I had to lie on my back on the hard floor of the waggon & was battered & jolted along for 36 hours but I took one of the small Shakespeare volumes with me in my pocket, & it helped me to forget my aching bones."[305]

In the following year he wrote to Saxon Sydney-Turner with an anecdote about Shakespeare in Ceylon: "Here an enterprising female has started a Shakespeare Reading Society. We read *As You Like It* on Friday. It was not quite as bad as it might have been & I had expected the worst. There was considerable difficulty over the word copulation. 'I press in here, Sir, amongst the rest of the country copulatives' was allowed to pass, because no one was quite sure whether it referred to grammar or sexual intercourse. It was only the weight of my assurance that it referred to the former that induced Touchstone not to leave it out. I was Jaques."[306] The tone of this communication is in tune with the spirit of their undergraduate exchanges, from the slightly defensive swipe at the "enterprising female" to the comic story about the word *copulation.* What is most of interest, though, is that Woolf did join the group, continuing in Ceylon the pleasure in reading Shakespeare aloud with others that he had enjoyed in the play-reading societies at Cambridge. His casting as the "melancholy Jaques," the play's philosopher and sentimental ironist, seems (and would probably have seemed to him) entirely appropriate.

As Woolf notes in his autobiography, when he returned to England in 1911 many things had begun to change. Friends now addressed each other by their first names rather than their surnames.[307] People often kissed when meeting instead of shaking hands, sexual and social frankness had become the expectation in mixed as well as all-male company, and "what came to be called Bloomsbury" was in the process of coming into existence.[308] He married Virginia Stephen in 1912.

In 1914 Woolf published his second novel, *The Wise Virgins.* His first novel, *The Village in the Jungle* (1913) had been based on his experiences in Ceylon. *The Wise Virgins,* set in London, was a social comedy—or social tragedy, depending upon your point of view—that told the story of a young Jewish man, Harry Davis, his love for the imaginative and artistic Camilla Lawrence, and his reluctant marriage to the far more ordinary—and sexually responsive—Gwen Garland.

Leonard Woolf's gifts as a novelist have been overshadowed by the brilliant career of his wife, but *The Wise Virgins* is an impressive fictional achievement in which—as also in the novels of Virginia Woolf—brief mentions of Shakespeare are used effectively to point up aspects of character. The small, plump barrister-cum-literary critic Arthur Woodhouse, a failed suitor to Camilla, "impelled by his restless little mind and his desire to talk," lectures his captive audience in the Lawrence household circle about the superiority of "simple" feelings to "civilized" ones: "We went off at a wrong tack in the Renaissance. Shakespeare hypnotized us and we've never got back."[309] Harry, having proposed to Camilla and been calmly refused ("I'm not in love with you, Harry"), suddenly sees all women passing in the street as repulsive and remembers a phrase from *King Lear:* "One imagined that 'forked animal' woman—a poor, thin, soft white body, forking out into two long, weedy white legs."[310] Camilla, shutting the door behind Harry, thinks to herself that perhaps she could not feel love and did not want to, comparing her situation (however obliquely) to Macbeth's: "These passions and deep desires only cribbed and cabined one from the romance of life."[311] And Gwen Garland, whose only literary reading comes from books Harry lends her, enjoys a small mental victory over her sisters as she thinks about "how people became clever and wrote books": "'The mystery of things'—she remembered that line in *Hamlet,* was it, or *King Lear*? which Harry had made her read. The mystery of things, the mystery of things, she murmured to herself, pleased a little to hear herself do it; she was different from May and Ethel, because surely they did not even recognize the mystery of things."[312] The phrase is spoken by Lear to Cordelia as he imagines, for a moment, escaping to a life with her in prison, away from the world.

Each of Woolf's Shakespeare references deftly skewers his subject, while providing minimal distraction from the main narrative. Arthur parades his knowledge of Shakespeare, Gwen clings to hers, and both Harry and Camilla enlist famous Shakespearean catchwords to underscore their own emotions. Together they offer a small master class in how Bloomsbury does Shakespeare.

The Hogarth Letters

In 1917 Leonard and Virginia Woolf founded the Hogarth Press, which would from that time publish all of Virginia's novels, as well as T. S. Eliot's *The Waste Land*, fiction by E. M. Forster and Vita Sackville-West, and the complete psychological works of Sigmund Freud. At least two other Hogarth Press books, by F. L. Lucas and George Rylands, were scholarly studies of literature that engaged directly with Shakespeare. As Hogarth's publisher and editor, Woolf reflected wryly on the glut of submissions. To someone who had recommended that they publish the work of a particular poet, he wrote to say that they had, in the end, turned it down. "The difficulty of deciding what to publish, out of the mass of 'poetry' one is sent, is very great, and I feel more and more that if Shakespeare presented himself in the basement to the Hogarth Press, it is even betting that he would be informed that his work 'interested us but we regret being unable to offer to publish it,' while Tupper [Martin Farquhar Tupper, a Victorian writer of sententious popular verse] was appearing in the Living Poets."[313]

The Woolfs initiated some projects specifically for the press. They solicited twelve of what would be called "Hogarth Letters" as part of a pamphlet series, later collected for a volume. Contributors were invited to "write the letter to anyone, living or dead, real or imaginary, on any subject," as Leonard wrote to E. M. Forster.[314] (The format, while familiar from ancient and Renaissance models, also resembles the scheme for a comic correspondence in the early years of what would become the Bloomsbury Group.)[315] Not surprisingly, Shakespeare makes cameo appearances in many of the *Hogarth Letters*. Raymond Mortimer, condescending to his imaginary addressee "Harriet," informs her that though schoolmasters and clergymen may seek him for "moral platitudes," the true "point of Shakespeare is not in the truths he states but in the way he states them, the imagery and the diction. All good pictures are painted as it were in verse. I think you get a better notion of what painters are up to by thinking of the poets than by reading all the lives of all the painters."[316] Francis Birrell, posing as a dissolute Englishman living in France and signing himself "Black Sheep," castigates his upright English cousin on the literary opinions of the Conservative politician Stanley Baldwin, who had, Black Sheep asserts, written in the *Times* "about how America was ruining the language of Shakespeare" when Baldwin "would not have understood a word of Shakespearian English had he heard it spoken, and who doesn't apparently know that the only places in which it is still spoken are certain parts of America."[317] Hugh Walpole, in his "Letter to a Modern Novelist," deftly skewers the fictive, pretentious, and presumptuous young author of a book called *The Camel with Four Humps:* "Is [the] simple genius for story-telling altogether so negligible," he asks rhetorically. "Homer had it, Chaucer had it, Dante had it, Shakespeare had it—mixed beautifully with other and possibly greater gifts but, all the same, none of these geniuses disdained it! Of this particular art there is no sign whatever in your *Camel.*"[318] The best known of these letters is Virginia Woolf's "Letter to a Young Poet," addressed to John Lehmann, in which she includes, as we have seen, one of her most compelling observations about the relationship between poetry and character: "Can you doubt that the reason why Shakespeare knew every sound and syllable in the language and could do precisely what he liked with grammar and syntax, was that Hamlet, Falstaff and Cleopatra rushed him into this knowledge; that the lords, officers, dependants, murderers and common soldiers of the plays insisted that he should say exactly what they felt in the words expressing their feelings? It was they who taught him to write, not the begetter of the Sonnets."[319]

In each of these cases, the mention of "Shakespeare" enables the writer to make an observation about *something else:* how to look at a painting; the philistinism of politicians; the absence of storytelling in modern fiction; the centrality of literary character. It's not that the observations the authors make about Shakespeare are unimportant, but rather that Shakespeare, as a cultural benchmark, can be brought into conversation with the other arts while simultaneously providing an opportunity for poetic or dramatic analysis. "Shakespeare" is the fixed foot on which the compass can rest while the other roams. If Roger Fry's unfinished letter to the inquisitive and persistent (and, again, presumably fictional) "Reginald," was, as has been conjectured, originally intended for this series, his vision of himself as Polonius would have fit well into the sequence.

Editing and Reviewing

While he continued to work as a publisher, Leonard Woolf took on a number of other demanding positions. In 1923 he was appointed the literary editor of the *Nation and Athenaeum,* which was then owned by Maynard Keynes, and he continued in that role until 1930. He began a column called "World of Books," and most evenings when he and Virginia were at home he "read a book for review or in connection with what I was writing."[320] Over the years, in the *Nation and Athenaeum* and elsewhere, he reviewed many books on Shakespeare, among them Samuel Butler's *Shakespeare's Sonnets Reconsidered; The Works of Shakespeare Chronologically Arranged,* with an introduction by Charles Whibley; Noel Douglas's *Replicas of Shakespeare's Sonnets;* John Bailey's *A Question of Taste* and David Nicol Smith's *Shakespeare in the Eighteenth Century* (reviewed jointly under the heading, "Is Shakespeare a Great Poet?"); George Gordon's *Shakespeare's English; The Works of Shakespeare,* volume 1, edited by Herbert Farjeon; and four volumes of J. Dover Wilson's *Facsimiles of the First Folio Text.*[321] For another writer, or in another time, the number, quality, and tone of these reviews might have qualified him as a recognized expert.

Sometimes Shakespeare even crept into reviews on ostensibly quite different subjects. When Woolf reviewed a book called *Twenty Thousand Years in Sing Sing,* by the prison warden Lewis E. Lawes, he quoted sympathetically from *King Lear.*[322] And much later, when he reviewed Michael Holroyd's 1968 biography of Lytton Strachey for the *New Statesman,* he turned to Shakespeare to support one disagreement he had with the author: "I do not think," Woolf wrote, "that he [Lytton] had any very strong emotions. . . . He was hardly ever completely serious when he had a pen in his hand, writing the tragedy or comedy of his perpetual love affairs to Maynard Keynes, James [Strachey], or me. . . . Mr Holroyd should remember what Rosalind said some 350 years ago: 'Men have died from time to time, and worms have eaten them, but not for love.'"[323]

Peggy Ashcroft

In his later years, Woolf's friendship with the actress Peggy Ashcroft brought him closer to the world of the theatre. The Woolfs had gone regularly to the theatre when they were in London, and one of the actresses they especially admired was Ashcroft. They were in the audience when she played Juliet at the New Theatre in December 1935, and they saw her again as Viola in *Twelfth Night* at the Phoenix in December 1938.

In 1940 Ashcroft married Jeremy Hutchinson, the barrister son of Mary and St John Hutchinson. (She had previously been married to Rupert Hart-Davis and to the theatre director Theodore Komisarjevsky.)[324] Marriage to Hutchinson brought her—belatedly—into the Bloomsbury orbit. Jeremy's mother, Mary, a celebrated hostess, had had a long relationship with Clive Bell, and Mary and St John were both friends of the Woolfs.[325] During the war, Peggy Ashcroft, Dadie Rylands, Maynard Keynes, Stephen Spender, and Natasha Litvin founded the

Apollo Society for poetry reading, launched at the Arts Theatre, Cambridge, in 1943, with financial support from Keynes. Ashcroft and Dadie Rylands remained close; they corresponded and traveled together, and she played a number of Shakespearean roles under his direction.

In the late 1950s, Woolf and his companion Trekkie Parsons got to know Ashcroft better, and over time he became a mentor as well as a fan. To help Peggy prepare for a production of Ibsen's *Rosmersholm* he gave her a copy of Freud's essay "Character Types Sometimes Met with in Psycho-analytic Work," which included a discussion of the incest secret in Ibsen's play, as well as two studies of Shakespearean characters.

Throughout her life Peggy Ashcroft had played major Shakespearean roles—Desdemona, Juliet, Imogen, Portia, Perdita, Viola, Miranda, Beatrice, Cordelia, Rosalind. As she grew older she still played some of the ingénue parts, but also a few more mature roles: Paulina in *The Winter's Tale,* Emilia in *Othello,* and the ageless Cleopatra. Her bravura performance of Margaret of Anjou in the 1963 *The Wars of the Roses,* John Barton's adaptation of the *Henry VI* plays and *Richard III,* directed by Peter Hall, led Woolf to write her that it was "the most wonderful thing I've ever seen on the stage as [Margaret] goes from youth to age," adding, "I must say that Shakespeare also came extraordinarily well out of it. His passion and at the same time his unblinking icy objective cynicism are terrific."[326] In 1959 he wrote to her that she was "far and away the best English actor I have seen," comparing her to Bernhardt, Duse, and Coquelin: "You stand with them."[327] Ten years later he offered another set of comparisons: "I once used to say to myself, 'Well, I've seen Sarah, Duse, Réjane and Ellen Terry,' but I now say to myself, 'Well, I've seen Sarah, Duse, Réjane and Peggy Ashcroft.' And you beat them all for range."[328] The friendship was important to them both. "Much of the fun that Leonard had in his eighties," says Victoria Glendinning, "came through his and Trekkie's friendship with Peggy Ashcroft at the height of her career."[329]

Situated as they are among the remarkably varied accomplishments of Leonard Woolf, his writings on Shakespeare have receded into the background. But Shakespeare was, from the Trinity College Shakespeare Society to the end of his life, a major influence on his work and on his thinking. The plays—read, quoted, discussed, and seen—were for him always a source of interest and pleasure. We might recall that Virginia once told him the only two people who really understood her were "you and Shakespeare."[330]

THE THEATRE CRITIC: DESMOND MacCARTHY

We have already encountered Desmond MacCarthy as the Cambridge friend (and fellow Apostle) who gave Leonard Woolf a miniature edition of Shakespeare when he departed for Ceylon, and the gregarious conversationalist who dropped in on Virginia to talk at length about Shakespeare. Her laconic diary entry from July 1926 reads merely, "Desmond came in; talked about Shakespeare," but she described his visit more fully in a letter to Vita Sackville-West: "Desmond turned up last night and rambled on for an hour about the character of Shakespeare—he was a smallish man, very nervous, with staring blueish gray eyes, highly excitable—did you know all this? he talked a great deal—Shakespeare: and Desmond and Virginia too."[331]

MacCarthy seems subsequently to have revised his view about the degree to which writers and scholars could accurately visualize the poet, suggesting instead that the more they look for his personality, the more they find only a reflection of themselves.[332]

The article in which he put forth this view, "Mr Shaw on Shakespeare," was first published in the *New Statesman* in 1914 and then reprinted in MacCarthy's 1918 collection of essays, *Remnants.* It begins with a striking image: "History has unfortunately hung the portrait of Shakespeare in a bad light. Like some dark, rich, glazed masterpiece in an ill-planned gallery, it seems to reflect not infrequently something of the features of those who peer curiously into it."[333] From here he launches into a series of brief characterizations of other writers on Shakespeare that anticipates, by more than a decade, T. S. Eliot's similar but more satiric version of the same trope in "Shakespeare and the Stoicism of Seneca." "Sir Sidney Lee's Shakespeare is essentially a steady man" who "gathered much comforting gear about him and died honoured, safe, satiated, and prosperous; Sir Leslie Stephen's a stoic who was no pipe for Fortune's fingers to play upon. Mr Frank Harris's Shakespeare, on the other hand, is . . . intellectual, bookish, and will-less," but with a "treble dose of sensuality," who "talked, laughed, drank, swaggered, worked, loved—above all, loved—wept, suffered, and wore himself out."[334]

And what of "Mr Shaw"? Shaw's Shakespeare, says MacCarthy, "could look the ugly facts of life in the face with a chuckle," and though sometimes moved by strong feelings, "whether for a woman, fame, riches, or for life itself," was capable of rising above those feelings. Shaw "thinks of genius as a kind of immunity from average human weakness, bringing with it an irrepressible gaiety of heart." In fact, says MacCarthy mildly, Shaw, the critic who had coined the terms *bardolatry* and *bardolator,* "remains after all among the bardolators: Shakespeare

Desmond MacCarthy, photograph by Lady Ottoline Morrell, 1923

was superhuman."[335] Given a choice between Shaw's Shakespeare and Harris's, MacCarthy unhesitatingly plumps for the latter: "To me it is easier to imagine Shakespeare as Mr Harris describes him, as a man even more at the mercy of all that tortures and beglamours than average mortals, with an enormous overplus of sensibility."[336] Whether this portrait reflects something of his own features he does not say.

Although his friends and his wife Molly all expected that he might write novels, MacCarthy became instead one of Britain's best-known drama critics and journalists, whose commentary on Shakespeare productions, focusing on the importance of the language and fidelity to the text, matched and underscored the views of other members of Bloomsbury. An original member of the play-reading Midnight Society, an enthusiast who loved the excitement of theatregoing, he was close not only to Strachey but also to many other Apostles, and notably to G. E. Moore—who would, at his request, be buried "beside Desmond" in the churchyard of St. Giles in Cambridge (now the Ascension Parish Burial Ground).[337] In 1903 MacCarthy began working as a freelance journalist and was appointed assistant literary editor, and then drama critic, of the Liberal weekly the *Speaker.* He joined the *New Statesman* as its drama critic in 1917, becoming its literary editor in 1920. His weekly column, published under the pen name Affable Hawk, became known for its literary judgment and cultural observation. He later wrote for several other periodicals, including the *Sunday Times.*

A New Kind of Theatre

When he met the innovative actor and director Harley Granville Barker, who had leased the Royal Court Theatre for three years beginning in 1904, MacCarthy quickly became an admirer and a friend. He saw that Granville Barker, in turning away from artificial and mannered performance toward naturalness in language and gesture, was inaugurating a new (or renewed) kind of theatre, with great consequences for Shakespeare on the stage. After the long dominance of figures like Henry Irving and Herbert Beerbohm Tree, this was a fresh approach, and a welcome one, since it focused attention on language rather than spectacle. As MacCarthy wrote in his book on the Court, "The players have been trained not to 'act.' . . . The surprisingly good quality of the acting has been mainly due to the fact that the producers have taken pains to see that the actors should have nothing inane or affected set them to say and do; and that the parts should be capable of being acted well, that is to say, naturally and sincerely, from beginning to end."[338] (The book's epigraph, an altered passage from *As You Like It* [3.2.27–30], was a characteristic piece of Bloomsbury/Shakespeare wit: "TOUCHSTONE: Wast ever at the Court, shepherd? / CORIN: No, truly. / TOUCHSTONE: Then thou art damned.")[339]

As early as 1906 MacCarthy laid out the standards to which he would hold directors and actors of Shakespeare. A production of *Othello* at the Lyric Theatre, starring Lewis Waller and the younger Henry Irving, concluded with Othello's suicide, cutting Lodovico's resonant rebuke to Iago ("Look on the tragic loading of this bed. / This is thy work") and his injunctions to Gratiano, Cassio, and the audience. By this truncation, MacCarthy declared in print, the final act of the play was was "utterly ruined."[340] He was equally dismissive of the Herbert

Beerbohm Tree production of *Antony and Cleopatra* staged at His Majesty's Theatre the same year, with Tree and Constance Collier in the title roles, because of the way the actors spoke their lines: "Anyone who is not stone deaf to the music of language," he wrote, or "who is even sleepily susceptible to the rhythm of speech, must have left the theatre contemptuous and cold."[341] As, very clearly, he had done.

Two back-to-back reviews of Granville Barker's *A Midsummer Night's Dream* in 1914 are likewise indicative. In the first, MacCarthy addresses the problem of producing poetic drama, much in the way that Lytton Strachey and Charles Lamb had done, noting that "some people whose imaginations demand absolute freedom" find any production imperfect; they "go to Shakespeare performances sometimes, sitting through them with resigned patience." (A producer, MacCarthy says, "cannot be expected to consider people who want *only* to use their ears in the theatre.")[342] As we've noted, he expressed the general Bloomsbury condemnation of a Shakespeare "smothered in scenery," observing that "Sir Herbert Tree considers any picture that can be called up by the poetry . . . to be relevant provided that it can be reconciled with the stage directions; and even if it cannot be, he often puts it in."[343]

On the brink of suggesting that the scenery in Granville Barker's production is similarly "distracting," he instead goes a second time to the Savoy, then reports in his column the following week that he has changed his mind. Even though some directorial and costume choices did not suit with MacCarthy's own sense of the play, he found on a second viewing that he was "immensely impressed by admirable qualities" in what he saw onstage. "I have always enjoyed *A Midsummer Night's Dream* as a poem, not a play," he says, but "what is remarkable about Mr Granville Barker's production is that it shows as has never been shown before, how dramatic also passages are which seem to the reader to be entirely lyrical." Though he "missed poetry at all sorts of points" and "Puck was a shock to me," he ultimately found that he had "given up [my] Puck, a phantom born of reading," to acknowledge the plausibility of Granville Barker's choice to show him as a "buffoon-sprite" full of "comic swagger." Granville Barker, after all, was a man of the theatre, and "the production is primarily a dramatist's production, not a poet's."[344] This judicious balance between the play read and the play acted is characteristic of MacCarthy's Shakespeare reviews, which always exhibit both a literary sensibility and a theatrical appreciation.

Perhaps most individual to him, however, is the way he approached the interpretation of Shakespearean character. In 1918 MacCarthy and the Woolfs had discussed the question of Shakespeare and modern psychology. Leonard, an early appreciator of Freud, seems to have argued for a sophisticated psychological understanding of Shakespeare's dramatic characters, while both Virginia and Desmond had maintained that a sense of their psychological complexity reflected the reader's viewpoint rather than the playwright's. Desmond, Virginia noted, "thought Othello & Desdemona very simple."[345] Reviewing the German scholar L. L. Schücking's *Character Problems in Shakespeare's Plays* in 1920, MacCarthy reinforced this position, arguing that modern attempts to interpret these as aspects of the speaker's character and motives rather than "indications to the audience how these characters are to be judged" are mistaken. As Schücking's book pointed out, "Shakespeare wrote for a naïve audience," and "one of the main principles of Shakespearean exegesis must therefore be to take literally, as mere plain statements, what the characters say about themselves and each other, and to avoid interpreting these comments as though the utterance of them threw subtle sidelights on the speaker's own character."[346] Likewise, "the monologue was a means of explaining the character to the audience; it was not an attempt at psychological realism."[347] When Iago calls himself a villain, when Lady Macbeth describes her own "cruelty," when Edmund praises Edgar, these are indications to the audience, not clues as to the internal thoughts or mental conflicts of the speaker.

In 1920 Affable Hawk published a review of Arnold Bennett's *Our Women*, leading to a correspondence with Virginia Woolf that was published in two issues of the *New Statesman*. Bennett's book had argued that "intellectually and creatively man is the superior of woman."[348] Woolf's reply was stinging, rich in the names of creative women from several centuries, and characteristically ironic ("I cannot claim to know Greek as Mr Bennett and Affable Hawk know it, but I have often been told that Sappho was a woman.") Affable Hawk at first stuck with his initial line of argument (even in areas where they might have some level of education, like "literature, poetry, music and painting," women "have hardly attained, with the possible exception of fiction, the highest achievements reached by men") but surrendered after a second and equally scathing blast. This was the exchange that elicited Woolf's powerful statement on the social and intellectual opportunities that were essential "for a Shakespeare to exist"—"that he shall have had predecessors in his art, shall make one of a group where art is freely discussed and practiced, and shall himself have the utmost of freedom of action and experience"—a description that, as we have already noted, seems to fit the circumstances of the women and men of Bloomsbury as well as of William (although not of "Judith") Shakespeare.[349]

Poetry and "Spontaneous Adroitness"

Like Lytton Strachey and Virginia Woolf, Desmond MacCarthy continually returned to the *poetry* of the plays—rather than their characterization, plot, or historical reference—as what made Shakespeare great. In a review of *Othello* at the Court Theatre in 1921, with Godfrey Tearle as Othello and Basil Rathbone as Iago, he once again found the biggest problem with the production was that it was unsuccessful "on the realistic level" and failed to foreground the centrality of the play's poetic language. "If Shakespearean actors act their parts as though the poetry were not the very soul of the play," he writes, "their performance . . . will not be the exhibition of a world's masterpiece. If the poetry of *Othello* is not felt, the play becomes an energetic, brutal, rather senseless melodrama, open to the most damaging criticism."[350]

Assessing a production of *Cymbeline,* he distinguishes between the experience of the reader and that of the playgoer, since the machinery of the play, with its "untidy, artificial, absurd" plot, "grinds and creaks with an intolerable insistence on the stage."[351] Even the passage of poetry that the young Virginia Stephen had singled out for praise seemed to him simultaneously marked by "splendor and failure." Imogen's line "Think that you are upon a rock; and now / Throw me again" was, he observes, "a line so meaningless that it has been suspected of corruption."[352] By contrast, in Posthumus's reply "Hang there like fruit, my soul, till the tree die," "never did passion and tenderness find more perfect expression in a single cry."[353] Sybil Thorndike in the role of Imogen reminded him, by the "perpetual lowering and then raising of the voice at the end of the sentence, which often destroys the verse," of a "kind governess setting down her pupils to their morning tasks."[354] The disparaging tone of this description is not entirely mitigated by MacCarthy's comment that Thorndike has too much personal dignity to "simulate" it on the stage, "just as a real gentleman or lady is often the worst hand at representing themselves."[355] But his critique of her verse readings is consistent with his claim at the outset, that *Cymbeline* is one of the plays that give him "most literary pleasure. There is in it an exquisite spontaneous adroitness in phrasing and cadence such as Shakespeare never excelled."[356] To speak the poetry with exaggerated and artificial emphasis, far from "spontaneous adroitness," was for Desmond MacCarthy, as for others in Bloomsbury, an unpardonable fault.

It is not a surprise, then, to find that MacCarthy responded positively to a production of the Marlowe Society at the Amateur Dramatic Club in Cambridge—an all-male performance of *Troilus and Cressida.* The portrayal of Cressida by "a young man with a neck like a pillar and a booming contralto voice" forces the audience to use their ears rather than their eyes: "You stare like a cow at the scene, but you listen like an intelligent human being to the *words.*"[357] The play was "as it should be, acted straight through with one rest, and on an apron stage." The performance as a whole exhibited "vigour and consistency of interpretation."[358] "Bravo, amateurs!" MacCarthy applauds in a parenthetical aside while crediting, in his last sentence, the vital contribution of a professional, the actor and theatre manager William Poel, whose Elizabethan Stage Society (1894–1905), featuring amateur casts, bare stages, and fidelity to the tone and spirit of the playwright's language, "set Shakespearean productions on the right path."[359]

This critical attention to speaking clearly and well continued to be a vital criterion for MacCarthy, with professionals as much as with amateurs. Reviewing a new production of *Hamlet* in March 1925, he found John Barrymore's enunciation and phrasing as Hamlet "excellently distinct. Every word he spoke (this is rare) was intelligible." Nonetheless, MacCarthy thought Barrymore's interpretation failed "in conveying Hamlet's bitter-gay, intellectual exhilaration," and felt strongly that it was a mistake of modern "stage-Hamlets" to insist on Hamlet's passion for Ophelia: "Hamlet was no lover," he asserts, repeating the point for emphasis: "Our actors play [the nunnery scene] as if it were a lover's quarrel! One which might end by Ophelia saying soothingly, 'Darling, you *know* you love me!'" He thought the closet scene between Hamlet and his mother "took on a Freudian significance," which was "a mistake and artistically uninteresting" contrasted with the real pathos of Ophelia's situation ("the pain of a girl, uneasy at being used for a purpose she does not understand—perhaps to the danger of the man she loves").[360] Again, as he did regarding the Lyric Theatre's *Othello,* he deplores the directorial habit of cutting a Shakespeare play to make for a dramatic curtain line: "'The play's the thing / Wherein I'll catch the conscience of the King,' is a splendid curtain, but damn curtains."[361] He thinks that Ophelia's burial was "badly stage-managed. Away with these white nuns!"—instead the corpse should be "borne in by a few rustics from the fields."[362] And he finds "no justification for the clutching, frantic physical tenderness which Mr Barrymore exhibits toward his mother." Had Barrymore looked at the First Quarto, MacCarthy informs his readers, noting parenthetically that "every actor should consult the quartos for lights upon Shakespearean parts," he would have found the queen saying, "He throws and tosses me about."[363] By contrast, he praises the portrayal of the ghost, "though several critics have crabbed him. I am sure Mr Thorpe is right in wailing out his lines with ominous monotony in a voice like the wind in a chimney."[364] The review is an example of MacCarthy at his confident best, combining scrupulous learning with stage smarts, textual knowledge, and theatre history.

In another review, called "Hamlets in General" (echoing the title of his earlier piece "Shylocks in General"), he describes a production indebted to the methods of Gordon Craig as "a distinct improvement upon any *Hamlet* I have seen," one "so interesting that when someday a history of stage Hamlets is written it should not be omitted," and quotes the painter Henry Fuseli's famous phrase about Blake: "damned good to steal from."[365] (The phrase was a favorite of his; he had also used it in "Shylocks" to describe, admiringly, the performance of the actor Maurice Moskovitch.)[366]

Despite taking a passing swipe at the work of literary scholars—"I do not recommend Shakespearean studies"—he mentions by name the American scholar Elmer (E. E.) Stoll, who supplied what was for him, apparently, surprising news: that the famous "delay" was a late addition to the story.[367] The idea of Hamlet "as a profound study in irresolution and a diseased will" was an innovation of "the Romantic Movement," he informs his readers; "to all earlier commentators Hamlet was a hero of brilliant dash in a story of revenge, courageous and resolute, who set about the slaying of his uncle as expeditely as the exigencies of the plot, the old plot, allowed."[368] That this should come as a surprise to MacCarthy seems, from a contemporary perspective, itself surprising, and he attempts to rebut it by citing passages from Seneca and Greek tragedy that accuse designated revengers of "sluggish" behavior, but his ultimate decision is to praise great works of art for being capable of growing and changing with the times. "Humanity is only interested in past ages and dead authors in so far as it can attribute to them its own passions and thoughts. That they are able to go on doing so—seeing now this, now that, in them—is the sign and proof of an immortal creation."[369] The note of modern progressive self-congratulation ("We of later days have read our sensitive bewilderments into a character which his creator designed more simply. . . . We ought to be thankful that we can read in a richer significance") replaces the different and arguably respect-worthy perceptions of the past ("even if Shakespeare would himself agree with Dr. Stoll").[370]

How might a reader of MacCarthy's criticism reconcile his insistence that the "amount of subtle speculation which has been wasted upon discrepancies in [Shakespeare's] character-drawing is appalling" with his thankfulness that today "we can read in a richer significance" than was the case in Shakespeare's time? Both views may coincide with his own beliefs. "Simple" and "literal" are words that recur throughout his discussions of how Shakespeare ought to be understood and presented onstage.

Doing It with Mirrors

The degree to which MacCarthy had become an influential figure for Shakespeareans may be underscored by returning to his views about the self-reflectiveness of biographical study, which had, by midcentury, apparently become something of a byword. In the preface to his book *Shakespeare's Lives,* first published in 1970, scholar Sam Schoenbaum alludes to MacCarthy's opinion, which bolstered his own conviction:

> I quickly recognized the truth of the observation that biography tends toward oblique self-portraiture. How much must this be so with respect to Shakespeare, where the sublimity of the subject ensures empathy and the impersonality of the life-record teases speculation! I remember once mentioning this pattern to the late John Crow in the familiar columned portico of the British Museum, and he reminded me that Desmond McCarthy [*sic*] had said somewhere that trying to work out Shakespeare's personality was like looking at a very dark glazed picture in the National Portrait Gallery: at first you see nothing, then you begin to recognize features, and then you realize that they are your own.[371]

This perception, says Schoenbaum, supplied him with a leitmotif for his project.[372]

The portrait analogy—from MacCarthy's 1914 essay on Shaw and Shakespeare—had undergone a few changes by the time the two scholars recalled it many years later. The unidentified "ill-planned gallery" became England's National Portrait Gallery, home of the Shakespeare portrait that is proudly designated Number 1 in the gallery's official list of works, despite the fact that it was neither the first portrait acquired nor the earliest in date. The gradual, ghostly emergence of the gazer's own features from the dark surface of the picture replaced the more immediate self-(mis)recognition of the curious, peering observer. If MacCarthy's original first sentence, "History has unfortunately hung the portrait of Shakespeare in a bad light," ends, as I think it may, with a deliberate play on the phrase "bad light" (poorly lit; unfavorable), then some of the wit has also been lost in translation. The very lack of a cited source probably increased the effect: an observation that Desmond MacCarthy "had said somewhere" here attains a quasi-proverbial status.[373]

MacCarthy's story of Shakespeare and reflected resemblance had, moreover, a slightly uncanny sequel in his own life. By what may be a fortuitous coincidence, he and his wife Molly spent their last years living in rented quarters in

Garrick's Villa, an early eighteenth-century house in Hampton Court refurbished by Robert Adam in 1775 as a country home for the Shakespearean actor David Garrick. Across the road was Garrick's Temple to Shakespeare, in which stands a statue of the playwright, its face modeled on Garrick's features. Perhaps—as MacCarthy suggested—some crossover between Shakespeare and any interpreter is inevitable, though it is seldom as blatant as Garrick's. But in Desmond MacCarthy's Shakespeare, too, we can discern the lineaments of the critic, as well as his view of the dramatist and his work: spontaneously adroit, and damned good to steal from.

THE DIRECTOR: GEORGE RYLANDS

The interest in Shakespeare shown by members of Bloomsbury enriched both their lives and their own varied practices. Whether they were novelists, poets, journalists, biographers, painters, philosophers, economists, dancers, or politicians, they read, cited, and watched Shakespeare because his works gave them pleasure and insight. They were thus in the best sense "amateurs"—lovers of Shakespeare's language and his plays and poems.

At the same time, there was at least one manifest professional "Shakespearean" in their midst: the director, actor, university don, theatrical producer, and CBE in Shakespearean studies, George Humphrey Wolferstan Rylands. The life and career of "Dadie" Rylands (his mispronunciation of "baby" as a small child became a lifelong and affectionate nickname) influenced how many in Bloomsbury experienced Shakespeare, just as their response to Shakespeare influenced his own. As his obituary noted, "It is clearly through Rylands that the Bloomsberries enter English theatre."[374]

A member of the Cambridge University English faculty, the director of dozens of Shakespeare productions, and the author of the Shakespeare anthology *The Ages of Man,* Rylands spent his life teaching, writing, and directing Shakespeare. His lifelong friends included Maynard Keynes, Virginia and Leonard Woolf, Lytton Strachey, and many others foundational to Bloomsbury as a cultural, philosophical, and intellectual movement. Keynes supported Dadie's selection as a Cambridge Apostle in 1921 and then his 1927 appointment as a fellow at King's College—a position he held throughout his long life.

At Cambridge Rylands taught many of the outstanding Shakespearean actors and directors of the twentieth century, among them Ian McKellen, John Barton, Derek Jacobi, Peter Hall, and Trevor Nunn. He had been, briefly, an assistant to the Woolfs at the Hogarth Press. (His name is perhaps best known to Woolfians—though unjustly, given his many subsequent achievements—as the host of the delectable lunch served to Virginia Woolf at King's College before she went on to the meager dinner offered by a woman's college.)[375] He not only produced and directed Marlowe performances, he often also acted in them, especially when undergraduate performers were scarce.

Rylands Onstage

Rylands's Shakespeare career began early. At Eton he was the first student to produce a play in the College School Hall. He starred as Viola in *Twelfth Night* and was awarded the Shakespeare Gold Medal. His gift for women's roles attracted attention, since in school and college productions, as in Shakespeare's theatre, men played all the parts. When the classics scholar John Sheppard—later to be provost at King's—interviewed Rylands in December 1920 he insisted that he leave Eton early in order to appear as Electra in a King's production of *The Oresteia.* He was a "ruthlessly dashing Diomedes" in a Marlowe Society production of *Troilus and Cressida* in 1922, heralding the return of that hitherto neglected play to the stage.[376] Two years later he would dazzle Cambridge audiences as the Duchess of Malfi. Rylands was "an eager and talented participant in University theatrical ventures," report Anne Olivier Bell and Andrew McNeillie. "Elected to the Society (Apostles), he was both an acute and personable recruit to the fraternity and had, inevitably, engaged the interest of both Maynard Keynes and Lytton Strachey."[377]

The newly founded English department at Cambridge, which Rylands was to join, was unique for its time in England in emphasizing not Anglo-Saxon literature but the relation of English poetry to Greek and Latin authors. As Noel Annan points out, "The first dons in the faculty were determined to meet the jibes of Bloomsbury and other writers that the last thing professors of literature ever asked themselves was why poems and novels touched the heart." And they also "took another notion from Bloomsbury. Why not examine what a writer is doing, what makes him tick, rather than pontificating about him, as the Victorian critics did."[378]

When he took over the direction of the Marlowe Society in 1928, Rylands focused attention on the language of early modern drama, making the Marlowe, Annan rightly notes, "the nursery where those who were to become famous in the theatre learnt to speak Shakespeare's verse."[379] "It was," writes Tim Cribb, "the university's Marlowe Society which was to be the main channel of his influence on English theatre. Through that channel flowed the principles of impersonality, balance, and the delivery of verse with neither the huff-and-puff of old-style rhetoric nor the clipped twittering of drawing-room comedy which were then the prevailing alternatives. These principles were first mooted by Lytton Strachey in reviews of earlier Marlowe productions and developed by Rylands in discussion with Strachey and other members of the Bloomsbury Group, especially Virginia Woolf."[380] As soon as the society decided to allow women to act in its plays, Rylands took advantage of the opportunity to stage a production of *Antony and Cleopatra.*

His production of *King Lear* in 1929, starring Michael Redgrave as Edgar, was praised by Strachey, who came up to Cambridge to see a rehearsal, and by John Lehmann, who called it "one of the most moving and beautiful of our time and without doubt the one truest to the spirit of the poetry."[381] During World War II, when undergraduate actors were less available, he often took part in his own Marlowe Society productions. In the mid-1940s Dadie Rylands could be seen onstage at the Cambridge Arts Theatre—built by Maynard Keynes, later managed by Rylands himself—in the roles of Othello, King Lear, Leontes, Caliban, and Macbeth. He also, by his own account, played Cordelia, Regan, Henry IV, and "the three ladies from Coriolanus."[382] An image of him as the Duchess of Malfi was the first Cecil Beaton photograph to appear in *Vogue.* And when his Marlowe Society *Measure for Measure* traveled to Berlin as part of a British cultural offensive during the Cold War, Rylands played Angelo, "perhaps the best of all his many performances."[383]

Over the course of his career, he directed a remarkable series of actors in his productions, from Cambridge students like Redgrave, Derek Jacobi, and Ian McKellen to professionals at the peak of their fame, such as John Gielgud and Peggy Ashcroft. But as Noel Annan writes, "It was not until Peter Hall became director of the Royal Shakespeare Company and formed a permanent company with a theatre in London as well as at Stratford-upon-Avon that the full effect of Rylands' work began to be seen."[384] John Barton, Dadie's former student, now a Shakespeare scholar at King's, joined Hall at the RSC, becoming a director and training the actors in speaking verse. During this vital period Rylands's views and practice would inform—and transform—Shakespeare productions at Stratford.

"The Young Man in the Basement"

After he graduated from Cambridge and before he returned there as a Fellow, Rylands worked briefly for Virginia and Leonard Woolf at the Hogarth Press

Virginia Woolf and Dadie Rylands, 1932

at the end of 1923 but, as Hermione Lee notes, "He lasted as a friend, not as an employee."[385] He had first met the Woolfs during a holiday at Studland, Dorset, where the other guests were Keynes, Lydia Lopokova, and Raymond Mortimer; it was on this occasion that the idea of his working at the press was first proposed.[386]

Virginia Woolf's affection for Dadie Rylands was strong and remained so over the years. He "became Dadie" ("Dady" in her initial spelling) the minute she first met him "at 10 A.M. Monday at Poole station" on September 11, 1923. (In the previous sentence of her diary he was referred to as "the poet Rylands"; in other diary entries she described him affectionately as a "young kitten" and a "corn flower.")[387] To one of her friends, a woman who had just met him, he was "that enchanting creature."[388] In a letter to the painter Jacques Raverat responding to his request for "gossip," Woolf offered among a list of short-takes, "Our Dadie is a very nice boy."[389] A little more than a month later she sent Jacques a longer account of the "very nice boy," again in terms couched to amuse. (The "basement" was the location of the Hogarth Press.)

> About the young man in the basement, George Rylands. Alas, he will soon cease to be in the basement, King's College requiring him to work harder at his dissertation, and so he will be going after Xmas to write upon Diction in Poetry, and so win a fellowship, and live at Cambridge and teach, which they now insist upon. . . . He is a semi-Neo Pagan perhaps. At King's they are all reminded of Rupert—partly his yellow hair, partly his poetry, which is not so good as Rupert's. He is a very charming spoilt boy, sprung of the rich who have no money, and so rather dazzled London and parties, and perhaps he scents himself; but at heart he is uncorrupted, (so I think—others disagree) and all the young and oldish men, like Eddie Marsh and so on, fall in love with him, and he dines out every night, and treats his lovers abominably. . . . A life in Cambridge seems to me a skeleton life, but then, it has to be.[390]

Women, too, regularly fell in love with Dadie. Topsy Lucas left her husband on his account, even though Rylands did not reciprocate her passionate commitment.[391] And his charm was the kind that lasts; Noel Annan recalls that as an undergraduate "I got to know him and became platonically devoted to him for the rest of his life."[392]

Leonard Woolf shared his wife's admiration of the "brilliant" young man who came to work with them when he was only twenty-two. "We were aiming very high when we took Dadie into the Press and began to turn him into a publisher," Woolf wrote. "Not unnaturally he did not stay long in the basement." They had known that he was waiting to see whether he got the fellowship at King's, and when he did, "much to our regret [he] left us for a distinguished career in the university, the arts, and the theatre."[393]

When Rylands asked Virginia Woolf if he could dedicate his book of poems *Russet and Taffeta* to her, she responded with pleasure ("and Old Woolf himself can find no objection to it. So we will do it").[394] The book was published by the Hogarth Press in 1925. The press also published a second volume, *Poems,* in 1931, as well as Rylands's book of literary criticism, *Words and Poetry* (1928), based on his fellowship dissertation.

By 1931 Virginia's letters, which in earlier years began "Dear Dadie" or "My dear Dadie," had become consistently addressed to "Dearest Dadie."[395] "Dearest Dadie," she wrote him in February 1932, "Of course we're coming to Hamlet. . . . I'm longing, without exaggeration, to see it."[396] The *Hamlet* production at the ADC—Rylands's first *Hamlet*—was praised by the reviewer for the *Times,* who found himself convinced, "most unexpectedly, that *Hamlet* is a play for the young."[397] The Woolfs drove to Cambridge to see it, and Virginia wrote Rylands the next day to tell him she was "dumfoundered [*sic*] at your brilliance as a producer."[398] The costumes and set evoked the Romantic period of the Napoleonic Wars—the time of Coleridge and Byron—avoiding both tired "Elizabethanism" and nondescript modern dress. E. M. Forster, in a review for the *Spectator,* was especially impressed by the way the young actors handled verse drama:

> They are not ashamed of poetry, for one thing. They neither brazen it out, like the professionals of the last generation, nor twitter past it like bats after the fashion of today. They do not regard poetry as the sign of a weak character, to be expiated at all costs. They actually say what Shakespeare said, and so they are a constant delight to the ear. Nor do they mistrust thought. Hamlet thinks his way through the soliloquies, he does not declaim them. Claudius thinks both in his villainies and in his prayers, the Gravedigger thinks, and Polonius thinks more seriously than anyone, though his conclusions are bizarre. And so we come away from Cambridge feeling that Shakespeare had not only a sense of beauty but a mind. When we go to see him displayed at immense cost at His Majesty's, shall we have the least notion that he possessed either?[399]

After Rylands had become a fellow at King's, he and Virginia kept up their conversations about Shakespeare and publishing, both in person and by letter. "I've been sent a volume of the Yale Shakespeare you told me of," she wrote him. "I wish the type wasn't American, that's all. They have also sent this prospectus—you see they have an interleaved edition too."[400] The Yale Shakespeare, issued in the period between 1918 and 1929, was a new entry into the world of Shakespeare publishing, combining text and critical annotation in its forty small, affordable hardback volumes. Each volume had a brief introduction, an index, and—of special note—the valuable innovation of brief glosses at the foot of the page explaining words, phrases, and other unfamiliar elements in the text. This procedure, now routinely followed in all modern editions, made the series one of the best known, and most successful, of the Yale Press's ventures—and may have been of special interest to Virginia Woolf, who herself ran a press.

On the whole Virginia preferred reading the plays—or hearing them read—to seeing them in performance. In March 1934 she and Leonard went to Cambridge to see Rylands's Marlowe Society production of *Antony and Cleopatra* at the Festival Theatre. In her diary she noted, "Lunch with Dadie" but privately rated the show "a dragging weak performance."[401] But when Rylands read selections from Shakespeare on the radio in the BBC series *The English Poets* on May

1, 1937, she sent him a postcard the next day: "You almost brought the Wolves to tears last night, reading Shakespeare so beautifully."[402] In December 1939 she noted that among the books she was reading was "Dadie's Shakespeare," probably his anthology *The Ages of Man: Shakespeare's Image of Man and Nature,* which was published that year.

Rylands and Strachey: Words and Poetry

Dadie Rylands's friendship with the Woolfs had developed as a result of his work with them at the Hogarth Press. His friendship with Lytton Strachey went back even further, to his undergraduate days. They met at Cambridge, first through Keynes and Sheppard and then in the weekly gatherings of the Apostles. Michael Holroyd notes in his biography of Strachey that "among those who became his friends and whom he began inviting back for weekends to Tidmarsh were George ('Dadie') Rylands, a feline, fair-haired Etonian of great poise and elegance of dress, with a flair for stagecraft."[403] From the mid-1920s on, Rylands was one of Strachey's chief confidants and a regular houseguest. In the late winter of 1927 Lytton reported that Dadie was at Ham Spray House "reading Shakespeare with a violent cold in the head."[404] A letter from Carrington to Sebastian Sprott gives a delightful sense of his persona: "This weekend we have Dadie . . . in his highest high brow mood. 'I don't think I can agree. You find in Shakespeare's sonnets . . .' comes through the window from Dadie on the verandah. 'It is essential that the poet, as indeed all writers, should use words etc. etc.'"

And later in the same letter:

> ("Listen to this: the expedition of my careless love outran the etc."[405] Then there is a very good commodity passage in *King John.* Listen to this. . . ." etc.)
>
> All this at 11 o'clock in the morning and it's been going on for 2 hours![406]

In 1930 Rylands and Strachey went to Rome together, "Dadie carrying with him a portable edition of Shakespeare, Lytton some novels of Trollope and most of Proust."[407] But Rylands was not only a good friend and a clever, attractive, companion, he was also an exceptionally gifted scholar-teacher, director, and actor. Lytton Strachey had attended a rehearsal of Rylands's *King Lear* in the spring of 1929, sending him, as we saw, a note of warm encouragement. (The *Lear* was Rylands's first Shakespeare production for the Marlowe Society; his twenty-fourth and last, in 1966, was *Measure for Measure.*) What was so striking, especially after the years in which actors like Irving and Macready had dominated the stage, was the *way* he read Shakespeare: as poetry, as words—not as a backstory for character motivation, a cue to action, a moral precept, or a clue about the personal life of the playwright.

When the Hogarth Press decided to publish Rylands's book *Words and Poetry* in 1928, Strachey readily agreed to provide the introduction. "There is one name that no English writer on English literature can hope, or wish, to avoid for more than a very few moments together," he declared with characteristic aplomb.

> Before we are aware of it, we all of us find that we are talking about Shakespeare. And Mr Rylands is no exception. Naturally, inevitably, he devotes the latter half of his book to a consideration of Shakespeare as a user of words, and to the history—the romance, one might almost say—of his adventures among them.
>
> It is curious that Shakespeare—by far the greatest word-master who ever lived—should have been so rarely treated from this point of view. . . . How very remarkable, for instance, is the development, which Mr Rylands points out to us,—a late and unexpected development—in Shakespeare's use of prose! How extremely interesting is the story of his dealings with words of classical derivation! The early youthful *engouement* for a romance vocabulary, the more mature severity, and the recoil towards Saxon influences, and then the sudden return to a premeditated and violent classicism—the splendid latinistic passion which, though it grew fainter with time, left such ineffaceable traces on all his later life!
>
> A drama might almost be made of it—and a drama that could hardly have passed unconsciously in Shakespeare's mind. The supreme artist must have known well enough what was happening among those innumerable little creatures who did his bidding with such rare felicity—his words. Did he, perhaps, for his own amusement, write an account of the whole affair? A series of sonnets . . .? If an allegory must be found in those baffling documents, why should not be this the solution of it? One can fancy that the beautiful youth was merely a literary expression for the classical vocabulary, while the dark lady personified the Saxon one.[408]

As Strachey goes on to note, there have been "many more far-fetched" theories about the sonnets. The introduction is framed by a deft reference to a story about Degas and Mallarmé, the former complaining to the latter that he can't seem to write a sonnet, even though he is "full of excellent ideas," and the latter replying succinctly, "My dear Degas, poetry is not written with ideas; it is written with words."[409] These words may be Mallarmé's, but the tone is unmistakably Strachey.

Rylands chose as an epigraph to *Words and Poetry* an observation by British poet and critic Lascelles Abercrombie: "what we call the magic of words—thereby pleasantly avoiding the necessity of thinking out what we really mean." In good Stracheyan fashion, he observes dryly that "even Mr Strachey, who tilts an eyebrow at sentiment, is ready to endow the poet with a magic wand," before setting forth the substance of his argument: "It behoves us to possess some first-hand knowledge of the scientific and emotional values of words: we must be able to analyse the meaning and appeal of the few score that make up our favorite sonnet."[410]

Read from the perspective of almost a century later, *Words and Poetry* has lost little of its freshness and none of its point. The sections on Shakespeare's poetic and dramatic development are closely reasoned, clearly and appealingly stated, and illustrated throughout with examples and comparisons that demonstrate an intimate, comfortable, and impressive knowledge of the play texts. "Language is the subject of *Love's Labour's Lost,*" he observes. "Shakespeare is still half enchanted by the golden net in which he is entangled." But soon, in this play as in others, we see "Shakespeare tilting at the diction of the day."[411] It is this reaction, Rylands suggests, that led "to the study of prose" and to "character and dramatic realism breaking through fashions and conventions." In Shakespeare's mature style—as in Jaques's twitting of Orlando in *As You Like It* for speaking in blank verse—characters begin to criticize over-ornate speech (though indeed they often do so in blank verse): Hotspur in *Henry IV, Part 1* complaining about the "popinjay with the pouncet box" on the battlefield, or sneering at the "mincing poetry" of the Welshman Owen Glendower. And here—as indeed throughout his book—Rylands clarifies his claims in a way that later critics have not always done: "I do not fall into the snare of identifying Shakespeare with his *dramatis personae* and making his views theirs; but these voices demanded a new medium, verse which will allow colloquial emphases and prose order, or else prose itself, the prose which Hamlet and Edmund and Iago were to speak."[412]

"It is not perhaps necessary to emphasise the quality of the prose in *Hamlet,*" he remarks, citing "What a piece of work is man" as well as "the meditations over Yorick's skull, the parable of the recorder, the renunciation of Ophelia." In his view, "It is the excellence and the importance of the prose which separates *Hamlet* from, and in many ways sets it above, all the other plays."[413] His close knowledge of the texts makes itself evident again and again. Commenting on Othello's "When I have pluck'd the rose, / I cannot give it vital growth again, / It needs must wither," Rylands observes, "After *Hamlet* the rose almost disappears; this is a notable exception."[414] Likewise, when he incorporates history into his account, it is always, and only, to underscore something about the tonality of the verse: the passing of a statute in 1606 forbidding the taking of God's name in vain on the stage leads to the use of "gods" rather than "God," making *Lear* "more Greek."[415]

Blank verse resumes its primacy in the late tragedies, preeminently in *Antony and Cleopatra.* "Shakespeare's first sublime character, Falstaff, was created in prose; Hamlet, his greatest, in both elements; Cleopatra, the third, in poetry."[416] At this point "his command of metre was such that he could use blank verse with more ease than prose, and experiment in syntax and arrangement of clauses without rattling his chains."[417]

As Strachey had done in his audacious essay "Shakespeare's Final Period," Rylands suggests in *Words and Poetry* that as Shakespeare continued to develop his style, language increasingly became the sole focus of his interest: "In the last period of all, the characters and the plot are sacrificed to the reckless power of expression; that is, to the poetry."[418] In the "final style" of Shakespeare, he says, in the late tragedies and final comedies or romances, "perhaps most important of all" is the syntax: "the condensation, exemplified by a fondness for ellipsis, inverted order, apposition, and parenthesis."[419] Thus, "Every speech provides instances of curious construction."[420] Meter and syntax are "no longer those of prose or verse"; instead, both seem "fused together and interchangeable."[421] Plot and character are subordinated: "Facts are often wedged in among poetic flourishes and speakers are in one line perfunctory, in the next leisurely and fanciful. In scenes where the story has to be lugged on its way, Shakespeare is like a peacock who picks his causal way and then quite suddenly unfurls the glory of his tail; sometimes there is only a glimpse, sometimes the full fan."[422]

Strachey had made a similar point in his early essay: "Never did Shakespeare's magnificence of diction reach more marvelous heights than in some of the speeches of Prospero, or his lyric art a purer beauty than in the songs of Ariel; nor is it only in these ethereal regions that the triumph of his language asserts itself."[423] But Strachey—characteristically—had been even more contentious in his famous claim about Shakespeare's frame of mind: "It is difficult to resist the conclusion that he was getting bored himself. Bored with people, bored with real life, bored with drama, bored, in fact, with everything except poetry and poetical dreams."[424] It is a claim he happily revisits two decades later, in his introduction to *Words and Poetry:*

> In Shakespeare's later works character has grown unindividual and unreal; drama has become conventional or operatic; the words remain more tremendously, more exquisitely, more thrillingly alive than ever—the excuse and the explanation of the rest. The little creatures had absolutely fascinated their master; he had become their slave. At their bidding he turned Coriolanus from a human being into a glorious gramophone; they spoke, and a fantastic confusion, a beautiful impossibility, involved the constructions of *The Winter's Tale* and *Cymbeline.* To please them, he called up out of nothingness, in *The Tempest,* an Island, not of Romance, but of Pure Style. At last, it was simply for style that Shakespeare lived; everything else had vanished.[425]

It's intriguing to compare this to the early view expressed by the young Virginia Stephen in a letter to her brother Thoby at Cambridge, when she asked him why the characters in *Cymbeline* were not "more human." "Really," she wrote, "they might have been cut out with a pair of scissors," although "of course they talk divinely."[426] Strachey's introduction to *Words and Poetry*—like his essay "Shakespeare's Final Period"—addresses the same perception about character and language, leading him to his theoretical ideas about late style.

A Poet's Testimony: John Lehmann

As an undergraduate, the poet and future publisher John Lehmann, who would later work at the Hogarth Press—and still later purchase Virginia Woolf's share of it—was strongly influenced by Rylands in his reading and especially in his appreciation of Shakespeare.

"Of George Rylands, one of the youngest dons of King's, I saw a good deal," Lehmann recalled. "His *Words and Poetry* was just the book I needed to read at the time . . . with its emphasis on the importance to a line of the weight, colour and overtones of every single word."[427] Lehmann "began to read some books of Shakespearean criticism, stirred by Wilson Knight's *The Wheel of Fire.* The more I read the more interested I became. . . . I therefore welcomed Dadie Rylands's suggestion that I should spend one long vacation working for the Charles Oldham Shakespeare scholarship. . . . My instinct was that I must *know* Shakespeare through and through."[428]

Lehmann's account of that youthful summer—viewed from the perspective of midlife—is rhapsodic: "The whole Shakespeare panorama unfolded before me like a new landscape or the further side of a mountain pass—new, because, though many details were already familiar enough to me, I had never seen it as a whole before—and my mind was changed by the experience. In no other way could I have understood that Shakespeare was the key to the whole of English literature, the master mind that determined its course and depth and vitality so fundamentally that we can hardly conceive what our imaginative life—perhaps even our moral values—would be like without him."[429] And again,

> No one had prepared me for this experience before Cambridge, nor would I, with my sceptical turn of mind, have been ready to believe what the necessity of reading every play (and every apocryphal play as well) two or three times in the order of writing—and following step by step how that order had been established—so miraculously presented to me: the incredible flowering of his genius and the immeasurable amplitude that flowering reached. Even if there had not been this revelation, which was almost like the revelation of a new dimension to existence, the summer would not have been lost. On the contrary, it was transformed into one of the most memorable summers of my life, because the whole of my surroundings seemed to exist within Shakespeare's vision.[430]

With his sister, the novelist Rosamond Lehmann, and her then husband, Wogan Philipps, he would sometimes drive over to Stratford, where "even in those days, before the great revival of Shakespearean production and acting we have enjoyed in the last dozen years," he wrote in 1955, "one could see productions that never lacked something to delight or illuminate."[431] To be in the countryside that had given rise to "Justice Shallow and Hotspur and Falstaff and the music that haunted a wood near Athens" was a special delight. "It was a time in my life when the identification of poet and landscape was one of the greatest sources of imaginative pleasure to me."[432]

Words and Prose

Virginia Woolf's appreciation for *Words and Poetry* was heightened by Rylands's praise for prose, the novelist's medium, as a literary mode.[433] Although when reading Shakespeare she would sometimes say that it was poetry she wanted, in many ways she aspired to be the Shakespeare of prose. We might recall here Virginia's remark in a letter to Vita, "I write prose, you write poetry," and Vita's quick and complimentary rejoinder: "There is 100% more poetry in one page of Mrs Dalloway . . . than in a whole section of my damned poem."[434] Dadie's theory that the early Shakespeare "reduced blank verse to the level of prose" and that in so doing he "found himself dramatically in prose" was a welcome and enabling idea.[435] Shakespeare "created in prose Rosalind and Beatrice," wrote Rylands, and "with invention and subtlety used prose to suggest certain *traits* of character, worldliness perhaps, or cynicism, or sense of humour"; in characters like Falstaff, Hamlet, Iago, and Edmund, "Shakespeare used prose for a more philosophical purpose."[436] "What would these two plays be," he asks about *Troilus and Cressida* and *Hamlet,* "without their prose scenes and characters?" In *Troilus,* "the long and excellent comedy scene in which the Trojan heroes pass over the stage, and the thumb-nail sketch of Helen and Paris"; in *Hamlet,* "all Hamlet's best scenes with his contemporaries Rosencrantz and Guildenstern, with Ophelia, with Osric, with the Players, with the Gravediggers." It is, Rylands contends, "the complete naturalness of the prose scenes which makes the soliloquies so convincing."[437]

To the author of *Mrs. Dalloway* and *To the Lighthouse* this description of the power of prose—and its near and necessary alliance with poetry—would surely have been welcome. In the essay "Poetry, Fiction, and the Future," published in 1927, Woolf had described Shakespeare's plays, in a compelling phrase, as "the perfectly elastic envelope of his thought."[438] She would also have recognized herself in Rylands's insistence on "Shakespeare's love of writing for its own sake" in his "final style," a period that he saw as extending from *Antony and Cleopatra* to *The Tempest.* Woolf's own "final style" in fiction, including her "playpoem" *The Waves* and the comical-tragical-historical tonal shifts of *Between the Acts,* juxtaposed poetry and prose with an assurance that profited from her previous novels—and, arguably, from Rylands's meticulous analysis of language.[439]

In 1931 she sent him a copy of *The Waves,* shortly afterward inviting his further thoughts on poetry and prose. Rylands wrote his "Dearest Virginia" to say that he was convinced *The Waves* was her masterpiece, comparing it to *Hamlet:* "It combines being unique and individual with expressing + epitomizing the spirit of the age: that is, both permanent + immediate value." Like the major poets—he mentions Pope, Byron, Shelley, Keats, and Wordsworth—she produces "voices for all time." "Yet so miraculously *The Waves* is fiction: the six characters emerge although their idiom is the same. . . . All with that fourth dimension which the Shakespearian soliloquy gave to his greatest creations."[440]

Many years later, returning to his comparison between the two writers, Rylands would suggest in a BBC TV interview that not only the content and the form but the speed and intensity of writing itself drew Woolf to Shakespeare. "I think this is one of the reasons why she felt the greatest admiration for Shakespeare and felt something in common with him. He wrote with this extreme rapidity, and she also when she was working worked at that rate absolutely—it came hot like lava from her."[441] (Here we might recall again Woolf's very similar comparison in her diary: "I read Shakespeare *directly* I have finished writing, when my mind is agape & red & hot. . . . I never yet knew how amazing his stretch & speed & word coining power is, until I felt it utterly outpace & outrace my own.")[442]

In 1937, Virginia Woolf was invited to do a radio broadcast in the BBC series *Words Fail Me.* In her talk, "Craftsmanship," she echoed some of Rylands's commentary in his own previous talk in the series, "The Language of Shakespeare."[443] Rylands said of Shakespeare, "His vocabulary is enormous and he thinks nothing of making new words or making old words do new things"; Woolf, after alluding to one of her favorite phrases in Shakespeare (Macbeth's "This my hand will rather / The multitudinous seas incarnadine, / Making the green one red" [2.2.61–63]), observes that "in the old days, of course, when English was a new language, writers could invent new words and use them," but today "you cannot use a brand new word in an old language because . . . a word is not a single and separate entity, but part of other words." How then, she asks, rhetorically, "can we combine the old words in new orders so that they survive, so they create beauty, so that they tell the truth? That is the question."[444] In addition to these remarks about old and new words, we can recognize in Woolf's pleasure at the partnering of *multitudinous/incarnadine/green one/red* her sympathy with Rylands's more extended observations in *Words and Poetry* on Shakespeare's use of "Latin polysyllables" in the later plays: "the introduction of the Latin element which made Shakespeare's style at once more abstract and more intellectual," and the way, in some cases, "Shakespeare used his new Latinisms for their own sake, for sound and novelty, more than for their sense."[445]

"The Thing Said and the Way in Which It Is Said": The Ages of Man

In 1939 Dadie Rylands set out to articulate in his introduction to *The Ages of Man* the benefits gained by putting together an anthology of Shakespeare. "What do we gain, and what do we lose?" in such an anthology, he asks, and then answers his own question. We lose "the form; that is, the plot, the whole" and "the theatrical effect." And "we must forget or neglect the characterisation." But "we receive in recompense and in isolation two elements: the thing said and the way in which it is said."[446]

The "words themselves," he reminds the reader, "are not ours but Shakespeare's. Yet each time we return to them, each time they rise up in our memory like ghosts and push us from our stools of self-complacency, we feel that double sense of recognition and surprise, a simultaneous release and identification."[447] It is for a moment disconcerting to find Rylands equating the reader to Macbeth, and Shakespeare to the ghost of Banquo. He could so easily have chosen another ghost, allowing us the vanity of imagining ourselves as Hamlet. But "self-complacency" is the danger here, recognition the remedy. Shakespeare scripts us, he suggests, in what we think and how we think it. We think through him. It is the same kind of perception that led Virginia Woolf to write of Shakespeare that "he is speaking our own thoughts."[448]

The Ages of Man anthology was Rylands's most popular and influential book. According to Noel Annan, it was packed in many soldiers' knapsacks during World War II.[449] Focusing on Shakespeare's poetry rather than on the action and plot of his drama, Rylands drew attention to the elements that were central for him while imagining, as one performer to another, the nature of the creative process. "Shakespeare never bends to himself a situation, a character, a passion. He catches it as it flies."[450] And, citing the editors of the First Folio: "'His mind and hand went together (Heminge and Condell tell us) and what he thought he uttered with that easiness that we have scarce received from him a blot in his papers.' Say rather his heart and voice went together. His language rings in our ears."[451]

The editorial revision here is striking and revealing: for Rylands it was "heart" and "voice" that made Shakespeare's language so singular and unforgettable. "He himself," recalled his friend Noel Annan, "had a light, resonant voice; he never dramatised or used elocutionary tricks and was always intelligible, taking care not to drop the voice at the end of a sentence. He was an exquisite reader. His lectures, though packed with material, were original in their effect, their delivery and their arrangement rather than in the argument itself or the method of analysis.... He was not a great actor: he did not move well; but he had a stage presence and he could hold an audience by his voice alone."[452] And as in the lecture hall, so on the stage. "Dadie took as his model in directing Shakespeare Granville Barker and the pioneer William Poel, who used no scenery, never cut the text and attended to the words. He was at his best," Annan thought, "with undergraduate actors. He did not waste time trying to get them to move like professionals or 'act.'"[453] His objective, and his great accomplishment, was to get the students to think about what the words meant rather than shouting or gesticulating to cover them—and also "to respect the interplay of rhythm and meter of the lines," a practice, or habit of mind, that would carry over to the great years of British midcentury Shakespeare, both in London and at Stratford.[454]

From 1957 to 1964 Rylands also supervised and brought to completion an enormous new undertaking: the plan to record in their entirety the works of William Shakespeare—performed by a mix of professional actors and Cambridge undergraduates, sponsored by the British Council, and in coordination with the Marlowe. This project stands as one of his, and the Marlowe's, greatest achievements, making the plays widely available to new listeners. And when John Gielgud brought *The Ages of Man* to television in 1966 after touring his one-man show throughout Britain, Europe, Australia, and the United States, it was watched by "multitudes who had never seen him at work on the stage or watched a Shakespeare play being professionally performed."[455] In these two cultural innovations, bringing Shakespeare's words to ever-wider audiences, Rylands ensured that his version of "Bloomsbury Shakespeare" would serve as a public good, a gift of experience, knowledge, work, and understanding—the result of years of collaboration and love.

THE PSYCHOANALYST: JAMES STRACHEY

James Strachey, elected to the Apostles in 1906, was at first known as "the Little Strachey" (his brother Lytton was "the Great Strachey"). He quickly began to campaign for the election of Rupert Brooke, whom he had known at Hillbrow School, and with whom, for many years, he was hopelessly in love. It was a time of theatrical excitement and innovation, with the presence of Harley Granville Barker at the Royal Court Theatre in Chelsea.

After Cambridge James worked as a secretary to his cousin, St. Loe Strachey, the editor of the *Spectator* (their professional relationship ended when James declared himself a pacifist during the war). His *Spectator* Shakespeare reviews, both from 1912, rival his brother's for ferocity and perception, and articulate very clearly what would be Bloomsbury's position on verse speaking and stage decor. Assessing Granville Barker's production of *The Winter's Tale,* which he judged, despite its failings, as "the most interesting Shakespearean revival that has been seen in London within the memory of this generation," the twenty-four-year-old James contrasts it with the errors of the past. "The tradition (if as such it can be described) of Shakespearean production in England for the last generation has been beneath contempt."

> The conventional method of delivering blank verse, as taught by the elocutionists, is so monotonous, so slow, and disregards so completely not only the sense but the feeling expressed in the lines, that an audience can

> scarcely be cajoled into listening for more than a few minutes at a time; and, since so much of Shakespeare is written in blank verse, the unhappy producer is forced to look elsewhere for means of holding his audience's attention. Accordingly, after cutting out a third of the play, "owing to the exigencies of time," he crowds the stage with elaborate scenery and clothes, he hires an orchestra to play slow music during the longer speeches, and every few minutes he arranges a piece of ingenious "business" to distract the audience from the longeurs of the words.

To make things even worse, the visual imagination of the "traditional producer" has "never got beyond the Royal Academy stage," and "accordingly his one idea for the scenery and dresses is photographic realism combined with archaeological correctness. His Julius Caesar must not merely wear a bald wig, but must be bald; and the palace of Theseus in *A Midsummer Night's Dream* must be furnished in precise accordance with Dr. Evans's latest Minoan discoveries."[456] (Readers who regard "political correctness" as a recent coinage may be especially amused by the dismissive term "archaeological correctness" in this diatribe from over a century ago.)

As for the specifics of Granville Barker's *Winter's Tale,* James Strachey has two criticisms to make. One has to do with "the decorative side of the production." He believes it was a mistake to hire two different artists to design the scenery and the costumes (Norman Wilkinson for the backdrops, Albert Rothenstein for the dresses). Both had experience in both, and giving the responsibility to one rather than splitting it between them would have made for a more harmonious visual presentation. The other problem comes with the actors' management of the poetry of the play, especially in the later scenes. Whereas the earlier parts of the play are dramatic and rhetorical, the language of the fourth act offers "scarcely anything but poetry, and poetry perhaps greater than Shakespeare ever wrote elsewhere." And in this case "Mr Barker's neglect of rhythm" also neglects the magic of the lines, so that Florizel's "When you do dance, I wish you / A wave o' th' sea, that you might ever do / Nothing but that, move still, still so / And own no other function" (4.4.140–43) sounds almost like "a piece of dialogue between two 'lyrics' in a musical comedy."[457]

Three months later, James published his second review, which began with a strong commendation. "If Mr Granville Barker's production of *The Winter's Tale* was no more than an interesting experiment, his *Twelfth Night,* which followed it at the Savoy Theatre, must be pronounced an almost unqualified success." Both the errors of the previous production had been corrected: the "division of labour between scene-painter and costume designer has been abolished," and the actors spoke their blank verse lines much better. On this second point, the reviewer tended to credit the author as much as the producer. "The language of *Twelfth Night* is for the most part straightforward, and has none of the Donne-like ultra-crabbedness of the later Shakespeare. This may explain much of the apparent increase in the actors' audibility. So too with the rhythm. The blank-verse of *Twelfth Night* runs smoothly; the stresses come in the expected places, for instance, and the lines are mostly of the Marlowe, or end-stopped, pattern. It was most particularly the enjambment that led to much disaster in *The Winter's Tale.*" With a few cavils, he was happy to recommend Barker's production to all comers. "The blasé devotee of musical comedy, the Shakespearean scholar who cannot tolerate Shakespeare on the stage, the revolutionary theatrical reformer, or the ordinary theatregoer who is none of all these, will delight in it." In short, wrote the youthful (and anonymous) reviewer, "we can think of no pleasanter way of spending three hours than by a visit to the Savoy."[458]

Strachey's bachelor flat in Bloomsbury was full of books. When Vanessa Bell lived there for a while with her children, the books, as Virginia Woolf noted, were "the incongruous part of the decoration, & Nessa professed great contempt for them. 'Of course, she said, there's Shakespeare & all that on the bottom shelf, but look at that! Doesn't that give James away?' He has all the right books, neatly arranged, but not interesting in the least—not, I mean, all lusty & queer like a writer's books."[459] "Shakespeare & all that" would remain among the "right books" for James when he embarked upon what would become his life's work—*The Standard Edition of the Complete Psychological Works of Sigmund Freud,* published in twenty-four volumes by the Hogarth Press.

After James's marriage to Alix Sargant-Florence in 1920, the couple traveled to Vienna and began psychoanalysis with Freud. James would return to London in 1922 and start seeing his own patients. Alix spent a year in Berlin, 1924–25, continuing her analysis with Karl Abraham. Freud, an admirer of Lytton's books, invited James and Alix to translate some of his own works into English, and after they returned to London they became practicing analysts, members of the Psycho-Analytic Society, and Freud's regular, and valued, English translators. The connection with Leonard and Virginia Woolf and the Hogarth Press made possible the publication project; the landmark *Standard Edition* is, in an important sense, a Bloomsbury achievement. As the editor of the *Standard Edition* of Freud and the literary executor of Lytton Strachey, James Strachey was to have an enormous influence upon Bloomsbury's legacy.

James Strachey, ca. 1917

Sigmund Freud had studied humanities at university before moving on to medicine, and his interest in literature and art strongly influenced his writing. His correspondence with his friend Wilhelm Fliess about *Hamlet* and the Oedipus complex dates from 1897, three years before the publication of *The Interpretation of Dreams.* He worked on an essay concerning *King Lear* and *The Merchant of Venice* in 1912, and in 1914 he wrote to Sandor Ferenczi that he had "begun to study Macbeth, which has long tormented me."[460] *Hamlet, Lear,* and *Macbeth* were among the Shakespeare plays that would appear regularly in his correspondence as well as in his psychoanalytic work. (Others that he would comment upon or quote from in his published writings, many more than once, include *Richard II, Richard III, Henry IV, Part 1* and *Part 2, Henry V, Love's Labour's Lost, Julius Caesar, The Merchant of Venice, A Midsummer Night's Dream, Much Ado About Nothing, Othello, Pericles, Romeo and Juliet, Timon of Athens,* and *The Tempest.*) After the First World War Freud found that more and more of his patients were from England or the United States, and he was "anxious about his English," especially his command of English idioms, as he told Ernest Jones.[461] The arrival in his life of the couple he would call "my excellent

English translators, Mr. and Mrs. James Strachey," would be of enormous service to him—and to the scholarly and reading public.[462]

In his general preface to the *Standard Edition* James Strachey quoted from Samuel Johnson's *Preface to Shakespeare* on the editorial choices that had faced him: "It is impossible for an expositor not to write too little for some and too much for others. He can only judge what is necessary from his own experience."[463] Freud, he observed, was "a striking example of a man equally at home in both of what have been called the 'two cultures'"; in addition to his scientific knowledge, "he was also widely read in the Greek and Latin classics as well as the literatures of his own language and those of England, France, Italy, and Spain."[464]

In his editor's introduction to the early *Project for a Scientific Psychology,* Strachey comments, "It was almost literally true of Freud that (as Ben Jonson says of Shakespeare) 'he never blotted a line.'"[465] Translating a theorist whose works often turned on puns, jokes, double meanings, and the significance of specific words or images was a special challenge, particularly when these ambiguities involved quotation or citation. For this purpose it was also greatly helpful for the translators to move comfortably between the "two cultures" of science and humanities as well as the "two cultures" of German and English.

During his analysis with Freud, James had written to Lytton to describe the experience: "Each day I spend an hour on the Prof's sofa," he reported. "It's sometimes extremely exciting and sometimes extremely unpleasant.... The Prof himself is most affable and as an artistic performer dazzling. . . . Almost every hour is made into an organic aesthetic whole. Sometimes the dramatic effect is absolutely shattering."[466] Phrases like "dramatic effect," "aesthetic whole," and "artistic performer" leap out at the reader, as does the idea that the hour is sometimes "extremely exciting" and sometimes "extremely unpleasant." The whole description has something in it of Prospero the magician, and even something of Shakespeare the playwright snapping up unconsidered trifles and making them into art. Lytton wondered, "In what language does it all go on?" and whether Freud made jokes ("Or only German ones?"), viewing the proceedings from afar as "a trifle-highly coloured," while also, characteristically, suggesting that he himself would never "suffer from *any* 'resistance,'" a key component of analysis.[467]

Among the works of Freud that address Shakespeare directly and were translated by James Strachey are *The Interpretation of Dreams, Jokes and Their Relation to the Unconscious,* and "Psychopathic Characters on the Stage" as well as Freud's *Autobiographical Study.* In 1935 Freud famously added a footnote to the *Study* in which he said that, having read J. Thomas Looney's *"Shakespeare" Identified* (1920) he "no longer believe[d] that William Shakespeare the actor from

Stratford was the author of the works which have so long been attributed to him."[468] To this note Strachey added—and printed in square brackets in the *Standard Edition*—a further note of his own, which I cite in full here, since it is indicative of the two writers and of their relationship to one another, and indeed to Shakespeare.

> When, in 1935, the English translator received the draft of this additional footnote, he was so much taken aback that he wrote to Freud asking him to reconsider it—not on the ground of the truth or otherwise of the theory, but of the effect the note was likely to have on the average English reader, particularly in view of the unfortunate name of the author of the book referred to. Freud's reply was most forbearing, as an excerpt from a translation of his letter will show. The letter is dated August 29, 1935. " . . . As regards the Shakespeare-Oxford note, your proposal puts me in the unusual position of showing myself as an opportunist. I cannot understand the English attitude to this question: Edward de Vere was certainly as good an Englishman as Will Shakspere. But since the matter is so remote from analytic interest, and since you set so much store on my being reticent, I am ready to cut out the note, or merely to insert a sentence such as 'For particular purposes I no longer wish to lay emphasis on this point.' Decide on this yourself. On the other hand, I should be glad to have the whole note retained in the American edition. The same sort of narcissistic defence need not be feared over there." Accordingly in the English edition of 1935 the footnote reads: "I have particular reasons for no longer wishing to lay any emphasis upon this point."[469]

Whether Freud and Strachey, both psychoanalysts, in fact believed that it was "remote from analytic interest" to suggest that an English nobleman rather than an actor from Stratford wrote the world's most famous plays is, perhaps, a question not to be asked of professionals who invented (Freud) or tacitly endorsed (Strachey) the concept of the family romance. But the scrupulosity of the editor—here identified merely as "the English translator," not with any more personal description—shows something of the seriousness with which he took his obligations to Freud and to his current and future readers.

THE APOSTATE: RUPERT BROOKE

Handsome and charismatic, educated at Rugby and Cambridge, a promising poet studying literature and the classics, Rupert Brooke was elected to the

Rupert Brooke, photograph by Sherril Schell, 1913

Apostles in 1908, the same year he was appointed stage manager—the equivalent of a modern director—for the newly formed Marlowe Dramatic Society. Brooke provided a connection between the Marlowe Society and Bloomsbury. He had been at prep school with James Strachey, who was for a while in love with him, and had praised him to Lytton. He knew Geoffrey Keynes, who recommended him to Maynard. On a reading holiday hosted by G. E. Moore, Lytton Strachey found him attractive and amusing. Virginia Stephen had known him when they were both children, and she later joined Rupert, Ka Cox, Maynard Keynes, and others on a camping trip to Devon. "I mean to throw myself into youth, sunshine, nature, primitive art. Cakes with sugar on the top, love, lust, paganism, general bawdiness, for a fortnight at least; and not write a line."[470]

But Brooke, whose relations with women were often intense and tormented, later turned against Bloomsbury with a vengeance. He lashed out at Lytton Strachey and became obsessed with what he regarded as Bloomsbury's poisonous atmosphere after a weekend when Lytton's friend Henry Lamb flirted successfully with Ka Cox, with whom Rupert was having an affair. To James, with whom he was supposed to travel to Scotland for a holiday, he wrote angrily, "To be a Strachey is to be blind—without a sense—towards good and bad, and clean and dirty; irrelevantly clever about a few things, dangerously infantile about many."[471] He later traveled to Tahiti and Fiji, where he found for a while a version of the simple life he (sometimes) sought.

Brooke's comments about Shakespeare varied in tone depending upon his audience. In some cases, often—but not always—with women, his tone was instructive and tutorial. To his cousin Erica Cotterill, six years his senior, who had asked him to suggest some books to read, he wrote from his retreat at Grantchester, near Cambridge, "I work at Shakespere, read, write all day, & now and then wander in the woods or by the river. I bathe every morning & sometimes by moonlight . . . & am as happy as the day's long. I am chiefly sorry for all you people in the world." He particularly resented the arrival of "dull bald bespectacled people" from the university who came to Grantchester to take tea. "The world smells of roses. Books? Pah!" and here he appends an annotated list of recommendations, beginning with the bible of Bloomsbury, G. E. Moore's *Principia Ethica,* which she is to read "very slowly & carefully, as you want to think." "Shakespeare's *Anthony & Cleopatra* is very good," he advised her. Also on the list were works by Roger Fry, Lowes Dickinson, Havelock Ellis, and E. M. Forster. Apparently her letter asked about other matters as well, since his closing sentence reads, "As for people in love with people of the same sex as themselves, I know all about it, & will tell you some time."[472]

He wrote to his friend Frances Cornford, a fellow Marlowe Society member who was working on a verse drama, advising her that "simplicity is not always expressed by simple lines, or complexity by elaborate blank verse." Marlowe's plays were all composed "in simple lines, *metrically,*" but "in *The Tempest* Shakespeare had left that *miles* behind him, and was writing immensely varied and complicated and suggestive and built-up verse." Nonetheless, responding to her interest in "simple lines," he points to a few from *The Tempest,* including "This music crept by me upon the waters" and Caliban's speech that begins "Be not afeard; this [*sic*] isle is full of noises."[473]

In another letter he counseled the politician and playwright Reginald Berkeley about melodrama and sentimentality: "W.S. himself did the melodramatic method, but how unexpectedly and how truly. Figure to yourself what a speech before death another would have given Othello—the lines of pathos, the regret, the despair, the prayers for forgiveness, the self-malediction . . . the too too easy phrases. Then read how Othello bids them repeat that he was this and that, and that once, for Venice' honour, he beat a Turk, 'took by the neck [*sic*] th' uncircumcised [*sic*] dog

And smote him—thus,'

And so stuck himself. Thus gentlemen die."[474]

The letter was written aboard ship as he sailed for Tahiti; Brooke is quoting from memory, which accounts for his errors in citation (though "uncircumcised" for "circumcised" betrays something about the limits of his cultural information). From Fiji he wrote a letter to the critic Edmund Gosse about the South Seas, with brief jokes about the porter in *Macbeth* and the companionship of Falstaff and Bardolph intermixed with warm but condescending observations about "these dear good people."[475]

At other times, however, Brooke could be less reverent and more transgressive about Shakespeare, especially when striving for effect. "This glutton, drunkard, poacher, agnostic, adulterer, and sodomite was England's greatest poet," Brooke wrote in one of his Grantchester notebooks. "I like telling the story of Shakespeare's love affairs. It shocks the Puritans, who want it hushed up. And it shocks the pro-Sodomites, who want to continue in a hazy pinkish belief that all great men were Sodomites. The truth is that some great men are sodomites and womanizers, Shakespeare, Angelo, etc."[476] Keith Hale suggests that these notes may have been made in preparation for a talk Brooke was to deliver, "William Shakespere: The Man and His Age," in September 1910. The event was to be held at the New Bilton Adult School in his hometown of Rugby—a possible but not entirely likely venue for tweaking either shockable Puritans or shockable sodomites.

On a similar theme he wrote to James Strachey with a comic proposal for editing Shakespeare to avoid impropriety, mimicking the editorial ellipses and substitutions of a previous and more censorious age. Hamlet's remonstrance to Gertrude, he thought, might be rewritten as "Nay but to live in the [perspiration] of an enseamed [room] [Hot] [with] [emotion], honeying and [flirting] over the [unpleasant place]."[477]

He took James's affection for granted and made few gestures to reciprocate. James wrote him in June 1911 asking him to visit for the weekend, urging him to "do what you want—read or write your poems—and let me just sit, or read? Is it impossible for you not to feel worried one way or another if I'm there? Couldn't I be simply furniture or an animal?"[478] Rupert's reply (declining the invitation) invoked the stage and Shakespeare.

> You see, from your point of view (you make out) you & I are in the centre of the stage, an interesting picture, a moving group. But from other points of view—mine or the stage crowd's—there are moments when I and somebody else, or two quite other people, are central. . . . If Emilia thought every action of Othello's had sole reference to her, if Laertes had such an idea of Hamlet, they must have made sad mistakes. It wasn't, for the moment, Emilia's or Laertes's tragedy. And I must plaintively insist that there are moments when—to my eyes—it's my tragedy and not yours, when—to my eyes—I'm being the chief character in my life, not the second one in yours.[479]

However appropriate the analysis, this must have stung. James wrote gamely back ("You're rather a sledge-hammer; you know,") remonstrating that "it wasn't because I thought we were together in the limelight that I wrote to you."[480] In the next short period they went together twice to see ballets by Diaghilev, and also to Westminster Abbey for the coronation. The friendship and the correspondence continued. But it was clear from this letter who was the tragic hero and who was not.

In a letter to Geoffrey Keynes, Brooke discussed the proposal for a production of *Macbeth* at the Marlowe. "I'd like something done, even that, perhaps," he told Keynes in 1910. "But I don't think Shakespeare or any of the Elizabethans wrote stuff that is bearable when acted."[481] It was at a Shakespeare performance at the Savoy Theatre, however—and one that appealed to him so much that he saw it twice—that Rupert Brooke fell in love with an actress playing her first starring role. "*Of course* I've seen *The Winter's Tale!*—the first night!," he wrote to his close friend Eddie Marsh in early October 1912. "And in fact I'm going to it again on Tuesday."[482] Directed by Harley Granville Barker, *The Winter's Tale* production at the Savoy in London, which opened on September 21, featured the young Cathleen Nesbitt in the role of Perdita, the innocent shepherdess who will turn out to be a princess and marry a prince. (This was the same production that James Strachey had reviewed for the *Spectator.*) Eddie Marsh arranged for Brooke and Nesbitt to meet, and for a while they were emotionally committed to one another, though (as she attests) they never became lovers.[483]

Later that year, when she had been cast as Olivia in *Twelfth Night*, he wrote her to describe it as a "thankless part" and to take a swipe at "your Mr Barker," who "says such damned silly things about Shakspere." Granville Barker had suggested that a celebrated line from *Antony and Cleopatra* ("O withered is the garland of the war!") did "not mean anything," and Brooke took this occasion to rail at him in absentia: "The swine! The goat! The actor-manager!"[484] Granville Barker had once been a hero to Brooke, who "sat next to him!!" after a lecture at Cambridge and found him "utterly divine." ("His profile is one of the nicest things in the world. And his voice!")[485] Now, like the personae of Bloomsbury, he was the object of vituperation.

Brooke's dissertation "John Webster and Elizabethan Drama," undertaken to earn him a fellowship at King's College, was published after his death. (Like many others at the time, Brooke uses *Elizabethan* to describe the early modern period that encompassed as well the reign of James I.) Perhaps more clearly than any incidental correspondence, the dissertation shows something of his attitude toward Shakespeare—though as some selections from Brooke's writing will make clear, "attitude" here carries a double meaning. Many of his views, written for his academic advisers and mentors, are also, characteristically, poses, gestures toward iconoclasm. This was, of course, also the effect of Lytton Strachey's early essay "Shakespeare's Final Period," arguably a more assured—and less anxious—achievement.

Brooke's assessment of the plays of Webster, Shakespeare, and their fellow dramatists is focused on the stage. Unlike Strachey, Woolf, and others in Bloomsbury, he demotes the text to a secondary place. The "appeal made by a performance of the kind of play *Hamlet* or *The Duchess of Malfi* is, comes through the eye," he insists. "Would one rather be blind or deaf at such a performance?"

> It is a comprehensible and common, but dangerous fault, to overemphasize the importance of the printed text to the whole play. It is true that the romantic halo and additions of beauty to the general lines of the play, came, in Elizabethan plays, very little in the things you could look at; almost entirely in the words. But the story itself was told visually as well as audibly. The Elizabethans were above all men of the theatre, and planned performances. It is important to keep that in mind when reading their "plays," always to be trying to visualise the whole performance from the text, and to judge it so, and always to look with suspicion on those who judge the text as literature.[486]

From a former undergraduate actor whose first appearance onstage was in the nonspeaking role of a herald, and who decided to take over the part of the Attendant Spirit in *Comus* from Reginald Pole because Pole "was not beautiful enough," such a viewpoint is perhaps not unexpected.[487] At the Marlowe Society Brooke had regarded himself as a "man of the theatre," a producer in the impresario mode of Henry Irving or Herbert Beerbohm Tree. Still, the vehemence in his tone is striking: the double emphasis on "always," the quotation marks around "plays," and the telltale word *suspicion.* This is Brooke contra Bloomsbury.

In the dissertation's semi-obligatory chapter "The Elizabethan Drama," Brooke quickly moves from assessment to polemic. History and chronicle plays are "dreary," though "critics have always idiotically thought it their duty to praise these histories; partly because Shakespeare, in obedience to popular demand, wrote some."[488] He concedes that "in his worst efforts Shakespeare always leaves touches of imagination and distinction," but nonetheless, "as a whole these histories are utterly worthless."[489] About the romantic comedies of the period he is equally scathing, and equally self-revealing: "Shakespeare threw a pink magic over them. But it should be left to girls' schools to think the comedies he obligingly tossed off exist in the same universe with his later tragedies. The whole stuff of this kind of play—disguises, sentimentality, girls in boys' clothes, southern romance—was very thin."[490] The best period, by contrast, was 1600–1610, when "nearly all the good stuff of Elizabethan drama" was written.[491]

And here Brooke launches into a passionate description that seems as much wishful autobiography as literary analysis:

> Boyhood passed. Imagination at this time suddenly woke to life. . . . Intellect was pressed into the service of the emotions, and the emotions were beaten into fantastic figures by the intellect. The nature of man became suddenly complex, and grew bitter at its own complexity. The lust of fame and the desire for immortality were racked by a perverse hunger for only oblivion. . . . Madness was curiously explored, and all the doubtful coasts between delirium and sanity. . . . The mind, intricately considering its extraordinary prison of flesh, pondered long on the exquisite transparency of the height of love and the long decomposition that death brings. . . . The veils of romanticism were stripped away; Tragedy and Farce stood out, for men to shudder or to roar.[492]

Brooke's early death—from an infected mosquito bite suffered as he was en route to fight at Gallipoli—led to a moment of national celebrity, in which, as the author of the "war sonnets," he was enshrined as the poet who spoke for English patriotism and sacrifice. In an obituary in the *Times,* partly written by Brooke's friend and sponsor Eddie Marsh, Winston Churchill praised him as a "poet-soldier," "joyous, fearless . . . with classic symmetry of mind and body" and "a heart devoid of hate for fellow-men."[493] Lytton Strachey, who had been so volubly attacked by Brooke, wrote to Duncan Grant, "It was impossible not to like him, and impossible not to hope that he might like one again; and now . . ."[494]

The obituary gave the cause of death as "sunstroke," presumably more tragic and less farcical than an insect bite. Nor did the nation fail to notice that Rupert Brooke died on Shakespeare's birthday, April 23—also celebrated as St. George's Day. A few years later, in an article in the *Times Literary Supplement,* Virginia Woolf noted "the peculiar irony of his canonisation" (he had never in fact made it to a battle) and expressed the hope that "those who knew him when scholarship or public life seemed more his bent than poetry will put their view on record and relieve his ghost of an unmerited and undesired burden of adulation."[495]

THE NEO-PAGANS AND THE RAVERATS

"Neo-Pagans" was Virginia Woolf's half-mocking, half-admiring description of the group that would later form around Brooke—influenced by Fabianism, committed to a notion of the simple life that included eating vegetables, camping out, taking long walks, and bathing naked together. Woolf did not invent the term (it had been applied to the Pre-Raphaelites and used by Edward Carpenter in his lectures on the "simple life"), but her invocation of it in a letter to Clive Bell in 1911 has stuck.[496]

Different in their interests and temperament from the more intellectual and skeptical members of Bloomsbury, the Neo-Pagans were equally complex in their personal interrelationships. Several had attended the progressive coeducational Bedales School, where work on the land and healthy, chaste naked bathing were part of the bohemian spirit of the place. They included many people whom Woolf would continue to know throughout her life: the Olivier sisters (Margery, Daphne, Bryn, and Noel), Justin Brooke (no relation to Rupert), Frances Cornford, Ka Cox, and Gwen and Jacques Raverat. Of these, it was the Raverats whose interests in Shakespeare deserve particular notice.

Gwen Darwin, the daughter of the astronomer and professor Sir George Darwin, was brought up in Cambridge among a host of other young Darwins, including her cousin Frances (later Frances Cornford). Her father read Shakespeare's history plays aloud to his children.[497] Jacques, a Frenchman, attended Bedales School, and was persuaded by the headmaster to play the part of Antonio in a school production of *The Tempest*—the beginning of a lifelong interest. As was the case with Virginia Woolf, Lytton Strachey, and others, it was Shakespeare's language, not the psychology of his characters, that caught his imagination. "I was in raptures at the magical atmosphere which so mysteriously enveloped the words and rhythms of its incomparable language," he wrote. "The association of two or three words, which in another's hands would be quite or-

Gwen Raverat, *King Lear for the Marlowe Society*, 1938 (program design)

dinary, in his wove a spell of great emotional power."[498] Some lines from the play always thereafter brought tears to his eyes.

A close friend of Rupert Brooke, Jacques, in later life a painter, met Gwen through the Marlowe Dramatic Society, in which they were both involved. Gwen, who was also to become a painter as well as a much-admired wood engraver, attended the Slade School and became friendly with the young Stephens in London, dining with Virginia and Adrian in Fitzroy Square and attending Vanessa Bell's Friday Club, of which she was soon secretary. With some friends she visited Rupert Brooke in Grantchester, where he greeted them "reading Shakespeare barefoot."[499] At the Marlowe Society she painted scenery for *Comus,* designed costumes for *Doctor Faustus* (in which Jacques played Mephistophilis), and produced program images. In this period she also made some small Shakespeare wood engravings, including the superb *King Lear, Kent, and Cordelia,* and many years later another exquisite small wood engraving, *Old Hamlet Poisoned in His Orchard,* which was used as the cover image for the production's program.

When Jacques wrote to his father to tell him that he wanted to marry Gwen, he said that she "had a proud soul, very fierce and strong," and that "you will love

Jacques Raverat, ca. 1924

her too, as one loves great things, Rembrandt or Shakespeare."[500] After their marriage they traveled to France, where Jacques, whose health was always a problem, received a serious diagnosis: he suffered from multiple sclerosis. Rejected by the army as physically unfit, he was living in Cornwall with Gwen, working on a fresco for the house of Francis and Frances Cornford, when they received the news of Rupert Brooke's death.

Raverat wrote to André Gide, whom he had known since 1910, "Rupert Brooke is dead. . . . Nothing will be able to replace exactly what he was for me. We had, he and I, many projects afoot. . . . His death, there, so near Greece and Troy. . . . Lines from *Troilus and Cressida* come to mind: 'Hector is dead. There is no more to say.'"[501] The line is Troilus's, spoken at the very end of the play

(5.11.22). But Jacques also wrote in a sketchbook two other lines from the same play: Cressida's "The grief is fine, full, perfect, that I taste" (4.5.3) and Troilus's "And sometimes we are devils to ourselves" (4.5.95).[502] Gide, replying to his letter, alluded to a planned project: "How well we will translate Shakespeare together."[503] This project, however, was never pursued.

A period of estrangement between the Raverats and Virginia Woolf was ended when Jacques wrote to Virginia in 1922. In the correspondence that ensued, Woolf mentions "how the Neo-paganism at that stage of my life annoyed me" but in her next letter, full of thoughts about writing and human relations, she calls him "my dear and adorable Jacques." In February 1925 she sent Jacques the proofs of *Mrs. Dalloway;* he was only the second reader of the novel, after Leonard. By that time Jacques's illness was very advanced. Gwen read him the proofs (omitting the sections on Septimus Smith's thoughts of suicide). He died on March 7. "I don't think you would believe how much it moves me that you and Jacques should have been reading Mrs Dalloway, and liking it," Woolf wrote to Gwen.[504] The renewed friendship between the two women continued until Woolf's death. When Gwen Raverat died, many years later, her tombstone was inscribed with the dirge from *Cymbeline* that sounds throughout *Mrs. Dalloway.*

CHAPTER 5

Mr. Eliot's Shakespeare

T. S. Eliot's relationship with members of the Bloomsbury Group began in 1916, when Bertrand Russell suggested that Clive Bell should get to know him, and Bell introduced him to Roger Fry, Lytton Strachey, Mary Hutchinson, and others. Russell also brought Eliot into contact with Ottoline Morrell and her guests at Garsington Manor. Virginia Woolf seems not to have met Eliot till 1918, and it was in October of that year that Leonard wrote to "Mr Eliot"—at the suggestion of Roger Fry—to invite him to publish his poems with the Hogarth Press.[1]

"When we first got to know Tom," Leonard wrote in his autobiography, "we liked him very much, but we were both a little afraid of him. He was very precise, cautious, and even inhibited."[2] The press published Eliot's *Poems* in November 1919 and *The Waste Land* in September 1923, in book form, the pages handset by Virginia Woolf.[3]

In the summer of 1922, just prior to its initial publication in Eliot's literary magazine the *Criterion,* he had come to Richmond and read the poem aloud to the Woolfs. "He sang it & chanted it [&] rhythmed it," Virginia noted. "It has great beauty & force of phrase; symmetry; & tensity. What connects it together, I'm not so sure.... One was left, however, with some strong emotion."[4]

What she does not comment on, either here or in connection with the earlier volume of poems, is how much Eliot's poetry engages with Shakespeare and his contemporaries. "Gerontion" begins with an epigraph from *Measure for Mea-*

T. S. Eliot and Virginia Woolf, photograph by Lady Ottoline Morrell, 1924

sure. The Waste Land includes famous citations from *Antony and Cleopatra* and *The Tempest,* a mention of Coriolanus, and a possible allusion to *Titus Andronicus,* as well as the name of a 1912 popular song, "That Shakespearian Rag." The Jacobean authors John Donne and John Webster are memorably characterized in "Whispers of Immortality." Eliot would go on to write *Essays on Elizabethan*

Drama as well as some of the most influential essays on Shakespeare of his time. But neither Virginia nor Leonard Woolf mentions these shared literary interests, although Virginia was always appreciatively alert when the talk turned to Shakespeare and would shortly publish in the first *Common Reader* essays such as "The Elizabethan Lumber Room" and "Notes on an Elizabethan Play."

Leonard reports that their friendship deepened over time, that "Eliot" became "Tom," and that Virginia "noted with regret that she was no longer frightened of him."[5] But for someone like Virginia, who wrote so often about her friends and Shakespeare, the absence of recorded Shakespeare conversations with "Tom" is a little surprising. There was one such conversation, as her diary explains, but it took place at the theatre and had unhappy results. On March 30, 1924, she went with Eliot to see *King Lear*, then playing at the Regent Theatre in a production by the Phoenix Society. They "both jeered & despised"—and then Eliot published, in the April issue of the *Criterion,* a "solemn & stately rebuke of those who jeer & despise."[6] Eliot's review, signed "Crites," declared the production "almost flawless" and offered a critique of the playgoers rather than the play: "It is commonly said that *King Lear* is not a play to be acted; as if any play could be better in the reading than in the representation. It is more likely, from the response of the audience, that *King Lear* is a work of such immense power that it offends and scandalizes ordinary citizens of both sexes."[7] Woolf was offended and scandalized by Eliot's volte-face, by the view that a play was never better read than seen and, presumably, by being grouped with "ordinary citizens of both sexes." She "taxed him, lightly," when she saw the review. He "sat tight & said that he meant what he wrote: then what does he mean by what he says? God knows." She concluded that he was "hole & cornerish, biting in the back, suspicious, elaborate, uneasy," and would probably only be "liberated" by "a douche of pure praise, which he can scarcely hope to get."[8]

Not meaning what you say was a major fault in Bloomsbury, the opposite of the frankness and freedom they considered a central tenet of their beliefs, a conviction inherited from the Apostles and from Moore. Relations between Eliot and Woolf would mend—this was an outburst rather than a breaking point—but she never thereafter wholly trusted his views. The conflict was exacerbated by the competition between the Woolfs and Eliot to recruit authors for their respective presses (Eliot had moved on to Faber). In September 1925 Woolf wrote, "Dignity is our line; & really as far as the poaching of authors goes, he won't harm us. Then there is the fascination of a breach; I mean, after feeling all this time conscious of something queer about him, it is more satisfactory to have it on the surface. Not that I want a breach: what I want is a revelation. But L. thinks the queer shifty creature will slip away now."[9]

Leonard's retrospective view of Eliot was, as we've noted, more generous, and when Eliot did get something close to the "douche of pure praise," he became, as Virginia had foreseen, more magisterial and less "hole & cornerish." But the openness and truth telling she valued—even as she herself was far from immune to occasional malicious gossip—was at odds with his self-protective style (exacerbated by his first wife's illness and his unhappy marriage). Moreover, his learnedness sometimes made her feel inadequate—an aspect of his persona she denigrated, perhaps defensively, as that of an "American schoolmaster."[10] Much later, when they were both immensely successful, she wrote to their mutual friend Ottoline Morrell, "Tom Eliot was here the other weekend, very mellow, charming and humane. I no longer feel a crashing vulgarian, an upstart illiterate in his presence—after 20 years thats something."[11] Like all her communications with Ottoline this was in part a performance, but it has a ring of truth.

Whether warned off by the *King Lear* contretemps or for other reasons, she seems not to have spent much time discussing Shakespeare with Eliot, or at least taking note of such conversations. Also, she didn't like his plays. When she and Leonard went to a production of *Romeo and Juliet* she contrasted it with *Murder in the Cathedral,* which they had seen a few weeks before: "How fresh, rich, various coloured—& then think of the pale New England morality murder."[12] (This language of color seems to have been part of her response to these plays. Eliot had given her a copy of his play to read, "which, having run through & tested my colour sense, I expect to be good." Her opinion changed either when she read the play more carefully or when she saw it performed.)[13] She continued to admire him as a poet and a fellow reader of poetry, but she thought Eliot's verse drama was a failure ("He's a lyric, not a dramatic," she wrote in her diary), while also freely acknowledging her sense of competitiveness with him (the poor reviews of *The Family Reunion* were "proof he's not a dramatist. . . . I'm of course for reasons I can't go into selfishly relieved").[14] T. S. Eliot, however significant his literary accomplishments, would not be Shakespeare's heir.

If the Woolfs did not spend much time discussing Shakespeare with Eliot, however, he himself had no hesitation in discussing—and writing about—the Shakespeare of another Bloomsbury author. Eliot's impressively learned—and indeed "magisterial"—essay, "Shakespeare and the Stoicism of Seneca," was initially presented as a talk to the Shakespeare Association in 1927, which may account in part for its vigorous tone and its several striking personal reflections.

The long opening paragraph is a tour de force, worth quoting in its entirety to allow for a sense of its content, tone, and highly effective pacing:

> The last few years have witnessed a number of recrudescences of Shakespeare. There is the fatigued Shakespeare, a retired Anglo-Indian, presented by Mr. Lytton Strachey; there is the messianic Shakespeare, bringing a new philosophy and a new system of yoga, presented by Mr. Middleton Murry; and there is the ferocious Shakespeare, a furious Samson, presented by Mr. Wyndham Lewis in his interesting book, *The Lion and the Fox*. On the whole, we may all agree that these manifestations are beneficial. In any case, so important as that of Shakespeare, it is good that we should from time to time change our minds. The last conventional Shakespeare is banished from the scene, and a variety of unconventional Shakespeares take his place. About anyone so great as Shakespeare, it is probable that we can never be right; and if we can never be right, it is better that we should from time to time change our way of being wrong. Whether Truth ultimately prevails is doubtful and has never been proved; but it is certain that nothing is more effective in driving out error than a new error. Whether Mr. Strachey, or Mr. Murry, or Mr. Lewis, is any nearer to the truth of Shakespeare than Rymer, or Morgann, or Webster, or Johnson, is uncertain; they are all certainly more sympathetic in this year 1927 than Coleridge, or Swinburne, or Dryden. If they do not give us the real Shakespeare—if there is one—they at least give us several up-to-date Shakespeares. If the only way to prove that Shakespeare did not feel and think exactly as people felt and thought in 1815, or in 1860, or in 1880, is to show that he felt and thought as we felt and thought in 1927, then we must accept gracefully that alternative.[15]

The triad of writers on Shakespeare in Eliot's teaser opening was manifestly neither random nor accidental. Each typified an approach—and each offered a target. Grouping them together provided a way for Eliot to transcend them.

The "fatigued Shakespeare, a retired Anglo-Indian," is a fascinating conflation of Strachey's famously "bored" Shakespeare as described in "Shakespeare's Final Period" and some details of the Strachey family biography. Lytton Strachey, born in 1880, was a very young man when he published the essay in 1904. But his father Sir Richard Strachey, then eighty-seven, had served in India in a variety of important capacities for most of his life until his retirement. (Leonard Woolf describes him at that time as "sitting all day long, summer and winter, in a great armchair before a blazing fire, reading a novel.")[16] Lytton's mother, the former Jane Grant, also came from "a distinguished Anglo-Indian family," and so many Stracheys had participated in the Indian government that there were occasional ironic mentions of the "government of the Stracheys."[17] All this would have been common knowledge, or gossip, in the sets in which T. S. Eliot had begun to move. His "fatigued Shakespeare" might otherwise have been situated elsewhere, perhaps at a seaside resort or spa favored by retired Englishmen.

It is perhaps worth noting here that Strachey had, in fact, got his own jab in first, in his 1925 Leslie Stephen Lecture on Pope. Commenting on Pope's early pastoral poetry, in which everything was "obvious" and the diction a "mass of clichés," he exclaims, "But what a relief! What a relief to have escaped for once from *le mot propre,* from subtle elaboration of diction and metre, from complicated states of mind, and all the profound obscurities of Shakespeare and Mr T. S. Eliot!"[18] Being coupled with Shakespeare was surely gratifying, but the "profound obscurities" seem already recognizable as Eliot's signature trope.

Lytton Strachey did not meet Eliot till the late 1910s, getting to know him through Ottoline Morrell at Garsington. After an initial resistance he came to like him, and joined in the Bloomsbury project to raise money so Eliot could quit his work at the bank to write full-time (the short-lived "Eliot Fellowship Plan"). Another rescue plan, spearheaded by Maynard Keynes, would have hired Eliot as the literary editor of the *Nation and Athenaeum* (owned by Keynes). Ultimately Eliot chose instead to take a position with a newly founded journal, the *Criterion,* "a paper which, standing for classicism in literature and religion, was alien to Lytton, Maynard, Virginia and Leonard."[19] Leonard, already overworked, became the *Nation and Athenaeum*'s literary editor.

John Middleton Murry was also a literary editor, previously at the *Athenaeum* (before its merger with the *Nation*) and later at the *Adelphi.* Initially Eliot, as the relative newcomer on the scene, had sought Murry's regard and patronage. By 1926 the position was reversed, with Eliot's reputation as a critic and editor far higher than Murry's. Their opposition was ideological as well as personal: Eliot the classicist, Murry, to use the period's designation, the romantic.

As for Wyndham Lewis, the artist and editor of *Blast,* the Vorticist journal, he had been Bloomsbury's vocal opponent since the fallout over the Omega Workshop, and was particularly vicious in his attacks on Lytton Strachey. Eliot met him through Ezra Pound, and Lewis later painted his portrait. *The Lion and the Fox: The Role of the Hero in the Plays of Shakespeare* had just been published in 1927 when Eliot delivered the first version of his essay to the Shakespeare Association. It is worth noting that only Lewis, of the three Shakespeare critics mentioned, merits an approving adjective ("interesting"). But Eliot's overall assessment, that the Shakespeare portrayed by these critics bears a close resemblance to the critics themselves, is persuasive—in particular and in general. "One of the chief reasons for questioning Mr. Strachey's Shakespeare, and Mr. Murry's, and Mr. Lewis's, is the remarkable resemblance which they bear to Mr. Strachey, Mr. Murry, and Mr. Lewis respectively. I have not a very clear idea of what Shakespeare was like. But I do not conceive him as very like either Mr. Strachey, or Mr. Murry, or Mr. Wyndham Lewis, or myself."[20] In this last phrase he is perhaps too modest, or at least mistaken, for the Shakespeare of T. S. Eliot—like the Shakespeares of Messrs Strachey, Murry, and Lewis—bears a close resemblance to the critic.

Eliot's Shakespeare in this essay is "classicist" in the ways indicated by his title. The influence of the Roman playwright Seneca, translated into English in the sixteenth century, is explained and "disinfect[ed]"—which is Eliot's way of preempting future critics on the topic: "My ambitions would be realized," he writes, if he could prevent a "Senecan Shakespeare" from "appearing at all."[21] In fact, as he will go on to make clear, Eliot's Shakespeare in this piece is as Flaubertian as it is Senecan, and again he will plant his flag: "I do not believe that any writer has exposed this *bovarysme,* this human will to see things as they are not, as clearly as Shakespeare."[22] Eliot's chief examples are all tragic heroes—Othello, Antony, Coriolanus. To underscore his ownership of this claim he once again offers an apologia ("I am ignorant whether anyone else has ever adopted this view, and it may appear subjective and fantastic in the extreme.")[23]

The most famous of his pronouncements in the essay, and the most disputed, is his declaration that in Othello's "last great speech" what he is really doing is "*cheering himself up.*" The words are printed in italics, unusual for Eliot. "Humility is the most difficult of all virtues to achieve," Eliot writes feelingly. "Nothing dies harder than the desire to think well of oneself. Othello succeeds in turning himself into a pathetic figure, by adopting an *aesthetic* rather than a moral attitude, dramatizing himself against his environment."[24] To this reader the commonsensical phrase "*cheering himself up,*" although it can be found in Shakespeare and other early writers, has a distinctly Stracheyan ring, as indeed does the opening gambit on the fatigued Anglo-Indian Shakespeare.[25]

"Dramatizing himself" had been, in effect, Eliot's verdict on Strachey as critic. Speculating on what would likely be "Mr Strachey's Montaigne," he observes that "all of Mr Strachey's favourite figures have a strong Strachey physiognomy."[26] But it is possible to hear in Eliot's tone, too, a certain resemblance to Strachey; as his friends and fellow Apostles often noticed, the Strachey voice, even if in print, could be catching. The signature statement of his 1919 essay on

Hamlet, "So far from being Shakespeare's masterpiece, the play is certainly an artistic failure," has much of the same *épater les bourgeois* tone as "Shakespeare's Final Period" (which likewise begins with a brisk put-down of other Shakespeare scholars).[27] That Eliot was pleased with the reaction can be seen from his blithe mention, in a letter to Ford Madox Ford, of having "outraged public opinion in England by my remarks."[28]

Perhaps most striking, however, is the kinship between Eliot's concept of Shakespeare and that of various members of the Bloomsbury Group. Once he is past the witty characterizations of his contemporaries, he settles into a clear exposition of what can and cannot be divined from the plays. They cannot, for example, tell us what Shakespeare thought about this thing or that thing. "The poet who 'thinks,'" he says, "is merely the poet who can express the emotional equivalent of thought. But he is not necessarily interested in the thought itself." Brushing aside Wyndham Lewis's claim that "we possess a great deal of evidence" about what Shakespeare thought of military glory and martial events, Eliot asks, "Do we? Or rather did Shakespeare think anything at all? He was occupied with turning human actions into poetry." And "I would suggest that none of the plays of Shakespeare has a 'meaning,' although it would be equally false to say that a play of Shakespeare is meaningless. All great poetry gives the illusion of a view of life."[29] His distinction between thinking and poetry in this essay accords with the anecdote Lytton Strachey tells about Mallarmé and Degas in his introduction to George Rylands's Shakespeare book ("My dear Degas, poetry is not written with ideas; it is written with words.")[30]

Eliot sent copies of "Shakespeare and the Stoicism of Seneca" to Murry and Lewis, both of whom briefly thanked him for sending it, and also to his friend and publisher Geoffrey Faber, who in his reply described Shakespeare as "the supreme combination of the 'ordinary man' with a miraculously gifted craftsman in words," and asked Eliot pointedly, "Are you conscious of your own excessive obscurity? Is it an unavoidable element in your poetry? or is it deliberate? Do you, in that case, write only for the intuitively gifted few?" Writing, as he says, as "the professional friend, rather than the critic," Faber urges Eliot "to make the way plainer for the earnest reader."[31] His example of Shakespeare's "unanalyzable power over language" is the "Winter Song" from *Love's Labour's Lost*—the same lyric that Roger Fry had singled out as "pure poetry" illustrative of the "irreducible essence of the work of art."[32] Quoting the verse, which begins "When icicles hang by the wall, / And Dick the shepherd blows his nail," Faber comments, simply, "Can that be beaten anywhere?"[33]

In 1928, while going through the proof sheets for *Elizabeth and Essex,* Lytton

Strachey read Eliot's essays on Shakespeare, which he thought offered "interesting remarks, but not quite enough."[34] Had he waited a few months and read Eliot's review of his book in the *Times Literary Supplement,* he might have changed his opinion since Eliot's admiring review was, as we've seen, full of perceptive comparisons between Shakespeare's dramatic technique and that of *Elizabeth and Essex.* The "fatigued" Strachey, like the "fatigued" Shakespeare parodied in the "Seneca" essay, is nowhere in sight. In *Elizabeth and Essex,* wrote Eliot, Strachey demonstrates a "cunning ability to accelerate or reduce the speed of his narrative" so that the reader, marveling at how this is done, wants "to read the book at a sitting."[35] The review is at several points illustrated by telling Shakespearean comparisons; while very clearly an analysis of Strachey's "dramatic gift," it is also a brief but knowledgeable and suggestive discussion of Shakespeare.

Lytton Strachey's death in January 1932 brought a close to these literary interactions, and other than with Strachey, Eliot seems not to have had much interchange about Shakespeare with his Bloomsbury acquaintances. Virginia Woolf, who typically notes such conversations in her diaries and letters, has nothing to say on the subject, though their friendship continued, together with her wariness. As his poetry and plays became more religious in content, she found them less to her taste. When she went to a performance of *Romeo and Juliet* shortly after seeing *Murder in the Cathedral,* she wrote to Julian Bell that Shakespeare's play "curled up Tom's Cathedral, and dropped it down the W.C.!"[36]

Where Eliot's interests most clearly diverge from those of Bloomsbury are in his religious belief and his sense that formal religion is central to life. "If anyone asked me about the good things in life," he wrote, "I should say, primarily, heroism and saintliness. But of course it is necessary to distinguish between the good *states* of a human being and the good *objects* before that human being. . . . The objects would be, roughly, God, the State (Commonwealth), and Humanity."[37] The contrast with the famous statement of G. E. Moore in his *Principia Ethica* could hardly be greater: "By far the most valuable things, which we know or can imagine, are certain states of consciousness, which may be roughly described as the pleasures of human intercourse and the enjoyment of beautiful objects."[38] This assertion would later be described by Maynard Keynes as Moore's "religion"—and also that of Bloomsbury.[39]

In his own definition of the good Eliot insists that "if one makes the relation of man to man (or still more to woman) the highest good, I maintain that it turns out a delusion and a cheat. But if two people (say a man and a woman in the greatest intimacy) love God still more than they love each other, then they enjoy greater love of each other than if they did not love God at all," adding that

"I have found my own love for a woman enhanced, intensified and purified by meditation on the Virgin."[40] On this and other points his conviction diverged enough from that of his Bloomsbury friends and acquaintances that their conversation and correspondence took other directions, often playful and purposefully entertaining. "Their friend T. S. Eliot," wrote Noel Annan, "was converted to Anglicanism, and distanced himself gently but decisively from Bloomsbury as a whole."[41] But the Woolfs retained their fondness for him, enjoying his quirks as well as his conversation. "He has his grandeur," Woolf noted after Eliot came to visit; he "has a humorous sardonic gift which mitigates his egotism. . . . A nice old friends evening."[42]

CHAPTER 6

Shakespeare at Charleston and Ham Spray

The Bloomsbury taste for theatricals and passionate arguments about art, literature, and Shakespeare continued to flourish when Bloomsbury spent time in the countryside: the Woolfs at Monks House, the Bells and Duncan Grant at Charleston, and Lytton Strachey and Carrington first at the Mill House in Tidmarsh and later at Ham Spray House in Wiltshire.

Clive Bell visited Charleston regularly even after he and Vanessa no longer lived together as husband and wife. He had been a Cambridge classmate and friend of many of the Apostles, though he was not himself a member of the society, and his lively interest in plays and performance there was one of the things that initially brought them together. All of the "Charlestonians," including Vanessa's three children, Julian, Quentin, and Angelica, were engaged with Shakespeare, whether through photographs, stage sets, reading, writing, or performance. Vanessa's family album contains some striking images of Angelica in Shakespearean roles. Duncan Grant designed costumes, properties, and a stunning stage curtain for Shakespeare productions.

At Ham Spray, Strachey often read Shakespeare aloud to Carrington, Ralph Partridge, Frances Marshall, and others. Frances, who later married Ralph, recorded in her diaries the many intersections of Shakespeare with their daily lives.

CLIVE BELL

Lady Ottoline Morrell remembered Clive Bell in the early years of his marriage as "that happy, flattering, good-tempered Autolycus holding out gay leaves for us to admire."[1] The description is entirely affectionate; Autolycus, the "snapper-up of unconsidered trifles" in *The Winter's Tale,* is a peddler, performer, trickster, and con man as well as enchanting company.

As an undergraduate at Cambridge, Bell had been proud of his role as the founder of the Midnight Society—and its successor, the X Society—which took as their mission the reading of neglected and prized "Elizabethan" plays. In 1907 he organized a Play-Reading Society in Bloomsbury on a similar model, which continued until the war. The repertoire included a number of lively—and sexy—Restoration plays as well as works by Jonson, Milton, and Shakespeare (*Henry IV, Part 1,* with Adrian Stephen as an impressive Falstaff, a part he had also played at Cambridge).[2] Virginia, Vanessa, Clive, Lytton, and Saxon Sydney-Turner were among the regular performers, and the parts they played seem occasionally to have offered a chance to act out, in fictional terms, some real-life relationships and interactions.

In the fall of 1903 Clive, Vanessa, and Virginia traveled together to Italy, and Virginia wrote a brief sketch of Clive that seems prescient in view of his later career. At public school, rebelling somewhat from his conventional upbringing as the "son of a substantial country family," he developed "a reputation for originality" and "took to reading," she says.

> He saw literature first as a long series of triumphs. When you had despatched Hamlet you were ready to attack Browning, & he had the sense in reading every book that he was providing himself with talismans to be used against the cheerful flattering people who teased him & admired him in the holidays. He was puzzled to discover how his knowledge was to be brought into play; & for the most part walked about stuffed up with it, or produced it with the most violent distortions which even his self love could not approve of altogether.
>
> He quoted Shakespeare in a shrill triumphant voice, when there was no occasion for it, & scorned the young lady who asked him the name of the author. Unfortunately, no one at the family table could carry on the discussion.[3]

This description is presumably based on Clive Bell's own account, although its

Clive Bell, photograph by Bassano Ltd., 1921

tone, however derived from sophisticated self-mockery, still reads as a fondly satirical portrait.

Bell's engagements with Shakespeare were sporadic, usually linked to another project or relationship. In his aesthetic treatise *Art* (1914), he described "the actual meaning of the words in Shakespeare's songs, the purest poetry in English," as "generally either trivial or trite. They are nursery-rhymes or drawing-room ditties." About the haunting lyric from *Twelfth Night,* "Come away, come away, death," he writes, "Could anything be more commonplace?" And of Ariel's "Hark, hark! I hear / The strains of strutting chanticleer," "What could be more nonsensical?" Bell's argument here is geared toward the claim that, though "poetry has its raptures, [it] does not transport us to that remote aesthetic beatitude in which, freed from humanity, we are upstayed by musical and pure visual form."[4] Earlier in the same book he had excoriated "the vulgar" for seeking realism in Shakespeare: "The conception, the thing that Shakespeare set himself to realise, was not a faithful presentation of life."[5] In both references there is an implied authoritative voice (perhaps not so distant from the "shrill triumphant voice" in which Virginia Stephen had described the young Bell quoting Shakespeare) that invokes the playwright by name, uses the name to support a generalized point, and then moves on.

In an article on watercolors exhibited in London galleries he observes, in the final line, that Klee's works shine "like a good deed in a naughty world." The phrase—from Portia in *The Merchant of Venice*—is unattributed and devoid of quotation marks; this, and its position as a punchline, seems to imply that the sophisticated readers of the *New Statesman and Nation* will recognize it if not as Portia, then at least as Shakespeare.[6] Similarly, in a discussion of money and national prestige, he contrasted the value of a Rembrandt painting in the national collection to a hypothetical discovery about Shakespearean authorship: if a scholar were to prove that some lines of *The Two Noble Kinsmen* were by Shakespeare rather than by Fletcher, he said, publishers would not profit from it, whereas an authentic Rembrandt immediately enhanced the museum's equity.[7]

The success of *Art* had made Clive Bell what today would be called a "public intellectual," and he took pleasure in the role. On February 8, 1945, he broadcast on the BBC Home Service (the predecessor of BBC 4) some brief remarks on Shakespeare's *Julius Caesar,* the first part of which was to be performed on the radio the following evening. It was not his favorite Shakespeare play, Bell told the audience, but listeners would find it exciting, and they would hear, among other things, Shakespeare's warning—which was again very timely—about the dangers of the mob.[8]

The most indicatively "Bloomsbury" of Bell's comments on Shakespeare, however, may be a remark he made to one of the women with whom he had a relationship that lasted for several years—Benita Jaeger, later known as Benita Armstrong.[9] Benita, a talented sculptor born and brought up in Germany, was advised by Clive on her reading of English classics. When she went to the Old Vic to see *Measure for Measure,* starring Charles Laughton, James Mason, and Flora Robson, she telephoned Clive to tell him how much she had enjoyed it. Though pleased, he nonetheless insisted on putting the experience in Bloomsbury perspective, telling her later that "*We,* of course, only *read* Shakespeare."[10]

The implied double stress on "we" and "read" underscores the importance to Bell of his continuing role as a member of Old Bloomsbury. In fact "they" did also go to see Shakespeare productions, especially after Maynard Keynes and Dadie Rylands became involved in the Cambridge theatre, but some of the Bloomsberries—notably Virginia Woolf—often preferred the text to the performance. Nonetheless, it was characteristic that Bell, at least on this occasion, declared himself an insider purist—or perhaps a purist insider. "Shakespeare" for him was, among other things, a mark of belonging.

VANESSA BELL

Like her siblings, Vanessa Stephen spent many evenings listening to their father read poetry and prose, and she remained an enthusiastic reader. She described her literary preferences, in a letter to Virginia, as "simple and domestic."[11] Her favorite author was Jane Austen, and at Charleston in the evenings she would sometimes read Dickens aloud to her own children.[12] From the Hyde Park days on, the sisters read aloud to one another; Vanessa later said she could still hear "much of George Eliot and Thackeray" in Virginia's voice.[13]

But her strongest passion, from the first, was for art. "Vanessa was always sketching and Virginia wrote and read," observed Virginia's friend in her early years, Violet Dickinson.[14] After Leslie's death, when the young Stephens moved to Bloomsbury and began to meet Thoby's Cambridge friends, Vanessa founded the Friday Club in 1905 as a discussion group for artists, the counterpart to Thoby's Thursday Evenings, which focused on politics, literature, and ideas.

Her views on Shakespeare were influenced by both her life and her commitment to painting. She read *Antony and Cleopatra* for the first time sometime around 1913, writing to Roger Fry that she thought she appreciated it more because she had had some experience of living.[15] As we've seen, she argued with Lytton Strachey about the "human interest" he found in *King Lear,* a play she thought "a rather mechanical and stilted affair with quite unreal relationships and feelings."[16] When Lytton read portions of *Eminent Victorians* to them at Charleston, she wrote Virginia, "It seems to me the Strachey mind is purely dramatic" and thus unsuited to the mode of biography—although she confessed that her judgment might be open to question since during much of the reading she and Duncan had been asleep.[17] Strachey was in fact a playwright as well as a biographer, starting from his undergraduate years, when he wrote *Essex: A Tragedy* in blank verse as an entry for the Stratford-upon-Avon Prize Competition. Clive and Vanessa visited him during that time, as did Virginia. ("I am preparing for my competition tragedy," he wrote Vanessa, inviting them to come for a weekend. "When it's finished I might read it at Gordon Square.")[18] Quentin Bell also remembers Lytton reading one of his plays at Charleston.

In a letter to Duncan Grant in 1917 Virginia Woolf wrote that her sister "has become a Shakespearean character in my mind, so that I often put her into action for my amusement."[19] She admired and envied (and sometimes was glad not to share) the complex family, farm, and artistic activities over which Vanessa held sway—as she put it in her letter, "the dirt, the itch, the brats, the paints."[20] But Vanessa thrived on the mix, running the house and the household with serene confidence.

Vanessa Bell, ca. 1913

During the years when her son Julian was at Cambridge, she went to see Dadie Rylands's Shakespeare productions at the Marlowe Society—sometimes arranging the visit to include a family lunch party where she could meet Julian's latest girlfriend. Vanessa and Angelica saw *Henry IV, Part 2*, with Michael Redgrave as Prince Hal, Donald Beves as Falstaff, and Dennis Robertson as Justice Shallow, and she went with Duncan Grant to see Rylands's production of *Hamlet*—the one that had left Virginia Woolf "dumfoundered" by its brilliance.

She also encouraged her children's interest in the plays. Traveling in France, she wrote to Helen Anrep that Angelica, newly out of school, was "a perfect travel companion," by turns high-spirited and reflective: "She reads Shakespeare at intervals and plays the piano in hotel drawing rooms."[21]

But Vanessa Bell's most direct material contribution to Shakespeare in Bloomsbury came, appropriately, in the form of visual evidence: photographs in her family albums. Like her fellow Bloomsbury painters, Vanessa avoided the descriptive and thematic literary scenes favored by both Pre-Raphaelites and Academicians. In her albums Shakespeare is represented instead by snapshots of family and friends in Shakespearean poses or tableaux. Her photographs of Angelica as Ophelia and as Cleopatra are among the most striking of these images, the first for its beauty, the second as a vivid illustration of the comic ardor that attended these home theatricals and charades.

DUNCAN GRANT

Duncan Grant's connection with Shakespeare onstage, though short-lived, is significant because of what it shows about his imaginative art making and also about Bloomsbury's integration of the decorative and performing arts. Grant was not only a painter but also a muralist, a designer of fabrics and objects, and a playful and inventive experimenter in a wide range of visual modes. A cousin of Lytton and James Strachey, Grant had in his childhood spent a good deal of time at the Strachey family home, 69 Lancaster Gate. Lady Strachey (his "Aunt Janie") read to the children from her favorite works of Elizabethan drama, and took the young Duncan, already interested in art, to the open studios of well-known painters on Picture Sunday. He seems to have benefited from both of these early opportunities.

When he went to Paris to live and work in 1907 Grant brought the works of Shakespeare with him, reading *Coriolanus* and *Timon of Athens* with special pleasure, writing to Lytton to share his thoughts.[22] A year later, planning a holiday in the Orkneys with Maynard Keynes, he sent Keynes a list of the books he had with him: the only work of English literature included in his list is Shakespeare.[23] He participated—with Adrian and Virginia Stephen, among others—in the famous *Dreadnought* Hoax in 1910; their costumes and makeup (Grant and Virginia were "Abyssinian princes") were planned in consultation with Willy Clarkson, the theatrical costumier. Throughout his life he made costumes for amateur theatricals performed by his friends, and he was a noted performer, often reducing his audience to helpless laughter. "I remember him suddenly transforming himself into Mrs Beerbohm Tree in the role of Lady Macbeth," reports Quentin Bell.[24] He played a wolfhound in a full-scale comic entertainment at Maynard Keynes's house in 1926, and when Virginia Woolf's satirical farce *Freshwater* was finally performed in 1935, he happily assumed the bearded role of the Victorian painter G. F. Watts.

Duncan Grant at Charleston, photograph by Vanessa Bell, ca. 1933–35

In April 1912 Harley Granville Barker invited Grant to make designs for a production of *Macbeth* to be mounted at the Savoy Theatre immediately following *The Winter's Tale.* Granville Barker had taken a lease on the Savoy, which was owned by H. B. Irving, one of the actor sons of the famed Victorian actor-manager Henry Irving. His goal was to change the way Shakespeare was seen—and heard—on the English stage after many years of extravagant productions that overwhelmed the language of the plays.

Rehearsals for both *The Winter's Tale* and *Macbeth* were held in the summer of 1912, and *The Winter's Tale* opened in September. It was an artistic but not a commercial success, and Granville Barker decided that the next production should be the more popular *Twelfth Night,* so plans for *Macbeth* were canceled, although they were renewed the following year.

Duncan Grant, Costume design for a Lord, from *Macbeth Sketchbook*

Grant worked on sketches and ideas for the production, and some of his costume designs for the play exist in the Charleston archives: a dress for Lady Macbeth, a costume for the witches, another for a lord.

He planned to use fabrics from the Omega Workshops for the lords' robes. (From July 1913 on he had been involved, together with Roger Fry and Vanessa Bell, in setting up the Omega, creating fabrics, screens, furniture, toys, and other decorative artifacts—in effect, stage settings for the home.) The influence seems to have gone in both directions, from *Macbeth* to the Omega as well as from the Omega to *Macbeth;* some of Grant's pottery pieces for the Omega Workshops resembled the "severe, angular pots" he had designed for the banqueting scene in *Macbeth.*[25]

On a page of notes Grant described some of the costume changes he planned for Macbeth and Lady Macbeth over the course of the play, following indications in the text. Lady Macbeth was to wear an orange/yellow dress in the opening scenes, and then by the fifth act to appear in a "grey crepe nightgown with dark blue cashmere wrapper spotted with dull Indian red," the red spots echoing the "out, damned spot" lines in the sleepwalking scene.[26] Macbeth himself was to appear in 2.1, the scene in which he resolves upon the murder ("Is this a dagger which I see before me"), in a fur-lined purple coat, gray silk undershirt, and red shoes. The account book for the Savoy Theatre lists, under "Stock in Hand," some scenery constructed for *Macbeth.*[27]

But despite these plans the production did not go forward. Meanwhile, Grant was finding the preparations for theatre design tiresome—too many visits to dressmakers and scene painters across Paris, temperamental actresses with opinions of their own, no time for his own work. Ultimately he quit, giving Granville Barker his drawings (for which he was "generously paid").[28]

A few years later, however, Grant was once again persuaded to participate in a Shakespearean project, and this one came to a more successful—indeed, a highly memorable—conclusion. He had become acquainted in Paris with the French director Jacques Copeau, the architect of a creative theatre renewal comparable to that taking place in England, and agreed in 1914 to design costumes and settings for a French production of *Twelfth Night.*[29] Copeau, working with a smaller theatre and a smaller budget at his Théâtre du Vieux-Colombier, had something very different in mind from Granville Barker's London *Twelfth Night* at the Savoy: "I imagine surroundings in every respect unobtrusive," he wrote to Grant, "all the amusement of form and colour being produced by the costumes and gestures of the actors."[30] Grant, already an aficionado of improvisation, was engaged by this vision and by the director's energy and imagination. If anything, Copeau surpassed his expectations; he would later say that in this collaboration he had "found the theatre of my dreams."[31] (The choice of play may have further influenced his enraptured response: after seeing a later production of *Twelfth Night* he wrote to Vanessa Bell that the play seemed "like the dreams of a very complicated person.")[32]

The production of *Nuit des rois* (*Twelfth Night*) in May 1914—featuring Louis Jouvet as Sir Andrew Aguecheek, Suzanne Bing as Viola, Blanche Albane as Olivia, Romain Bouquet as Sir Toby Belch, and Copeau himself as Malvolio—was a huge success, both with critics and with the public. Up to ten minutes before the curtain rose, Grant was dashing among the actors with a palette and paintbrush, adding final details to their costumes.[33] His designs avoided the faux authenticity of period hats, swords, and hairstyles in favor of floating fabrics and visually striking shapes; Viola emerging from the sea in the opening scene was, in Copeau's description, "veiled in pink, a palm-leaf fan in her hand."[34] As for the performance of the play in French, in a faithful translation by Théodore Lascaris specifically commissioned for the production by Copeau, Grant experienced it as a "revelation": "more used to hearing Shakespeare read aloud, he realized that even in translation it did not lose its music."[35] Like others in the Bloomsbury Group, Duncan Grant regarded Shakespeare above all as a poet.

This was Copeau's vision as well. His praise of his ensemble sounded very much like the praise of the Marlowe Society's actors being offered in the same

Duncan Grant, Stage curtain design for Jacques Copeau's production of *Twelfth Night,* 1913

years by Lytton Strachey (and Desmond MacCarthy): "They hardly step between us and the poet, giving our imagination every kind of liberty and pleasure."[36] Many who saw the production agreed: Claude Debussy wrote to Copeau that after the curtain fell he was "astonished not to see Shakespeare make his appearance at the end of the play."[37] Granville Barker was led to acknowledge that some French actors could now perform Shakespeare better than English ones.[38] As for the scenery, Copeau again shared the views of the Bloomsbury critics: "Much too long a time has Shakespeare been disfigured by adapters who, under pretext of having him profit from the 'progress' of our [stage] mechanics, altered the design of his works and slowed down its movement by changes of set." He urged instead "an austerity in staging," the achievement of all the best eras of dramatic art.[39]

The *Twelfth Night* production had changed the history of French theatre. When war came, and Copeau sent out a financial appeal for the artists of the Vieux-Columbier now engaged in the fighting and for the unemployed actresses of the troupe at home, an American he had never met came to see him and gave him 200 francs, saying—as Copeau reported in a letter to his colleague Jouvet—

"I have seen Shakespeare played in all Europe and in America. I have never seen anything which resembles even remotely your production of *Twelfth Night*."[40]

The war put an end to the promising collaboration between Jacques Copeau and Duncan Grant, as it did to so many things (though Copeau's theatre continued to thrive). Grant designed strikingly original costumes and scenery for J. T. Sheppard's productions of Euripides' *Cyclops* (1923) and Aristophanes' *The Birds* (1924) at Cambridge, but he never again dressed the stage for a Shakespeare play.

JULIAN BELL

The poet and publisher John Lehmann recalled his friendship with Julian Bell, a fellow poet, as "the most intimate intellectual friendship of my Cambridge years." Julian had "a conviction that the arguments he defended had the authority of graven tablets of the law: the tablets of Bloomsbury," Lehmann remembered. "He had had a Quaker schooling, followed by a period in France, but Bloomsbury had been his real education."[41] In part through the influence of Lytton Strachey, Julian had become a passionate enthusiast of the eighteenth century: "Pope was finally established as his god of poetry, and his rage descended, with ludicrous and wilful exaggeration, on Shakespeare."[42]

During one Cambridge vacation, at the instruction of critic and scholar F. L. Lucas, Julian read all of Shakespeare's plays. He then wrote a letter to Lehmann declaring that he found Shakespeare to be "a person so utterly lacking in all notions of construction, half whose lines mean nothing at all, and who has only the vaguest notion of metre."[43]

Lehmann replied in a long letter of his own, and "in refuting his criticisms of Shakespeare called to my aid two of his favorite modern critics, Lytton Strachey and Charles Mauron, and flung at him as many quotations from his own seventeenth and eighteenth century authors—Dryden, Dr. Johnson, and even Pope—as I could remember, all praising Shakespeare for the qualities Julian denied him."[44]

This literary dispute was clearly enjoyed by both young men. On another occasion, when Lehmann visited Julian at Charleston during university holidays and the other members of the family were away, "After dinner we both laid our pens down, and took up again the endless argument of Pope versus Shakespeare."[45] The friendship and the correspondence continued until Julian's death in 1937, when he was hit by bomb fragments as a volunteer in the ambulance corps during the Spanish Civil War.

QUENTIN BELL

As an early and enthusiastic participant in Bloomsbury theatricals, for which he often served as scene designer and/or playwright, Quentin Bell was familiar with Shakespeare as both image and text. It was a language in which he had grown up. In a successful career as a painter, sculptor, potter, and professor of the history and theory of art, he published a number of Bloomsbury memoirs as well as his two-volume biography of his aunt, Virginia Woolf.

In what he describes as a "youthful aesthetic experience," he was moved by the plot of *King Lear* when—as a boy at Charleston—he first encountered it. He had been lying by the pond reading the Lambs' *Tales from Shakespeare,* he recalled, "and had struck King Lear. I came to the end and was deeply perturbed; I should have known better even then, but somehow I had imagined that stories end happily. Lear doesn't. It seemed all wrong. And yet at heart, I felt without at all being able to explain it, the beauty of a story in which it is the good who are punished."[46] Vanessa, in her conversation with Lytton Strachey, had thought the plot of *Lear* artificial and pointless. Her son found it not only moving but instructive.

Quentin Bell's first published book, *On Human Finery,* a study of clothing and fashion through the ages, wittily illustrates the way fashion distorts cultural vision by presenting some images of Shakespearean costume from the past. A Lady Macbeth dressed as a "highly fashionable person" with huge billowing panniers, or side hoops, in the style of 1770, is recognizable today only because she is "armed with a couple of daggers," but "it was thus that the eighteenth century treated Shakespeare."[47] In the period, a woman dressed in this fashion took up three times the space of a man. Likewise, an image of Cleopatra receiving the homage of Antony in a scene from Shakespeare's play can be identified by "her hair style, her waist, her full, tiered skirts" as an actress performing "in the 1840s, in fact, in 1849." Yet audiences at the time would not, he suggests, have thought "how very 1849" but simply "how becoming."[48] The history of stage costume, his book contends, is compounded of beauty and what is essentially an invisible modernism; only when a style falls out of fashion does it seem to belong to a defining historical period. It's intriguing to compare these comments on costume to Virginia Woolf's observations in "Anon," the study of the history of English literature that she left unfinished at her death. "Elizabethan clothes have had too much attention from the historical novelist, and too little from the psychologist," Woolf wrote.

> What desire was it that prompted this extraordinary display? There must have been some protest, some desire to affirm something, behind the

> slashed cloaks; the stiff ruffs; the wrought chains and the loops of pearls. The cost was great; the discomfort appalling; yet the fashion prevailed. Was it perhaps, the mark of an anonymous, unrecorded age to enforce the individual; to make one's physical body as bright, as definite, as marked as possible? Fame must be concentrated in the body; since the other kind of fame, the publicity of the paper, of the photograph, was denied them. Did the eloquence of dress speak, when the art of verbal speech was still unformed?[49]

Quentin Bell's familiarity with Shakespeare emerges strikingly in his writing; he often uses a Shakespearean phrase, without comment or quotation marks, in the course of a casual description. This unobtrusively allusive style is clearly visible in *Elders and Betters,* a book of Bloomsbury portraits and reminiscences published in 1995 in the United Kingdom and later in the United States under the title *Bloomsbury Recalled.* The index of *Elders and Betters* contains no listings under "Shakespeare." There is one explicit reference to a named Shakespearean character, when Bell is describing Duncan Grant: "Duncan was always capable of taking on a role and playing it with art and conviction. I remember him suddenly transforming himself into Mrs Beerbohm Tree in the role of Lady Macbeth."[50] But virtually all the Shakespearean allusions in this memoir are glancing, telling, witty—and unacknowledged. Here are some examples:

- One day Vanessa Bell found to her annoyance that Barbara Hiles and Nicholas Bagenal "had made a willow cabin at her gate"—that is, they had pitched a tent about twenty yards from the Charleston farmhouse.[51]
- At a particularly raucous adolescent gathering, Rachel MacCarthy, the daughter of Desmond and Molly MacCarthy, sat "in the middle of it all, like patience on a monument."[52]
- Lady Ottoline Morrell, whose parties at Garsington attracted Bloomsbury's members but invited their scorn, was "stupendous, gorgeous, a little overwhelming and highly dramatic. Her voice was in a sense musical, she roared like any sucking dove, rolling her words along her vast Hapsburg jaw in a thrilling manner."[53]
- After the end of the First World War, the women's suffrage activists Emmeline and Christabel Pankhurst "found their occupation gone."[54]
- Mary Butts's stories about ghosts and vampires, especially when she

had had a pipe or two of opium, were so intriguing that "although I do not usually feel the urge to call spirits from the vasty deep, she talked so well that for the moment I would suspend disbelief and enjoy her fantasies."[55]

- Before he became head of the Department of Fine Art at Leeds, he was shown "the local habitation of the new department which was then being built."[56]
- Discussing the arguments about war and pacificism in Virginia Woolf's *Three Guineas,* as well as her views of women's potential in *A Room of One's Own,* he offers "a word of thanks that Virginia should not live to see a female Prime Minister joyfully leading her country into a short but bloody war fought over 'a little patch of ground that hath in it no profit but the name.'"[57]
- Similarly, in *Charleston: A Bloomsbury House and Garden,* a book of photographs and reminiscences co-written with his daughter and published after his death, Bell describes the time when the house was first opened to visitors in the 1980s and they expected a few to come each week. What happened, however, was that the public came "not single . . . but in battalions" (*Hamlet* 4.5.74–75), rushing the guides off their feet—a wry reference to King Claudius's lament that when sorrows come, they come in clusters rather than one by one.[58]

The tacit expectation in these memoirs is that readers will catch the references, but they are not there to be "caught"—Quentin Bell's incorporation of Shakespeare into his descriptions is simply a way of using effective language, including some of the best-known phrases in English, to characterize individuals and events. Just in this way did the young Lytton Strachey write to his friend Leonard Woolf in the first years of the century, using phrases like "patterns of bright gold" from *The Merchant of Venice* and "far, far wide" from *King Lear* to describe his own thoughts and feelings.[59] If there is a Bloomsbury style of Shakespearean allusion—one passed on to the next generation—this is it.

ANGELICA BELL GARNETT

Growing up at Charleston, Angelica Bell remembered the costumes and amateur theatricals with special fondness. One summer when Vanessa and Duncan went abroad, they lent the house to Marjorie Strachey, the sister of Lytton and

James, who was then teaching a small group of pupils, mostly the children of Bloomsbury friends.

> Marjorie's greatest gift, as far as we were concerned, was for theatricals. Grace, our cook, once came on her striding up and down in one of the chalk pits—a natural amphitheatre—book in hand, reciting the part of Macbeth to the rabbits and plovers. It was her idea that we should give a performance of *A Midsummer Night's Dream* under the elm trees at the back of the house where, as well as trees, there were great dung heaps several feet high. Undeterred, Marjorie strode around as Theseus, in an exiguous Greek tunic. Vanessa, returned from Paris, painted and stitched bits of book muslin for fairies' wings, and Roger Fry designed an ass's head worn by Helen Anrep's daughter, Anastasia, as Bottom. Elizabeth [Raverat], our beauty, was Hippolyta, and I was a skinny Peaseblossom. Photographs taken at the time show us grinning inanely in the grass, evidently without much idea of what it was all about, but enjoying ourselves.[60]

The free-spirited Marjorie, two years younger than Lytton, had posed nude for Vanessa in 1913 and was famed at Bloomsbury parties for her ribald versions of nursery rhymes. She was also a scholar and author as well as "a teacher of genius."[61] Angelica's description of her "striding" up and down as Macbeth and Theseus suggests that she might be another model for Woolf's Miss La Trobe in *Between the Acts.*

Vanessa's photograph albums record a number of these performances and tableaux over the ensuing years. In one Angelica poses as Cleopatra, with her friend Eve Younger as Charmian in the death scene from *Antony and Cleopatra.*[62] "I am amazed at the tolerance with which everyone lent themselves to my overwhelming desire for dramatic situations," she would write much later. But in fact "dressing up" for private theatricals was part of her Bloomsbury heritage.[63]

A group of particularly beautiful photographs of Angelica as Ophelia, taken at Charleston around 1935, show her floating peacefully in the water, eyes closed, her right hand clutching a stick for support. To get the proper angle, Vanessa was obliged to balance on a boat in the Charleston pond.[64] The likeness of the pose to Millais's famous version of the same scene is striking and effective.

The Ophelia images may also be related, in both time and subject matter, to the performance of Woolf's comic farce *Freshwater,* privately staged for a Bloomsbury audience at Vanessa's London studio in January of the same year. Much to the delight of the applauding spectators, Angelica played the part of Ellen Terry,

Marjorie Strachey's summer school: *A Midsummer Night's Dream,* Anastasia (Baba) Anrep as Bottom, in a mask thought to have been made by Roger Fry; Angelica Bell as Peaseblossom, photograph attributed to Vanessa Bell, 1925

married at sixteen to the much older painter G. F. Watts, and in Woolf's play falsely presumed to have been "found drowned."

Found Drowned (c. 1848–50) is the title of one of Watts's social realist paintings about the problems of mid-Victorian society; the subject is that of a young woman, presumably a prostitute, who has taken her own life.[65] According to one biographer, when Terry ran off with Edward Godwin in 1868, she left a two-word note attached to Watts's photograph: "Found Drowned."[66] In Watts's *Found Drowned* the woman's head lies to the right of the frame, not the left as in the Millais painting and the Bell Ophelia photograph; she is presumed to be a prostitute, not a virginal young girl, and she is partially covered in a piece of red cloth, whereas Angelica-as-Ophelia wears white. The time is night, not day; the landscape is gritty and urban, not romantic and rural. And yet the images speak powerfully to one another.[67]

At this point in her life Angelica was considering a career as an actress, and for a time she studied drama at Michel Saint-Denis's London Theatre Studio.

Angelica Bell as Peaseblossom, photograph attributed to Vanessa Bell, 1925

Eve Younger as Charmian (*center*) and Angelica Bell as Cleopatra (*foreground*) in Shakespeare's *Antony and Cleopatra,* photograph attributed to Vanessa Bell, late 1930s

Angelica Bell as Ophelia, at Charleston, photograph attributed to Vanessa Bell, ca. 1935

John Everett Millais, *Ophelia*, 1852 (detail)

G. F. Watts, *Found Drowned*, 1848–50

Vanessa Bell wrote to her son Julian that Angelica "seems absolutely bent now on going on the stage."[68] Saint-Denis was the nephew of Jacques Copeau, with whom Duncan Grant had worked at the Théâtre du Vieux-Colombier on their innovative production of *Twelfth Night.* Later he would co-direct the Royal Shakespeare Company and found a new theatre school at the Old Vic.[69] As Angelica notes in her own memoir, "I discovered that I had a stage presence, and enjoyed exploiting it."[70]

Even after she turned her main attention to painting she retained an interest in theatre and in Shakespeare. In August 1940 Virginia Woolf wrote to her enthusiastically about a planned production of *A Midsummer Night's Dream* for the Women's Institute of Rodmell that Angelica was to direct.[71] The girl who had played Peaseblossom years before would now be in charge of the show.

DORA CARRINGTON

The English painter and decorative artist Dora de Houghton Carrington—known always by her surname, since she regarded "Dora" as "vulgar and sentimental"—lived with Lytton Strachey at the Mill House in Tidmarsh near Pangbourne in Berkshire, and then at the larger Ham Spray House in Wiltshire.[72] In the evenings and when they were out walking in the countryside Strachey read many of his favorite plays aloud: *King Lear, Henry IV, Romeo and Juliet, Othello,* Marlowe's *Tamburlaine,* and Webster's *The White Devil.* Lytton read well, and

Lytton Strachey and Dora Carrington, 1920s

his listeners, whether singly or in groups, found him an effective interpreter, at times comic, at others deeply moving. In a letter to her brother Noel in the summer of 1918 Carrington wrote, "The day being fine went for a walk with Lytton who read Shakespeare sonnets to me in a delectable dell, sheltered by tall beech trees." Nothing in English verse she thought, with the exception of Milton, could "touch in exquisite beauty and form those sonnets."[73]

Shakespeare and Strachey would also figure, in a small and curious way, in the complex relationship between Carrington and the painter Mark Gertler. Although Carrington told him that she was in love with Strachey and broke off their affair, she never entirely lost touch with Gertler, and in the spring of 1917 she wrote him that she had "just been reading *King Lear* by Shakespeare. I think it his best work." When she went to visit him, she brought her copy of *Lear* with her. Afterward he wrote her, "I enjoyed our last meeting so much. How nice of you to read *King Lear* to me."[74] Their relationship was renewed, though Gertler's jealousy did not abate.

A year later, now living with Strachey at Tidmarsh, Carrington wrote to Gertler—after a long period in which they did not correspond—"In the evening Lytton has been reading *King Lear* to me. The completion of it made me dreadfully sad last night. But what a stupendous work of art it is!"[75] She does not mention the role *Lear* had had in their own earlier friendship.

But hearing the play as Strachey read it to her in December 1918 was clearly meaningful to her. When her father died shortly afterward and she went back home to mourn, she lamented in a letter to Lytton that her mother and sister were "hard human beings without feelings" who sat and discussed his will and his coffin "like two pieces of furniture conversing. The piano and the marble mantelpiece could not have felt less." Carrington wanted to bolt but had to remain until the funeral. She described herself in her letter as "the daughter of Lear."[76]

After Ralph Partridge joined the household Carrington wrote a friend that Lytton loved to read the classics with him, especially Shakespeare and the metaphysical poets, and that under Lytton's tutelage Ralph had changed his Oxford studies from law to English literature.[77] To give a sense of the ease with which these friends quipped about and through Shakespeare, we might note that the tall, burly Partridge, who tended to avoid his sisters, described them to his Bloomsbury friends "as Goneril and Regan, with himself as Little Cordelia."[78]

At Lytton's urging, Carrington married Ralph in 1921, and the three of them continued to live together. After Ralph met Frances Marshall and they fell in love, the four of them began occasionally to spend weekends together at Ham Spray. When Carrington painted her famous portrait of Lytton Strachey—reclining at ease, holding a book in his long thin fingers—he posed for her while reading aloud from Donne and Shakespeare.[79] After he died she read Shakespeare sonnets in bed at night before her suicide seven weeks later.[80]

FRANCES PARTRIDGE

"My father was over fifty in 1900, when I was born," writes the Bloomsbury diarist Frances Partridge on the first page of a book she called *Memories*. "His head was already a pink polished dome surrounded by a fringe of white hair, and his high forehead and neatly trimmed beard gave him a little the look of Shakespeare's bust."[81]

The bust of Shakespeare in Holy Trinity Church in Stratford—as contrasted with the various engraved and painted portraits—is not usually regarded as particularly handsome; the critic John Dover Wilson famously said it resembled a "self-satisfied pork butcher" and, as we've seen, after a visit to Stratford, Virginia Woolf described it in her diary as the "florid foolish bust."[82] But there is nothing of the pork butcher (or the fool) in Partridge's further description of her father, William Marshall: "He was tall and broad-shouldered, and dressed himself with old-fashioned elegance—his tie, for instance, being a wide strip of brocaded silk passed through an opal ring."[83]

The glancing mention of Shakespeare, occurring as it does in the early pages of her memoir, may well be an actual memory from childhood. But it also offers a clue to what might be called intellectual parentage—and also, looking ahead, to the literary interests of the adult memoirist. In fact the young Frances also associated Shakespeare with her mother and her mother's interest in theatre. The actor Sir Johnston Forbes-Robertson and his wife, Gertrude Elliott, were frequent dinner guests at their house, she recalls. "In fact I think my mother was a little in love with him, and I was taken to see him as Hamlet when I was nine."[84]

This, then, is the frame, very lightly sketched. Parents who were associated in her memory with the kind of culture that valued Shakespeare. Family friends who included not only Forbes-Robertson and his wife but also "the classical scholar Jane Harrison," who was a major founding figure at the Marlowe Society in Cambridge.[85]

Memories, which would be published in the United States under the title *Love in Bloomsbury,* recounts some of Frances Marshall's early experiences, culminating in her marriage to Ralph Partridge. It is a tale, as she terms it, of both "Old Bloomsbury" and "Young Bloomsbury," the coming together of individuals and generations.

Frances Marshall attended the progressive Bedales School, to which many Bloomsbury families had ties; her best friend, and the reason she was drawn to Bedales, was Julia Strachey, the daughter of Oliver and the niece of Lytton. Frances studied moral sciences (philosophy, psychology, logic, and ethics) and English at Newnham College, Cambridge. At Cambridge she met a number of people who were likewise connected to Bloomsbury, including G. E. Moore, author of the *Principia Ethica,* by then "a middle-aged, middle-sized, greyish man, who sat on the hearthrug holding his ankles in both hands and tying himself in knots, while he endeavoured to pinpoint 'what one exactly *meant.*'"[86] She finished her work at Cambridge in 1921, although because of the university's rules against awarding degrees to women, she did not formally receive her degree until 1998, at the age of ninety-eight.

Frances met other members of the Bloomsbury Group—of which she quickly became a part—when she worked at Francis Birrell and David Garnett's bookstore on Curzon Street in London. (Bunny Garnett would marry her sister Ray.) Among those she knew and spent time with were Roger Fry, Maynard Keynes, Duncan Grant, Desmond and Molly MacCarthy, Vanessa and Clive Bell, Adrian and Karin Stephen, and Virginia Woolf. "These," she recalled thinking, were the sort of people I would like to know and have friends among, more than any others I had come across. I was instantly captivated and thrilled by them. It was as if a lot of doors had suddenly opened."[87] Ralph Partridge, whom she was just beginning to know, was then working for the Hogarth Press. Dadie Rylands also became a close friend, as did James and Alix Strachey. At their invitation Frances later became the indexer for their landmark edition of Freud's complete works, published by Hogarth.

Ralph Partridge had lived with Lytton Strachey and Dora Carrington, first at Tidmarsh and then at Ham Spray, in an arrangement that for a time suited them all; he married Carrington in 1921, but the household continued as it had before. In 1923 Lytton told Virginia Woolf "tenderly, tremulously," that he was in love with Ralph, whose "extraordinary simplicity" he compared to that of Othello.[88] Later, after her relationship with Ralph had begun, Frances would join them for some weekends at Ham Spray—not without some resistance from Lytton—and she and Ralph also began to live together in London.

In her diary from 1927, she provides a Shakespearean vignette that underscores both the power of Strachey as a reader and the importance this had for Carrington. After dinner one evening Frances was happily reading a book about Byron and his love affairs, and she thought to herself, "Oh, how I hope there's no reading aloud," at which point Carrington said "in her most coaxing tone, 'Lytton, would you read to us, do you think?'" Strachey hesitated and was about to say no, but, urged on by the gathering, was soon "taking down a volume of Shakespeare from the shelf."

> He started on a Falstaff scene in a rather unconvincing manner. I put down *Astarte* and began mending my dressing gown. Bit by bit I found myself melting. Falstaff's charm was working on me. I laughed aloud at a joke; I was enjoying myself. Was Lytton really reading much better? And what a delightful character Pistol was. Lytton was picking scenes from here and there, and reading with gusto, his voice now deep and rich as velvet, now soaring to near treble, while all the time his long elegant left hand made pouncing movements in the air. Now Falstaff was dying, "his nose as sharp as a pen." The reading was over.[89]

Like many others in Bloomsbury, Frances Partridge generally preferred reading the plays to seeing them onstage. In March 1928 she traveled to Cambridge from London, reporting in her diary, "Read *Coriolanus* all the way down in the train, in preparation for the Marlowe Society's performance. It's far from my favorite Shakespeare play, but I enjoyed reading it more than the performance—

the usual affair of clanking soldiers, shouting crowds, and comic characters with permanently bent knees and cockney accents."[90] The director of the production was Frank Birch, whose style was more physical and less textual than that of Dadie Rylands.

Frances and Ralph married in 1933, and Ham Spray—which Ralph and Lytton had bought together—was their home until Ralph's death in 1960. All her life Frances retained some cherished objects from that time, including Carrington's famous painting of Lytton Strachey, some of Lytton's furniture, and several paintings by Duncan Grant.

Shakespeare appears as an incidental reference point a number of times in the diary that Frances kept at Ham Spray during World War II. Alec Penrose, who had taken a house in the country, called to ask "what he should do with his first and second Shakespeare folios. Should he bury them? Does he really want them to survive him?"[91] When the pig they had been raising for food in a time of rationing was butchered, they "sat up till midnight making the brawn. Head, heart, trotters, et cetera, were all boiled in a cauldron," and then, "seated round the table with our visitors, like the witches in *Macbeth,* we hand-picked it and chopped it, removing first an eye and then a tooth."[92] Alix Strachey reports that her mother, resisting the installation of a modern water closet in her house, "waved her arms and shouted, with her white hair flying like King Lear's: 'My whole life work is destroyed!'"[93] And when Frances and her young son Burgo go off to watch a nearby road being tarred, "a man with a curly mop of bright yellow hair, looking like a Shakespearean clown, let him use his shovel" and talked to them about when the war might be over. "Not so far off neither" was his opinion. "It's the food shortage. If we could starve every soul in the country, that would be the best thing. You have to be cruel to be kind!"[94] Partridge doesn't flag this last line as Hamlet's (3.4.176), but I wonder whether it—perhaps together with the shovel—is what put the "Shakespearean clown" in her head. None of these mentions of Shakespeare are anything like literary criticism, and they are not intended as such. Rather, what they show—as was also the case with Quentin Bell's memoirs—is the way a group of people at a certain time in their lives (and in history) thought easily, comfortably, and naturally with and through Shakespeare.

There were, of course, also encounters with scholars and critics. In a much later diary, published as *Everything to Lose,* Frances Partridge notes with pleasure the visit to Ham Spray in June 1960 of "Professor Dick Sanders [Charles Richard Sanders] of Duke University, who is writing about Lytton and all the Stracheys." During the course of his stay "we got on to Shakespeare, and were in complete agreement that *Othello* was the best play that he or probably anyone else ever wrote."[95] When she went "to hear Dadie speak on Shakespeare and Troy at the Royal Institution" she found it "very, very fascinating. . . . He read his quotations in a voice of intense vitality and emotion, leaving me convinced that Elizabethan literature was a dazzlingly exciting, tremendously inspiring affair. Nothing of the don, nothing arid about him—just this splendid, infectious enthusiasm."[96]

In 1965 a visit from Gerald Brennan, Ralph's old friend, whom she had known for forty years, led her to comment on "the continuance of his essential characteristics. Imagination but no judgment; or rather, those judgments he makes are rooted in emotion. During dinner he began saying how *boring* Shakespeare was. His plays were completely undramatic; no one could sit through *Hamlet,* he preferred Pinter or *Who's Afraid of Virginia Woolf?*"[97] To a reader of these diaries, aware that Partridge had known Virginia Woolf since the 1920s, to come upon this reference is slightly disconcerting. (In *Memories* Partridge, who seems not to have been afraid of anyone, calls her "the alarming Virginia").[98] Leonard Woolf, another long-lived member of Old Bloomsbury, had in 1962 given Edward Albee permission to use Virginia's name in the title of his play.[99] Nonetheless, the apparently casual introduction of *Who's Afraid of Virginia Woolf?* in this mid-century conversational context strikes the ear with curious force.

The following year on April 21, two days from the traditional date of Shakespeare's birthday, Partridge was invited by her friends Lionel and Margaret Penrose to a dinner given by the "Anti-Shakespeare Society," an event that she characterized in the diary as "a large gathering of solid, intelligent-looking middle-aged and elderly people in evening dress." Her extended account is worth reading for both tone and content:

> There was a strong element of *snobbery* about the supporters of Oxford, though I don't know if they thought Shakespeare's two noble descendants—both of whom made speeches—were worthy offshoots. The Duke, a pink-faced youngish man with an unbridled smile, excused himself for not bringing up a portrait of Oxford from his country seat, but gave no reason. The "man Shack-speer" or "the man of Stratford" was mentioned several times with smug and pitying smiles. I asked Lionel what on earth all the eminent scholars who thought Shakespeare wrote Shakespeare had to gain by their beliefs if they weren't true? And he muttered something about vested interests, Establishment and scholars always being heated. . . . Indeed, not a single argument was produced except for Sir

> John Russell declaring that *The Tempest* was obviously not by "Shakespeare" (it was written after Oxford's death) one reason being that the "cloud-capped towers" speech plainly showed that he didn't believe in an afterlife, while the author of *Hamlet* did. One speaker alluded to Shakespeare's ambivalent sexual tastes, and Mr Christmas Humphreys briskly waved aside any idea of his being "cissy." In fact, everyone was completely woolly-minded.[100]

When she mentioned to Sir John Russell, "a hatchet-faced legal light," that she too "was descended from Oxford (which is true) he looked at me in ludicrous amazement."[101]

Lionel Penrose was a Cambridge Apostle, a psychiatrist, and the Galton Professor of Genetics at University College, London; his wife Margaret had been Frances's friend at the Bedales School and at Newnham. She found them stimulating, intelligent, genial, and loving, though she wondered how "so clever a man as Lionel" could think "Shakespeare's plays were written by a syndicate."[102]

A Christmas visit with David and Rachel Cecil in 1971 was again enlivened by discussion—and debate—about Shakespeare. Rachel was the daughter of Molly and Desmond MacCarthy, and David, a literary critic, biographer, and the author of many books, including one on Shakespeare, had been professor of English literature at Oxford until his retirement the previous year. In her diary, Frances described a conversation with David about Hamlet's religious beliefs. "He thought his excuse for not killing Claudius when praying (that in that case he would send him to heaven) was genuine, and didn't see that if so, it was much beastlier, or even less Christian, I would say, than one can conceive of Hamlet ever being. Nor would he hear of Hamlet having been tormented by speculative doubt. So he seemed to me to miss the whole point of his character, turning him into a bigoted fanatic and doing so with a somewhat fanatical gleam in his eye."[103] Later, she reports, they resolved their differences, at least to her satisfaction. "I read Hamlet all yesterday afternoon and talked to David again, finding a meeting point about Claudius. Now I've gone on to *Othello.* Woke in the night and read more. It seems insane to read anything else, when there is always inexhaustible Shakespeare."[104] Even the weather seemed to endorse this view. "Snow and Shakespeare combine to freeze and preserve my existence here in a way that is marvelously soothing."[105]

"Inexhaustible Shakespeare." "Preserve my existence." "Marvelously soothing." To argue about Shakespeare in the daytime and to read him at night, to shelter from the winter weather with Shakespeare's works at hand—this again is the essence of what we might call Bloomsbury Shakespeare.

Coda

BLOOMSBURY'S SHAKESPEARE

Now he is ourselves.

—VIRGINIA WOOLF, "Anon"

In discussing the writing of the Bloomsbury Group and their followers, I have alluded in passing to something I called Bloomsbury Shakespeare. But what might be meant by such a phrase?

For all that they had in common, the men and women of the Bloomsbury Group were strong-minded individuals, each with his or her own perspective on Shakespeare. Yet on many points these views tended to concur. They were not, in the main, interested in the historical Shakespeare—"Shakespeare the man"—nor in the politics of Elizabethan or Jacobean England, nor yet in the religious beliefs (or unbeliefs) voiced in the plays. Though they bought, and treasured, many editions of the plays, they were not primarily concerned with what today is called "material culture" or book history. The Shakespeare they admired, read, quoted, and sometimes performed was a poet, a stylist, a wordsmith, and a thinker. What they valued above all was his language—what George Rylands described as "the thing said and the way in which it is said."[1] Having read the plays for pleasure, they remembered and cited them whenever a phrase or a passage seemed to them to express their own ideas or feelings. Whether their citations of Shakespeare were made in private diaries, letters to friends, or published work, they created what was in effect a network of shared reference, much as if they were alluding to the work of a brilliantly gifted contemporary whom they had known since childhood. As they were, and as they had.

Bloomsbury's Shakespeare was not the occasion for extravagant theatrical spectacle, nor a conveyer of manners and morals, nor yet a "historicist" figure whose plays engaged with early modern politics and culture. Instead, first and foremost, Shakespeare was—like them—a writer, whose language became theirs, whose characters were modern without being anachronistic, whose expressions of emotion, from love to loss, enabled the expression of their own. When Lytton Strachey rejects the posturing declamation of actors like Henry Irving or Herbert Beerbohm Tree, when Roger Fry excoriates the elaborate "architecturally-correct" scenery of Lawrence Alma Tadema, they are refocusing attention on Shakespeare's language and characters, away from a kind of spectacle that seemed both to distrust the power of the play and to overpower it. When Virginia Woolf compares herself to Shakespeare and finds him quicker or better than she is, what is chiefly notable is that she regards him as a fellow craftsman, not a father or a god.

As a young girl Virginia had read A. C. Bradley's lectures on Shakespearean tragedy.[2] Many years later, in *A Room of One's Own,* she quoted, and gently mocked, George Trevelyan's social history of England in Shakespeare's time. But when David Garnett, then the literary editor of the *New Statesman,* suggested that Woolf might review a book on Shakespeare, she wrote him a graceful note declining the opportunity: "If anyone could induce me to write about Shakespeare, it would be you; perhaps I will one day; but apart from wanting to write something quite different at the moment (entirely different from Shakespeare) I have a kind of feeling that unless one is possessed of the truth, or is a garrulous old busybody, from America, one ought to hold one's tongue. So I will: I mean I wont."[3] She did, of course, "write about Shakespeare" all the time, but her interest was not in scholarly work. Leonard Woolf regularly reviewed books on Shakespeare in his weekly columns, and so, in his early years as a journalist, did Lytton Strachey. But the closest Virginia came to doing so was probably her review of Professor Walter Raleigh's letters, in which she objected so strenuously to his facetiousness in referring to the playwright as "Billy Shax." ("Yet there is no doubt, Walter Raleigh was one of the best Professors of Literature of our time; he did brilliantly whatever it is that Professors are supposed to do.")[4]

"Bloomsbury had no love for academies," Noel Annan has remarked, noting that Lytton Strachey often insinuated that the worst enemies of literature were the so-called scholars of literature at the universities.[5] After the enormous success of *Eminent Victorians* and *Queen Victoria* and his first collection of literary essays, *Books and Characters,* Strachey was invited to become a member of the Academic Committee of the Royal Society of Literature. In response, he wrote Edmund Gosse that though there were arguments to be made in favor of "Academics and similar bodies," he felt he would "really be out of place in one," adding that "if I am ever able to do any service to Literature, it will be as an entirely independent person and not as a member of a group."[6] With the advantage of hindsight we might observe that it was as a member of a different group that he is now often remembered. But a voluntary group of friends was for him—and for all of them—the obverse of a committee or an academy, especially when it came to their views on literature and the arts.

Virginia Woolf was not disposed to admire the academic analysis of literature, and her attitude elicited a correspondingly combative response from some university teachers of English, notably Q. D. and F. R. Leavis. The Cambridge of the Leavises was, Woolf thought, simply "priggish": "All they can do is to schoolmaster."[7] But the Woolfs' young friend Dadie Rylands became a teacher of English at Cambridge, as did F. L. ("Peter") Lucas, who had been a classicist before he turned to graduate study in English. Both were Apostles; both published books with the Hogarth Press. The divide was not simply between town and gown, or established members of the "upper middle class" and emergent strivers, or "amateur" and "professional": Virginia Woolf was herself very much a professional writer, whose interactions with the works of Shakespeare, though they indeed gave her enormous pleasure, also had—as we have seen—a profound effect upon her novels. The "Bloomsbury Shakespeare," if we can hypothesize such a thing, was not so much anti-academic (Woolf never bothered to reply to Queenie Leavis's diatribes) as extra-academic. Picking up a phrase from Desmond MacCarthy, Leavis dismissively called the Bloomsbury way of reading "adventuring among masterpieces."[8] But adventuring, in its Elizabethan sense, was far from child's play. It meant exploration and discovery and new worlds. To adventure was to dare, to venture, to take a risk—indeed, to risk oneself. This they did in their professional and in their personal lives, with Shakespeare always in—and on—their minds.

Theatre historians have drawn attention to a change in the way we refer to the experience of attending a play. In Shakespeare's time one went to "hear" the play; only later did theatregoers begin to speak of "seeing" or "watching" *Romeo and Juliet.* But there is a third term that needs to be introduced into this history, the word *read* and the process of *reading.* To read a Shakespeare play was not a secondary experience, a substitute for the real thing; it *was* the real thing. This was the case for many members of Bloomsbury, whether the reading was solitary, tête-à-tête, or in a group, and whether it was a first encounter with a play or a return to a much-loved favorite. Dadie Rylands directed plays; Maynard Keynes built and sponsored theatres. Both James and Lytton Strachey reviewed plays, and Desmond MacCarthy made doing so his career. But for all of them, as for Virginia Woolf, who cherished her private time with Shakespeare, reading was the quintessential activity, the one that brought the reader closest to the language of the play and therefore to the playwright. "Shall I read King Lear?" she wrote one day in her diary. "Do I want such a strain on the emotions? I think I do."[9] Shakespeare was at once a stimulus to and a pacifier for the passions. "Anyone who is left alone in a tumultuous frame of mind is quite likely to (sit up) read(ing) Shakespeare," she thought. "In ten minutes or so the personal cobwebs are blown clean away. The vigour of the language is too overwhelming."[10]

"I think heaven must be one continuous unexhausted reading," Woolf wrote to her friend Ethel Smyth.[11] To Vita Sackville-West, she described it as erotic: "Love is so physical, & so's reading."[12] But reading Shakespeare was a pleasure of a special order. "Remote and extravagant as some of Shakespeare's images seem," she observes, "at the moment of reading they seem the cap and culmination of the thought; its final expression."[13] And "Anyone who has read a poem with pleasure will remember the sudden conviction, the sudden recollection (for it seems sometimes as if we were about to say, or had in some previous existence already said, what Shakespeare is actually now saying), which accompany the reading of poetry."[14] This sense of Shakespearean uncanniness or déjà vu is very like that described by George Rylands in his introduction to *The Ages of Man:* "The words themselves . . . are not ours but Shakespeare's. Yet each time we return to them . . . we feel that double sense of recognition and surprise, a simultaneous release and intensification."[15] Both Woolf and Rylands are, in context, specifically discussing Shakespeare's plays as *poetry.* It is not plot, action, or character that creates this sensation but words. In another oddly compelling affirmation of the reading process, she says that "the existence of life in another human being is as difficult to realise as a play of Shakespeare when the book is shut."[16]

As we have already noticed, she connected the historical emergence of "the reader" with the closing of the theatres in England during the English Civil War. "The curious faculty of making houses and countries visible, and men and women and their emotions, from marks on a printed page was undeveloped so long as the play was dominant." The reader, she suggests, "comes into existence some time at the end of the sixteenth century, and his life history could we discover it would be worth writing, for the effect it had upon literature. At some point the ear must have lost its acuteness; at another his eye must have become dull. . . . As time goes on the reader becomes distinct from the spectator. His sense of words and their associations develops. A word spelt in the old spelling brings in associations."[17]

Acknowledging that "the power to make places and houses, men and women and their thoughts and emotions visible on the printed page is always changing," Woolf took note of the emergence of what were then new media, capable of attracting—or distracting—the reader: "The cinema is now developing his eyes; the Broadcast is developing his ear." But her preferred model remained the reader who is able to consider what he reads "at a remove from the thing treated" because it is then that "we develop faculties that the play left dormant. Now the reader is completely in being. He can pause; he can ponder; he can compare. . . . He can read what is directly on the page, or, drawing aside, can read what is not written.[18]

George Rylands had described his *Ages of Man* anthology as "intended first and foremost for the common reader, who may care to carry in his luggage, if not in his head, something more than *To be or not to be* and *To-morrow and to-morrow and to-morrow* and *The quality of mercy is not strained*."[19] The twenty-first-century reader who could confidently identify the last of these phrases as Portia's would perhaps be slightly uncommon, statistically speaking. One thing that has happened is that the "reader" is no longer to be assumed to be reading Shakespeare unless he or she is at school, preparing to see a production or, perhaps later in life, belongs to a Shakespeare play-reading society.

In the days before cinema, radio, and television became dominant sources of entertainment, reading Shakespeare aloud in the evenings was a popular recreation in some upper- and upper-middle-class households. As we have seen, Lytton Strachey read Shakespeare to Carrington and their friends at Tidmarsh and Ham Spray. Lady Ottoline Morrell, a famous society hostess, wrote rhapsodically in her memoirs about quieter moments with her husband: "Then there float to me stray remembered lines from *Richard II* and *Antony and Cleopatra* that Philip has been reading to me, transplanting me into a world of poetic life where I am happy and at home."[20] In 1937 Maynard Keynes, ever alert to opportunities to bring commerce together with culture, proposed that "really good reading out loud" was a programming possibility for the BBC: "This is something on which so many of us were brought up and is one of the best things to be communicated to the greater public."[21] British detective novels from the 1930s and 1940s—and some as late as the 1960s—still described the kinds of social gatherings in which people compete with one another to recall and cite passages on "Shakespeare's bells," literary nightingales, or "Awful Lines from Shakespeare"—passages gleaned and remembered from their reading.[22] But the custom of spending an evening reading aloud to one's friends and family has not survived the competition of electronic media—nor, for the most part, has the private recreational reading of Shakespeare's plays.

A century of academic scholarship and technological revolution has changed, inevitably and probably irreversibly, how Shakespeare is read, studied, performed, researched, and "searched." It would be surprising today to find a similarly professionally diverse group of individuals—novelists, biographers, economists, political theorists, artists, professors—sharing their thoughts and ideas with one another in writing or in conversation by quoting from Shakespeare. It might be equally surprising, given the modern emphasis on specialization, to find that many of them had read the plays for pleasure either as children or as adults. We are a long way from the time when the world's best economist, ill in bed, could listen with pleasure to a radio broadcast of *As You Like It* because he knew the play by heart.

Shakespeare does appear regularly these days in works of fiction and drama, from revivals of *West Side Story* to novels that rewrite the plays to situate them in new times and places. The balance has shifted, though, to adaptation, where what remains is the plot and the characters, and what is changed, or lost, is Shakespeare's language. (This is of course what Shakespeare himself did in drawing upon his fictional and historical sources.) One pertinent example was the project known as the Hogarth Shakespeare, developed by Penguin/Random House, which now own the "Hogarth" name. The series, timed to coincide with the four hundredth anniversary of the playwright's death, commissioned a set of novels by famous novelists to retell tales from Shakespeare, "modernizing" them in date and setting to appeal to a twenty-first-century audience. Words like *modernize, update,* and *reimagine* were used to describe both the series and the individual novels.[23] The initial plan was to rewrite the entire Shakespeare canon, but after the first seven novels the series was apparently discontinued.

Many other similar "retellings" of the plays have been published in recent years, as have plays and novels about Shakespeare's wife, his son, and others in his reimagined social world, and some have been best sellers. In fact, "retellings" of Shakespeare have a long history, as exemplified by Mary Cowden Clarke's highly popular series of tales, *The Girlhood of Shakespeare's Heroines* (1850–52). Shakespeare's name sells. But as Adam Gopnik has noted, "The *story* content of a Shakespeare play is the least content it has."[24] For Virginia Woolf the plot was not what was Shakespearean. In her novels, there are no Shakespeare characters—no avatars of Shylock, Falstaff, or Lady Macbeth, unless we count Mrs. Swithin's longing to be Cleopatra. When someone who might be "Sh—p—re" is sighted, he looks nothing like the Stratford bust or the Droeshout engraving. Shakespeare is present in Woolf's fiction instead through her use of haunting leitmotifs, allusions, and lines of verse, together with sketches of gently mocked enthusiasts and equally gently mocked detractors, versions of the self-avowed Shakespeare lovers and Shakespeare haters she records so vividly in her diaries.

Twenty-first-century revisions of Shakespeare's plots, by contrast, often focus on issues of interest and concern to contemporary readers (race, immigration, antisemitism, feminism, sex and gender). *Romeo and Juliet, Hamlet, Macbeth,* and *King Lear* are now often memes or macros, signifying by their titles—not always by key phrases or passages—broad general ideas like young love, introspection, vaulting ambition, or old age. In universities and colleges early modernists study the plays with close attention to historical detail; literary critics and journalists often seek—and identify—Shakespearean parallels with current events, often of a minatory or foreboding (or occasionally comic) nature. But for nonspecialists the easy, knowledgeable, comfortable—and comforting—familiarity with Shakespeare shared by the Bloomsbury Group would be very difficult to find today.

To read these writers through their interest in, and reliance upon, Shakespeare is to give us new insights into both Shakespeare and Bloomsbury. Their frames of reference are life, the plays, and what Virginia Woolf, writing about the special literary province of Shakespeare, called "the passions of the human heart."[25] Their method of reading—more difficult to emulate than it may first appear—is consonant with the advice Lytton Strachey once offered to aspiring actors: "The first rule for acting Shakespeare is to trust him."[26] The same kind of "trust"—a firm belief in reliability and truth, a willingness to speak frankly and retain mutual affection and respect, a conviction that something was of manifest value—was what bound together the friends who came to be known as Bloomsbury. To trust Shakespeare as they did, to share with him and through him their most profound emotions and thoughts, is perhaps the clearest demonstration of his standing among them.

In 1943, long after the years that first brought the Bloomsbury Group to prominence, Vanessa Bell painted a portrait of the Memoir Club. Shown seated in the room are eleven people: Duncan Grant, Leonard Woolf, Vanessa Bell, Clive Bell, David Garnett, Maynard and Lydia Keynes, Desmond and Molly MacCarthy, Quentin Bell, and E. M. Forster. On the wall behind them are three portraits, images of much-loved members who had died since the club's first meeting in 1920: Virginia Woolf (painted by Duncan Grant), Lytton Strachey (painted by Duncan Grant), and Roger Fry (painted by Vanessa Bell). Many of those in the room are middle-aged. Quentin Bell alone represents the younger

Vanessa Bell, *The Memoir Club,* ca. 1943

generation, while the three figures enshrined on the gallery wall remain forever in their prime. A compelling group study, *The Memoir Club* is an homage to Bloomsbury, past and present.

But let us look again.

In Bell's design, the portraits on the wall are set a little to the right of center. To the left, above the heads of Leonard Woolf and Clive Bell, the artist has left a space. Is there another portrait that might be placed there? Another figure closely linked to Bloomsbury, who lives on in the minds of the assembled members of the Memoir Club, and whose influence is strongly felt in their work? For me, this empty space on the wall marks the place of Shakespeare in Bloomsbury: once again "absent-present," as Virginia Woolf had described him, yet—like the other absent members who preside with undimmed brilliance over this gathering of friends—keenly remembered, always present in mind and heart.

Notes

INTRODUCTION

1. *The Diary of Virginia Woolf,* vol. 2: *1920–1924,* ed. Anne Olivier Bell and Andrew McNeillie (New York: Harcourt Brace, 1980), 222–23 (January 7, 1923). Leonard Woolf cites this party in *Downhill All the Way,* the third volume of his autobiography, as an example of the "social excitement" Virginia showed at such events. Leonard Woolf, *Downhill All the Way: An Autobiography of the Years 1919 to 1939* (New York: Harvest, 1967), 115–17. Those who attended on that occasion included Clive Bell, Duncan Grant, Roger Fry, Lytton Strachey, David ("Bunny") Garnett, and Lydia Lopokova. "I kept thinking of Shakespeare," Virginia wrote afterward to her friend Molly MacCarthy. "We were so mellowly and good fellowly; not any intensity, or bitterness, but all serene and melodious." Virginia Woolf to Molly MacCarthy, January 19, 1923, in Woolf, *A Change of Perspective: The Letters of Virginia Woolf,* vol. 3: *1923–28,* ed. Nigel Nicolson and Joanne Trautmann Banks (London: Hogarth, 1994), 6 (letter 1348).
2. Even the shabbiness is somehow linked in her mind with Shakespeare, who appears in *Orlando*—published that same year—as a shabby man with a high forehead, lost in thought and holding a pen.
3. Virginia Woolf, "The Intellectual Status of Women," in *Diary,* 2:339 (appendix 3).
4. Many important and perceptive studies have traced Woolf's reading in and commentary on Shakespeare. Alice Fox places Woolf in the context of her fascination with the Elizabethan period and its literature (Fox, *Virginia Woolf and the Literature of the English Renaissance* [Oxford: Clarendon, 1990]). Theodore Leinwand compares Woolf's Shakespeare to that of poets from Coleridge and Keats to Allen Ginsberg and Ted Hughes (Leinwand, *The Great William: Writers Reading Shakespeare* [Chicago: University of

Chicago Press, 2016]). Christina Froula, in a powerful essay and then in a capacious and equally resonant book, points to Woolf's early—and enduring—sense of herself as Shakespeare's "true inheritor," charting her sibling rivalry (first with her brother Thoby, then with "Judith" Shakespeare's brother William) and the abiding presence of Shakespeare in her novels and diaries (Froula, "Virginia Woolf as Shakespeare's Sister: Chapters in a Woman Writer's Autobiography," in *Women's Re-Visions of Shakespeare: On the Responses of Dickinson, Woolf, Rich, H.D., George Eliot, and Others,* ed. Marianne Novy [Urbana: University of Illinois Press, 1990]; Froula, *Virginia Woolf and the Bloomsbury Avant-Garde* [New York: Columbia University Press, 2005]). Sandra Gilbert and Susan Gubar see her as central to the emergence of the woman writer in the twentieth century (Gilbert and Gubar, *No Man's Land,* vol. 2: *Sexchanges* [New Haven: Yale University Press, 1989]). Cary DiPietro juxtaposes Woolf's interest in Shakespeare to that of figures like Wilde, Shaw, T. S. Eliot, and Edward Gordon Craig (DiPietro, *Shakespeare and Modernism* [Cambridge: Cambridge University Press, 2006]). Those critics who have suggested that Woolf "never published an essay about Shakespeare" (Carol Hanbury MacKay, "The Thackeray Connection: Virginia Woolf's Aunt Anny," in *Virginia Woolf and Bloomsbury,* ed. Jane Marcus [London: Macmillan, 1987], 80) or that "she avoided discussing Shakespeare" and "his work remained a significant silence at the core of her literary canon" (Julia Briggs, *Virginia Woolf, An Inner Life* [London: Harcourt, 2005], 122) are looking for a specific work of literary criticism rather than considering the entirety of her writing life, from diaries and essays to fiction, in all of which she regularly addresses and engages with Shakespeare.

5. Virginia Woolf, "Old Bloomsbury," in Woolf, *Moments of Being: Autobiographical Writings,* ed. Jeanne Schulkind (London: Pimlico, 2002), 48. The 1928 date is convincingly established by S. P. Rosenbaum, correcting an earlier estimation that Woolf read "Old Bloomsbury" to the Memoir Club "in about 1922." S. P. Rosenbaum, *The Bloomsbury Group Memoir Club,* ed. James M. Haule (New York: Palgrave Macmillan, 2014), 151.
6. Virginia Woolf to Saxon Sydney-Turner, February 25, 1918, in Woolf, *The Flight of the Mind: The Letters of Virginia Woolf,* vol. 1: *1888–1912,* ed. Nigel Nicolson and Joanne Trautmann Banks (London: Hogarth, 1993), 220–21 (letter 910).
7. *The Diary of Virginia Woolf,* vol. 4: *1931–1935,* ed. Anne Olivier Bell and Andrew McNeillie (New York: Harcourt Brace, 1983), 235 (August 4, 1934). A week later, when Saxon came to stay, she still associated him with Shakespeare ("odd that I should think of 'honey-sweet Queen' in connection with him; it is what Pandarus calls Helen in *Troilus and Cressida.* But he has grown rather pink & chubby in face, & very mellow & in fact charming in mind"). Woolf, *Diary,* 4:236 (August 12, 1934). *Troilus and Cressida* 3.1.136. Helen calls Pandarus "honey-sweet lord" at line 60.
8. *The Diary of Virginia Woolf,* vol. 3: *1925–1930,* ed. Anne Olivier Bell and Andrew McNeillie (New York: Harcourt Brace, 1980), 96 (July 22, 1926).
9. Ibid., 4:357 (December 11, 1935).
10. David Garnett, *The Flowers of the Forest* (London: Chatto & Windus, 1955), 161.
11. *The Diary of Virginia Woolf,* vol. 1: *1915–1919,* ed. Anne Olivier Bell (New York: Harcourt Brace, 1977), 248 (March 5, 1919).
12. Ibid., 2:320 (August 15, 1924).

13. Ibid., 4:229 (July 21, 1934).
14. Ibid., 3:300–301 (April 13, 1930).
15. Ibid., 4:165 (June 26, 1933).
16. Ibid., 2:143 (November 16, 1921).
17. Ibid., 4:332 (July 16, 1935).
18. Ibid., 2:273 (November 3, 1923).
19. Ibid., 1:259 (March 22, 1919).
20. Ibid., 3:8–9 (April 8, 1925).
21. Virginia Woolf, *Mrs. Dalloway* (1925; London: Penguin, 1992), 37–38. She quotes *Othello* 2.1.186–87.
22. *The Diary of Virginia Woolf,* vol. 5: *1936–1941,* ed. Anne Olivier Bell and Andrew McNeillie (New York: Harcourt Brace, 1985), 190 (December 11, 1938).
23. Virginia Woolf to Ethel Smyth, May 9, 1931, in Woolf, *A Reflection of the Other Person: The Letters of Virginia Woolf,* vol. 4: *1929–1931,* ed. Nigel Nicolson and Joanne Trautmann (London: Chatto & Windus, 1981), 327 (letter 2370).
24. See Leonard Woolf to Lytton Strachey, March 20, 1901, suggesting that the book of Job "is absolute perfection and *can only* rank with Plato and Shakespeare," in *Letters of Leonard Woolf,* ed. Frederic Spotts (London: Bloomsbury, 1989), 13, 13n.
25. Leonard Woolf to Humbert Wolfe, March 25, 1929, in Spotts, *Letters of Leonard Woolf,* 300. The poem he turned down was by T. S. Eliot, and though Woolf thought it had promise, he also thought it unformed "and, to be honest, it bored me."
26. Roger Fry, to Helen Anrep, May 5, 1930, in *Letters of Roger Fry,* ed. Denys Sutton, 2 vols. (London: Chatto & Windus, 1972), 2:648.
27. Ibid., 2:369.
28. John Maynard Keynes to Lytton Strachey, January 25, 1906, quoted in Robert Skidelsky, *John Maynard Keynes: Hopes Betrayed, 1883–1920* (London: Papermac, 1992), 138.
29. Woolf, *Diary,* 3:266 (September 11, 1923).
30. Virginia Woolf to Lytton Strachey, January 26, 1926, in Woolf, *The Sickle Side of the Moon: The Letters of Virginia Woolf,* vol. 5: *1932–1935,* ed. Nigel Nicolson and Joanne Trautmann Banks (London: Hogarth, 1994), 234 (letter 161).
31. G. E. Moore, *Principia Ethica* (1903; Cambridge: Cambridge University Press, 1922), 158, chapter 6, section 113.
32. Woolf, *Diary,* 4:219 (May 9, 1934).
33. Clive Bell, *Old Friends* (1956; London: Cassell, 1988), 137.
34. Leonard Woolf, *Downhill All the Way,* 22.
35. Ibid., 23–24.
36. Ibid., 25.

CHAPTER 1. SHAKESPEARE IN VICTORIAN BLOOMSBURY

1. Colin Ford, *Julia Margaret Cameron: A Critical Biography* (Los Angeles: J. Paul Getty Museum, 2003), 26. S. P. Rosenbaum uses *Victorian Bloomsbury* as the title of a book subtitled *Early Literary History of the Bloomsbury Group* (New York: St. Martin's, 1987), which has a fine section on Leslie Stephen as well. A second volume is *Edwardian Bloomsbury,* with the same subtitle and focus. My own use of the phrase, as will be clear from

the context, is more directed toward issues of lineage, heritage, and influence, especially with reference to Shakespeare.

2. Virginia Woolf, "Julia Margaret Cameron," in *Victorian Photographs of Famous Men and Fair Women* (London: Hogarth, 1926), reprinted in *The Essays of Virginia Woolf,* vol. 4: *1925–1928,* ed. Andrew McNeillie (New York: Harcourt, 1994), 377; Una Ashworth Taylor, *Guests and Memories: Annals of a Seaside Villa* (Oxford: Oxford University Press, 1924), 217; Woolf, "'Pattledom,'" in *Essays,* 4:280–81.
3. Wilfred Blunt says that the nickname was invented by Sophia Pattle Dalrymple, the youngest of the seven Pattle sisters. "It seemed impossible to call him 'George,' still more so 'Fred.'" Blunt, *England's Michelangelo: A Biography of George Frederic Watts* (1975; London: Columbus, 1989), 70, 75.
4. A. M. W. Stirling, *A Painter of Dreams: The Life of Roddam Spencer Stanhope* (London: John Lane, 1916), quoted in Blunt, *England's Michelangelo,* 77.
5. Ellen Terry, *The Story of My Life* (London: Hutchinson, 1908), 53.
6. Vanessa Bell, letter to Virginia Stephen, August 11, 1908, in *Selected Letters of Vanessa Bell,* ed. Regina Marler (London: Bloomsbury, 1993), 67.
7. Leslie Stephen, *Mausoleum Book* (Oxford: Clarendon, 1977), 30: "And then there used to be Leighton, now Sir Frederick, in all his glory; and Val Prinsep and his friends, who looked terribly smart to me; and [the opera singer] Mrs Sartoris, who had been Adelaide Kemble, who like the rest of her family was alarming and could talk music and the drama and other mysteries."
8. Virginia Woolf, "Sketch of the Past" (1939–40) in *Moments of Being: Autobiographical Writings,* ed. Jeanne Schulkind (London: Pimlico, 2002), 159.
9. Leonard Woolf, *Sowing: An Autobiography of the Years 1880 to 1904* (New York: Harvest, 1960), 131.
10. Thoby Prinsep also leased a plot of land in Kensington and gave part of it to Watts, who built a house there; inevitably, it became known as "new Little Holland House."
11. Woolf, "Julia Margaret Cameron," 4:382.
12. John Batchelor, *Tennyson: To Strive, to Seek, to Find* (London: Vintage, 2014), 261.
13. V. C. Scott O'Connor, "Mrs. Cameron, Her Friends, and Her Photographs," *Century Magazine* 55, no. 1 (November 1897): 3. Quoted in Ford, *Julia Margaret Cameron,* 20.
14. Hallam Tennyson, *Alfred Lord Tennyson: A Memoir / by His Son,* 2 vols. (London: Macmillan, 1897–98), 1:48.
15. Ibid., 1:35.
16. Ibid., 1:42.
17. Alfred Tennyson to Emily Sellwood, ca. June 8, 1840, in *The Letters of Alfred Lord Tennyson,* 3 vols., ed. Cecil Y. Lang and Edgar F. Shannon (Oxford: Clarendon, 1990), 1:182.
18. Batchelor, *Tennyson,* 285.
19. Hallam Tennyson, *Memoir,* 1:396.
20. Anny Thackeray Ritchie, in Hallam Tennyson, *Memoir,* 2:151.
21. Hallam Tennyson, *Memoir,* 2:291.
22. Ibid.
23. Ibid.

24. Ibid., 2:290. The other two are Cordelia's reply to Lear in the first act of *King Lear* and Perdita's acknowledgment that she will never part from Florizel in *The Winter's Tale.*
25. Hallam Tennyson to Queen Victoria, October 13, 1892, in *Dear and Honoured Lady: The Correspondence of Queen Victoria and Alfred Tennyson,* ed. Hope Dyson and Charles Tennyson (London: Macmillan, 1969), 142–43.
26. Virginia Woolf to Thoby Stephen, November 5, 1901, in Woolf, *The Flight of the Mind: The Letters of Virginia Woolf,* vol. 1: *1888–1912,* ed. Nigel Nicolson and Joanne Trautmann Banks (London: Hogarth, 1993), 45 (letter 39).
27. Virginia Woolf, *Jacob's Room* (1922; New York: Harcourt, 2008), 132.
28. Julia Margaret Cameron to "Mr Digby," n.d., quoted in Hallam, Tennyson, *Memoir,* 2:84, cited in Ford, *Julia Margaret Cameron,* 33.
29. Woolf, "Julia Margaret Cameron," 4:375–86.
30. Blunt, *England's Michelangelo,* 127.
31. Ibid., 131.
32. Woolf, "Julia Margaret Cameron," 4:381; Julia Margaret Cameron, "Annals of My Glass House," in *Julia Margaret Cameron,* by Herself, Virginia Woolf, and Roger Fry (London: Pallas Athene, 2016), 55.
33. A photograph, *Jephthah and His Daughter* (1868), with unidentified sitters also presents a father-daughter duo, and although Cameron was presumably thinking of the biblical story, we could note that Hamlet accuses Polonius of being a Jephthah, using his daughter, Ophelia, for a plot and a purpose she does not fully comprehend (*Hamlet* 2.2.403, 410, 411). In Cameron's "Jephthah" image both father and daughter seem shell-shocked, appalled at the disaster that has overtaken them. Jephthah and his daughter was a popular topic in the period, mentioned in poems by Byron and Tennyson and painted by Doré and Millais. But it's the likeness to the other images of old bearded men and "innocent" young girls that is striking here. On the other hand, a warning note against a too complacent understanding of this power relation can be seen in the 1874 double portrait *Vivien and Merlin.* The visual iconography is similar—a young woman gazes upward into the face of a white-bearded patriarch, her hand touching his neck. But in this case Vivien is seducing Merlin, her mentor, into giving her a spell that will undo his power and lead to his imprisonment. Following Tennyson's version of the story, Cameron casts Vivien as the aggressor—not, as in Malory, a pure young girl at the mercy of an amorous older man.
34. Sidney Lee, *A Life of William Shakespeare* (1898; Royston: Oracle, 1996), 256.
35. Woolf, "Julia Margaret Cameron," 4:380–81.
36. Cameron, "Glass House," 56.
37. Stuart Sillars, *Shakespeare, Time, and the Victorians* (Cambridge: Cambridge University Press, 2012), 163. Sir Henry Cotton had a distinguished career in the Indian civil service, became an MP, and campaigned for Indian rights. He and his wife, Lady Mary Cotton, had four children and lived into the second decade of the twentieth century.
38. Ford, *Julia Margaret Cameron,* 116.
39. Philip Prodger, *Victorian Giants: The Birth of Art Photography* (London: National Portrait Gallery, 2018), 163.

40. Virginia Woolf's mother, Julia Duckworth Stephen, who sat for Watts and Burne-Jones, knew Millais, and as a frequent model for her aunt Julia Cameron would have been familiar with all the Ophelia images of the time. One of Woolf's cherished memories of Julia Stephen was her responsiveness to the sound of poetic language. "She had an instinctive, not a trained mind," Woolf wrote. "But her instinct, for books at least, seems to me to have been strong, and I liked it, for she gave a jump, I remember, when reading *Hamlet* aloud to her I misread 'sliver' as 'silver'—she jumped as my father jumped at a false quantity when we read Virgil with him" (Woolf, "Sketch," 97). The passage Virginia had been reading to her mother is the description of Ophelia's death by drowning: "clamb'ring to hand, an envious sliver broke, / When down her weedy trophies and herself / Fell in the weeping brook" (4.7.144–47). Like so many of Woolf's mentions of death by drowning—and there are many, direct and implied, in the novels and diaries—this memory seems retrospectively indicative and uncanny. Why, of all the times that she must have read to her mother, does she especially remember this one?
41. Mark Bills and Barbara Bryant, *G. F. Watts, Victorian Visionary: Highlights from the Watts Gallery Collection* (New Haven: Yale University Press, 2008), 153.
42. Ibid., 155.
43. Ibid.; Tom Taylor, in the *Times,* May 2, 1878, 7.
44. "If the stage was a picture, the actor also had to be a picture, in other words to act pictorially, for this was the only acting style appropriate to the circumstances of production," says Michael Booth, suggesting that a "perfect example of this union between art and acting style is Ellen Terry." Booth, "Pictorial Acting and Ellen Terry," in *Shakespeare and the Victorian Stage,* ed. Richard Foulkes (Cambridge: Cambridge University Press, 1986), 83–85; W. Graham Robertson, *Time Was: The Reminiscences of W. Graham Robertson* (London: Hamish Hamilton, 1931), 54.
45. Woolf, "Ellen Terry," in *The Essays of Virginia Woolf,* vol. 6: *1933–1941,* ed. Stuart N. Clarke (London: Hogarth, 2011), 285. Initially published in the *New Statesman and Nation,* February 1941.
46. Ibid., 6:289.
47. Ibid.
48. Ibid., 6:290.
49. Katherine Cockin, *Edith Craig and the Theatres of Art* (London: Bloomsbury, 2017), 238.

CHAPTER 2. SHAKESPEARE AS A (VICTORIAN) MAN

1. Virginia Woolf, "Impressions of Sir Leslie Stephen" (1906), in *The Essays of Virginia Woolf,* vol. 1: *1904–1912,* ed. Andrew McNeillie (New York: Harcourt, Brace, Jovanovich, 1989), 128–29.
2. Noel Annan, *Leslie Stephen: The Godless Victorian* (New York: Random House, 1984), 330.
3. Woolf, "Impressions of Sir Leslie Stephen," 1:129.
4. Virginia Woolf, "Leslie Stephen, the Philosopher at Home: A Daughter's Memories," *Times,* November 28, 1932, 15–16, in *The Essays of Virginia Woolf,* vol. 5: *1929–1932,* ed. Stuart N. Clarke (London: Hogarth, 2009), 585–86.

5. *The Diary of Virginia Woolf,* vol. 3: *1925–1930,* ed. Anne Olivier Bell and Andrew McNeillie (New York: Harcourt Brace, 1980), 182 (April 24, 1928).
6. Virginia Woolf, "Sketch of the Past," in *Moments of Being: Autobiographical Writings,* ed. Jeanne Schulkind (London: Pimlico, 2002), 120.
7. Stephen edited the first twenty-six volumes, Lee the remaining thirty-seven, as well as the two supplements of 1901 and 1912. Annan, *Leslie Stephen,* 85–86.
8. Leslie Stephen, "The Study of English Literature," in *Men, Books, and Mountains,* ed. S.O.A. Ullmann (London: Hogarth, 1956), 18. Originally published in the *Cornhill Magazine* in 1887. The idea of the author as a personal friend has had its predictable ups and downs in the works of subsequent generations of literary critics. Wayne C. Booth's *The Company We Keep: An Ethics of Fiction* (Berkeley: University of California Press, 1988) is a strong voice in favor as, more recently, is Blakey Vermeule's *Why Do We Care About Literary Characters?* (Baltimore: Johns Hopkins University Press, 2010).
9. Stephen, "The Study of English Literature," 17.
10. Ibid. His daughter Virginia would claim, with equal certainty, that the right time to read *Hamlet* was "between the ages of twenty and twenty-five." "On Being Ill," a signed essay in T. S. Eliot's *New Criterion,* January 26, 1926, in *The Essays of Virginia Woolf,* vol. 4: *1925–1928,* ed. Andrew McNeillie (New York: Harcourt, 1994), 325.
11. Stephen, "The Study of English Literature," 38.
12. Leslie Stephen, "Did Shakespeare Write Bacon?" *National Review,* 1901, reprinted in *Men, Books, and Mountains,* 74–80.
13. Leslie Stephen, "Massinger," in *Hours in a Library* (London: John Murray, 1899), 2:147.
14. Ibid., 148.
15. Ibid., 167.
16. Ibid., 168–69.
17. Ibid., 173.
18. Leslie Stephen, "Shakespeare as a Man," in *Studies of a Biographer,* vol. 4 (London: Duckworth, 1902), 1–44; George [*sic*] Brandes, *William Shakespeare: A Critical Study,* trans. William Archer, Mary Morison, and Diana White (London: Heinemann, 1898); Sidney Lee, *A Life of William Shakespeare* (1898; Royston: Oracle, 1996).
19. Lee, *A Life of William Shakespeare,* v–vi.
20. Stuart Sillars notes that "a curious parallel exists" between Brandes and "Lee's own identity. Born Simon Lazarus [*sic;* Paul Levy, *The Letters of Lytton Strachey* (London: Viking 2005), 42 says Lee's birth name was Solomon Lazarus Levi], he was advised by Benjamin Jowett to change his name when an exhibitioner at Balliol College, Oxford. It is a curious reflection on the prejudices of Victorian England that a Jewish Prime Minister was quite acceptable, but for an aspiring young scholar such an identity was thought a hindrance. And thus Lee, in his own assumed identity, did more than any other single figure to construct and propagate the identity of the great English dramatist." Sillars, *Shakespeare and the Victorians* (Oxford: Oxford University Press, 2013), 144–45. In this regard, however, it is also worth pointing out that Brandes's full name was Georg Morris Cohen Brandes; and that he too came from a Jewish family background.
21. Woolf, "Sketch," 120; Leslie Stephen, *Mausoleum Book* (Oxford: Clarendon, 1977), 76n.
22. Annan, *Leslie Stephen,* 5–6.

23. In his essay "Shakespeare's Final Period," Lytton Strachey would quote the vision of the scholar F. J. Furnivall, who imagined Shakespeare in retirement: "At last, in his Stratford home again, peace came to him, Miranda and Perdita in their lovely freshness and charm greeted him, and he was laid by his quiet Avon side." Strachey, *Books and Characters* (London: Chatto & Windus, 1922), 42.
24. Annan, *Leslie Stephen,* 110.
25. Virginia Woolf, "Reminiscences," in *Moments of Being,* 16.
26. Stephen, *Mausoleum Book,* 102–3.
27. Annan, *Leslie Stephen,* 121.
28. Virginia Woolf, *Virginia Woolf's Reading Notebooks,* ed. Brenda R. Silver (Princeton: Princeton University Press, 1983), 149. Silver dates this note somewhere between January 1909 and March 1911.
29. Woolf, "Sketch," 117.
30. Woolf, *Diary,* 3:208 (November 28, 1928).
31. Hermione Lee, *Virginia Woolf* (New York: Vintage, 1999), 146. She was not, of course, the only intellectually curious daughter in the period to find herself in this situation. Isabel Fry, a younger sister of Roger, had been "refused permission to study at Cambridge on the grounds that her father's conversation was education enough." She went on to found two successful experimental schools and to serve as headmistress for both. Michael Holroyd, *Lytton Strachey* (1994; London: Pimlico, 2011), 166.
32. The "liberal arts" traditionally included both the trivium—grammar, logic, and rhetoric—and the quadrivium—arithmetic, geometry, music, and astronomy.
33. "Recorded in a little diary she kept during 1897 are the books he chose for her to read when she was fifteen; Froude's *Carlyle,* Creighton's *Queen Elizabeth,* Lockhart's *Life of Scott,* Carlyle's *Reminiscences,* James Stephen's *Essays in Ecclesiastical Biography,* J. R. Russell's *Poems,* Campbell's *Life of Coleridge,* Carlyle's *Life of Sterling,* Pepys's *Diary,* Macaulay's *History,* Carlyle's *French Revolution,* Carlyle's *Cromwell,* Arnold's *History of Rome,* Froude's *History of England* and his own *Life of Fawcett.* These books he expected her to discuss with him—'But my dear, if it's worth reading, it's worth reading twice.'" Annan, *Leslie Stephen,* 131.
34. Woolf, *Diary,* 3:271 (December 8, 1929). For more on Woolf's passion for Elizabethan culture and travel narratives, see Alice Fox, *Virginia Woolf and the Literature of the English Renaissance* (Oxford: Clarendon, 1990).
35. Virginia Woolf, *A Reflection of the Other Person: The Letters of Virginia Woolf,* vol. 4, ed. Nigel Nicolson and Joanne Troutmann (London: Chatto & Windus, 1981), 27.
36. Woolf, "Sketch," 116.
37. Annan, *Leslie Stephen,* 17.
38. Derek Hudson, *Lewis Carroll: An Illustrated Biography* (New York: Clarkson N. Potter, 1977), 165. Dodgson's dates are 1832–98; Leslie Stephen was born in the same year and died six years later, in 1904.
39. Ellen Terry, *The Story of My Life* (London: Hutchinson, 1908), 356–57. (It might be noted parenthetically, however, that when Terry began her affair with Edward Godwin, with whom she had two children, Dodgson dropped her for religious reasons, only resuming their correspondence and friendship many years later.)

40. Woolf, "Sketch," 122.
41. When Watts sent her portrait to the Royal Academy to display in 1880, he sedately titled it *The Dean's Daughter;* her father, the Very Reverend William Corbet Le Breton, was a churchman—though a rather scandalous one—on the island of Jersey.
42. Abraham Hayward, in the *Times,* December 17, 1882, quoted in Laura Beatty, *Lillie Langtry: Manners, Masks and Morals* (London: Vintage, 1999), 219.
43. Noel B. Gerson, *Lillie Langtry: A Biography of her Life and Loves* (Leeds: Sapere, 1971), 170; Beatty, *Lillie Langtry,* 274.
44. Quoted in S. P. Rosenbaum, *Victorian Bloomsbury: The Early Literary History of the Bloomsbury Group* (London: St. Martin's, 1994), 123.
45. Frederic William Maitland, *The Life and Letters of Leslie Stephen* (London: Duckworth, 1906), 482–83.
46. *The Diary of Virginia Woolf,* vol. 4: *1931–1935,* ed. Anne Olivier Bell and Andrew McNeillie (New York: Harcourt Brace, 1983), 79 (February 29, 1932). In the following entry, on March 3, Woolf describes her second thoughts—she could refurbish six lectures from her work in progress, "Phases of Fiction," and "win the esteem of my sex, with a few weeks work," but decided against it in part because she resisted "the lecturing manner: its jocosity, its emphasis," and it would take her away from her current work on *The Waves.* Leonard was against the idea, although Vanessa was for it. There is no sense here that she had any feminist resistance to the idea of lecturing at Trinity; in fact she imagined that some "friendly don" there would encourage her to accept, and thought she might discuss the matter the following weekend with their friend Dadie Rylands, a fellow at King's.
47. E. M. Forster, *Virginia Woolf* (New York: Harcourt, Brace, 1942), 5–6.

CHAPTER 3. THE SHAKESPEARES OF VIRGINIA WOOLF

1. Virginia Woolf, *Orlando: A Biography* (1928; London: Penguin, 1993), 215.
2. Virginia Stephen to Thoby Stephen, November 5, 1901, in Woolf, *The Flight of the Mind: The Letters of Virginia Woolf,* vol. 1: *1888–1912,* ed. Nigel Nicolson and Joanne Trautmann Banks (London: Hogarth, 1993), 45 (letter 39).
3. Ibid.
4. Hallam Tennyson, *Alfred Lord Tennyson: A Memoir by His Son,* 2 vols. (London: Macmillan, 1897), 2:425–29.
5. Virginia Woolf, *Jacob's Room* (1922; New York: Harcourt, 2008), 132.
6. Leslie Stephen, "The Study of English Literature," in *Men, Books, and Mountains,* ed. S.O.A. Ullmann (London: Hogarth, 1956), 38.
7. Virginia Stephen to Thoby Stephen, May 1903, in Woolf, *The Flight of the Mind,* 76.
8. Sidney Lee, *A Life of William Shakespeare* (1898; Royston: Oracle, 1996), vi.
9. Robert Browning, "House," in Browning, *Pacchiarotto and How He Worked in Distemper, with Other Poems* (Boston: Osgood, 1877).
10. Oscar Wilde, "The Portrait of Mr W.H.," *Blackwood's Magazine,* July 1889.
11. As we'll see, a year after Virginia's question to her brother Thoby about Sidney Lee's "sonnet theory," Lytton Strachey would have a "rather wonderful" conversation with his mother about the sonnets, reported in a 1904 letter to Leonard Woolf, in which he railed

against "that fiend Sydney [*sic*] Lee, who—whatever Shakespeare may have been—was certainly a bugger." Lytton Strachey to Leonard Woolf, December 21, 1904, in *The Letters of Lytton Strachey,* ed. Paul Levy (London: Viking 2005), 44.

12. The typescript of "Sketch of the Past" leaves a blank for the title of the play.
13. Virginia Woolf, "Sketch of the Past," in *Moments of Being: Autobiographical Writings,* ed. Jeanne Schulkind (London: Pimlico, 2002), 141–42.
14. Woolf, "Sketch," 143.
15. Virginia Woolf, "Indiscretions," *Vogue,* late November 1924, in *The Essays of Virginia Woolf,* vol. 3: *1919–1924,* ed. Andrew McNeillie (New York: Harcourt, Brace, Jovanovich, 1988), 460.
16. Virginia Woolf, *Virginia Woolf's Reading Notebooks,* ed. Brenda R. Silver (Princeton: Princeton University Press, 1982), 149.
17. Virginia Stephen to Lytton Strachey, November 20, 1908, in Woolf, *The Flight of the Mind,* 274 (letter 456).
18. Woolf, *Reading Notebooks,* 149–50.
19. *The Diary of Virginia Woolf,* vol. 1: *1915–1919,* ed. Anne Olivier Bell (New York: Harcourt Brace, 1977), 192–93 (September 10, 1918).
20. Ibid., 1:193.
21. Ibid.
22. Ibid.
23. Virginia Woolf to Katherine Arnold-Porter, August 12, 1919, in Woolf, *The Flight of the Mind,* 383 (letter 1073). Before her marriage, Arnold-Porter was known as Ka Cox.
24. "I'm reading Murry on Shakespeare," she would inform her nephew Julian Bell. "Much though I hate him, I think he has a kind of warm suppleness which makes him take certain impressions very subtly." Virginia Woolf to Julian Bell, May 2, 1936, in *Leave the Letters till We're Dead: The Letters of Virginia Woolf,* vol. 6: *1936–1941,* ed. Nigel Nicolson and Joanne Trautmann (London: Chatto & Windus, 1983), 33 (letter 3126). Her earlier refusal to read Murry's book was expressed in a letter to Ottoline Morrell, July 17, 1935, in Woolf, *The Sickle Side of the Moon: The Letters of Virginia Woolf,* vol. 5: *1932–1935,* ed. Nigel Nicolson and Joanne Trautmann Banks (London: Hogarth, 1994), 418 (letter 3048). "I've not read Shakespeare, and I cant. Why let that smell pervade him even for a moment."
25. Woolf, *Diary,* 1:75 (November 11, 1917).
26. Ibid., 1:194 (September 18, 1918).
27. Ibid., 1:283 (June 18, 1919).
28. *The Diary of Virginia Woolf,* vol. 4: *1931–1935,* ed. Anne Olivier Bell and Andrew McNeillie (New York: Harcourt Brace, 1983), 333 (July 19, 1935).
29. Virginia Woolf to E. M. Forster, January 19, 1936, in *Leave the Letters till We're Dead,* 7 (letter 3099).
30. Virginia Woolf to T. S. Eliot, February 9, 1938, ibid., 213 (letter 3364).
31. Virginia Woolf to Angelica Bell, June 2, 1930, in Woolf, *A Reflection of the Other Person: The Letters of Virginia Woolf,* vol. 4, ed. Nigel Nicolson and Joanne Troutmann (London: Chatto & Windus, 1981), 173 (letter 2185).

32. Virginia Woolf to Julian Bell, December 1, 1935, in Woolf, *The Sickle Side of the Moon,* 449 (letter 3085).
33. Herbert Farjeon, in Richard Findlater, *These Our Actors—A Celebration of the Theatre Acting of Peggy Ashcroft, John Gielgud, Laurence Olivier, Ralph Richardson* (London: Elm Tree Books, 1983), 57.
34. The rope-and-basket analogy is to the so-called Indian rope trick, which had intrigued stage magicians in England. See, for example, Will Goldston, "The Secret of the Indian Rope Trick," *Sunday Express,* March 17, 1935; *Listener* (London), January 30, 1935; Peter Lamont, *The Rise of the Indian Rope Trick: Biography of a Legend* (London: Little, Brown, 2004).
35. *The Diary of Virginia Woolf,* vol. 3: *1925–1930,* ed. Anne Olivier Bell and Andrew McNeillie (New York: Harcourt Brace, 1980), 182 (April 24, 1928).
36. Ibid., 3:300–301 (April 13, 1930).
37. "When I did name her brothers, then fresh tears / Stood on her cheeks, as doth the honey-dew / Upon a gather'd lily almost wither'd" (*Titus Andronicus* 3.1.111–13).
38. Woolf, *Diary,* 3:104 (July 31, 1926).
39. Virginia Woolf to John Lehmann, August 1, 1935, in Woolf, *The Sickle Side of the Moon,* 422 (letter 3055). The article does not seem to have been published.
40. *Diary,* 4:207 (April 17, 1934).
41. Virginia Woolf to Hugh Walpole, September 12, 1932, in Woolf, *The Sickle Side of the Moon,* 103–4 (letter 2634). The title of the anthology was *The Waverly Pageant.*
42. Virginia Woolf to George Rylands, September 27, 1934, ibid., 335 (letter 2936).
43. Virginia Woolf to Quentin Bell, February 17, 1930, in Woolf, *A Reflection of the Other Person,* 142 (letter 2145).
44. Virginia Woolf to V. Sackville-West, July 8, 1931, ibid., 356 (letter 2403).
45. Woolf, *Diary,* 3:300 (October 27, 1928).
46. Ibid., 4:356 (December 10, 1935).
47. Hermione Lee, *Virginia Woolf* (1996; New York: Vintage, 1999), 672.
48. *The Diary of Virginia Woolf,* vol. 5: *1936–1941,* ed. Anne Olivier Bell and Andrew McNeillie (New York: Harcourt Brace, 1985), 42 (December 10, 1936).
49. Ibid., 5:265–66 (February 9, 1940).
50. Ibid., 5:293 (June 9, 1940).
51. Ibid., 5:298 (June 22, 1940).
52. Virginia Woolf to Ethel Smyth, February 1, 1941, in Woolf, *Leave the Letters till We're Dead,* 466 (letter 3685).
53. Nigel Nicolson, *Portrait of a Marriage* (1973; London: Weidenfeld & Nicolson, 1992), 186.
54. *The Diary of Virginia Woolf,* vol. 2: *1920–1924,* ed. Anne Olivier Bell and Andrew McNeillie (New York: Harcourt Brace, 1980), 306 (July 5, 1924).
55. Ibid., 2:320 (August 15, 1924).
56. Virginia Woolf to Vita Sackville-West, September 1, 1925, in *The Letters of Vita Sackville-West to Virginia Woolf,* ed. Louise DeSalvo and Mitchell A. Leaska (London: Virago, 1997), 70; Vita Sackville-West to Virginia Woolf, September 2, 1925, ibid., 71.

57. Vita Sackville-West to Virginia Woolf, January 8, 1926, ibid., 91.
58. Vita Sackville-West to Virginia Woolf, June 17, 1926, ibid., 142.
59. Ibid.
60. Virginia Woolf to Vita Sackville-West, January 31, 1927, ibid., 186–87.
61. Virginia Woolf to Vita Sackville-West, August 30, 1928, in Woolf, *A Change of Perspective: The Letters of Virginia Woolf,* vol. 3: *1923–28,* ed. Nigel Nicolson and Joanne Trautmann Banks (London: Hogarth, 1994), 520.
62. Vita Sackville-West to Virginia Woolf, August 31, 1928, in *Letters of Vita Sackville-West to Virginia Woolf,* 296.
63. Vita Sackville-West to Virginia Woolf, October 5, 1928, ibid., 302.
64. Vita Sackville-West to Virginia Woolf, November 29, 1928, ibid., 312–13. Other occasional Shakespeare quotations, less fraught, are often also out of context; of Herbert Read's literary criticism (probably his 1926 essay "What Is a Poem") she writes to Woolf, "I tried to read Read on poetry—Words, words, words,—and all polysyllabic."
65. Woolf, *Diary,* 4:219–20 (May 9, 1934).
66. On "absent presence" in poststructuralism, see Jacques Derrida, *Of Grammatology,* trans. Gayatri Chakravorty Spivak (1976; rev. ed., Baltimore: Johns Hopkins University Press, 2016), for example, 167: "The sign, the image, the representation, which come to supplement the absent presence are the illusions that sidetrack us."
67. Virginia Woolf to Vita Sackville-West, May 10, 1934, in Woolf, *The Sickle Side of the Moon,* 302.
68. V. Sackville West, *Knole and the Sackvilles* (London: Ernest Benn, 1976), 57–59.
69. Ibid., 58.
70. Virginia Woolf to Ethel Smyth, July 4, 1931, in Woolf, *A Reflection of the Other Person,* 353 (letter 2400).
71. Virginia Woolf to Ethel Smyth, August 22, 1933, in Woolf, *The Sickle Side of the Moon,* 218 (letter 2783).
72. Virginia Woolf to Ethel Smyth, July 29, 1934, ibid., 320 (letter 2915).
73. Virginia Woolf to Ethel Smyth, March 14, 1935, ibid., 378 (letter 3000).
74. Virginia Woolf to Ethel Smyth, November 26, 1935, ibid., 447 (letter 3084).
75. Virginia Woolf to Ethel Smyth, February 2, 1936, in *Leave the Letters till We're Dead,* 11 (letter 3103).
76. Virginia Woolf to Ethel Smyth, September 18, 1936, ibid., 73 (September 18, 1936).
77. Virginia Woolf to Ethel Smyth, April 23, 1938, ibid., 224–25 (letter 3382).
78. Virginia Woolf to Ethel Smyth, June 26, 1938, ibid., 246 (letter 3408).
79. Virginia Woolf to Ethel Smyth, October 3, 1938, ibid., 278 (letter 3348).
80. Virginia Woolf to Ethel Smyth, November 14, 1940, ibid., 444–45 (letter 3658). The Shakespeare reference is from *Macbeth* 3.2, Macbeth's comparison of kinds of men to kinds of dogs. Hermione Lee notes the "alarming conjunction" of "wanting to be immersed in the savage water and wanting to be anonymous and featureless" in Lee, *Virginia Woolf,* 740.
81. Virginia Woolf to Ethel Smyth, February 1, 1941, in Woolf, *Leave the Letters till We're Dead,* 466 (letter 3685).

82. Keats, "Ode to a Nightingale," stanza 3:

> Fade far away, dissolve, and quite forget
> What thou among the leaves hast never known,
> The weariness, the fever, and the fret
> Here, where men sit and hear each other groan;
> Where palsy shakes a few, sad, last gray hairs,
> Where youth grows pale, and spectre-thin, and dies;
> Where but to think is to be full of sorrow
> And leaden-eyed despairs.

83. Virginia Woolf, "Charlotte Brontë," in *The Essays of Virginia Woolf,* vol. 2: *1912–1918,* ed. Andrew McNeillie (London: Hogarth, 1987), 27. Originally published in the *Times Literary Supplement,* April 13, 1916, the centenary of Brontë's birth.
84. T. S. Eliot, "Tradition and the Individual Talent" (1919), in *Selected Essays* (1932; London: Faber & Faber, 1999), 16.
85. "On Re-reading Novels," *Times Literary Supplement,* July 20, 1922, in Woolf, *Essays,* 3:337.
86. Virginia Woolf, "Social Life in England," review of *Social Life in England, 1750–1850,* by F. J. Foakes Jackson, *Times Literary Supplement,* December 21, 1916, in Woolf, *Essays,* 2:65.
87. Virginia Woolf, *The Voyage Out* (1915; London: Penguin, 1992), 299.
88. Virginia Woolf, "On Being Ill," a signed essay in T. S. Eliot's *New Criterion,* January 26, 1926, in *The Essays of Virginia Woolf,* vol. 4: *1925–1928,* ed. Andrew McNeillie (New York: Harcourt, 1994), 4:325.
89. "Poetry, Fiction, and the Future," signed essay published in two parts in the *New York Herald Tribune,* August 14, 1927, ibid., 4:431.
90. Ibid., 4:436.
91. Virginia Woolf, "A Letter to a Young Poet," in Woolf, *The Death of the Moth and Other Essays* (London: Harcourt, 1942), 223–24. Originally published in the *Yale Review,* June 1932, and then in *The Hogarth Letters,* vol. 8 (London: Hogarth, 1932).
92. Virginia Woolf to Julian Bell, December 1, 1935, in Woolf, *The Sickle Side of the Moon,* 449 (letter 3085).
93. Virginia Woolf, "Editions-de-Luxe," review of *A Midsommer Night's Dreame,* intro. Harley Granville-Barker, and *Studio Plays: Three Experiments in Dramatic Form,* by Clifford Bax, *Nation and Athenaeum,* August 23, 1924, in Woolf, *Essays,* 3:439. The actor, playwright, and director Harley Granville Barker was born in 1877, the son of Albert James Barker and Mary Elizabeth Bozzi-Granville. Christened Harley Granville Barker, he was known throughout most of his stage career as Granville Barker and was often referred to by his surname, Barker. After World War I, when he left theatrical performance and became a critic and theorist, he added a hyphen and restored Harley as his first name; his books from 1921, including his prefaces to Shakespeare and *A Midsommer Night's Dreame,* were published under the name Harley Granville-Barker. I have retained the unhyphenated spelling of "Granville Barker" in references to the prewar and wartime

period, since the Bloomsbury figures who wrote about him at that time spelled it that way, both in their private communications and in print. For more on his life and work in the theatre, see Dennis Kennedy, *Granville Barker and the Dream of Theatre* (Cambridge: Cambridge University Press, 1985).

94. Virginia Woolf, "The Strange Elizabethans," written specifically for *The Second Common Reader* (1932), in *The Essays of Virginia Woolf,* vol. 5: *1929–1932,* ed. Stuart N. Clarke (London: Hogarth, 2009), 336.
95. Virginia Woolf, "The Art of Biography," in *The Essays of Virginia Woolf,* vol. 6: *1933–1941,* ed. Stuart N. Clarke (London: Hogarth, 2011), 184. First published in the *Atlantic Monthly,* April 1939, 506–10, reprinted in *The Death of the Moth and Other Essays* (New York: Harcourt Brace Jovanovich, 1974), 192.
96. Virginia Woolf, "Personalities," in Woolf, *Essays,* 6:439. Initially published in Leonard Woolf, ed., *The Moment and Other Essays* (London: Hogarth, 1947), 137.
97. A. C. Bradley, *Shakespearean Tragedy: Hamlet, Othello, King Lear, Macbeth* (1904; Greenwich, CT: Fawcett, 1965), 16.
98. Woolf, *Orlando,* 215.
99. Virginia Woolf to Ethel Smyth, April 24, 1931, in Woolf, *A Reflection of the Other Person,* 321 (letter 2363).
100. Brenda Silver, "'Anon' and 'The Reader': Virginia Woolf's Last Essays," *Twentieth Century Literature* 25, nos. 3–4 (Fall–Winter 1979): 356–441; Woolf, *Essays,* 6:580–607.
101. Ibid., 6:598.
102. Ibid., 6:598–99.
103. Roland Barthes, "The Death of the Author," trans. Richard Howard, in *A Roland Barthes Reader,* ed. Susan Sontag (New York: Vintage, 1993).
104. Woolf, *Essays,* 6:600.
105. Ibid.
106. Ibid., 6:601.
107. Leslie Stephen, *Samuel Johnson* (London: Macmillan, 1888), 178.
108. On this point see Christine Froula. "Virginia Woolf as Shakespeare's Sister: Chapters in a Woman Writer's Autobiography," in *Women's Re-Visions of Shakespeare: On the Responses of Dickinson, Woolf, Rich, H.D., George Eliot, and Others,* ed. Marianne Novy (Urbana: University of Illinois Press, 1990); Christine Froula, *Virginia Woolf and the Bloomsbury Avant-Garde* (New York: Columbia University Press, 2005).
109. Many years ago, before he became a major Shakespeare critic, Bloom mentioned to me that he was not very interested in Shakespeare because Shakespeare was not anxious.
110. Recall her comment "Shre surpasses literature altogether." Woolf, *Diary,* 3:301 (April 13, 1930).
111. Ibid.
112. Ibid., 3:208–9 (November 28, 1928).
113. Woolf, *The Voyage Out,* 214; 254.
114. Ibid., 46.
115. Ibid., 277.
116. Ibid., 141.
117. Ibid., 185.

118. Virginia Woolf to Leonard Woolf, dated "Tuesday," probably written on March 18, 1941, quoted in Lee, *Virginia Woolf,* 744.
119. Virginia Woolf, *The Mark on the Wall* (London: Hogarth, 1919), 4.
120. E. M. Forster, *Aspects of the Novel* (1927; London: Penguin, 2005), 34–35; Affable Hawk, *New Statesman,* April 9, 1921, 18.
121. Woolf, *The Mark on the Wall,* 5.
122. Virginia Woolf to Ethel Smyth, October 16, 1930, in Woolf, *A Reflection of the Other Person,* 231 (letter 2254).
123. Ibid., quoted in Virginia Woolf, *The Complete Shorter Fiction,* ed. Susan Dick (New York: Harvest, 1989), 2.
124. Virginia Woolf to Ethel Smyth, October 16, 1930, in Woolf, *A Reflection of the Other Person,* 231 (letter 2254).
125. Frances Spalding, "Vanessa, Virginia, and the Modern Portrait," in *Vanessa Bell,* ed. Sarah Milroy and Ian A. C. Dejardin (London: Philip Wilson, 2018), 69.
126. Virginia Woolf, *Night and Day,* ed. Julia Briggs (1919; London: Penguin, 1992), 258–59.
127. Ibid., 259.
128. Ibid.
129. Ibid., 260.
130. Ibid.
131. Ibid., 38.
132. Ibid., 59.
133. Ibid., 113, 115.
134. Ibid., 114.
135. Frances Spalding, *Vanessa Bell: Portrait of the Bloomsbury Artist* (1983; London: Tauris Parke, 2016), 189–90.
136. Woolf, *Night and Day,* 146.
137. Ibid., 80.
138. Ibid., 424–25.
139. Ibid., 96.
140. Ibid., 364.
141. Ibid., 408.
142. For example, an unsigned review in the *Times Literary Supplement,* October 30, 1919.
143. Virginia Woolf, letter to Ethel Smyth, September 18, 1936, in Woolf, *Leave the Letters till We're Dead,* 73 (letter 3173).
144. Woolf, *Night and Day,* 408.
145. Ibid., 80, 126.
146. Ibid., 122.
147. Virginia Woolf, "Craftsmanship," in Woolf, *Essays,* 6:95. Originally published in the *Listener,* May 5, 1937, reprinted in Woolf, *The Death of the Moth and Other Essays,* 203.
148. Woolf, *Night and Day,* 125.
149. Ibid., 127.
150. Julia Briggs, in her notes to the Penguin edition of *Night and Day,* 443, says "there may be a subliminal link," and I think this is right. But whether the link is conscious or

unconscious, it is telling, and it also makes clear how closely Woolf read, and knew, the language of the plays.

151. Ibid., 425.
152. Woolf, *Diary,* 2:23 (January 26, 1920).
153. Ibid., 2:186 (July 26, 1922).
154. Woolf, *Jacob's Room,* 170.
155. Woolf, *Reading Notebooks,* 235.
156. Woolf, *Jacob's Room,* 34.
157. Ibid., 46.
158. Ibid.
159. Ibid., 47.
160. This oblique reference to a death by drowning is one of several that can be found in Woolf's writings, often, as here, without a sense of pain or loss. Another, already noted, is the brief mention of Millais's *Ophelia* in *Night and Day:* "Some say it is the best picture he ever painted" (126).
161. Woolf, *Jacob's Room,* 79–81.
162. Ibid., 128.
163. Ibid., 90–91.
164. Ibid., 92.
165. Ibid., 88.
166. Ibid., 110.
167. Ibid., 113.
168. Ibid., 114.
169. Ibid., 131.
170. Ibid., 132.
171. Ibid., 170.
172. Ibid., 170.
173. See Woolf, "Sketch," 42n.
174. Virginia Woolf, "Impressions at Bayreuth," *Times,* August 21, 1909, in *The Essays of Virginia Woolf,* vol. 1: *1904–1912,* ed. Andrew McNeillie (New York: Harcourt, Brace, Jovanovich, 1989), 290.
175. Ibid., 1:291.
176. Virginia Woolf, letter to Katherine Cox, May 16, 1913, in *The Question of Things Happening: The Letters of Virginia Woolf,* vol. 2: *1912–1922,* ed. Nigel Nicolson and Joanne Trautmann (London: Chatto & Windus, 1980), 26 (letter 668).
177. Leonard Woolf, *Beginning Again: An Autobiography of the Years 1911 to 1918* (1963, 1964; New York: Harvest, 1972), 50.
178. Virginia Woolf, *Mrs. Dalloway* (1925; London: Penguin, 1992), 82.
179. Ibid., 198.
180. Ibid.
181. Ibid., 10.
182. Hatchards describes itself today as a "unique British institution" dating from 1797 whose customers have been "the literary, political, artistic and social lions of their day" ("History," www.hatchards.co.uk).

183. Woolf, *Mrs. Dalloway,* 32.
184. Ibid., 33.
185. Ibid., 43.
186. Ibid., 153.
187. Ibid., 201.
188. Ibid., 108.
189. Ibid., 204.
190. Ibid., 202.
191. Ibid., 37–38.
192. Ibid., 38.
193. Ibid., 188.
194. Ibid., 199.
195. Ibid., 207.
196. Ibid., 197.
197. Woolf, *Diary,* 3:8–9 (April 8, 1925).
198. Ibid., 3:9 (April 19, 1925).
199. Ibid., 2:273 (November 3, 1923).
200. Woolf, *Mrs. Dalloway,* 93.
201. Woolf, *Reading Notebooks,* 224–25.
202. Woolf, *Mrs. Dalloway,* 94.
203. Ibid., 98.
204. Ibid., 160–61.
205. Virginia Woolf to Jacques Raverat, November 4, 1923, in Woolf, *A Change of Perspective,* 76 (letter 1432).
206. Lee, *Virginia Woolf,* 465.
207. Woolf, *Mrs. Dalloway,* 97.
208. Ibid., 97.
209. Ibid., 100.
210. Ibid., 102–3.
211. Ibid., 153.
212. Ibid.
213. Woolf, "Old Bloomsbury," delivered to the Memoir Club in 1922, in Woolf, *Moments of Being,* 45.
214. Woolf, *Mrs. Dalloway,* 162.
215. Ibid., 154.
216. Ibid., 160.
217. Ibid., 203.
218. Ibid.
219. Virginia Woolf, *Mrs. Dalloway,* ed. Bonnie Kim Scott (Orlando, FL: Harvest, 2005), xlix, 181.
220. Woolf, *Mrs. Dalloway* (Penguin edition), 213.
221. Virginia Woolf, *To the Lighthouse,* ed. David Bradshaw (1927; Oxford: Oxford University Press, 2006), 64.
222. Ibid., 65.

223. Ibid., 142.
224. Ibid., 143.
225. Ibid., 143.
226. Ibid., 103, 191n.
227. Leslie Stephen, *Mausoleum Book* (Oxford: Clarendon, 1977), 93.
228. Woolf, *To the Lighthouse,* 32.
229. James Boswell, *The Life of Samuel Johnson* (1791; London: Penguin, 2008), 248.
230. Woolf, *To the Lighthouse,* 127.
231. Ibid., 32.
232. Ibid., 96, 97.
233. Ibid., 98.
234. Ibid., 98.
235. Ibid., 100.
236. Nicolson, *Portrait of a Marriage,* 186.
237. Woolf, *Orlando,* 16.
238. Ibid., 54.
239. *OED,* s.v. "front," II.7.g., I.1.a. Now defined as "a person, organization, etc., that serves as a cover for subversive or illegal activities," the term *front* began, appropriately enough, as a poetical word for "forehead." See *Hamlet* 3.4.54–55: "See what a grace was seated on this brow— / Hyperion's curls, the front of Jove himself."
240. Woolf, *Orlando,* 56.
241. Virginia Woolf, "Not One of Us," signed review of *Shelley: His Life and Work,* by Walter Edwin Peck, *New York Herald Tribune,* October 23, 1927, in Woolf, *Essays,* 4:465–71.
242. Woolf, *Orlando,* 56–57.
243. Ibid., 117.
244. Ibid., 215.
245. John Aubrey, *Brief Lives,* quoted in Lee, *A Life of William Shakespeare,* 286.
246. Lee, *A Life of William Shakespeare,* 286.
247. Ibid., 287.
248. Ibid., 289.
249. Woolf, *Orlando,* 61.
250. Ibid., 62.
251. Ibid., 63.
252. Ibid., 62.
253. "Virginia Woolf, "A Professor of Life," in Woolf, *Essays,* 4:343. This signed review of *The Letters of Sir Walter Raleigh,* edited by Lady Raleigh with a preface by D. Nichol Smith, originally appeared in *Vogue* in early May 1926. Raleigh was a family friend of the Stracheys and had been an early mentor to Lytton Strachey at University College Liverpool.
254. Virginia Woolf to Vita Sackville-West, February 17, 1926, in Woolf, *A Change of Perspective* (letter 1621).
255. Woolf, *Orlando,* 75.
256. Ibid., 123, 124.

257. Woolf, *Diary,* 3:182 (April 24, 1928).
258. Woolf, *Orlando,* 40–41.
259. Ibid., 41.
260. Woolf, *Diary,* 3:143 (June 30, 1927).
261. For example, *A Midsummer Night's Dream* 2.1.162–64.
262. Woolf, *Orlando,* 51.
263. Ibid., 56, 57.
264. Ibid., 116.
265. Ibid., 153.
266. Ibid., 197.
267. Ibid.
268. Leonard Woolf, *Sowing: An Autobiography of the Years 1880 to 1904* (New York: Harvest, 1960), 202. Three of the four Oxford volumes contained the works of Shakespeare—William Shakespeare, *The Oxford Miniature Edition: The Comedies, the Tragedies, the Histories, Poems, and Sonnets,* ed. W. J. Craig (London: Oxford University Press, 1903).
269. Woolf, *Orlando,* 47.
270. Virginia Woolf, "The New Biography," signed review in the *New York Herald Tribune,* October 30, 1927, published in Woolf, *Granite and Rainbow* (New York: Harvest, 1975), 149, reprinted in Woolf, *Essays,* 4:473.
271. Sidney Lee, *Principles of Biography* (Cambridge: Cambridge University Press, 1911), 25–26.
272. Woolf, "The New Biography," 478.
273. Harold Nicolson, *Some People* (London: Constable, 1927).
274. Woolf, "The New Biography," 473, 475, 478.
275. "Nature . . . has played so many queer tricks upon us, making us so unequally of clay and diamonds, or rainbow and granite . . . the poet has a butcher's face and the butcher a poet's nature." Woolf, *Orlando,* 55. Woolf's narrator at this point breaks the frame to give the date: "even now (the first of November, 1927)."
276. Ibid., 68.
277. Ibid., 11.
278. Virginia Woolf, *A Room of One's Own* (1929; Orlando, FL: Harcourt, 2005), 110.
279. Ibid., 26.
280. Ibid., 28–29.
281. Ibid., 41.
282. Ibid., 42.
283. Ibid., 43.
284. Leonard Woolf to Lytton Strachey, April 8, 1902, in *Letters of Leonard Woolf,* ed. Frederic Spotts (London: Bloomsbury, 1989), 23.
285. F. L. Lucas, *Tragedy: In Relation to Aristotle's Poetics* (1928; London: Hogarth, 1953), 114–15; Woolf, *Room,* 43n.
286. Woolf, *Room,* 46.
287. Ibid.
288. Ibid., 47–48.
289. Ibid., 48. Since Woolf's time scholars have studied and taught dramatic works by women

in the period, like Elizabeth Carey's *Mariam,* but Woolf reflects then current scholarship when she says that Judith Shakespeare's stage plays, were they to have been written, "would have gone unsigned" (49).

290. Ibid., 112.
291. Ibid., 82.
292. Ibid., 50.
293. Ibid., 56.
294. Ibid., 94.
295. Ibid., 88.
296. Virginia Woolf, "Coleridge as Critic," review of *The Table Talk and Omniana,* by Samuel Taylor Coleridge, *Times Literary Supplement,* February 7, 1918, in Woolf, *Essays,* 2:222.
297. Samuel Taylor Coleridge, "Table Talk," in Coleridge, *The Table Talk and Omniana* (Oxford: Oxford University Press, 1917), 201 (September 1, 1832). Coleridge does not mention Shakespeare in this passage; his example is Swedenborg. For Coleridge on Shakespeare in *The Table Talk,* we have "Shakespeare's poetry is characterless; that is, it does not reflect the individual Shakespeare," 92 (May 12, 1830); "Shakespeare is universal and in fact has no *manner,*" 213 (February 17, 1833); "How well do we seem to know Chaucer! How absolutely nothing do we know of Shakespeare!" and "Shakespeare is of no age," 294–95 (March 15, 1834).
298. Woolf, *Room,* 97.
299. Woolf, *Orlando,* 178–79.
300. Ottoline Morrell, *Ottoline: The Early Memoirs of Lady Ottoline Morrell,* ed. Robert Gathorne-Hardy (London: Faber & Faber, 1963), 180.
301. Woolf, *Diary,* 3:203 (November 7, 1928).
302. Ibid., 2:320 (August 15, 1924).
303. Ibid., 3:312 (August 20, 1930).
304. Virginia Woolf, *The Waves* (1931; New York: Harvest, 2006), 94.
305. Ibid., 214.
306. Woolf, *Diary,* 3:303 (May 1, 1930).
307. Woolf, *The Waves,* 220; Lee, *Virginia Woolf,* 753. Leonard thought *The Waves* "a masterpiece" and "the best of your books" when she first gave it to him to read (Woolf, *Diary,* 4:36 [July 19, 1931]) and seems to have maintained that view, listing it first in his autobiography when he was describing those of her books he thought of "a work of art or a work of genius." The others were *To the Lighthouse* and *Between the Acts.* Leonard Woolf, *Downhill All the Way: An Autobiography of the Years 1919 to 1939* (New York: Harvest, 1967), 146–47.
308. The voluble Bernard, who cannot seem to write something that expresses him as well as his speaking does, corresponds to Desmond MacCarthy; Louis the outsider, with his Australian accent and his banker father, is associated with T. S. Eliot, an American from St. Louis who himself worked in a bank; Susan, who loves the countryside, with Vanessa; Neville, who loves Percival, with Lytton Strachey; Jinny perhaps with Mary Hutchinson; the silent, heroic, "godlike" Percival, whom all the "boasting boys" copy at school, whom Neville loves, and who dies young, with Virginia Woolf's brother Thoby

Stephen. When she wrote the final words of *The Waves,* the invocation "O Death," she thought of Thoby. "It is done; & I have been sitting these 15 minutes in a state of glory, & calm, & some tears, thinking of Thoby & if I could write Julian Thoby Stephen 1881–1906 on the first page. I suppose not." Woolf, *Diary,* 4:10 (February 7, 1931).

309. Woolf, *The Waves,* 130.
310. Ibid., 184.
311. Ibid., 190.
312. Ibid., 25–26.
313. Ibid., 212, 217.
314. Ibid., 115, 116. Later (119) she will call them "my penny bunch, my penny bunch of violets," which she has "torn up by the roots from the pavement of Oxford Street."
315. Ibid., 63.
316. Ibid., 216. Bernard omits the pathos of the scene, in which Lear desperately—and wrongly—imagines that he and Cordelia can live safely together in prison: "So we'll live, / And pray, and sing, and tell old tales, and laugh / At gilded butterflies, and hear poor rogues / Talk of court news . . . And take upon's the mystery of things, / As if we were God's spies" (5.3.11–17).
317. "Fear no more th' heat o' th' sun" (*Cymbeline* 4.2.259).
318. Woolf, *The Waves,* 143.
319. Ibid., 209–10. "Pillicock sat on Pillicock hill" is a fragment of an old rhyme chanted by Edgar as Poor Tom in *King Lear* (3.4.73); "Come away, come away death" is Feste's sublime song in *Twelfth Night* (2.4.50).
320. Woolf, *The Waves,* 192. "Let me not to the marriage of true minds" is the first line of Shakespeare's Sonnet 116.
321. Ibid., 202.
322. Virginia Woolf, "Character in Fiction"(1924), in *Essays,* 3:420–38.
323. Virginia Woolf, *Flush* (1933; London: Vintage, 1991), 83.
324. This phrase—and less frequently "the educated man's sister"—are invoked constantly and with conscious wry humor throughout the essay, as Woolf describes the limits placed by society (the Victorian father, the Church, high-performing male professionals, and so on) on women like herself. Queenie Leavis, in her review of *Three Guineas,* failed signally to recognize the self-parodic tone that the phrase gathers as it recurs throughout the essay, and (mis)read it as a claim of class exclusiveness rather than as the irony characteristic of Woolf's double-edged critique. Woolf, of course, as the daughter of Leslie Stephen and the sister of Thoby and Adrian, was both the "daughter" and the "sister" she mentions so regularly.
325. Virginia Woolf, *Three Guineas,* in Woolf, *A Room of One's Own and Three Guineas,* ed. Anna Snaith (Oxford: Oxford University Press, 2015), 176. Other possible *Hamlet* allusions, of a very general kind, include "no certainty in heaven above or on earth below" (95) and "so rank does it stink" (134), both marked by Snaith. For the second quotation, see 235–37n38.
326. Woolf, *Diary,* 5:165 (September 1, 1938).
327. *Three Guineas* engendered a number of "hostile responses" from her friends and allies. As Hermione Lee summarizes, "Keynes thought it silly. Leonard (though he picked his

words with care), thought it her worst book. Most of her friends were embarrassed by it, and few of them passed comment. The next generation of her male readers and friends," including Nigel Nicolson and Quentin Bell, "followed suit." Lee, *Virginia Woolf,* 680.

328. A nascent dictator "curled up like a caterpillar on a leaf" (Woolf, *Three Guineas,* 135); the public world "forces us to circle, like caterpillars head to tail" (156).
329. Ibid., 226–27n30.
330. Q. D. Leavis, "Caterpillars of the Commonwealth, Unite!" *Scrutiny,* September 1938, 207.
331. Ibid., 209.
332. Ibid., 208.
333. Woolf, *Three Guineas,* 226.
334. Noel Annan, *The Dons: Mentors, Eccentrics, and Geniuses* (Chicago: University of Chicago Press, 1999), 172–73.
335. Virginia Woolf to Julian Bell, December 1, 1935, in Woolf, *The Sickle Side of the Moon,* 450 (letter 3085).
336. Woolf, *The Years* (1939; Orlando, FL: Harvest, 2008) 185–86.
337. Ibid., 177.
338. Ibid., 269.
339. Woolf, *Diary,* 3:300 (October 27, 1928).
340. Ibid., 3:125 (January 23, 1927).
341. Woolf, *The Years,* 328.
342. Lucas, *Tragedy,* 152.
343. Woolf, *The Years,* 329.
344. Ibid., 388–89.
345. Ibid., 387–88.
346. Ibid., 412.
347. Virginia Woolf to Margaret Llewelyn Davies, April 6, 1940, in Woolf, *Leave the Letters till We're Dead,* 391 (letter 3597).
348. Virginia Woolf, *Between the Acts* (1941; London: Penguin, 2019), 102, 92. Shakespeare's Bottom, of course, had an ass's head and a man's body rather than a man's head and a donkey's hindquarters, but the allusion seems clear; the "village idiot" may be thought to be already equipped with the head of an "ass."
349. Ibid., 16.
350. Michael Holroyd, *A Strange Eventful History: The Dramatic Lives of Ellen Terry, Henry Irving, and Their Remarkable Families* (New York: Picador, 2008), 532.
351. Vita Sackville-West to Virginia Woolf, May 30, 1938, in *The Letters of Vita Sackville-West to Virginia Woolf,* 439.
352. Woolf, *Between the Acts,* 94.
353. Michael Dobson, *The Making of the National Poet* (Oxford: Clarendon, 1992), 226.
354. Woolf, *Between the Acts,* 16, 36.
355. Ibid., 128.
356. Ibid., 54.
357. Ibid., 118–19.

358. Woolf, *Diary,* 5:164 (August 28, 1938); ellipses in original.
359. Virginia Woolf to Ethel Smyth, October 3, 1938, in Woolf, *Leave the Letters till We're Dead,* 278.
360. Woolf, *Between the Acts,* 26.
361. Ibid., 73.
362. Ibid., 111–12.
363. Ibid., 114.
364. Ibid., 127.
365. Ibid., 125.
366. Woolf, *Diary,* 3:300 (October 27, 1928).
367. Woolf, *Between the Acts,* 52.
368. Ibid., 62.
369. Ibid., 56.
370. Ibid. "Look where they come" (*Antony and Cleopatra* 1.1.10).
371. "Vex not his ghost. O, let him pass! He hates him / That would upon the rack of this tough world / Stretch him out longer" (*King Lear* 5.3.312–14). Woolf, *Between the Acts,* 57.
372. "The heavens rain odours on you" (*Twelfth Night* 3.1.77); "Look, love, what envious streaks / do lace the severing clouds in yonder east. / Night's candles are burnt out" (*Romeo and Juliet* 3.5.6–8). Woolf, *Between the Acts,* 57.
373. Woolf, *Between the Acts,* 61.
374. Ibid., 53.
375. Ibid., 35.
376. Ibid., 104.
377. Lytton Strachey, "Shakespeare and the Musical Glasses," in *Unpublished Works of Lytton Strachey: Early Papers,* ed. Todd Avery (London: Routledge, 2011), 133.
378. Aldous Huxley, *Point Counter Point* (1928; London: Vintage 2018), 364. Huxley's novel is a roman à clef whose characters are thinly veiled portrayals of many people Woolf knew (Augustus John, Ottoline Morrell, Katherine Mansfield, John Middleton Murry, and others). The Woolfs' old friend S. S. Koteliansky ("Kot") had urged her to read it, saying it was "a painful book, a horrid book," but "typical of the age." Woolf, *Diary,* 3:217–18 (January 4, 1929).
379. Woolf, *Between the Acts,* 92.
380. Ibid., 61.
381. Ibid., 32.
382. Ibid., 35.
383. Ibid., 66.
384. Ibid., 110.
385. Ibid., 126.
386. Ibid., 130.
387. Ibid., 25–26.
388. Ibid., 43–44.
389. Ibid., 46.
390. Ibid., 122.

391. Ibid., 123.
392. Ibid.
393. Ibid., 46.
394. Virginia Woolf to Vita Sackville-West, February 17, 1926, in Woolf, *A Change of Perspective,* 242 (letter 1621); Woolf, "A Professor of Life," in Woolf, *Essays,* 4:343.
395. Woolf, *Diary,* 3:74 (April 11, 1926).
396. Woolf, *Between the Acts,* 122–23.

CHAPTER 4. SHAKESPEARE AMONG THE APOSTLES

1. In Leonard Woolf, *Sowing: An Autobiography of the Years 1880 to 1904* (New York: Harvest, 1960), between pp. 102 and 103.
2. Robert Skidelsky, *John Maynard Keynes: Hopes Betrayed, 1883–1920* (London: Papermac), 117.
3. Arthur Sidgwick, Eleanor Sidgwick, and Henry Sidgwick, *Henry Sidgwick: A Memoir* (London: Macmillan, 1906), quoted in Woolf, *Sowing,* 129–30.
4. Leonard Woolf, *Downhill All the Way: An Autobiography of the Years 1919 to 1939* (New York: Harvest, 1967), 114.
5. John Maynard Keynes, "My Early Beliefs" (1938), in *The Essential Keynes,* ed. Robert Skidelsky (London: Penguin, 2015), 13.
6. E. M. Forster, *Goldsworthy Lowes Dickinson* (1934; New York: Harvest, 1962). "Dickinson loved England, he felt its scenery to be trembling on the verge of an exquisite mythology which only Shakespeare has evoked and he only incidentally" (67). Dickinson's book *From King to King* (1891) "illustrates his belief that history should be a form of art, and that it had never been better treated than by Shakespeare" (79).
7. Leonard Woolf, *Beginning Again: An Autobiography of the Years 1911 to 1918* (1963, 1964; New York: Harvest, 1972), 21.
8. Lytton Strachey, introduction to *Words and Poetry,* by George H. W. Rylands (London: Hogarth, 1928), xiii.
9. Charles Richard Sanders, *The Strachey Family, 1588–1932: Their Writings and Literary Associations* (New York: Greenwood, 1968), 268.
10. Michael Holroyd, *Lytton Strachey* (1994; London: Pimlico, 2011), 24.
11. Ibid., 33.
12. Ibid.
13. Robert Skidelsky, *English Progressive Schools* (Harmondsworth, UK: Penguin, 1969), 105.
14. Lytton Strachey, "Diary" (1898), in *Lytton Strachey by Himself,* ed. Michael Holroyd (1971; London: Abacus, 2005), 118.
15. John Keats to Benjamin Bailey, November 22, 1817, in John Keats, *Selected Letters,* ed. John Barnard (London: Penguin, 2014), 69.
16. John Keats to George and Tom Keats, December 27 (?), 1817, ibid., 79.
17. Clive Bell, *Old Friends* (1956; London: Cassell, 1988), 26.
18. Holroyd, *Lytton Strachey,* 384.
19. Vanessa Bell to Hilton Young, April 15, 1915, in *Selected Letters of Vanessa Bell,* ed. Regina Marler (London: Bloomsbury, 1994), 176.

20. Holroyd, *Lytton Strachey,* 93.
21. Bell, *Old Friends,* 26.
22. Lytton Strachey to Leonard Woolf, November 21, 1906, in *The Letters of Lytton Strachey,* ed. Paul Levy (London: Viking, 2005), 114.
23. Lytton Strachey to Leonard Woolf, December 21, 1900, ibid., 3.
24. Lytton Strachey, "Conversation and Conversations," in *Unpublished Works of Lytton Strachey: Early Papers,* ed. Todd Avery (London: Routledge, 2011), 11.
25. Ibid., 14.
26. Ibid., 15.
27. "Cleopatra and Mrs Humphry Ward" and "Salter and Cleopatra: An Imaginary Conversation," in *Unpublished Works of Lytton Strachey,* 147–49, 153–57.
28. In a letter to Leonard Woolf he reports a chance meeting at an art gallery where Salter detects a likeness between the painting of an old woman by Frans Hals and the statesman Lord Haldane: "He must be her reincarnation." Lytton Strachey to Leonard Woolf, November 10, 1906, in *Letters of Lytton Strachey,* 112.
29. Lytton Strachey, "Ought the Father to Grow a Beard?" in *The Shorter Strachey,* ed. Michael Holroyd and Paul Levy (Oxford: Oxford University Press, 1980), 14.
30. Ibid., 17.
31. Ibid., 16, 15, 19.
32. Ibid., 19.
33. Lytton Strachey, "Christ or Caliban," in *Unpublished Works of Lytton Strachey,* 24.
34. Lytton Strachey, "The Praise of Shakespeare," unsigned review, *Spectator,* June 4, 1904.
35. Strachey to Roger Senhouse, February 11, 1927, from Ham Spray House, in *Letters of Lytton Strachey,* 560. The quotation here is from Enobarbus's account of the meeting of Antony and Cleopatra at Cydnus; although Lytton is not here cast as Cleopatra, it's perhaps notable that Carrington is Antony.
36. Strachey, "The Praise of Shakespeare."
37. Lytton Strachey, "King Lear" (May 23, 1908), in Lytton Strachey, *Spectatorial Essays,* ed. James Strachey (London: Chatto & Windus, 1964), 67.
38. Ibid.
39. William Butler Yeats, "Emotion of Multitude," in *Ideas of Good and Evil* (London: Bullen, 1903), 340. Half a century later, Leonard Woolf would make a similar suggestion to Angus Wilson, proposing that there was a class of literary work that dealt "with the relations of human beings to one another and also to the universe." Among his examples were *King Lear, The Tempest,* and Virginia Woolf's *The Waves.* Leonard Woolf to Angus Wilson, March 8, 1962, in Leonard Woolf, *Letters of Leonard Woolf,* ed. Frederic Spotts (London: Bloomsbury, 1989), 520.
40. Strachey, "King Lear," 69.
41. Holroyd, *Lytton Strachey,* 264.
42. Lytton Strachey, "Voltaire's Tragedies," in *Books and Characters* (London: Chatto & Windus, 1922), 123.
43. Holroyd, *Lytton Strachey,* 282.
44. Tim Cribb, *Bloomsbury and British Theatre: The Marlowe Story* (Cambridge: Salt, 2007), 67.

45. *Independent Review* 3 (August 1904). Described by Michael Holroyd as "an intellectual monthly largely financed by the Trevelyans, with a strong Apostolic input" (*Lytton Strachey,* 122), the *Independent Review* also published essays by Strachey on Blake and Sir Thomas Browne. "Shakespeare's Final Period" was republished in Strachey, *Books and Characters.*
46. Gordon McMullan, *Shakespeare and the Idea of Late Writing: Authorship in the Proximity of Death* (Cambridge: Cambridge University Press, 2007), 162.
47. Strachey, "Shakespeare's Final Period," in *Books and Characters,* 42–43.
48. Ibid., 49.
49. Ibid.
50. Ibid., 50.
51. Ibid., 46–47.
52. Ibid., 47.
53. Ibid., 51.
54. Ibid., 52.
55. Strachey would use the word again in *Eminent Victorians* in his comments on Lord Hartington, who felt "it was a bore not to do the proper thing. He was usually bored—for one reason or another; but this particular form of boredom he found more intense than all the rest. He would take endless pains to avoid it." What "bored" Hartington in this case was his feeling that he should do something to rescue General Gordon. *Eminent Victorians* (1918; London: Penguin, 1986), 245–46.
56. Russ McDonald, *Shakespeare's Late Style* (Cambridge: Cambridge University Press, 2006), 12.
57. Ibid., 15.
58. Strachey, "Shakespeare's Final Period," 54.
59. Ibid., 55.
60. Ibid.
61. Ibid., 56.
62. S. Schoenbaum, *Shakespeare's Lives* (1970; Oxford: Oxford University Press, 1991), 665; McMullan, *Shakespeare and the Idea of Late Writing,* 162.
63. Alan Bell and Katherine Duncan-Jones, "Sir Sidney Lee," in *New Dictionary of National Biography,* October 8, 2009, https://doi.org.10.1093/ref:odnb/34470.
64. Lytton Strachey to Leonard Woolf, December 21, 1904, in *Letters of Lytton Strachey,* 42–44.
65. Sanders, *The Strachey Family,* 251.
66. Virginia Woolf to Vanessa Bell, February 11, 1917, in Virginia Woolf, *The Question of Things Happening: The Letters of Virginia Woolf,* vol. 2: *1912–1922,* ed. Nigel Nicolson and Joanne Trautmann (London: Chatto & Windus, 1980), 144 (letter 824).
67. Sanders, *The Strachey Family,* 263.
68. Holroyd, *Lytton Strachey,* 7.
69. Strachey to Leonard Woolf, December 21, 1904, in *Letters of Lytton Strachey,* 44.
70. Lytton Strachey, "Shakespeare's Sonnets," *Spectator,* February 4, 1905, reprinted in *Spectatorial Essays,* 72.

71. Ibid., 73.
72. Ibid., 74.
73. The lines are from *Titus Andronicus,* 3.1.214–15. The speaker is Titus's brother Marcus. Titus, having been duped into cutting off his hand in the vain hope of exchanging it for the lives of two of his sons, is trying to console his daughter, the handless, tongueless, and ravished Lavinia, when Marcus intervenes. That Strachey has (hurriedly) consulted a Shakespeare concordance for "extremes" seems the most likely reason for this curious, and wholly unnecessary, quotation. He may also have been attracted by the salutation "brother" in an Apostolic spirit, though the quotation could hardly be less germane.
74. Strachey, "Shakespeare's Sonnets," 75.
75. Sidney Lee, *A Life of William Shakespeare* (1898; Royston: Oracle, 1996), 158–59.
76. Ibid., 158.
77. Ibid., 159.
78. Lytton Strachey to John Maynard Keynes, August 13, 1909, quoted in Frances Spalding, *Duncan Grant: A Biography* (London: Pimlico, 1998), 80.
79. Strachey, "Shakespeare's Sonnets," 74.
80. James Strachey, "'The Winter's Tale' at the Savoy," *Spectator,* September 28, 1912; "'Twelfth Night' at the Savoy," *Spectator,* December 14, 1912. Both unsigned, as was the *Spectator* practice.
81. Marjorie Colville Strachey, "King Lear at the Théâtre Antoine," *Independent Review* 8 (March 1906): 319–25; Mrs. St. Loe Strachey, "The Shakespeare Ball Souvenir," *Spectator,* April 20, 1912, 626.
82. St. Loe Strachey, *The Adventure of Living: A Subjective Autobiography* (New York: Putnam, 1922), 303.
83. James Strachey, preface to Lytton Strachey, *Spectatorial Essays,* 7.
84. St. Loe Strachey, speech to the English-Speaking Union, April 23, 1925, Parliamentary Archives, STR/39/3.
85. James Strachey, preface, 7.
86. Lytton Strachey, "Shakespeare's First Editors," *Spectator,* June 22, 1907, in Strachey, *Spectatorial Essays,* 54.
87. Ibid., 55.
88. Ibid., 56.
89. Ibid.
90. Ibid., 57.
91. Ibid., 58.
92. Ibid., 56.
93. Ibid., 55–56.
94. Lytton Strachey, "Shakespeare on Johnson," *Spectator,* August 1, 1908, in Strachey, *Spectatorial Essays,* 60.
95. Ibid., 61.
96. Ibid., 62.
97. Ibid., 61.
98. Ibid., 63–64.

99. Ibid., 62–63.
100. Lytton Strachey, "Shakespeare on the Stage," *Spectator,* April 25, 1908, in Strachey, *Spectatorial Essays,* 184.
101. Ibid., 184–85.
102. Ibid., 186.
103. Ibid., 186–87.
104. Ibid., 187.
105. Ibid., 188.
106. Cribb, *Bloomsbury and British Theatre,* 19.
107. Ibid., 26.
108. Ibid., 18.
109. Lytton Strachey, "*Comus* at Cambridge," *Spectator,* July 18, 1908.
110. Lytton Strachey, "Shakespeare at Cambridge," *Athenaeum,* June 20, 1919, reprinted in *Characters and Commentaries* (1933) and in Strachey, *Literary Essays* (New York: Harvest), 20.
111. Ibid., 21.
112. Ibid., 22–23.
113. Carrington to Sebastian Sprott, March 14, 1928, in Carrington, *Letters and Extracts from Her Diaries,* ed. David Garnett (London: Jonathan Cape, 1970), 388.
114. Lytton Strachey to Roger Senhouse, April 21, 1931, in *Letters of Lytton Strachey,* 641–42.
115. *The Diary of Virginia Woolf,* vol. 2: *1920–1924,* ed. Anne Olivier Bell and Andrew McNeillie (New York: Harcourt Brace, 1980), 243 (June 4, 1923). In the same conversation Strachey told her he was in love with Ralph Partridge, comparing Ralph's "extraordinary simplicity" with that of Othello.
116. Strachey, *Eminent Victorians,* 22.
117. Ibid., 34–35.
118. Ibid., 85.
119. Ibid., 126–127.
120. Ibid., 213.
121. Ibid., 235.
122. Ibid.
123. Ibid., 240.
124. Ibid.
125. Ibid., 266.
126. Lytton Strachey, *Queen Victoria* (1921; London: Penguin, 2000), 63.
127. Ibid., 229.
128. Ibid., 208, 212.
129. A. N. Wilson, *Prince Albert: The Man Who Saved the Monarchy* (London: Atlantic, 2019), 292.
130. Ibid.
131. Lytton Strachey, *Elizabeth and Essex: A Tragical History* (1928; New York: Harvest, 1969), 8.
132. T. S. Eliot, "Elizabeth and Essex," *Times Literary Supplement,* December 6, 1928, 959.
133. Ibid.

134. Ibid.
135. Ibid.
136. Francis Birrell, "Souvenirs et réflexions sur Lytton Strachey," *La revue hebdomadaire,* July, 1932, 402–3; Desmond MacCarthy, "Lytton Strachey and the Art of Biography," "ca 1934," in Desmond MacCarthy, *Memories* (London: MacGibbon & Kee, 1953), 47–48.
137. Holroyd, *Lytton Strachey,* 609. Although "Elizabeth is no Cleopatra," he says, both women were famously changeable as well as imperious and seductive, "the Queen of England's variations of mind and temper making a dramatic equivalent to the 'infinite variety' of the Queen of Egypt."
138. Ibid.
139. Lytton Strachey, "A New History of Rome," unsigned review in the *Spectator,* January 2, 1909, 20–21, reprinted in Strachey, *Spectatorial Essays,* 17. John Dryden's *All for Love; or, The World Well Lost* (1677) was based on Shakespeare's *Antony and Cleopatra.*
140. Bertrand Russell, *Autobiography* (London: Unwin, 1978), 70.
141. Eliot, "Elizabeth and Essex."
142. Sigmund Freud to Lytton Strachey, December 25, 1928, trans. James Strachey, quoted in Holroyd, *Lytton Strachey,* 615. James Strachey translated the letter for Lytton; James and Alix Strachey were Freud's English editors and translators, and Lytton had dedicated his biography to James.
143. Sigmund Freud to Lytton Strachey, December 25, 1928, in *Bloomsbury/Freud: The Letters of James and Alix Strachey, 1924–1925,* ed. Perry Meisel and Walter Kendrick (London: Chatto & Windus, 1986), appendix 2, p. 333. This section of the letter was translated by Walter Kendrick (the full text of the James Strachey translation is no longer available).
144. Sigmund Freud, "Some Character-Types Met with in Psycho-Analytic Work" (1916), in *The Standard Edition of the Complete Psychological Works of Sigmund Freud* (1966; London: Vintage, 2001), 14:324.
145. George W. Trevelyan to Lytton Strachey, November 25, 1928, quoted in Holroyd, *Lytton Strachey,* 614.
146. Woolf, *Diary,* 3:208 (November 28, 1928).
147. Holroyd, *Lytton Strachey,* 616.
148. Woolf, *Diary,* 3:208–9 (November 28, 1928).
149. Ibid., 208.
150. Strachey, *Elizabeth and Essex,* 20, 263–64.
151. Ibid., 279.
152. *The Diary of Virginia Woolf,* vol. 3: *1925–1930,* ed. Anne Olivier Bell and Andrew McNeillie (New York: Harcourt Brace, 1980), 233–34 (June 25, 1929).
153. Ibid., 3:234.
154. Holroyd, *Lytton Strachey,* 612.
155. Strachey, *Elizabeth and Essex.* The full-length portrait of Essex from the portrait at Woburn Abbey is on p. 41. Michael Holroyd notes that Strachey rejected the "extremely intellectual" portrait of Essex at Trinity College, Cambridge, in favor of the "more idealized likeness" from Woburn Abbey. Holroyd, *Lytton Strachey,* 76n12. The

frontispiece portrait of Elizabeth is reproduced from a painting in the National Portrait Gallery. Elizabeth's hands, for which she was famous, have a certain resemblance to Strachey's as they appear in Carrington's 1916 portrait.

156. Ibid., 110.
157. Ibid., 286.
158. Ibid., 110.
159. Virginia Woolf to Lytton Strachey, December 10, 1931, in Woolf, *A Reflection of the Other Person,* 412 (letter 2481).
160. *Diary,* 4:55–56 (December 27, 1931).
161. The *Othello* essay, which exists only in fragmentary form, was published posthumously in *Characters and Commentaries.*
162. Woolf, *Diary,* 4:82 (March 12, 1932).
163. Roger Fry to Helen Anrep, May 5, 1930, in *Letters of Roger Fry,* ed. Denys Sutton, 2 vols. (London: Chatto & Windus, 1972), 2:648.
164. George Rylands, "Maynard Keynes: A Personal Note," in *Maynard Keynes: Collector of Pictures, Books, and Manuscripts,* ed. David Scrase and Peter Croft (Cambridge: King's College, 1983), 7.
165. Florence Ada Keynes, *Gathering Up the Threads: A Study in Family Biography* (Cambridge: Heffer, 1950), 61.
166. Robert Skidelsky, *John Maynard Keynes, 1883–1946: Economist, Philosopher, Statesman* (New York: Penguin, 2003), 471.
167. Keynes, *Gathering Up the Threads,* 73.
168. John Maynard Keynes to Bernard Swithinbank, April 18, 1905, quoted in Skidelsky, *John Maynard Keynes: Hopes Betrayed,* 130.
169. John Maynard Keynes to Lytton Strachey, January 25, 1906, quoted ibid., 138.
170. John Maynard Keynes, "Egoism," quoted ibid., 150.
171. Skidelsky, *John Maynard Keynes: Hopes Betrayed,* 168.
172. Rylands, "Maynard Keynes: A Personal Note," 8.
173. Woolf, *Diary,* 2:266 (September 11, 1923).
174. John Maynard Keynes, *The Applied Theory of Money,* in *The Collected Writings of John Maynard Keynes,* vol. 6: *A Treatise on Money, in Two Volumes* (London: Macmillan 1971), 137n.
175. Ibid., 137.
176. John Maynard Keynes, "Newton the Man," in *The Collected Writings of John Maynard Keynes,* vol. 10: *Essays in Biography* (London: Macmillan, 1933), 379.
177. John Maynard Keynes, *The Economic Consequences of the Peace* (1919; New York: Skyhorse, 2007), 27.
178. David Hunter Miller, review of *A Revision of the Treaty,* by John Maynard Keynes, *New York Times Book Review and Magazine,* March 5, 1922. Quoted in Martin Harries, *Scare Quotes in Shakespeare* (Stanford: Stanford University Press, 2000), 133–34.
179. John Maynard Keynes, letter to the editor of the *New York Times Book Review and Magazine,* April 23, 1922, in *The Collected Writings of John Maynard Keynes,* vol. 17: *Activities, 1920–1922,* ed. Elizabeth Johnson (London: Macmillan, 1977), 300–301.
180. Harries, *Scare Quotes in Shakespeare,* 134.

181. David Hunter Miller, reply to John Maynard Keynes, *New York Times Book Review and Magazine,* April 23, 1922, in Keynes, *Collected Writings,* 17:302.
182. John Maynard Keynes, "A Positive Peace Programme," *New Statesman and Nation,* March 25, 1938, in *The Collected Writings of John Maynard Keynes,* vol. 18: *Social, Political, and Literary Writings,* ed. Donald Moggridge (London: Macmillan, 1982), 100. See *Macbeth* 1.7.43–44. The speaker is Lady Macbeth.
183. Skidelsky, *John Maynard Keynes, 1883–1946,* 337; Keynes, letter to the *Times,* February 14, 1923, in *The Collected Writings of John Maynard Keynes,* vol. 19, ed. Donald Moggridge (London: Macmillan, 1981), 79.
184. John Maynard Keynes, "Thomas Robert Malthus," in *Collected Writings,* 10:107.
185. Keynes, *Collected Writings,* 19:142–43.
186. Jevons, journal entry, April 25, 1863, quoted in Keynes, "William Stanley Jevons," in *Collected Writings,* 10:115. Sonnet 66 reads:

> Tired with all these, for restful death I cry,
> As, to behold desert a beggar born,
> And needy nothing trimmed in jollity,
> And purest faith unhappily forsworn,
> And gilded honour shamefully misplaced,
> And maiden virtue rudely strumpeted,
> And right perfection wrongfully disgraced,
> And strength by limping sway disabled,
> And art made tongue-tied by authority,
> And folly, doctor-like, controlling skill,
> And simple truth miscalled simplicity,
> And captive good attending captain ill:
> Tired with all these, from these would I be gone,
> Save that, to die, I leave my love alone.

187. Jevons, journal entry, April 25, 1863, quoted in Keynes, "William Stanley Jevons," 10:115.
188. Keynes, "William Stanley Jevons," ibid., 10:109.
189. Keynes, "Preface to the First Edition," ibid., 10:xix.
190. Keynes, "Thomas Robert Malthus," 10:91, 91n.
191. N. G. Annan, "The Intellectual Aristocracy," in *Studies in Social History: A Tribute to GM Trevelyan,* ed. J. H. Plumb (London: Longmans, Green, 1955), 243–87. Annan uses the phrases "aristocracy of intellect" (243), "English intelligentsia" (244), and "new intelligentsia" (246) in addition to his title phrase; in his conclusion he remarks upon a "new class emerging in society" (284) and the "paradox of an intelligentsia which appears to conform rather than to rebel against the rest of society" (285). Annan, a King's man and Apostle of a later generation, became provost of King's College, serving in that role from 1956 to 1966.
192. Robert Skidelsky, *John Maynard Keynes: The Economist as Savior, 1920–1937* (London: Penguin, 1995), 8. "He was never an egalitarian," Skidelsky says. "Even his orthodox belief in equality of opportunity was tempered by the thought that 'certain small [family]

"connections" have produced eminent characters out of all proportion to their size.'" Keynes, "The Great Villiers Connection," in *Collected Writings,* 10:63.

193. Alfred Marshall, quoted in Keynes, "Alfred Marshall," in *Collected Writings,* 10:65.
194. Mary Paley Marshall, quoted in Keynes, "Mary Paley Marshall," ibid., 10:235.
195. Keynes, "Trotsky on England" (*Nation and Athenaeum,* March 27, 1926), ibid., 64; Keynes, "Einstein," ibid., 382. The "brief sketch of Einstein," as the editors describe it, was found among Keynes's papers, headed "My Visit to Berlin," June 22, 1926. Keynes did not publish it in his 1933 edition of *Essays in Biography,* and presumably for good reason: the sketch expresses attitudes toward "German political Jews" and Jews who "have all the money and the power and the brains" that are manifestly antisemitic—so much so that the editors of the 1972 edition (Richard Kahn, Roy Harrod, Austin Robinson, and Donald Moggridge) have appended an editorial note suggesting that "any modern reader . . . should be reminded that when Hitler, a few years later, began to persecute the Jews, Keynes was one of those most active in succoring the Jewish refugees (382). Almost a hundred years later the sketch remains deeply disturbing, but it is part of the record. The comparison between Einstein and Shakespeare, like a later comparison in the same piece between Einstein's mind and Newton's, is certainly intended as a high compliment.
196. Cribb, *Bloomsbury and British Theatre,* 47.
197. Ibid., 48.
198. Sinclair McKay, *The Secret Life of Bletchley Park* (London: Aurum, 2011), 13, 100.
199. Lydia Lopokova to John Maynard Keynes, August 14, 1922, in *Lydia and Maynard: Letters Between Lydia Lopokova and John Maynard Keynes,* ed. Polly Hill and Richard Keynes (London: Andre Deutsch, 1989), 50.
200. Lydia Lopokova to John Maynard Keynes, April 22, 1923, ibid., 85.
201. "But from thine eyes my knowledge I derive / And, constant stars, in them I read such art, / As truth and beauty shall together thrive." Lydia Lopokova to John Maynard Keynes, April 21, 1923, ibid., 84.
202. Lydia Lopokova to John Maynard Keynes, May 5, 1923, ibid., 87.
203. Lydia Lopokova to John Maynard Keynes, October 13, 1923, ibid., 110.
204. John Maynard Keynes to Lydia Lopokova, October 26, 1923, ibid., 116.
205. Lydia Lopokova to John Maynard Keynes, October 27, 1923, ibid., 117.
206. John Maynard Keynes to Lydia Lopokova, November 28, 1824, December 1, 1924, ibid., 263, 267.
207. John Maynard Keynes to Lydia Lopokova, February 22, 1924, ibid., 161; Lydia Lopokova to John Maynard Keynes, March 3, 1924, ibid., 167.
208. Lydia Lopokova to John Maynard Keynes, October 27, 1924, November 12, 1924, November 15, 1924, ibid., 242, 252, 254.
209. Lydia Lopokova to John Maynard Keynes, March 7, 1925, ibid., 299. Sir Oliver Lodge was a well-known scientist who worked on electricity and radio. He was interested in telepathy and psychical research, and after one of his sons died in World War I he tried to reach him through a medium, becoming a Christian Spiritualist and writing a bestselling book about his son's experiences in the spirit world. Lodge was a friend of Arthur Conan Doyle, who also lost a son in the war and became a Spiritualist.

210. Virginia Woolf, *Diary,* 3:18 (May 9, 1925).
211. Skidelsky, *John Maynard Keynes, 1883–1946,* 358–59.
212. John Maynard Keynes to Lydia Lopokova, October 19, 1928, in Judith Mackrell, *Bloomsbury Ballerina* (London: Weidenfeld & Nicolson, 2008), 326.
213. Dennis Arundell, "Lopokova as an Actress," in *Lydia Lopokova,* ed. Milo Keynes (London: Weidenfeld & Nicolson, 1983), 123.
214. Cited in Skidelsky, *John Maynard Keynes: The Economist as Savior,* 296, 667n64.
215. Arundell, "Lopokova as an Actress," 123.
216. Ibid.
217. Ibid., 124. In his essay, published in a book edited by Milo Keynes, the nephew of Lydia and Maynard Keynes, Dennis Arundell attributes this review to Birrell. Andrew McNeillie, however, prints it in volume 4 of *The Essays of Virginia Woolf* under the title "Plays and Pictures" (*Essays,* 4:564). He describes it as "a notice in the N&A, 17 November, 1928," and says that the Woolfs went to see the production on November 10 (564n1). There is no mention of this in Virginia Woolf's *Diary* (volume 3), which includes for Saturday, November 10, 1928, a long discussion of the *Well of Loneliness* trial she had attended the previous day. The next diary entry is not until November 25. On Monday, July 11, 1927, however, Leonard Woolf (but not Virginia) went to Cambridge to see Lydia dance in Stravinsky's *L'histoire du soldat,* an entertainment—in English—that would also be part of the production in November of the following year. Virginia wrote in her *Diary* for that day, "I'm missing Lydia & Stravinsky" (*Diary,* 3:147, 147n7).
218. All reviews quoted in Arundell, "Lopokova as an Actress," 126–27.
219. Virginia Woolf to Ethel Smyth, July 31, 1933, in Virginia Woolf, *The Sickle Side of the Moon: Letters of Virginia Woolf,* vol. 5: *1932–1935,* ed. Nigel Nicolson and Joanne Trautmann Banks (London: Hogarth, 1994), 209 (letter 2769).
220. Virginia Woolf to Francis Birrell, September 3, 1933, ibid., 222 (letter 2787).
221. Woolf, *Diary,* 4:179 (September 10, 1933).
222. Virginia Woolf to Ethel Smyth, September 14, 1933, in Woolf, *The Sickle Side of the Moon,* 225 (letter 2792).
223. Ibid., 227n1.
224. Virginia Woolf to Quentin Bell, September 19, 1933, ibid., 227 (letter 2795).
225. Quoted in Arundell, "Lopokova as an Actress," 129.
226. Ibid.
227. Mackrell, *Bloomsbury Ballerina,* 335.
228. Lydia Lopokova to John Maynard Keynes, April 20, 1933, ibid., 335.
229. Woolf, *Diary,* 4:179 (September 23, 1933).
230. Virginia Woolf, "'Twelfth Night' at the Old Vic," in *The Essays of Virginia Woolf,* vol. 6: *1933–1941,* ed. Stuart N. Clarke (London: Hogarth, 2011), 5–6. The review was initially published in the *New Statesman and Nation,* September 30, 1933, and reprinted in *The Death of the Moth and Other Essays* (New York: Harcourt Brace Jovanovich, 1974), 45, 47–50.
231. Woolf, *Essays,* 6:6.
232. Ibid., 6:7.
233. Woolf, *Diary,* 4:180 (September 23, 1933).

234. Virginia Woolf to Ottoline Morrell, October 7, 1933, in *The Sickle Side of the Moon,* 230.
235. Virginia Woolf to Quentin Bell, October 14, 1933, in Woolf, *The Sickle Side of the Moon,* 235 (letter 2806). The evening before, she and Leonard had been to see Tyrone Guthrie's production of *The Cherry Orchard,* about which she told Quentin, "We don't think on the whole the Cherry Orchard can be acted by the English," although "they acted very well."
236. On March 8, 1934, Virginia Woolf wrote to Quentin Bell about "Lydias Dolls house, which was a triumphant success, much to our surprise. Dear Old Maynard was—this is exactly true—streaming tears; and I kissed him in the stalls between the acts; really, she was a marvel, not only a light leaf in the wind, but edged, profound, and her English was exactly what Ibsen meant—it gave the right aroma. So shes in the 7th Heaven and runs about kissing and crying." Ibid., 282 (letter 2863).
237. John Maynard Keynes to Lydia Lopokova, November 20, 1933, in Skidelsky, *John Maynard Keynes: The Economist as Savior,* 503.
238. Ibid.
239. Robert Skidelsky, *John Maynard Keynes: Fighting for Freedom, 1937–1946* (London: Penguin, 2002), 288n.
240. John Maynard Keynes to Sir Stephen Tallents, July 12, 1937, in Keynes, *Collected Writings,* 18:351.
241. Kenneth Clark, *The Other Half: A Self-Portrait* (London: Book Club Associates, 1978), 26.
242. Rylands, "Maynard Keynes: A Personal Note," 8.
243. Frances Partridge, *Love in Bloomsbury* (1981; London: Tauris Parke, 2014), 82.
244. Virginia Woolf, *Roger Fry: A Biography* (1940; London: Vintage, 2003), 64.
245. Roger Fry to G. L. Dickinson, February 15, 1891, in *Letters of Roger Fry,* 1:124 (letter 26).
246. Roger Fry to G. L. Dickinson, March 4, 1891, ibid., 1:128 (letter 28). "Anthony" was—and is—an acceptable variant of "Antony" in the play's title role, especially among British scholars. The Anthony who played opposite Duse, and was her offstage lover at the time, was Flavio Andò. The production traveled to the Lyric Theatre in London in June 1893 for three performances (in Italian).
247. Roger Fry to G. L. Dickinson, November 7, 1891, ibid., 1:148–49 (letter 45). Ada Rehan, praised by Oscar Wilde, Mark Twain, and G. B. Shaw, was the star of Augustin Daly's company. Famous for her roles played in breeches, Rehan was also an icon for a kind of femininity that was regarded as both attractive and respectable. The drama critic William Winter described her performance as "the best representation of *Rosalind* that has been seen in our time." William Winter, *Shakespeare on the Stage* (London: T. Fisher Unwin, 1912), 214.
248. Woolf, *Roger Fry,* 51.
249. Roger Fry to G. L. Dickinson, January 24, 1889, in *Letters of Roger Fry,* 1:122–23 (letter 23).
250. Desmond MacCarthy, "The Production of Poetic Drama," February 14, 1914, in MacCarthy, *Drama* (London: Putnam, 1940), 8.
251. Roger Fry, "The Case of the Late Sir Lawrence Alma Tadema, O.M.," *Nation,* January 18, 1913, 666–67, reprinted in *A Roger Fry Reader,* ed. Christopher Reed (Chicago: University of Chicago Press, 1996), 147–49.

252. Ibid., 149.
253. Woolf, Roger *Fry,* 186. Alma Tadema's name was spelled with or without a hyphen; I have retained the spelling used in each of the works I cite. Tadema was his family's surname; he was born in the Netherlands and named Lourens Alma Tadema, after his godfather Lourens Alma. He settled permanently in London in 1870 and, as Lawrence Alma-Tadema, he was knighted by Queen Victoria in 1899. Modern art historians often refer to him as Tadema. R. J. Barrow says that "Alma was incorporated into the surname by the artist for the purpose of having his name appear at the beginning of exhibition catalogues, under A rather than under T" (R. J. Barrow, *Lawrence Alma-Tadema* [London: Phaedon, 2001]), 10.
254. Woolf, Roger *Fry,* 186.
255. Ibid.
256. Ibid., 187.
257. Edward Gordon Craig, *Catalogue of an Exhibition of Some Drawings and Models for "Macbeth" and Other Plays by Edward Gordon Craig* (exhibition no. 147) (London: Ernest Brown and Philips, the Leicester Galleries, 1911).
258. Roger Fry, "Mr Gordon Craig's Stage Designs," in *The Roger Fry Reader,* 287. Reprinted from the *Nation,* September 16, 1911, 871.
259. Ibid., 287.
260. Ibid., 288.
261. Ibid., 289.
262. Ibid.
263. Edward Gordon Craig, *Shakespeare's Plays* (1908; rev. ed. 1912), in *Craig on Theatre,* ed. J. Michael Walton (London: Methuen, 1999), 165.
264. Cited ibid.
265. Edward Gordon Craig, "On *The Tempest*" (1924), ibid., 165.
266. Ibid., 166.
267. Woolf, *Roger Fry,* 51.
268. Ibid., 106.
269. Roger Fry, "Claude," in *Vision and Design,* ed. J. B. Bullen (1920; Mineola: Dover, 1981), 156. First published in the *Burlington Magazine* 11 (August 1907): 267–98. Bridges's comment is from his introduction to *Poems of John Keats,* ed. G. Thorn Drury (London, 1896), 1:xci. The quotation is part of a larger comparison in which Bridges explicitly compares Keats and Shakespeare in describing "the highest gift of all in poetry, that which sets poetry above the other arts": "I mean the power of concentrating all the far-reaching resources of language on one point, so that a single and apparently effortless expression rejoices the aesthetic imagination at the moment when it is most expectant and exacting, and at the same time astonishes the intellect with a new aspect of truth. This is only found in the greatest poets, and is rare in them; and it is no doubt for the possession of this power that Keats has often been likened to Shakespeare, and very justly, for Shakespeare is of all poets the greatest master of it" (xci–xcii).
270. Roger Fry, "Rembrandt: An Interpretation," in *The Roger Fry Reader,* 366. Reprinted from *Apollo,* March 1962, 42–55.
271. Ibid., 369.

272. Ibid.
273. Ibid., 372.
274. Roger Fry, "An Essay in Aesthetics," in *Vision and Design,* 19. Originally published in the *New Quarterly* 2 (April 1909): 171–90.
275. Ibid., 15.
276. Woolf, *Roger Fry,* 52.
277. Roger Fry to G. L. Dickinson, February 18, 1913, in *Letters of Roger Fry,* 1:362 (letter 331).
278. Rylands, *Words and Poetry,* 171.
279. Strachey, introduction to Rylands, *Words and Poetry,* xv–xvi. Both Rylands and Strachey are, to some extent, reframing Strachey's much earlier and more combustible claim from his essay "Shakespeare's Final Period," originally published in 1904, that by the time he wrote his last plays Shakespeare was "no longer interested . . . in what happens, or who says what, so long as he can find place for a faultless lyric, or a new, unimagined rhythmical effect, or a grand and mystic speech" (52).
280. Strachey, introduction to Rylands, *Words and Poetry,* xv; Fry, "A New Theory of Art," in *The Roger Fry Reader,* 159. Reprinted from the *Nation,* March 7, 1914.
281. As S. P. Rosenbaum points out, a previous use of this phrase can be found in A. C. Bradley's 1901 inaugural lecture as the Oxford Professor of Poetry, "Poetry for Poetry's Sake": "What you apprehend may be called indifferently as expressed meaning or a significant form." Bradley, *Oxford Lectures on Poetry* (London: Macmillan, 1965), 19. "It is interesting," notes Rosenbaum, "in the light of how this . . . phrase became famous as a formalist theory of painting, that it was first used as a description of literature." Rosenbaum, *Victorian Bloomsbury: The Early Literary History of the Bloomsbury Group* (New York: St. Martin's, 1994), 32–33.
282. Frances Spalding, *Roger Fry: Art and Life* (Norwich: Black Dog, 1999), 156.
283. Virginia Woolf to Julian Bell, December 1, 1935, in Woolf, *The Sickle Side of the Moon,* 449. The phrases in quotation marks are Woolf's, not Fry's; she is paraphrasing his letter, not quoting it.
284. Fry, "A New Theory of Art," 159.
285. The reference to the poem as Shakespeare's "Winter Song" implies that it is to be considered on its own rather than as part of *Love's Labour's Lost.* This was not uncommon in the period. In Arthur Quiller-Couch's 1906 *Oxford Book of English Verse* the poem is printed as the second half of "Spring and Winter." Like other lyrics from Shakespeare's plays, it appears in the anthology as a stand-alone poem, with no indication that it comes from a play. (The same is true of Ariel's songs from *The Tempest,* printed as a suite of poems under the heading "Fairy Land"; Feste's "O mistress mine" from *Twelfth Night,* retitled "Sweet and Twenty"; and so on.) *The Oxford Book of English Verse,* ed. A. T. Quiller-Couch (Oxford: Clarendon, 1906), 176–77, 178–80, 180–81.

    In *Love's Labour's Lost* the poem has no formal title but is presented instead as a comic afterpiece (analogous to the Pyramus and Thisbe play in *A Midsummer Night's Dream*) produced by lesser characters for the entertainment of the nobility. Like many such verses, it is part of a contrapuntal "dialogue," this one "compiled in praise of the owl and the cuckoo" (5.2.863–64). The two singers are called "Ver, the spring," and "Hiems, winter."

The "Winter Song" does indeed describe homely "English" things ("When icicles hang by the wall, / And Dick the shepherd blows his nail, / And Tom bears logs into the hall, / And milk comes frozen home in pail" [5.2.887–90]), but in its complementary relation to the "Spring Song" and in the reflection that the two songs offer upon *Love's Labour's Lost*—which is set at the French court of the king of Navarre, peopled with playful, self-regarding, and time-wasting nobles—it offers a larger commentary as well.

The play ends in death, both actual—the offstage death of the king of France—and symbolic: the lovers' courtship is put on hold, and the most outspoken of the young lords is sent to "jest a twelve-month in an hospital" to prove the worthiness of his love. "To move wild laughter in the throat of death?— / It is impossible," he complains (5.2.848, 831–32) before submitting to his mistress's command. (Her instruction to him is salutary: "A jest's prosperity lies in the ear / Of him that hears it, never in the tongue / Of him that makes it" [838–40].) But the seasonal songs promise renewal, while embedding some harsher realism in among the lyric pleasures: the bird of spring is the cuckoo, harbinger of cuckoldry, the bird of winter the "staring owl," whose note, however, is "merry." The cycle of the seasons will go on, even as the king's life—and the play—come to an end.

286. Roger Fry to Goldsworthy Lowes Dickinson, January 5, 1921, in *Letters of Roger Fry,* 2:501 (letter 493).
287. Ibid., 2:500–501. G. M. Trevelyan's younger brother, R. C. (Bob), a poet, was Fry's close friend and former housemate with whom he often over the years discussed poetry and prosody.
288. Ibid., 2:500–501.
289. Ibid., 2:501.
290. Virginia Woolf, *Diary,* 1:80 (November 22, 1917).
291. Vanessa Bell to Roger Fry, June 1916, in *Selected Letters of Vanessa Bell,* 199 (letter IV-18).
292. Roger Fry to Helen Anrep, July 11, 1928, in *Letters of Roger Fry,* 629.
293. Sutton's editorial note, ibid., 695.
294. Roger Fry to "Reginald," ibid., 696–97 (letter 713).
295. On this question, the master interrogator is Jorge Luis Borges in works like "Everything and Nothing."
296. Virginia Woolf, "Old Bloomsbury," in *Moments of Being: Autobiographical Writings,* ed. Jeanne Schulkind (London: Pimlico, 2002), 48–50.
297. Woolf, *Letters of Leonard Woolf,* 13n.
298. Leonard Woolf to Lytton Strachey, March 20, 1901, ibid., 13.
299. "Elles ont toutes les deux des coeurs de roche." "Then let them anatomize Regan; see what breeds about her heart. Is there any cause in nature that makes these hard hearts?" Lytton Strachey to Leonard Woolf, March 30, 1902, in *Letters of Lytton Strachey,* 9.
300. Leonard Woolf to Lytton Strachey, April 8, 1902, ibid., 22.
301. Ibid., 22–23.

302. Leonard Woolf, "Othello or Lord Byron?" October 31, 1903, cited in Victoria Glendinning, *Leonard Woolf: A Biography* (Berkeley: Counterpoint, 2008), 60–61. Moore's *Principia Ethica* was published in September 1903 and Woolf, like many of his friends, had been immediately taken by it; on October 12 he wrote to Lytton Strachey, "I've just got his book; it *is* magnificent!" S. P. Rosenbaum, *Victorian Bloomsbury: The Early Literary History of the Bloomsbury Group* (London: St. Martin's, 1994), 259.
303. Leonard Woolf, "Shakespearian Studies," unsigned review, *Spectator,* November 5, 1904.
304. Woolf, *Sowing,* 202.
305. Leonard Woolf to Desmond MacCarthy, February 26, 1905, in *Letters of Leonard Woolf,* 80.
306. Leonard Woolf to Saxon Sydney-Turner, June 24, 1906, ibid., 119.
307. Leonard Woolf, *Beginning Again,* 35; Leonard Woolf, *The Wise Virgins* (London: Edward Arnold, 1914), 27, 90.
308. Woolf, *Beginning Again,* 21.
309. Woolf, *The Wise Virgins,* 104.
310. Ibid., 179.
311. Ibid., 184.
312. Ibid., 197.
313. Leonard Woolf to Humbert Wolfe, March 25, 1929, in *Letters of Leonard Woolf,* 300.
314. Leonard Woolf to E. M. Forster, March 13, 1931, ibid., 304.
315. The idea was that each would write as an imaginary character. Lytton Strachey wrote as Vane Hatherly to Virginia Stephen on January 31, 1909; Virginia replied as Eleanor Hadyng, a Yorkshire woman. Clive and Vanessa were to be James and Clarissa Philips, Saxon Sydney-Turner, Mr. Ilchester, Ottoline Morrell, Caroline, Lady Eastnor, and so on. In this case the collected correspondence was to become a novel, but the scheme fell apart after the first two letters. Virginia Woolf to Lytton Strachey, January 28, 1909, and February 1, 1909, in Woolf, *The Flight of the Mind: Letters of Virginia Woolf,* vol. 1: *1888–1912,* ed. Nigel Nicolson and Joanne Trautmann Banks (London: Hogarth, 1993), 381, 381n, 382 (letters 469 and 470).
316. Raymond Mortimer, "The French Pictures: A Letter to Harriet" (1932), reprinted in *The Hogarth Letters* (Athens: University of Georgia Press, 1986), 102.
317. Francis Birrell, "A Letter from a Black Sheep" (1932), reprinted ibid., 124.
318. Hugh Walpole, "A Letter to a Modern Novelist" (1932), reprinted ibid., 252.
319. Virginia Woolf, "A Letter to a Young Poet "(1932), reprinted ibid., 233.
320. Leonard Woolf, *The Journey Not the Arrival Matters: An Autobiography of the Years 1939 to 1969* (New York: Harvest, 1969), 130.
321. Samuel Butler, *Shakespeare's Sonnets Reconsidered* (*Nation and Athenaeum,* December 12, 1925, 414); *The Works of Shakespeare Chronologically Arranged,* with an introduction by Charles Whibley (*Nation and Athenaeum,* January 9, 1926, 530); Noel Douglas, *Replicas of Shakespeare's Sonnets* (*Nation and Athenaeum,* October 30, 1926, 148); John Bailey, *Question of Taste* and David Nichol Smith, *Shakespeare in the Eighteenth Century* (*Nation and Athenaeum,* June 30, 1928, 402); George Gordon, *Shakespeare's English* (*Nation and Athenaeum,* August 25, 1928, 679); *The Works of Shakespeare,* vol. 1, ed. Herbert Farjeon (Cambridge: Cambridge University Press, 1929); *Antony and Cleo-*

patra, Julius Caesar, As You Like It, The Winter's Tale, in J. Dover Wilson, ed., *Facsimiles of the First Folio Text (Nation and Athenaeum,* April 6, 1929, 22).

322. Leonard Woolf, review of Lewis E. Lawes, *Twenty Thousand Years in Sing Sing* (*New Statesman and Nation,* July 9, 1932, 44); Leila Luedeking and Michael Edmonds, eds., *Leonard Woolf, a Bibliography* (Winchester: St. Paul's Bibliographies, 1992), 219.

323. Leonard Woolf, *New Statesman,* February 23, 1968. Holroyd's polite demurral in the introduction to a new edition of his biography reminds the reader that in Shakespeare's tragedies both men and women did die of love. Holroyd, *Lytton Strachey,* xxxi.

324. Ashcroft's lovers over the years had included Paul Robeson, the French director Michel Saint-Denis, and the painter—and former actor—Walter Sickert, a friend of the Stephens, Bells, and Woolfs. Sickert's portrait of Peggy Ashcroft hung for many years in the home she shared with Hutchinson, Manor Lodge, Frognal, Hampstead. It is now in the Tate Gallery.

325. Virginia Woolf records in her diary a Bloomsbury party where "Lydia [Lopokova] danced; there were charades; Sickert acted Hamlet," noting that "Shakespeare I thought would have liked us all tonight." Mary Hutchinson was at this party with Clive Bell. Woolf, *Diary,* 2:223 (January 7, 1923).

326. Leonard Woolf to Dame Peggy Ashcroft, January 29, 1964, in *Letters of Leonard Woolf,* 527.

327. Leonard Woolf to Dame Peggy Ashcroft, November 8, 1959, ibid., 510.

328. Leonard Woolf to Dame Peggy Ashcroft, February 5, 1969, ibid., 572. It's not clear that he really meant to omit Ellen Terry; in a postscript he adds, "I don't think Réjane was really as good as the other three," which could mean Bernhardt, Duse, and Ashcroft but could also mean the "other three" he had previously mentioned, Bernhardt, Duse, and Terry.

329. Glendinning, *Leonard Woolf,* 395. In the weeks before his death, when he found it difficult to read and preferred to see only Trekkie, Peggy, and a few other close friends, Peggy was the one person he wanted to have read aloud to him. She had made a recording for him of the last words of *The Waves,* the novel that he thought was clearly Virginia Woolf's greatest (432). At his cremation the day after he died, Peggy read Milton's "Lycidas," a poem Woolf knew by heart (435).

330. Virginia Woolf to Ethel Smyth, May 9, 1931, in Woolf, *A Reflection of the Other Person,* 327 (letter 2370).

331. Woolf, *Diary,* 3:96 (July 22, 1926); Virginia Woolf to Vita Sackville-West, July 1926, in Woolf, *The Sickle Side of the Moon,* 281 (letter 1656). MacCarthy would be teasingly mentioned in Woolf's novel in a description of Orlando's period of disfavor during the reign of King James: "He was exiled from Court; in deep disgrace with the most powerful nobles of his time; the Irish house of Desmond was justly enraged; the King had already trouble enough with the Irish not to relish this further addition."

332. Schoenbaum, *Shakespeare's Lives,* viii.

333. Desmond MacCarthy, "Mr Shaw on Shakespeare," *New Statesman,* June 20, 1914, reprinted in MacCarthy, *Remnants* (London: Constable, 1918), 202.

334. Ibid., 202–4.

335. Ibid., 206. *OED,* s.v. "bardolatry."

336. MacCarthy, "Mr Shaw on Shakespeare," 208.
337. Hugh and Mirabel Cecil, *Clever Hearts: Desmond and Molly MacCarthy, a Biography* (London: Gollancz, 1990), 302.
338. Desmond MacCarthy, *The Court Theatre, 1904–1907* (London: A. H. Bullen, 1907), reprinted in *Desmond MacCarthy's "The Court Theatre, 1904–1907": A Commentary and Criticism,* ed. Stanley Weintraub (Coral Gables, FL: University of Miami Press, 1966), 13.
339. The original passage begins "Wast ever in court, shepherd?"
340. Desmond MacCarthy, quoted in Cecil and Cecil, *Clever Hearts,* 71.
341. Desmond MacCarthy, quoted ibid.
342. MacCarthy, "The Production of Poetic Drama," 5.
343. Ibid., 7–8.
344. MacCarthy, "*A Midsummer Night's Dream,*" *New Statesman,* February 21, 1914, in *Drama,* 11, 12, 13.
345. *The Diary of Virginia Woolf,* vol. 1: *1915–1919,* ed. Anne Olivier Bell (New York: Harcourt Brace, 1977), 114 (January 27, 1918).
346. MacCarthy, "Shakespearean Criticism," *New Statesman,* November 25, 1922, in *Drama* 31, 32.
347. Ibid., 31.
348. Quoted in Woolf, *Diary,* 2:69n, in reference to a diary entry for September 26, 1920.
349. Woolf, "The Intellectual Status of Women," in *Diary,* 2:339–42 (appendix 3). Quotations from Affable Hawk as well as from Virginia Woolf are included in this appendix.
350. MacCarthy, "*Othello,*" *New Statesman,* May 7, 1921, in *Drama,* 23.
351. MacCarthy, "*Cymbeline* and Other Plays," *New Statesman,* September 22, 1923, in *Drama,* 37.
352. The Victorian scholar Edward Dowden proposed replacing "rock" with "lock," a wrestling hold. Most modern editions (but not Norton/Oxford) retain "rock," glossing the reading with references to medieval and Renaissance tales of women leaping from high cliffs to prove their devotion. See Arden Shakespeare Third Series, *Cymbeline,* ed. Valerie Wayne (London: Bloomsbury, 2017), 363n.
353. MacCarthy, "*Cymbeline* and Other Plays," 37.
354. Ibid., 38.
355. Ibid.
356. Ibid., 36.
357. Desmond MacCarthy, "*Troilus and Cressida,*" March 18, 1922, *New Statesman,* in *Drama,* 167.
358. Ibid., 169.
359. Ibid., 170.
360. MacCarthy, "The New Hamlet," *New Statesman,* March 7, 1925, ibid., 40.
361. Ibid., 41.
362. Ibid., 46.
363. Ibid., 41. "Whenas he came, I first bespake him fair, / But then he throws and tosses me about, / As one forgetting that I was his mother." *The First Quarto of Hamlet,* ed. Kathleen O. Irace (Cambridge: Cambridge University Press, 1998) 11.104–6.
364. MacCarthy, "The New Hamlet," 45.

365. MacCarthy, "Hamlets in General," *New Statesman,* March 8, 1930, in *Drama,* 48.
366. MacCarthy, "Shylocks Past and Present," January 24, 1920, *New Statesman,* ibid., 15.
367. MacCarthy, "Hamlets in General," 51.
368. Ibid., 52.
369. Ibid., 53.
370. Ibid., 52–53.
371. Schoenbaum, *Shakespeare's Lives,* viii.
372. Prefaces traditionally do not include footnotes or endnotes, and this one is no exception. This reference is the only time Desmond MacCarthy is mentioned in Schoenbaum's book, although Crow appears twice in other connections. "Reminded me" implies prior knowledge, but there is no direct citation, and MacCarthy's name is misspelled, unusual for so meticulous a scholar. When this passage is quoted in journals or online John Crow's role is usually elided, so that Schoenbaum seems to be remembering it directly rather than merely citing a chat with a friend.
373. The locution—Desmond MacCarthy "had said somewhere"—echoes, though doubtless unintentionally, another famous unsourced quote: "Hegel remarks somewhere that all facts and personages of great importance occur, as it were, twice. He forgot to add: the first time as tragedy, the second as farce" (Karl Marx, *The Eighteenth Brumaire of Louis Bonaparte* [New York: International Publishers, 1994], 15). What may be most relevant here is that MacCarthy's name—like Hegel's—seems to function as a sign that conveys authority.
374. T. J. Cribb, "Obituary: George Rylands," *Independent,* January 20, 1999.
375. Virginia Woolf, *A Room of One's Own,* in *A Room of One's Own and Three Guineas,* ed. Anna Snaith (Oxford: Oxford University Press, 2015), 8, 256n. The impression Woolf gives in her narrative is that she was alone on this occasion, but in fact Rylands's other luncheon guests on October 21, 1928, included Leonard Woolf and Vanessa and Angelica Bell.
376. Cribb, "Obituary." Between 1734 and 1898 there are no recorded performances of *Troilus and Cressida,* but in the twentieth century it became a popular stage vehicle for political and social commentary, and it has often been produced in recent years.
377. Woolf, *Diary,* 2:258n19.
378. Noel Annan, *The Dons: Mentors, Eccentrics, and Geniuses* (Chicago: University of Chicago Press, 1999), 171–72.
379. Ibid., 174.
380. Cribb, "Obituary."
381. Quoted in Cribb, *Bloomsbury and British Theatre,* 67.
382. Valerie Grosvenor Myer, "O for a muse of fire: Dr. George Rylands," *Guardian,* January 19, 1999.
383. Cribb, *Bloomsbury and British Theatre,* 87.
384. Annan, *The Dons,* 175.
385. Hermione Lee, *Virginia Woolf* (1996; New York: Vintage, 1999), 458.
386. Virginia Woolf, *A Change of Perspective: The Letters of Virginia Woolf,* vol. 3: *1923–1928,* ed. Nigel Nicolson and Joanne Trautmann Banks (London: Hogarth, 1994), 70n.
387. Woolf, *Diary,* 2:266 (September 11, 1923), 2:258 (July 28, 1923).

388. The friend was Elena Rathbone Richmond, wife of the editor of the *Times Literary Supplement* and a longtime acquaintance of the Stephen family. Woolf, *Diary,* 2:326 (December 21, 1924).
389. Virginia Woolf to Jacques Raverat, October 3, 1924, in *A Change of Perspective,* 137 (letter 1501).
390. Virginia Woolf to Jacques Raverat, November 29, 1924, ibid., 145 (letter 1515).
391. Cribb, *Bloomsbury and British Theatre,* 59. See also Annan, *The Dons,* 180.
392. Annan, *The Dons,* 181.
393. Woolf, *Downhill All the Way,* 172.
394. *Russet and Taffeta,* published by the Hogarth Press in December 1925. Virginia Woolf to George Rylands, July 20, 1925, in *A Change of Perspective,* 94 (letter 1568).
395. For example, Virginia Woolf to George Rylands, November 22, 1931, in Woolf, *A Reflection of the Other Person,* 408 (letter 2474). See also letter 2408, November 12, 1931, which begins "Yes, dearest Dadie, it was my intention to extract a letter from you."
396. Virginia Woolf to George Rylands, February 28, 1932, in Woolf, *The Sickle Side of the Moon,* 24 (letter 2536).
397. Quoted in Cribb, *Bloomsbury and British Theatre,* 71.
398. Virginia Woolf to George Rylands, March 15, 1932, in Woolf, *A Reflection of the Other Person,* 34 (letter 2554).
399. E. M. Forster, "'Hamlet,' by the Marlowe Society, at Cambridge," *Spectator,* March 12, 1932, 16.
400. Virginia Woolf to George Rylands, February 28, 1932, in Woolf, *A Reflection of the Other Person,* 24 (letter 2536). In letter 2529, February 19, 1932, to Helen McAfee, the managing editor of the *Yale Review,* Woolf expressed her thanks for a "delightful volume" from the Yale Shakespeare series that McAfee had sent at her request, adding that she had "sent on the information to a friend—a Fellow of Kings—who first spoke to me about it." Woolf, *The Sickle Side of the Moon,* 20. The Yale Shakespeare was edited by Professors Wilbur L. Cross and C. F. Tucker Brooke. "It wouldn't be much of an exaggeration to say that TYS bears much of the same relation to Yale as the Bible did to the presses at Oxford and Cambridge," remarked John G. Ryden, director of the Yale University Press from 1979 to 2002. "It was the most enduring publication of the first fifty years." Quoted in Nicholas A. Basbanes, *A World of Letters: Yale University Press, 1908–2008* (New Haven: Yale University Press, 2008), 21.
401. Woolf, *Diary,* 4:20 (March 19, 1934).
402. Virginia Woolf to George Rylands, May 2, 1937, in Woolf, *Leave the Letters till We're Dead: The Letters of Virginia Woolf,* vol. 6: *1936–1941,* ed. Nigel Nicolson and Joanne Trautmann (London: Chatto & Windus, 1983), 125 (letter 3243 [postcard]).
403. Holroyd, *Lytton Strachey,* 501.
404. Ibid., 569.
405. The lines from Macbeth actually read slightly differently: "The expedition of my violent love / Outran the pauser, reason" (2.3.107–8).
406. Carrington to Sebastian Sprott, [Sunday], July 1930, in Dora Carrington, *Carrington's Letters,* ed. Anne Chisholm (London: Vintage, 2017), 374.
407. Holroyd, *Lytton Strachey,* 644.

408. Strachey, introduction to Rylands, *Words and Poetry,* xiii–xv.
409. Ibid., xi.
410. Rylands, *Words and Poetry,* 17.
411. Ibid., 144–45.
412. Ibid., 147–48.
413. Ibid., 159.
414. Ibid., 220.
415. Ibid., 222.
416. Ibid., 159.
417. Ibid., 214.
418. Ibid., 171.
419. Ibid., 222.
420. Ibid., 224.
421. Ibid., 161.
422. Ibid., 223.
423. Strachey, "Shakespeare's Final Period," 53.
424. Ibid., 52.
425. Strachey, introduction to Rylands, *Words and Poetry,* xv–xvi.
426. Virginia Woolf to Thoby Stephen, November 5, 1901, in Woolf, *The Flight of the Mind,* 45 (letter 39).
427. John Lehmann, *The Whispering Gallery: Autobiography,* vol. 1 (London: Longmans, Green, 1955), 140.
428. Ibid., 154.
429. Ibid., 155.
430. Ibid.
431. Ibid., 155–56.
432. Ibid., 156.
433. On Woolf, Rylands, and prose, see Emily Kopley, "Virginia Woolf's Conversations with George Rylands: Context for *A Room of One's Own* and 'Craftsmanship,'" *Review of English Studies* 67, no. 282 (November 2026): 946–49.
434. Virginia Woolf to Vita Sackville-West, September 1, 1925, in *The Letters of Vita Sackville-West to Virginia Woolf,* ed. Louise DeSalvo and Mitchell A. Leaska (London: Virago, 1997), 70; Vita Sackville-West to Virginia Woolf, September 2, 1925, ibid., 71.
435. Rylands, *Words and Poetry,* 154, 165.
436. Ibid., 164–65.
437. Ibid., 158–59.
438. Virginia Woolf, "Poetry, Fiction, and the Future," in Woolf, *Essays,* 4:431. Originally published in the *New York Herald Tribune* in two installments, August 14 and 21, 1927. Based on a paper Woolf read to the Oxford University English Club, May 18, 1927.
439. Woolf, *Diary,* 3:203 (November 7, 1928).
440. George Rylands to Virginia Woolf, ALS, Monks House Papers, SxMs18/1/D/132, quoted in Kopley, "Virginia Woolf's Conversations with George Rylands," 954–55.
441. George Rylands, interviewed in the BBC TV documentary *Virginia Woolf: A Night's Darkness, a Day's Sail,* January 18, 1970 (*YouTube,* December 15, 2015), quoted in Kop-

ley, "Virginia Woolf's Conversations with George Rylands," 961, from Joan Russell Noble, ed., *Recollections of Virginia Woolf* (London: 1972), 138.

442. Woolf, *Diary,* 3:300–301 (April 13, 1930).
443. Kopley, "Virginia Woolf's Conversations with George Rylands," 962–64. Kopley notes a number of parallel phrases in the two radio talks. George Rylands, "The Language of Shakespeare," *Listener,* March 24, 1937, 542–44; Virginia Woolf, "Craftsmanship," *Listener,* May 5, 1937, 868–69, reprinted in Woolf, *Essays,* 6:91–102.
444. Woolf, "Craftsmanship," 95.
445. Rylands, *Words and Poetry,* 190, 191, 201.
446. George Rylands, introduction to *The Ages of Man: Shakespeare's Image of Man and Nature,* ed. George Rylands (1939; London: Mercury, 1962), xv–xvi.
447. Ibid., xvi.
448. Virginia Woolf, "The Reader," in Woolf, *Essays,* 6:598.
449. Annan, *The Dons,* 174.
450. Rylands, introduction to *The Ages of Man,* xvii.
451. Ibid.
452. Annan, *The Dons,* 179.
453. Ibid., 177.
454. Noel Annan, *Our Age* (London: Fontana, 1991), 6.
455. Richard Findlater, *These Our Actors: A Celebration of the Theatre Acting of Peggy Ashcroft, John Gielgud, Laurence Olivier, Ralph Richardson* (London: Elm Tree Books, 1983), 75.
456. James Strachey, "'The Winter's Tale' at the Savoy," unsigned review, *Spectator,* September 28, 1912, 18.
457. Ibid. It was in this production, incidentally, that Rupert Brooke first saw Cathleen Nesbitt in the part of Perdita and fell in love with her. Cribb, *Bloomsbury and British Theatre,* 26.
458. James Strachey, "'Twelfth Night' at the Savoy," unsigned review, *Spectator,* December 14, 1912, 18.
459. Woolf, *Diary,* 1:305 (October 11, 1919).
460. Peter Gay, *Freud: A Life for Our Time* (1988; New York: Norton, 2006), 314.
461. Ibid., 388.
462. Sigmund Freud, *Collected Papers,* vol. 3 (London: Hogarth Press, 1953), 21n; Holroyd, *Lytton Strachey,* 609.
463. James Strachey, general preface to *The Standard Edition of the Complete Psychological Works of Sigmund Freud,* 1:xvi; Samuel Johnson, *Preface to Shakespeare,* 1765.
464. Strachey, general preface, *Standard Edition,* 1:xvi.
465. James Strachey, introduction to the *Project for a Scientific Psychology,* in *The Standard Edition of the Complete Psychological Works of Sigmund Freud,* 1:287.
466. James Strachey to Lytton Strachey, November 6, 1920, quoted in Holroyd, *Lytton Strachey,* 481.
467. Lytton Strachey to James Strachey, November 24, 1920, in *Letters of Lytton Strachey,* 475–76.

468. Sigmund Freud, *An Autobiographical Study* (1925; English translation 1935), in *The Standard Edition of the Complete Psychological Works of Sigmund Freud,* 20:63–64n.
469. Ibid., 64n.
470. Virginia Woolf to Clive Bell, April 18, 1911, in Woolf, *The Flight of the Mind,* 462 (letter 566).
471. Rupert Brooke to James Strachey, August 6, 1912, in *Friends and Apostles: The Correspondence of Rupert Brooke and James Strachey,* ed. Keith Hale (New Haven: Yale University Press, 1998), 258–59.
472. Rupert Brooke to Erica Cotterill, July 1909, in *The Letters of Rupert Brooke,* ed. Geoffrey Keynes (London: Faber & Faber, 1968), 173.
473. Rupert Brooke to Frances Cornford, November 1909, ibid., 196–97.
474. Rupert Brooke to Reginald Berkeley, December 1913, ibid., 549.
475. Rupert Brooke to Edmund Gosse, November 19, 1913, ibid., 530–31.
476. Hale, *Friends and Apostles,* 134n3.
477. Rupert Brooke to James Strachey, March 28, 1911, in *Letters of Rupert Brooke,* 168.
478. James Strachey to Rupert Brooke, June 16, 1911, ibid., 182.
479. Rupert Brooke to James Strachey, June 19, 1911, ibid., 182–83.
480. James Strachey to Rupert Brooke, June 19, 1911, ibid., 183–84.
481. Rupert Brooke to Geoffrey Keynes, March 7, 1910, ibid., 226.
482. Rupert Brooke to Edward Marsh, October 4, 1912, ibid., 405.
483. Paul Delany, *Fatal Glamour: The Life of Rupert Brooke* (Montreal: McGill-Queen's University Press, 2015), 218.
484. Rupert Brooke to Cathleen Nesbitt, November 24, 1913, in *Letters of Rupert Brooke,* 536.
485. Rupert Brooke to Erica Cotterill, November 28, 1907, ibid., 115.
486. Rupert Brooke, *John Webster and the Elizabethan Drama* (London: Sidgwick & Jackson, 1917), 23.
487. Tim Cribb, *Bloomsbury and British Theatre,* 20.
488. Brooke, *John Webster,* 57.
489. Ibid., 58.
490. Ibid., 58–59.
491. Ibid., 60.
492. Ibid., 62–63.
493. Obituary of Rupert Brooke, *Times,* April 1, 1915.
494. Lytton Strachey to Duncan Grant, April 25, 1915, cited in Holroyd, *Lytton Strachey,* 320.
495. Virginia Woolf, "The New Crusade," in *The Essays of Virginia Woolf,* vol. 2: *1912–1918,* ed. Andrew McNeillie (London: Hogarth, 1987), 203. Originally published in the *Times Literary Supplement,* December 27, 1917.
496. Virginia Woolf to Clive Bell, April 18, 1911, in Woolf, *The Flight of the Mind,* 460 (letter 566). "At any moment my Neo Pagan Cox may descend," she wrote, describing Katharine ("Ka") Cox.
497. Frances Spalding, *Gwen Raverat: Friends, Family, and Affections* (London: Harvill, 2001), 61.

498. Jacques Raverat, unpublished autobiographical memoir, quoted ibid., 130.
499. Spalding, *Gwen Raverat,* 164.
500. Jacques Raverat to Georges Raverat, March 2, 1911, quoted ibid., 180–81.
501. Jacques Raverat to André Gide, April 25, 1915, quoted ibid., 244.
502. Ibid.
503. André Gide to Jacques Raverat, April 1915, quoted ibid., 247.
504. Virginia Woolf to Gwen Raverat, March 11, 1925, in Woolf, *A Change of Perspective,* 172 (letter 1541).

CHAPTER 5. MR. ELIOT'S SHAKESPEARE

1. *The Diary of Virginia Woolf,* vol. 1: *1915–1919,* ed. Anne Olivier Bell (New York: Harcourt Brace, 1977), 210n (October 28, 1918); Leonard Woolf to T. S. Eliot, October 19, 1918, in *The Letters of T. S. Eliot,* rev. ed., ed. Valerie Eliot and Hugh Haughton (London: Faber, 2009), 1:285.
2. Leonard Woolf, *Beginning Again: An Autobiography of the Years 1911 to 1918* (1963, 1964; New York: Harvest, 1972), 242, 243.
3. *The Waste Land* was first published in the United Kingdom in the inaugural issue of Eliot's literary magazine the *Criterion* in October 1922. In the United States it appeared in the *Dial* in November 1922 and was then published as a book in December 1922 by Boni & Liveright. The Hogarth Press version was the first in book form in the United Kingdom.
4. *The Diary of Virginia Woolf,* vol. 2: *1920–1924,* ed. Anne Olivier Bell and Andrew McNeillie (New York: Harcourt Brace, 1980), 178 (June 23, 1922).
5. Leonard Woolf, *Downhill All the Way: An Autobiography of the Years 1919 to 1939* (New York: Harvest, 1967), 111.
6. Woolf, *Diary,* 2:302 (May 5, 1924).
7. T. S. Eliot ("Crites"), "Commentary," *Criterion,* April 1924.
8. Woolf, *Diary,* 2:302 (May 5, 1924).
9. *The Diary of Virginia Woolf,* vol. 3: *1925–1930,* ed. Anne Olivier Bell and Andrew McNeillie (New York: Harcourt Brace, 1980), 45 (September 30, 1925).
10. Ibid., 2:302 (May 5, 1924).
11. Virginia Woolf to Ottoline Morrell, October 4, 1935, in Woolf, *The Sickle Side of the Moon: The Letters of Virginia Woolf,* vol. 5: *1932–1935,* ed. Nigel Nicolson and Joanne Trautmann Banks (London: Hogarth, 1994), 428 (letter 3066).
12. *The Diary of Virginia Woolf,* vol. 4: *1931–1935,* ed. Anne Olivier Bell and Andrew McNeillie (New York: Harcourt Brace, 1983), 356 (December 4, 1935).
13. Ibid., 4:323 (June 18, 1935).
14. *The Diary of Virginia Woolf,* vol. 5: *1936–1941,* ed. Anne Olivier Bell and Andrew McNeillie (New York: Harcourt Brace, 1985), 5:210 (March 22, 1939).
15. T. S. Eliot, "Shakespeare and the Stoicism of Seneca" (1927), in Eliot, *Selected Essays* (1932, 1934, 1951; London: Faber, 1999), 126.
16. Leonard Woolf, *Sowing: An Autobiography of the Years 1880 to 1904* (New York: Harvest, 1960), 188.
17. Ibid.; T. H. Holditch, "Obituary: General Sir Richard Strachey," *Geographical Journal*

31, no. 3 (March 1908): 342–44. For more on the Stracheys, see Barbara Caine, *Bombay to Bloomsbury: A Biography of the Strachey Family* (Oxford: Oxford University Press, 2005).

18. Lytton Strachey, "Pope," in *Characters and Commentaries* (London: Chatto & Windus, 1933), 290.
19. Michael Holroyd, *Lytton Strachey* (1994; London: Pimlico, 2011), 460.
20. T. S. Eliot, "Shakespeare and the Stoicism of Seneca," 128.
21. Ibid., 129.
22. Ibid., 131.
23. Ibid., 130.
24. Ibid., 130–31.
25. "My sovereign lord, cheer up yourself, look up" (*Henry IV, Part 2* 4.3.113). Strachey and Leonard Woolf had many years before corresponded about *Madame Bovary,* which Woolf thought at the time was "the saddest & most beautiful book" he had ever read. Leonard Woolf to Lytton Strachey, September 19, 1907, in *Letters of Leonard Woolf,* ed. Frederic Spotts (London: Bloomsbury, 1989), 132. Strachey replied on October 19 that he could no longer bring himself to "care for any of that" and now found it difficult "to taste real life in fiction." Woolf's letter had contained an account of a hanging in Ceylon over which he had to preside, ex officio, and Strachey experienced what he called "your hanging letter" as sobering and frightening. Strachey, *The Letters of Lytton Strachey,* ed. Paul Levy (London: Viking, 2005), 135–36.
26. Eliot, "Shakespeare and the Stoicism of Seneca," 128.
27. T. S. Eliot, "Hamlet," in *Selected Essays,* 143. Othello was another of Strachey's "favourite figures," and he several times mentioned plans to write about the play. In an uncompleted essay published after his death, he describes Othello as the converse of Oedipus: "a great soul" but "simple-minded, unsuspicious, easily thrown off his mental balance, a creature eminently susceptible to deceit. The tragedy here is not ironical but pathetic." Lytton Strachey, "Othello" (1931), in *Characters and Commentaries,* 310. Holroyd, *Lytton Strachey,* 662; Woolf, *Diary,* 2:243 (June 4, 1923).
28. T. S. Eliot to Ford Madox Ford, February 2, 1923, in Eliot, *Letters of T. S. Eliot,* vol. 2: *1923–1925* (London: Faber, 2009), 34.
29. Eliot, "Shakespeare and the Stoicism of Seneca," 135.
30. Lytton Strachey, introduction to George H. W. Rylands, *Words and Poetry* (London: Hogarth, 1928), xi.
31. Geoffrey Faber to T. S. Eliot, September 15, 1927, in Eliot, *The Letters of T. S. Eliot,* vol. 3: *1926–1927* (London: Faber, 2012), 708, 709.
32. Roger Fry to Goldsworthy Lowes Dickinson, January 5, 1921, in *Letters of Roger Fry,* ed. Denys Sutton, 2 vols. (London: Chatto & Windus, 1972), 2:500–501 (letter 493).
33. Faber to Eliot, September 15, 1927, in Eliot, *Letters,* 3:708–9.
34. Quoted in Holroyd, *Lytton Strachey,* 599.
35. T. S. Eliot, "Elizabeth and Essex," *Times Literary Supplement,* December 6, 1928, 959.
36. Virginia Woolf to Julian Bell, December 6, 1935, in *The Sickle Side of the Moon,* 449.
37. T. S. Eliot to Geoffrey Faber, September 18, 1927, in Eliot, *Letters of T. S. Eliot,* 2:711.
38. G. E. Moore, *Principia Ethica* (1903; Mineola, NY: Dover, 2004), 188.

39. Keynes, "My Early Beliefs" (1938) in *The Essential Keynes,* ed. Robert Skidelsky (London: Penguin, 2015), 13–14.
40. Eliot to Faber, September 18, 1927.
41. Noel Annan, "Bloomsbury and the Leavises," in *Virginia Woolf and Bloomsbury,* ed. Jane Marcus (London: Macmillan, 1987), 26.
42. Woolf, *Diary,* 5:192–93 (December 19, 1938).

CHAPTER 6. SHAKESPEARE AT CHARLESTON AND HAM SPRAY

1. Ottoline Morrell, *Ottoline: The Early Memoirs of Lady Ottoline Morrell,* ed. Robert Gathorne-Hardy (London: Faber & Faber, 1963), 179.
2. Hermione Lee, *Virginia Woolf* (1996; New York: Vintage, 1999), 248.
3. Virginia Woolf, *A Passionate Apprentice: The Early Journals, 1897–1909,* ed. Mitchell A. Leaska (New York: Harcourt, Brace, Jovanovich, 1990), 383–84.
4. Clive Bell, *Art* (1914; New York: Putnam, 1958), 110–11.
5. Ibid., 52–53.
6. Clive Bell, "Water-colours Ancient and Modern," *New Statesman and Nation,* March 15, 1941, 271, cited in Mark Hussey, *Clive Bell and the Making of Modernism* (London: Bloomsbury, 2021), 382.
7. Clive Bell, "Art and Expertise," *Cornhill Magazine* 161 (April 1945): 296–300, cited in Hussey, *Clive Bell and the Making of Modernism,* 377.
8. Hussey, *Clive Bell and the Making of Modernism,* 367. The program was broadcast from 9:55 to 10:10 p.m. (*Radio Times,* February 8, 1945).
9. In 1932 she married the British artist John Armstrong. After divorcing Armstrong, she married George Russell Strauss, a Labor politician, and became Lady Strauss.
10. Quoted in Frances Spalding, *Vanessa Bell: Portrait of the Bloomsbury Artist* (1983; London: Tauris Parke, 2016), 243. Frances Spalding interviewed Benita Armstrong in preparing her book; the anecdote, not footnoted, seems to have come from their conversation. See Spalding's acknowledgements (xxi).
11. Vanessa Bell to Virginia Woolf, June 5, 1917, quoted in Diane Filby Gillespie, *The Sisters' Arts: The Writing and Painting of Virginia Woolf and Vanessa Bell* (Syracuse: Syracuse University Press, 1988), 150.
12. Spalding, *Vanessa Bell,* 101, 362, 166.
13. Quoted in Gillespie, *The Sisters' Arts,* 150.
14. Quoted in Spalding, *Vanessa Bell,* 32.
15. Vanessa Bell to Roger Fry, in Gillespie, *The Sisters' Arts,* 150.
16. Vanessa Bell to Roger Fry, June 1916, in *Selected Letters of Vanessa Bell,* ed. Regina Marler (London: Bloomsbury, 1994), 199 (letter IV-18).
17. Vanessa Bell to Virginia Woolf, April 4, 1918, in Spalding, *Vanessa Bell,* 166–67.
18. Lytton Strachey to Vanessa Bell, October 21, 1909, in Strachey, *The Letters of Lytton Strachey,* ed. Paul Levy (London: Viking 2005), 189.
19. Virginia Woolf to Duncan Grant, March 6, 1917, in *The Question of Things Happening: The Letters of Virginia Woolf,* vol. 2: *1912–1922,* ed. Nigel Nicolson and Joanne Trautmann (London: Chatto & Windus, 1980), 145 (letter 825).
20. Ibid., 145.

21. Vanessa Bell to Helen Anrep, April 19, 1936, in Spalding, *Vanessa Bell,* 270.
22. Frances Spalding, *Duncan Grant: A Biography* (London: Pimlico, 1998), 59.
23. Ibid., 70.
24. Quentin Bell, *Elders and Betters* (London: Pimlico, 1997), 64.
25. Ibid., 142.
26. "New honours come upon him, like our strange garments," *Charleston Attic,* February 2, 2016. Duncan Grant sketchbook pages, Charleston Attic Collections, Angelica Garnett Gift.
27. Spalding, *Duncan Grant,* 133–34.
28. Ibid., 133, from an unpublished Grant manuscript.
29. Copeau had been invited by Roger Fry to the Second Post-Impressionist Exhibition in October 1912 in London, where he may have seen some of Grant's paintings.
30. Quoted in Spalding, *Duncan Grant,* 146, from Grant, "Jacques Copeau," unpublished manuscript.
31. Quoted ibid., 148.
32. Duncan Grant to Vanessa Bell, January 1, 1924, quoted in Spalding, *Duncan Grant,* 256. Vanessa Bell's comments on his *Twelfth Night* work with Copeau were restricted to complaints about the inconvenience of its production schedule: "I shall come on Friday I think, but you will be gone I suppose. It's a bore about your play." Vanessa Bell to Duncan Grant, January 14, 1914, in *Selected Letters of Vanessa Bell,* 153. The next month she urged him to return to the Omega Workshop, where arrangements were ongoing: "It sounds too beastly, your having to wait on in Paris, for most likely the play will only be put off again I suppose. I think you ought to come back and then Copeau can send for you to come back again when it's really settled." Vanessa Bell to Duncan Grant, February 25, 1914, in *Selected Letters of Vanessa Bell,* 155.
33. John Rudlin, *Jacques Copeau* (Cambridge: Cambridge University Press, 1986), 15; Maurice Kurtz, *Jacques Copeau: Biography of a Theater* (Carbondale: Southern Illinois University Press, 1999), 28.
34. Michel Saint-Denis, *Training for the Theatre* (New York: Theatre Arts, 1982), 34; Copeau, *Souvenirs du Vieux-Columbier* (Paris: Nouvelle Editions Latines, 1931), 35–40, both quoted in Rudlin, *Jacques Copeau,* 16.
35. Spalding, *Duncan Grant,* 147.
36. Copeau, quoted in Kurtz, *Jacques Copeau,* 29.
37. Claude Debussy to Jacques Copeau, November 24, 1916, in Debussy, *A New French Theater in America, 1917–1918* (New York, 1917), n.p.
38. Kurtz, *Jacques Copeau,* 29.
39. Quoted ibid., 30, from the introduction to Copeau's *Les tragédies de Shakespeare.*
40. Copeau to Jouvet, quoted ibid., 43.
41. John Lehmann, *The Whispering Gallery: Autobiography,* vol. 1 (London: Longmans, Green, 1955), 141.
42. Ibid., 144.
43. Ibid.
44. Ibid., 145.
45. Ibid., 149.

46. Quentin Bell, "The Garden," in Quentin Bell and Virginia Nicholson, *Charleston: A Bloomsbury House and Garden* (London: Frances Lincoln, 1997), 128.
47. Quentin Bell, *On Human Finery* (1945; London: Hogarth, 1976), 76.
48. Ibid., 87.
49. Virginia Woolf, "Anon," in *The Essays of Virginia Woolf,* vol. 6: *1933–1941,* ed. Stuart N. Clarke (London: Hogarth, 2011), 588. Adapted from Brenda Silver, "'Anon' and 'The Reader': Virginia Woolf's Last Essays," *Twentieth Century Literature* 25, nos. 3–4 (Fall–Winter, 1979): 356–441.
50. Bell, *Elders and Betters,* 64.
51. Ibid., 40 (*Twelfth Night* 1.5.237).
52. Ibid., 131 (*Twelfth Night* 2.4.113).
53. Ibid., 161 (*A Midsummer Night's Dream* 1.2.68).
54. Ibid., 170 (*Othello* 3.5.362).
55. Ibid., 197 (*Henry IV, Part 1* 3.1.51).
56. Ibid., 188 (*A Midsummer Night's Dream* 5.1.17).
57. Ibid., 220 (*Hamlet* 4.4.17–18).
58. Quentin Bell, "A Vanished World," in Bell and Nicholson, *Charleston,* 22.
59. Lytton Strachey to Leonard Woolf, August 23, 1901; Lytton Strachey to Leonard Woolf, July 19, 1907, in *Letters of Lytton Strachey,* 4, 132.
60. Angelica Garnett, "The Earthly Paradise," in *Charleston, Past and Present,* by Quentin Bell, Angelica Garnett, Henrietta Garnett, and Richard Shone, rev. ed. (London: Hogarth, 1993), 124.
61. Quentin Bell, headnote to "Charleston, 1925–1926," in *Vanessa Bell's Family Album,* compiled by Quentin Bell and Angelica Garnett (London: Jill Norman & Hobhouse, 1981), 77.
62. Richard Shone, *The Art of Bloomsbury* (Princeton: Princeton University Press, 1999), 28.
63. Angelica Garnett, *Vanessa Bell's Family Album,* 124. Many of the Bloomsbury adults—not only Duncan Grant, who loved dressing up, but also Roger Fry, Virginia and Leonard Woolf, Francis Birrell, Lydia Lopokova Keynes, and the dancer Frederick Ashton—were willing, even in some cases eager, to perform in Charleston theatricals. Fry appeared on one occasion as the White Rabbit, Duncan on another as a Spanish dancer. In a play called *A Guided Tour of Charleston,* written by Quentin Bell and set one hundred years into the future, the actors were the tourists, and the audience members pieces of Charleston furniture: Maynard Keynes was a safe, Clive Bell was an eighteenth-century chair, and the Woolfs were two bookcases, labeled Fact (Leonard) and Fiction (Virginia). Lee, *Virginia Woolf,* 662. Angelica also famously appears in exotic costume as Sasha the Russian Princess in *Orlando.*
64. Spalding, *Vanessa Bell,* 279.
65. The literary inspiration for Watts's painting was a popular poem by Thomas Hood, *The Bridge of Sighs.* See Mark Bills and Barbara Bryant, *G. F. Watts: Victorian Visionary* (London: Yale University Press, 2008), 114.
66. Tom Prideaux, *Love or Nothing: The Life and Times of Ellen Terry* (New York: Scribner's, 1975), 71–73. Laura Barker Taylor—the wife of Tom Taylor, critic, playwright, and longtime supporter of Terry—wrote to her husband in response to a letter from him that

Terry's "foolish talk of drowning herself etc. I can well understand but I can scarcely forgive the melodramatic act of sticking the 'found drowned' in the corner of Watt's photograph." Undated letter, sometime in mid-October 1868, quoted ibid., 73.

67. As noted above, Watts had painted Ellen Terry as Ophelia in 1864.
68. Vanessa Bell to Julian Bell, June 9, 1935, in *Selected Letters of Vanessa Bell,* 392 (letter VII-16).
69. It was then, he said, that he came to understand "how poetry is better able to express reality than the so-called 'realistic' language of everyday life; and how style is the only penetrating instrument of authentic 'realism,' whatever the period." It was important to him, as he emphasized, that theatre should reach all audiences, not just a privileged few: the seats in the gallery at the Old Vic cost sixpence, and every night the wooden benches "were filled with working people" who took away from a four-hour production of *Hamlet* both story and sound: the pleasure of being "soaked in words," the "intermingling of various elements in which sense cannot be separated from form." Michel Saint-Denis, *Theatre: The Rediscovery of Style* (London: Heinemann, 1960), 26–27.
70. Angelica Garnett, *Deceived with Kindness: A Bloomsbury Childhood* (1984; London: Pimlico, 1995), 88. Within the year Vanessa wrote excitedly to Julian to say that Angelica had been offered the lead in a play to be produced in a West End theatre in the fall, but the school bound its acting students by contract not to appear in public while studying there, so the offer would have to be declined. Vanessa Bell to Julian Bell, June 9, 1935, in *Selected Letters of Vanessa Bell,* 392 (letter VII-16).
71. Virginia Woolf to Angelica Bell, August 27, 1940, in *Leave the Letters till We're Dead: The Letters of Virginia Woolf,* vol. 6: *1936–1941,* ed. Nigel Nicolson and Joanne Trautmann (London: Chatto & Windus, 1983), 422 (letter 3636).
72. Jane Hill, *The Art of Dora Carrington* (London: Herbert, 1994), 11.
73. Dora Carrington to Noel Carrington [summer 1918], in Dora Carrington, *Carrington's Letters,* ed. Anne Chisholm (London: Vintage, 2017), 91.
74. Carrington to Mark Gertler, April 28, 1917; Gertler to Carrington, May 15, 1917, quoted in Michael Holroyd, *Lytton Strachey* (1994; London: Pimlico, 2011), 390.
75. Carrington to Mark Gertler, December 1918, in Carrington, *Carrington's Letters,* 107. He wrote back to her; her response, on December 8, says, "It's very odd how natural it seemed to see a letter in your writing again, and after a whole year!" (107).
76. Carrington to Lytton Strachey, December 1918, ibid., 108–9.
77. Dora Carrington to Gerald Brennan, quoted in Anne Chisholm, *Frances Partridge, the Biography* (London: Phoenix, 2009), 65.
78. Chisholm, *Frances Partridge,* 191.
79. Holroyd, *Lytton Strachey,* 374.
80. Carrington to Margaret Waley, February 1932, in Carrington, *Letters and Extracts from Her Diaries,* ed. David Garnett (London: Cape, 1970), 496.
81. Frances Partridge, *Memories* (1981; London: Robin Clark, 1982), 11.
82. John Dover Wilson, *The Essential Shakespeare* (Cambridge: Cambridge University Press, 1932), 6; *The Diary of Virginia Woolf,* vol. 4: *1931–1935,* ed. Anne Olivier Bell and Andrew McNeillie (New York: Harcourt Brace, 1983), 219 (May 9, 1934).
83. Partridge, *Memories,* 4.

84. Ibid., 17. Forbes-Robertson, one of the great Victorian Shakespeare actors, was born in 1853. He played many leading roles in Shakespeare's plays, including Romeo, Othello, and Leontes, but his first appearance as Hamlet was not until 1897. By the time the young Frances Marshall was taken to see Forbes-Robertson's Hamlet he would have been fifty-six. George Bernard Shaw, a great fan, thought his performance on that occasion definitive: "Nothing half so charming has been seen by this generation. It will bear seeing again and again," he wrote in the *Saturday Review* on October 2, 1897. George Bernard Shaw, *Shaw on Shakespeare* (New York: Dutton, 1961), 85.
85. Partridge, *Memories,* 24. On Jane Ellen Harrison and the Marlowe, see Tim Cribb, *Bloomsbury and British Theatre: The Marlowe Story* (Cambridge: Salt, 2007), 13.
86. Partridge, *Memories,* 67, 66.
87. Ibid., 75.
88. *The Diary of Virginia Woolf,* vol. 2: *1920–1924,* ed. Anne Olivier Bell and Andrew McNeillie (New York: Harcourt Brace, 1980), 243 (June 4, 1923). After a visit from Carrington Woolf had characterized him rather differently in her private diary, as a "village Don Juan"; Leonard described him as a "male bully." Ibid., 2:186 (July 28, 1922).
89. Partridge, *Memories,* 127.
90. Frances Partridge, *A Pacifist's War: Diaries, 1939–1945* (1978; London: Phoenix, 1999), 147 (March 3–4, 1928).
91. Partridge, *A Pacifist's War,* 40 (May 15, 1940).
92. Ibid., 147–48 (October 21, 1942).
93. Ibid., 170 (September 2–9, 1943).
94. Ibid., 58 (September 5, 1940).
95. Frances Partridge, *Diaries, 1939–1972,* ed. Rebecca Wilson (London: Phoenix, 2000), 298 (June 28, 1960). Originally published in the diary volume *Everything to Lose, 1945–1960.*
96. Ibid., 373 (March 23, 1963). Originally published in the diary volume *Hanging On, 1960–1963.*
97. Ibid., 453 (August 21, 1965). Originally published in the diary volume *Other People, 1963–1966.*
98. Partridge, *Memories,* 77.
99. Victoria Glendinning, *Leonard Woolf: A Biography* (Berkeley: Counterpoint, 2008), 396.
100. Partridge, *Diaries, 1939–1972,* 481–82 (April 21, 1966). Originally published in the diary volume *Other People, 1963–1966.* Shakespeare's birthday is traditionally celebrated on April 23. It's not clear whether the "Anti-Shakespeare" dinner was scheduled for an adjacent date on purpose.
101. Ibid., 481–82.
102. Ibid., 483 (May 9, 1966). She discussed the matter with Bunny Garnett, who had "tackled Lionel on the Shakespeare question at a Cranium [Club] dinner." The Cranium was an all-male club begun by Garnett in the 1920s to stimulate conversation; Ralph had been a member, although he seldom attended. At age eighty-two Frances would become one of the first two women admitted to this "old Bloomsbury stronghold."

The other was Barbara Strachey, the daughter of Oliver and Ray (Costelloe) Strachey (Chisholm, *Frances Partridge,* 333).

103. Partridge, *Diaries, 1939–1972,* 649 (Boxing Day [December 26], 1970). Originally published in the diary volume *Life Regained, 1970–1972.*
104. Ibid., 650 (December 2, 1970).
105. Ibid., 650 (December 28, 1970).

CODA

1. George Rylands, ed., *The Ages of Man: Shakespeare's Image of Man and Nature* (1939; London: Mercury, 1962), xv–xvi.
2. Virginia Woolf, *Virginia Woolf's Reading Notebooks,* ed. Brenda R. Silver (Princeton: Princeton University Press, 1982), 149.
3. Virginia Woolf to David Garnett, December 10, 1933, in Woolf, *The Sickle Side of the Moon: The Letters of Virginia Woolf,* vol. 5: *1932–1935,* ed. Nigel Nicolson and Joanne Trautmann Banks (London: Hogarth, 1994), 257 (letter 2831).
4. Virginia Woolf, "A Professor of Life," in *The Essays of Virginia Woolf,* vol. 4: *1925–1928,* ed. Andrew McNeillie (New York: Harcourt, 1994), 343. This signed review of *The Letters of Sir Walter Raleigh,* edited by Lady Raleigh with a preface by D. Nichol Smith, originally appeared in *Vogue* in early May 1926.
5. Noel Annan, "Bloomsbury and the Leavises," in *Virginia Woolf and Bloomsbury,* ed. Jane Marcus (London: Macmillan, 1987), 26.
6. Lytton Strachey to Edmund Gosse, December 30, 1922, in Michael Holroyd, *Lytton Strachey* (1994; London: Pimlico, 2011), 503.
7. *The Diary of Virginia Woolf,* vol. 4: *1931–1935,* ed. Anne Olivier Bell and Andrew McNeillie (New York: Harcourt Brace, 1983), 337 (September 4, 1935).
8. Q. D. Leavis, "Leslie Stephen: Cambridge Critic," *Scrutiny,* March 1939, 415.
9. *The Diary of Virginia Woolf,* vol. 2: *1920–1924,* ed. Anne Olivier Bell and Andrew McNeillie (New York: Harcourt Brace, 1980), 143 (November 16, 1921).
10. Virginia Woolf, "Byron and Mrs Briggs," in *The Essays of Virginia Woolf,* vol. 3: *1919–1924,* ed. Andrew McNeillie (New York: Harcourt, Brace, Jovanovich, 1988), 496.
11. Virginia Woolf to Ethel Smyth, July 29, 1934, in Woolf, *The Sickle Side of the Moon,* 319 (letter 2915).
12. Virginia Woolf to Vita Sackville-West, December 29, 1928, in Woolf, *A Change of Perspective: The Letters of Virginia Woolf,* vol. 3: *1923–1928,* ed. Nigel Nicolson and Joanne Trautmann Banks (London: Hogarth, 1994), 570 (letter 1976).
13. Virginia Woolf, "How Should One Read a Book?" (1926) in Woolf, *Essays,* 4:396.
14. Ibid.
15. Rylands, introduction to *The Ages of Man,* xvi.
16. *The Diary of Virginia Woolf,* vol. 1: *1915–1919,* ed. Anne Olivier Bell (New York: Harcourt Brace, 1977), 186 (August 27, 1918).
17. Virginia Woolf, "The Reader," in *The Essays of Virginia Woolf,* vol. 6: *1933–1941,* ed. Stuart N. Clarke (London: Hogarth, 2011), 600.
18. Ibid., 6:601.

19. Rylands, introduction to *The Ages of Man,* xviii.
20. Ottoline Morrell, *Ottoline: The Early Memoirs of Lady Ottoline Morrell,* ed. Robert Gathorne-Hardy (London: Faber & Faber, 1963), 197.
21. John Maynard Keynes to Sir Stephen Tallents, July 12, 1937, in *The Collected Writings of John Maynard Keynes,* vol. 18: *Social, Political, and Literary Writings,* ed. Donald Moggridge (London: Macmillan, 1982), 351.
22. Michael Innes, *There Came Both Mist and Snow* (1940; London: Ipso Books, 2017), 22–24, 4–5; Edmund Crispin, *The Moving Toyshop* (1946; Penguin: London, 1958), 205.
23. Adam Gopnik, "Why Rewrite Shakespeare?" *New Yorker,* October 17, 2015; Alexandra Alter, "Novelists Reimagine and Update Shakespeare's Plays," *New York Times,* October 5, 2015.
24. Gopnik, "Why Rewrite Shakespeare?"
25. Woolf, *Diary,* 1:193 (September 10, 1918).
26. Lytton Strachey, "Shakespeare at Cambridge," *Athenaeum,* June 20, 1919. Reprinted in Lytton Strachey, *Characters and Commentaries* (1933) and in Lytton Strachey, *Literary Essays* (New York: Harcourt Brace Jovanovich, 1969), 23.

Acknowledgments

Writing this book has given me the welcome opportunity to bring together two of my lifelong intellectual passions. I have taught and written about Shakespeare throughout my career, but in many ways I have always been a "modernist," engaged and informed by the writers, artists, and critics of the twentieth century.

My interest in the Bloomsbury Group probably began in my teens, when I found, and devoured, a secondhand copy of the recently published correspondence between Virginia Woolf and Lytton Strachey. At that (pre-internet) time, letters and telephone calls were the way we kept in touch with friends, and my friends from that period may well recall the influence of the Woolf-Strachey tone on my own epistolary style. Many years later a course I taught at Harvard renewed and extended my fascination with Bloomsbury. I am grateful to the students in that course, and especially to Dr. Michelle Taylor, who was then the graduate teaching assistant, for encouraging and furthering my ideas. I was especially struck, as we read and viewed the works of these brilliant writers, artists, and theorists, with how often Shakespeare came up in their discussions.

In 2019–20 a fellowship from the John Simon Guggenheim Memorial Foundation allowed me to develop my thoughts on this intriguing conjunction into a draft of this book. I thank the foundation, and Harvard University, for giving me the time and space to refine and articulate these ideas. My warm thanks as well to Michael Dobson, David Kastan, and Phyllis Rose for their support of this project, and for their counsel and expertise.

At Yale University Press Jennifer Banks has been an enormously perceptive and helpful editor, consistently both generous and wise. My wonderful agent Bill Clegg brought the book to Yale, for which I am extremely grateful. I am indebted as well to the anonymous readers of the manuscript for their invaluable suggestions, most of which I have tried to implement. Susan Laity, the production editor, has guided the book with skill and care throughout the process, providing both warm support and valuable advice. Robin DuBlanc has been an exemplary copyeditor, knowledgeable, meticulous, and thorough. Melissa Flamson worked tirelessly to locate and secure art and text permissions, without which the present volume could not have been produced. Her research was essential in structuring the book's visual narrative. The kind assistance of the many archives and collections that granted rights to the visual images is noted, with gratitude, in the photo credits. I would like especially to thank Thomas Davies, the assistant archivist of King's College, Cambridge, and Matthew Wittmann, the curator of the Harvard Theatre Collection.

Credits

TEXT

"Anon" and "The Reader," from *The Essays of Virginia Woolf,* Volume 6: *1933–1941,* by Virginia Woolf published by The Hogarth Press. Copyright © Anne Olivier Bell and Angelica Garnett 2011. Reproduced by Permission of The Random House Group Limited, and with approval from The Society of Authors as the Literary Representative of the Estate of Virginia Woolf. Adapted from Brenda Silver, "'Anon' and 'The Reader': Virginia Woolf's Last Essays," in *Twentieth-Century Literature,* vol. 25, nos. 3–4, pp. 356–441. Copyright 1979, Hofstra University. All rights reserved. Republished by permission of the copyright holder, and the present publisher, Duke University Press. www.dukeupress.edu.

From *Between the Acts* by Virginia Woolf. Copyright © 1941 by Harcourt, Inc. Copyright renewed © 1969 by Leonard Woolf. Used by permission of HarperCollins Publishers, and with approval from The Society of Authors as the Literary Representative of the Estate of Virginia Woolf.

From *The Diary of Virginia Woolf,* Volume 1. Diary copyright © by Quentin Bell and Angelica Garnett. Used by permission of HarperCollins Publishers, and with approval from The Society of Authors as the Literary Representative of the Estate of Virginia Woolf.

From *The Diary of Virginia Woolf,* Volume 2. Diary and Appendices I and II copyright © 1978 by Quentin Bell and Angelica Garnett. Used by permission of HarperCollins Publishers, and with approval from The Society of Authors as the Literary Representative of the Estate of Virginia Woolf.

From *The Diary of Virginia Woolf,* Volume 3. Diary and Appendix II copyright © 1980 by Quentin Bell and Angelica Garnett. Used by permission of HarperCollins Publishers, and with approval from The Society of Authors as the Literary Representative of the Estate of Virginia Woolf.

From *The Diary of Virginia Woolf,* Volume 4. Diary copyright © 1982 by Quentin Bell and Angelica Garnett. Used by permission of HarperCollins Publishers, and with approval from The Society of Authors as the Literary Representative of the Estate of Virginia Woolf.

From *The Diary of Virginia Woolf,* Volume 5. Diary copyright © 1984 by Quentin Bell and Angelica Garnett. Used by permission of HarperCollins Publishers, and with approval from The Society of Authors as the Literary Representative of the Estate of Virginia Woolf.

From *Essays of Virginia Woolf,* Volume 4: *1925–1928.* Text by Virginia Woolf copyright © Quentin Bell and Angelica Garnett 1925, 1926, 1928, 1994. Used by permission of HarperCollins Publishers, and with approval from The Society of Authors as the Literary Representative of the Estate of Virginia Woolf.

From *The Letters of Virginia Woolf,* Volume 5, ed. Nigel Nicolson. Letters copyright © 1979 by Quentin Bell and Angelica Garnett. Used by permission of HarperCollins Publishers, and with approval from The Society of Authors as the Literary Representative of the Estate of Virginia Woolf. From *The Sickle Side of the Moon: The Letters of Virginia Woolf,* Volume V: *1932–1935* by Virginia Woolf, published by Chatto & Windus. Copyright © Quentin Bell and Angelica Garnett 1994. Reproduced by Permission of The Random House Group Limited.

From *The Letters of Virginia Woolf,* Volume 6, ed. Nigel Nicolson. Letters copyright © 1980 by Quentin Bell and Angelica Garnett. Used by permission of HarperCollins Publishers, and with approval from The Society of Authors as the Literary Representative of the Estate of Virginia Woolf. From *Leave the Letters till We're Dead: The Letters of Virginia Woolf,* Volume VI: *1936–1941,* by Virginia Woolf, published by Chatto & Windus. Copyright © Quentin Bell and Angelica Garnett 1983. Reproduced by Permission of The Random House Group Limited.

From "Personalities" and "Ellen Terry" from *The Moment and Other Essays* by Virginia Woolf. Copyright © 1947 by Harcourt Brace & Company. Copyright renewed 1976 by Harcourt Brace & Company and Marjorie T. Parsons. Used by permission of HarperCollins Publishers, and with approval from The Society of Authors as the Literary Representative of the Estate of Virginia Woolf.

From *A Room of One's Own* by Virginia Woolf. Copyright © 1929 by Harcourt, Inc. Copyright renewed 1957 by Leonard Woolf. Foreword copyright © 1981 by Mary Gordon. Used by permission of HarperCollins Publishers, and with approval from The Society of Authors as the Literary Representative of the Estate of Virginia Woolf.

"A Sketch of the Past," from *Moments of Being* by Virginia Woolf. Text copyright ©

by Quentin Bell and Angelica Garnett 1985, 1976. First edition published in Great Britain by Sussex University Press, 1976, revised and enlarged edition published by The Hogarth Press, 1985, Pimlico 2002. Reproduced by Permission of The Random House Group Limited. "A Sketch of the Past," from *Moments of Being* by Virginia Woolf. Text copyright © 1985, 1976 by Quentin Bell and Angelica Garnett. Introduction and editorial matter copyright © 1985, 1976 by Jeanne Schulkind. Preface copyright © 1985 by Jeanne Schulkind. Used by permission of HarperCollins Publishers, and with approval from The Society of Authors as the Literary Representative of the Estate of Virginia Woolf.

From "'Twelfth Night,' at the Old Vic," "Craftsmanship," and "The Art of Biography" from *The Death of the Moth and Other Essays* by Virginia Woolf. Copyright © 1942 by HarperCollins Publishers, renewed 1970 by Marjorie T. Parsons. Used by permission of HarperCollins Publishers, and with approval from The Society of Authors as the Literary Representative of the Estate of Virginia Woolf.

From *The Waves* by Virginia Woolf. Copyright © 1931 by Harcourt, Inc. Copyright renewed 1959 by Leonard Woolf. Used by permission of HarperCollins Publishers, and with approval from The Society of Authors as the Literary Representative of the Estate of Virginia Woolf.

From *The Years* by Virginia Woolf. Copyright © 1937 by Harcourt Brace & Company. Copyright renewed by Leonard Woolf. Used by permission of HarperCollins Publishers, and with approval from The Society of Authors as the Literary Representative of the Estate of Virginia Woolf.

IMAGES

1. Shakespeare in Victorian Bloomsbury

Alfred, Lord Tennyson, photograph by Julia Margaret Cameron, ca. 1865 (David Hunter McAlpin Fund, 1966, The Metropolitan Museum of Art).

Julia Margaret Cameron, photograph by Robert Faulkner, early 1860s (© National Portrait Gallery, London).

Julia Margaret Cameron, *Friar Laurence and Juliet,* 1865 (Henry Taylor and Mary Hillier) (© Victoria and Albert Museum, London).

Julia Margaret Cameron, *Prospero and Miranda,* 1865 (Henry Taylor and Mary Ryan) (© Victoria and Albert Museum, London).

Julia Margaret Cameron, *King Lear Allotting His Kingdom to His Three Daughters,* 1872 (Lorina Liddell, Edith Liddell, Charles Hay Cameron and Alice Liddell) (Bequest of Maurice B. Sendak, 2012, The Metropolitan Museum of Art).

Julia Margaret Cameron, *Romeo and Juliet,* 1867 (Henry John Stedman Cotton and Mary Ryan) (National Science & Media Museum / Science & Society PL. © Science Museum Group.).

Julia Margaret Cameron, *Ophelia Study No. 2,* 1867 (Mary Pinnock) (Album / Alamy Stock Photo).

Julia Margaret Cameron, *Ophelia,* 1874 (Emily Peacock). (Artokoloro / Alamy Stock Photo).

G. F. Watts, *Ophelia,* 1863–64, ca. 1877–80 (Watts Gallery, Compton, Surrey, UK © Watts Gallery / © Trustees of Watts Gallery / Bridgeman Images).

Ellen Terry as Ophelia in *Hamlet,* photograph by Window & Grove, 1878 (© National Portrait Gallery, London).

2. Shakespeare as a (Victorian) Man

Virginia Stephen and Sir Leslie Stephen, photograph by George Charles Beresford, 1902 (© National Portrait Gallery, London).

Lillie Langtry as Rosalind in *As You Like It,* photograph by Napoleon Sarony, 1882 (© National Portrait Gallery, London).

3. The Shakespeares of Virginia Woolf

Virginia Stephen, photograph by George Charles Beresford, 1902 (© National Portrait Gallery, London).

Thoby Stephen, photograph by George Charles Beresford, 1906 (© National Portrait Gallery, London).

Vita Sackville-West, photograph by Howard Coster, ca. 1927 (© National Portrait Gallery, London).

"Chairs that Shakespeare might have sat on" in the Brown Gallery, Knole (The History Collection / Alamy Stock Photo).

Dame Ethel Mary Smyth, photograph by Bassano Ltd., 1927 (© National Portrait Gallery, London).

Virginia Woolf, ca. 1933 (Central Press / Hulton Archive, via Getty Images).

4. Shakespeare Among the Apostles

The Shakespeare Society, Trinity College, Cambridge, 1901 (including Thoby Stephen, Leonard Woolf, Lytton Strachey) (From Leonard Woolf, *Sowing* [London: Hogarth, 1960], 96. Photo courtesy Harvard Library.).

Lytton Strachey, photograph possibly by Dora Carrington, mid-1920s (detail) (© National Portrait Gallery, London).

Lytton Strachey and Virginia Woolf, photograph by Lady Ottoline Morrell, 1923 (detail; original includes Goldsworthy Lowes Dickinson). (Virginia Woolf Monk's House photograph album, MS Thr 561 [2], Harvard Theatre Collection, Houghton Library, Harvard University).

John Maynard Keynes, photograph by Walter Stoneman, 1930 (© National Portrait Gallery, London).

John Maynard Keynes and Lydia Lopokova, ca. 1922–23 (Courtesy King's College Archive Centre, The Papers of John Maynard Keynes: JMK/PP/94/195).

Michael Redgrave, Lydia Lopokova Keynes, and Dadie Rylands in Shakespeare's

A Lover's Complaint, photograph by Cecil Beaton, ca. 1930 (Courtesy King's College Archive Centre, Rylands Papers: GHWR/5/91. Cecil Beaton Archive, © Condé Nast.).

Lydia Lopokova Keynes with the cast of *Twelfth Night,* photograph from *The Times,* September 18, 1933 (The Times / News Licensing. Courtesy King's College Archive Centre, The Papers of Lydia Lopokova Keynes: LLK/1/5/3.).

Roger Fry, photograph by Alvin Langdon Coburn, 1913 (© The Universal Order. Photo courtesy of National Portrait Gallery, London.)

Leonard Woolf, photograph by Alfred Harris, 1927 (Lebrecht Music & Arts / Alamy Stock Photo).

Desmond MacCarthy, photograph by Lady Ottoline Morrell, 1923 (© National Portrait Gallery, London).

Virginia Woolf and Dadie Rylands, 1932 (Virginia Woolf Monk's House photograph album, MS Thr 560, Harvard Theatre Collection, Houghton Library, Harvard University).

James Strachey, ca. 1917, photographer unknown (© National Portrait Gallery, London).

Rupert Brooke, photograph by Sherril Schell, 1913 (© reserved; collection National Portrait Gallery, London).

Gwen Raverat, *King Lear for the Marlowe Society,* 1938 (program design). (Courtesy of the Raverat Archive @ www.raverat.com.)

Jacques Raverat, ca. 1924 (Virginia Woolf Monk's House photograph album, MS Thr 564 [118]. Harvard Theatre Collection, Houghton Library, Harvard University).

5. Mr. Eliot's Shakespeare

T. S. Eliot and Virginia Woolf, photograph by Lady Ottoline Morrell, 1924 (© National Portrait Gallery, London).

6. Shakespeare at Charleston and Ham Spray

Clive Bell, photograph by Bassano Ltd., 1921 (© National Portrait Gallery, London).

Vanessa Bell sitting on a chair outside her studio, ca. 1913. (Vanessa Bell Collection, Tate Archive. Presented by Angelica Garnett, 1981 and 1988–92. © Tate.)

Duncan Grant sitting on a table, barefoot, outside the drawing room at "Charleston," East Sussex, photograph by Vanessa Bell, ca. 1933–35. (Vanessa Bell Collection, Tate Archive. Presented by Angelica Garnett, 1981 and 1988–92. © Tate.)

Duncan Grant, Costume design for a Lord, from *Macbeth Sketchbook* (© Estate of Duncan Grant. All rights reserved, DACS 2022. Photograph © The Charleston Trust.).

Duncan Grant, Stage curtain design for Jacques Copeau's production of *Twelfth Night,* 1913 (© Estate of Duncan Grant. All rights reserved, DACS 2022. Photo © The Samuel Courtauld Trust, The Courtauld Gallery, London / Bridgeman Images.)

Marjorie Strachey's summer school: *A Midsummer Night's Dream,* Anastasia (Baba) Anrep as Bottom, in a mask thought to have been made by Roger Fry; Angelica Bell as

Peaseblossom, photograph attributed to Vanessa Bell, 1925 (From *Vanessa Bell's Family Album,* compiled by Quentin Bell and Angelica Garnett [London: Jill Norman and Hobhouse, LTD, 1981], p. 78 top. © Tate.).

Marjorie Strachey's summer school: *A Midsummer Night's Dream,* Angelica Bell as Peaseblossom, photograph attributed to Vanessa Bell, 1925. (From *Vanessa Bell's Family Album,* compiled by Quentin Bell and Angelica Garnett [London: Jill Norman and Hobhouse, LTD, 1981], p. 78 bottom. © Tate.).

Eve Younger as Charmian and Angelica Bell as Cleopatra in Shakespeare's *Antony and Cleopatra,* photograph attributed to Vanessa Bell, late 1930s (Vanessa Bell's photograph albums, Tate Gallery. © Tate. Digital image courtesy of the Paul Mellon Centre. Published in Vanessa Bell, *Duncan Grant: 'Famous Women' Dinner Service,* ed. Hana Leaper [Paul Mellon Centre, 2017], p. 40.).

Angelica Bell as Ophelia, Charleston, photograph attributed to Vanessa Bell, ca. 1935 (Vanessa Bell Album 8, p. 16, AA37. © Tate.).

John Everett Millais, *Ophelia,* 1852 (detail) (Photo © Peter Barritt / World Pictures / age fotostock).

G. F. Watts, *Found Drowned,* 1848–50. (VTR / Alamy Stock Photo).

Lytton Strachey and Dora Carrington, 1920s (© National Portrait Gallery, London).

Coda

Vanessa Bell, *The Memoir Club,* ca. 1943 (National Portrait Gallery, London. © Estate of Vanessa Bell. All rights reserved, DACS 2022.).

Index

Note: Page numbers in *italics* refer to figures.